THE LOEB CLASSICAL LIBRARY

FOUNDED BY JAMES LOEB, LL.D.

EDITED BY

E. H. WARMINGTON, M.A., F.R.HIST.SOC.

FORMER EDITORS

†T. E. PAGE, C.H., LITT.D. †E. CAPPS, PH.D., LL.D.
†W. H. D. ROUSE, LITT.D. L. A. POST, L.H.D.

LIVY

I

BOOKS I AND II

LIVY

IN FOURTEEN VOLUMES

I

BOOKS I AND II

WITH AN ENGLISH TRANSLATION BY

B. O. FOSTER, Ph.D.
OF STANFORD UNIVERSITY

CAMBRIDGE, MASSACHUSETTS
HARVARD UNIVERSITY PRESS
LONDON
WILLIAM HEINEMANN LTD
MCMLXVII

First printed 1919
Reprinted 1925, 1939, 1952, 1957, 1961, 1967

TO

A. L. F.

Printed in Great Britain

CONTENTS

	PAGE
TRANSLATOR'S PREFACE	vii
INTRODUCTION	ix
BOOK I	1
SUMMARY OF BOOK I	211
BOOK II	217
SUMMARY OF BOOK II	435
INDEX	441 |†
MAPS—	
ROME IN THE REGAL PERIOD	*At end*
WESTERN CENTRAL ITALY	,,

TRANSLATOR'S PREFACE

The Latin text of this volume has been set up from that of the ninth edition (1908) of Book I., and the eighth edition (1894) of Book II., by Weissenborn and Müller, except that the *Periochae* have been reprinted from the text of Rossbach (1910). But the spelling is that adopted by Professors Conway and Walters in their critical edition of Books I.–V. (Oxford, 1914), which is the source also of a number of readings which differ from those given in the Weissenborn-Müller text, and has furnished, besides, the materials from which the textual notes have been drawn up. I have aimed to indicate every instance where the reading printed does not rest on the authority of one or more of the good MSS., and to give the author of the emendation. The MSS. are often cited by the symbols given in the Oxford edition, but for brevity's sake I have usually employed two of my own, viz. Ω and ϛ. The former means "such of the good MSS. as are not cited for other readings," the latter "one or more of the inferior MSS. and early printed editions." Anyone who wishes more specific information regarding the source of a variant will consult

PREFACE

the elaborate apparatus of the Oxford text, whose editors have placed all students of the first decade under lasting obligations by their thorough and minute report of the MSS. With the publication of their second volume there will be available for the first time an adequate diplomatic basis for the criticism of Books I.–X.

I have utilized throughout the translations by Philemon Holland, George Baker, and Canon Roberts, and have occasionally borrowed a happy expression from the commentaries of Edwards, Conway, and others, mentioned in the introduction. The unpretentious notes in the college edition of my former teacher, the late Professor Greenough, have been particularly useful in pointing out the significance of the word-order.

Acknowledgments are also due to my colleagues, Professors Fairclough, Hempl, Cooper, and Briggs, and to Professor Noyes of the University of California, each of whom has given me some good suggestions.

B. O. F.

STANFORD UNIVERSITY, CALIFORNIA.
1919.

INTRODUCTION

I

FROM entries in Jerome's re-working of the *Chronicle* of Eusebius we learn that Titus Livius the Patavian was born in 59 B.C., the year of Caesar's first consulship, and died in his native town (the modern Padua) in 17 A.D. Of his parents nothing is known. They were presumably well-to-do, for their son received the training in Greek and Latin literature and in rhetoric which constituted the standard curriculum of that time, and was afterwards able to devote a long life to the unremunerative work of writing. That he was by birth an aristocrat is no more than an inference from his outstanding sympathy with the senatorial party. Livy's childhood witnessed the conquest of Gaul and Caesar's rapid rise to lordship over the Roman world. These early years he doubtless passed in his northern home. Patavium laid claim to great antiquity. Livy tells us himself in his opening chapter the legend of its founding by the Trojan Antenor, and elsewhere describes with unmistakable satisfaction the vain attempt of the Spartan Cleonymus (in 302 B.C.) to

INTRODUCTION

subdue the Patavians.[1] They defended themselves with equal vigour and success against the aggressions of the Etruscans and the inroads of the Gauls, and in the war with Hannibal cast in their lot with Rome. In 49 B.C., when Livy was ten years old, the town became a Roman municipality and its citizens were enrolled in the Fabian tribe. The place was a great centre of trade, especially in wool,[2] and under Augustus was perhaps the wealthiest city in Italy, next to Rome,[3] to which in some respects it presented a striking contrast, since the Patavians maintained the simple manners and strict morality which had long gone out of fashion in the cosmopolitan capital.[4] We cannot say how old Livy was when he left Patavium, but it is probable that his tastes and character had been permanently influenced by the old-world traditions of his native town. Did he go to Rome with the intention of pursuing there the career of a rhetorician and subsequently become interested in historical studies? It may have been

[1] Liv. x. ii. There were many living in his own day, Livy says, who had seen the beaks of the ships captured from Cleonymus, which were preserved as trophies in the temple of Juno.

[2] Martial, XIV. cxliii., speaks of the thickness of Patavian tunics.

[3] Strabo, III. clxix. and v. ccxiii.; *cf.* Nissen, *Italische Landeskunde*, 2, p. 220.

[4] Plin. *Epist.* I. xiv. 6, says of a young protégé: "His maternal grandmother is Sarrana Procula, from the municipality of Patavium. You know the manners of the place; yet Serrana is a pattern of strictness even to the Patavians."

INTRODUCTION

so. Perhaps he had already resolved to write history and wished to make use of the libraries and other sources of information which were lacking in a provincial town. Certain passages in his earlier books[1] indicate that he was already familiar with the City when he began his great work, about 27 B.C.,[2] and a reference to a conversation with Augustus in Book IV. seems to argue that it was not long till he was on a friendly footing with the Emperor.[3] He doubtless continued to reside in Rome, with occasional visits to Patavium and other places in Italy, till near the end of his long life.

Livy seems never to have held any public office, but to have given himself up entirely to literature. Seneca says that he wrote dialogues which one might classify under history as well as under philosophy, besides books which were professedly philosophical.[4] And Quintilian quotes a letter from Livy to his son which was very likely an essay on the training of the orator, for in the passage cited he advises the young man to read Demosthenes and Cicero, and then such as most nearly resembled

---

[1] *e.g.* I. iv. 5 ; I. viii. 5 ; I. xxvi. 13.

[2] It could not well have been earlier than 27, for in I. xix. 3 and IV. xx. 7 Octavian is mentioned with the title of Augustus, which the senate only conferred on him in January of that year. Nor may we put the date much later, for in mentioning the occasions on which the temple of Janus had been closed (I. xix. 3) Livy has nothing to say of the second of the two closings which took place in his own life-time,— namely that of 25 B.C.

[3] Liv. IV. xx. 7.   [4] Sen. *Epist.* 100. 9.

INTRODUCTION

them.[1] So, in another place, Quintilian tells us that he finds in Livy that there was a certain teacher who bade his pupils *obscure* what they said.[2] It may have been in this same essay that he made the criticism on Sallust which seemed to the elder Seneca to be unjust,—that he had not only appropriated a sentence from Thucydides but had spoilt it in the process.[3] And there is another passage in Seneca where Livy is credited with having quoted approvingly a *mot* of the rhetorician Miltiades against orators who affected archaic and sordid words, which may also be an echo of the letter.[4] If Livy was about thirty-two years old when he began to write history it is probable that this essay was composed some years later, for it is unlikely to have been written before the son was about sixteen.[5] We may therefore think of the historian as putting aside his magnum opus for a season, to be of use in the education of the boy, who, whether or no he profited by his father's instructions in rhetoric, at all events became a writer, and is twice named by the elder Pliny as one of his authorities, in Books V. and VI. of the *Natural History*, which deal with geography. In a sepulchral inscription found in Padua, which may be that of our Livy, two sons are named—Titus Livius Priscus and Titus Livius Longus,—and their

---

[1] Quint. x. i. 39 (*cf.* II. v. 20).
[2] Quint. VIII. ii. 18. [3] Sen. *Controv.* IX. i. 14.
[4] *Ibid.* IX. ii. 26.
[5] Schanz, *Geschichte der römischen Litteratur*, ii³. 1, p. 419.

mother's name is given as Cassia.[1] The only other item of information we possess about the family is supplied by the elder Seneca, who mentions a son-in-law, named Lucius Magius, as a declaimer who had some following for a time, though men rather endured him for the sake of his father-in-law than praised him for his own.[2]

Of Livy's social life in Rome we know nothing more than that he enjoyed the friendship of Augustus, and probably, as we have seen, from an early date in his stay in Rome.[3] The intimacy was apparently maintained till the end of the Emperor's life, for it cannot have been much before A.D. 14 that Livy, as related by Suetonius,[4] advised his patron's grand-nephew Claudius (born 9 B.C.) to take up the writing of history. The good relations subsisting between the Emperor and the historian do honour to the sense and candour of both. Livy gloried in the history of the republic, yet he could but acquiesce in the new order of things. And the moral and religious reforms of Augustus, his wish to revive the traditions of an elder day, his respect for the forms inherited from a time when Rome was really governed by a senate, must have commanded Livy's hearty approval. On the other

---

[1] *C.I.L.* v. 2975 (=Dessau, *Inscriptiones Latinae Selectae*, 2919): T. Livius C. f. sibi et / suis / T. Livio T. f. Prisco f., / T. Livio T. f. Longo f., / Cassiae Sex. f. Primae / uxori.

[2] Sen. *Controv.* x. *praef.* 2.

[3] It is just possible that the conversation with Augustus mentioned in IV. xx. 7 took place at some time after the original publication of that book, and that the reference was inserted later. [4] Suet. *Claud.* xli.

INTRODUCTION

side, when Livy's great history was appealing to men's patriotism and displaying the ideal Rome as no other literary work (with the possible exception of the contemporaneous *Aeneid*) had ever done, it was easy for the Emperor to smile at the scholar's exaggerated admiration of Pompey,[1] and even to overlook the frankness of his query whether more of good or of harm had come to the state from the birth of Julius Caesar.[2] Livy died three years after Augustus, in 17 A.D., at the ripe age of 76. If he continued working at his history up to the last he had devoted more than 40 years to the gigantic enterprise. Jerome says that he died in Patavium. We can only conjecture whether he was overtaken by death while making a visit to his old home, or had retired thither, with the coming in of the new régime, to spend his declining years. The latter is perhaps the more likely assumption. The character of Tiberius can have possessed little claim to the sympathy of Livy, and life in Rome may well have lost its charm for him, now that his old patron was no more.

---

[1] Tacitus, *Ann.* IV. xxxiv., describing the trial of Cremutius Cordus for lèse-majesté on the ground that he had published annals in which he praised Brutus and styled Cassius the "last of the Romans," makes Cremutius say in his defence: "Titus Livius, pre-eminent for eloquence and candour, so lauded Pompey that Augustus called him a Pompeian; yet it made no difference in their friendship."

[2] Sen. *Nat. Quaest.* v. xviii. 4.

INTRODUCTION

II

Livy seems to have called his history simply *Ab Urbe Condita*, "From the Founding of the City,"[1] just as Tacitus was later to call his Annals *Ab Excessu Divi Augusti*, "From the death of the Divine Augustus." He began with the legend of Aeneas, and brought his narrative down to the death of Drusus (and the defeat of Quintilius Varus?[2]) in 9 B.C. There is no reason to think that Livy intended, as some have supposed, to go on to the death of Augustus. In the preface to one of the lost books he remarked that he had already earned enough of reputation and might have ceased to write, were it not that his restless spirit was sustained by work.[3] He probably toiled on till his strength failed him, with no fixed goal in view, giving his history to the public in parts, as these were severally completed. The following table, taken from Schanz,[4] is an attempt to reconstruct these instalments:

Books I.-V. From the founding of the City to its conquest by the Gauls (387–386 B.C.).

---

[1] Livy once refers to his work as "my annals" (*in meos annales*, XLIII. xiii. 2), and Pliny, *N.H. praef.* 16, speaks of a certain volume of Livy's "histories," but these are merely generic names.

[2] The *Periocha* of Book CXLII. ends with these events, but the mention of Varus, which is found in only one MS., is generally regarded as a late addition. Its genuineness is, however, upheld by Rossbach, in his edition, *ad loc.*

[3] Plin. *l.c.*

[4] *Geschichte der römischen Litteratur*, ii³. 1, p. 421.

INTRODUCTION

VI.–XV. To the subjugation of Italy (265 B.C.).

XVI.–XX. The Punic wars to the beginning of the war with Hannibal (219 B.C.).

XXI.–XXX. The war with Hannibal (to 201 B.C.).

XXXI.–XL. To the death of King Philip of Macedon (179 B.C.).

XLI.–LXX. To the outbreak of the Social War (91 B.C.).

LXXI.–LXXX. The Social War to the death of Marius (86 B.C.).

LXXXI.–XC. To the death of Sulla (78 B.C.).

XCI.–CVIII. From the war with Sertorius to the Gallic War (58 B.C.).

CIX.–CXVI. From the beginning of the Civil Wars to the death of Caesar (44 B.C.).

CXVII.–CXXXIII. To the death of Antony and Cleopatra (30 B.C.).

CXXXIV–CXLII. The principate of Augustus to the death of Drusus (9 B.C.).

It will be noticed that certain portions fall naturally into decades (notably XXI.–XXX.), or pentads (*e.g.* I.–V.). Elsewhere, and particularly in that part of the work which deals with the writer's own times, no such symmetry is discernible. Later however it became the uniform practice of the copyists to divide the history into decades. This is clearly seen in the wholly distinct and independent MS. tradition of the several surviving sections.

Only about a quarter of the whole work has been

INTRODUCTION

preserved. We have the Preface and Books I.-X., covering the period from Aeneas to the year 293 B.C.; Books XXI.-XXX. describing the Second Punic War; and Books XXXI.-XLV., which continue the story of Rome's conquests down to the year 167 B.C. and the victories of Lucius Aemilius Paulus.[1]

For the loss of the other books the existence from the first century of our era of a handy abridgment is no doubt largely responsible. It is to this Martial alludes in the following distich (XIV. cxc.):

> Pellibus exiguis artatur Livius ingens,
> Quem mea non totum bibliotheca capit.[2]

If we had this *Epitome*[3] it would be some slight compensation for the disappearance of the original books, but we have only a compend of it, the so-called *Periochae*, and certain excerpts thought to have been made from another summary of it, no longer extant, which scholars refer to as the *Chronicon*, to wit, the fragments of the *Oxyrhynchus Papyrus*, the *Prodigiorum Liber* of Obsequens, and the consular lists of Cassiodorius.

The *Periochae*, or summaries of the several Books (only CXXXVI. and CXXXVII. are wanting), are the

[1] Books XLI.-XLV. contain many lacunae.
[2] Thus translated by Professor Duff:
> In vellum small huge Livy now is dressed;
> My bookshelves could not hold him uncompressed.
[3] See Schanz, *op. cit.* ii³. 1, pp. 425-428. H. A. Sanders, "The Lost Epitome of Livy" (in *Roman Historical Sources and Institutions*, p. 257), makes the interesting suggestion that it may have been written by Livy's son.

INTRODUCTION

most valuable of these sources for supplying the gaps in our text of Livy. Their author narrates briefly what seem to him the leading events in each book, adding a reference to other matters treated in the original.[1] The *Periochae* are thus a kind of compromise between a book of excerpts for the use of readers who for any reason could not or would not go to the unabridged Livy, and a table of contents for the convenience of those who did.[2] They are usually printed with editions of Livy, and are included in this one. It may be noted here that *Per. I.* exists in a double recension, of which B appears from its style to be of a piece with those of all the other books, while A is thought to have come from the *Chronicon*.

In 1903 a papyrus was discovered at Oxyrhynchus which contained fragments of a compend of Roman history which was based on Livy, though it seems not to have been taken from Livy directly but from the *Chronicon*, which was also, as we have said, the source of Obsequens and Cassiodorius. The MS. is assigned to the third century, and the book must therefore have been composed in that or a still earlier period. It contains eight columns of uncial writing. Of these 1–3 preserve a selection of the events recorded in Livy, Books XXXVII.–XL., (which we have), while 4–8 deal with the subject-

---

[1] See *e.g.* the last sentence of *Per. II.*, p. 438.
[2] Schanz, p. 425.

INTRODUCTION

matter of Books XLVIII.–LV. But there is a column gone between column 6 and column 7, which treated of the years 143 and 142 B.C.

Magnus Aurelius Cassiodorius Senator lived about 480 to 575, and was Consul in 514, under Theodoric. Among his writings was a chronicle, from Adam to A.D. 519. For the earlier periods he used Eusebius and Jerome, but from the expulsion of Tarquinius to A.D. 31 he names as his authorities Titus Livius and Aufidius Bassus. His list of consuls for this period shows kinship with the *Oxyrhynchus Papyrus* and Obsequens.

In his *Prodigiorum Liber* Julius Obsequens enumerates in chronological order the portents which occurred from the year 190 to the year 12 B.C. In its original form the catalogue probably began, as the title in the MS. indicates,[1] with the year 249. The little book is of unknown date: Schanz thinks it is a product of the fourth century of our era, when paganism made its last struggle against Christianity.[2] Rossbach inclines to a somewhat earlier date.[3] In any case Rossbach has shown that the author was a believer in prodigies, and therefore a pagan.

[1] Iulii Obsequentis *Ab Anno Urbis Conditae DV Prodigiorum Liber*.
[2] Schanz, *Röm. Lit.* iv². 1, p. 85.
[3] See his edition, p. xxxiii.

INTRODUCTION

III

In his preface to the whole work Livy gives a satisfactory account of his conception of history and the ends he himself had in view. He begins with an apology for adding to the already large number of Roman histories. Those who attempt this theme hope, he says, to surpass their predecessors either in accuracy or style, and it is doing Livy no injustice to infer that in his own case it was the belief that he could make the story of Rome more vivid and readable than anyone had yet done which gave him the courage to undertake the task. But whether he succeeds or not, he will be glad, he tells us, to have done what he could for the memory of the foremost people of the world. He recognizes the immense labour which confronts him, in consequence of the more than seven hundred years which he must deal with, and admits that it will be labour thrown away on most of his readers, who will have little patience with the earlier history in their eagerness to be reading of the civil wars and the events of their own generation. " I myself, on the contrary," he continues—and the sentiment reveals at once the man's romantic spirit— "shall seek in this an additional reward for my toil, that I may turn my back upon the evils which our age has witnessed for so many years, so long at least as I am absorbed in the recollection of the brave days

INTRODUCTION

of old."[1] He refers to the marvellous tales which were associated with the founding of the City as to matters of no great consequence. He declines to vouch for their authenticity, though he means to set them down as he finds them; and he apparently regards them as possessing a certain symbolic truth, at least. But the really important thing in Rome's history is the way her power was founded on morality and discipline, waxed mighty with the maintenance of these, and was now fallen upon evil days through their decay. For the use of historical study lies in its application to life. The story of a great people is fraught with examples and warnings, both for the individual and for the state. And no nation is better worth studying than Rome, for in none did righteousness and primitive simplicity so long resist the encroachments of wealth and luxury.

It was the ethical aspect of history then that chiefly appealed to Livy, and he chose Rome for his subject because the rise of the Roman empire seemed to him the best example of the fruition of those qualities which he wished to inculcate. To do this he must first of all win the interest of his readers, and if morality is his goal style is certainly the road by which he hopes to lead men towards it. We must therefore fix our attention on these two things if we would approach Livy's work in the spirit of his

[1] In another passage (XLIII. xiii. 2) Livy tells us that when he is writing of old-world things his spirit somehow becomes old-fashioned.

INTRODUCTION

ancient readers, and understand their almost unqualified approval of it.

For Livy's success was both immediate and lasting. I have already referred to the frank way in which he himself recognized his fame, in the preface to one of the books of his History, and the younger Pliny tells a delightful story of an enthusiastic Spanish admirer who travelled from Cadiz to Rome solely to behold the great writer, and having gratified his curiosity returned forthwith to his home.[1] Livy's magnanimity was warmly praised by the elder Seneca, who said that he was by nature a most candid judge of all great talents,[2] and it is a striking testimony to the justice of this observation that the modern reader's admiration for Hannibal is largely a reflection of Livy's, which all his prejudice against Rome's most formidable enemy could not altogether stifle. Tacitus too admired Livy, whom he considered the most eloquent of the older historians, as Fabius Rusticus was of the more recent.[3] Quintilian compared him with Herodotus, and spoke of the wonderful fascination of his narrative, his great fairness, and the inexpressible eloquence of the speeches, in which everything was suited not only to the circumstances but to the speaker.[4] Quintilian also praised his represent-

---

[1] Plin. *Ep.* II. iii. 8.   [2] Sen. *Suas.* vi. 22.

[3] *Agric.* x. and the passage already quoted from the *Annals* (IV. xxxiv.).

[4] Quint. *Inst. Or.* x. i. 101. There are some 400 of these inserted speeches in the extant text, some consisting of only

INTRODUCTION

ation of the emotions, particularly the gentler ones, in which field he said he had no superior. Livy shared with Virgil the honour of being the most widely read of Latin writers, and in consequence incurred the resentment of the mad Caligula, who lacked but little of casting out their works and their portraits from all the libraries, alleging of Livy that he was verbose and careless.[1] Even Quintilian could tax him with prolixity,[2] though he seems to have owned that it was but the defect of a quality, for he elsewhere speaks of his "milky richness."[3] The only other jarring note in the general chorus of admiration is sounded by the critic Asinius Pollio, who reproached Livy's style with "Patavinity," by which he perhaps meant that it was tainted with an occasional word or idiom peculiar to the historian's native dialect.[4] Owing chiefly to its intrinsic excellence, but partly no doubt to the accidental circumstance that it covered the whole field of Roman History, Livy's work became the standard source-book from which later writers were to draw their materials. We have already seen how it was epitomized and excerpted. Other writers who took their historical data from Livy were Lucan

---

a few lines, while others run to a length of several pages. Under Domitian a certain Mettius Pompusius made a collection of speeches by kings and generals which he took from Livy (Suet. *Dom.* x. 3).

[1] Suet. *Calig.* xxxiv. (*cf.* Schanz, p. 439.)
[2] Quint. *Inst. Or.* VIII. iii. 53.   [3] *Ibid.* x. i. 32.
[4] *Ibid.* VIII. i. 3. Pollio was also severe upon Caesar, Cicero, Catullus and Sallust !

INTRODUCTION

and Silius Italicus, Asconius, Valerius Maximus, Frontinus, Florus, and the Greeks Cassius Dio and Plutarch. Avienus, in the fourth century, turned Livy into iambic senarii, a *tour de force* which has not come down to us.[1] In the fifth he is cited by Pope Gelasius,[2] and the grammarian Priscian used him in the sixth. Comparatively little read in the Middle Ages, Livy found a warm admirer in Dante, who used him in the second book of his *De Monarchia,* and in the *Divina Commedia* refers to him naively as " Livio . . . che non erra."[3] The Italians of the Renaissance seized upon Livy's History with avidity. The poet Beccadelli sold a country-place to enable him to purchase a copy by the hand of Poggio. Petrarch was among those who hoped for the recovery of the lost decades, and Pope Nicholas V. exerted himself without avail to discover them. With the emendations in Books XXI.–XXVI. by Laurentius Valla[4] the critical study of the text was inaugurated. The year 1469 saw the first printed edition of the History, which was produced in Rome. Early in the sixteenth century Machiavelli wrote his famous *Discorsi sul Primo Libro delle Deche di Tito Livio.* It is not too much to say that from the Revival of Learning to the present time Livy has been generally recognized as one of the world's great writers. The English scholar Munro pronounced him owner of what is

[1] Servius on Virg. *Aen.* x. 388, Schanz, IV^2. i. p. 20.
[2] Hertz, *Frag.* 12 (in his edition of Livy).
[3] *Inferno,* xxviii. 12.   [4] Born in Rome, 1407.

INTRODUCTION

"perhaps the greatest prose style that has ever been written in any age or language,"[1] and his history seemed to Niebuhr a "a colossal masterpiece."[2]

The qualities which gave Livy his lofty place in literature are easily discovered. He was a high-minded patriot, inspired with a genuine desire to promote the welfare of his country. An idealist of the most pronounced type, he was endowed—as not all idealists are—with a breadth of sympathy which enabled him to judge men with charity, and to discern in the most diverse characters whatever admirable traits they might possess. In him a passionate love of noble deeds and a rare insight into the workings of the mind and heart were united with a strength of imagination which enabled him to clothe the shadowy names of Rome's old worthies with the flesh and blood of living men. Finally, his mastery of all the resources of language is only equalled by his never-failing tact and sense of fitness in the use of them.[3] It is difficult to describe in a few words so complex an instrument

---

[1] *Criticisms and Elucidations of Catullus*, London, 1905[2], p. 232.

[2] See the Introduction to his *Roman History*. I have taken most of the material for this paragraph from Schanz, pp. 438–441.

[3] Wachsmuth, *Einleitung in das Studium der alten Geschichte*, p. 591. Wachsmuth says: "No one even now can escape the magic of his enthralling narrative, and to his countrymen, whether contemporary or of a later generation, his style must have been absolutely fascinating. We are not surprised that Latin-speaking mankind in the time of the Empire saw the ancient history of Rome almost exclusively through the eyes of Livy."

INTRODUCTION

as Livy's style. Perhaps it might fairly be said that it is distinguished by the attributes of warmth and amplitude. The Livian period, less formal and regular than that of Cicero, whom Livy so greatly admired,[1] is fully as intricate, and reveals an amazing sensitiveness to the rhetorical possibilities inherent in word-order.[2] To the first decade, and especially Book I., Livy has, consciously no doubt, given a slightly archaic and poetical colour, in keeping with the subject-matter[3]; and his extraordinary faculty for visualizing and dramatizing the men and events of Roman story reminds us even more insistently of Quintilian's dictum that history is a kind of prose poetry.[4]

Yet despite his many remarkable gifts it is only too clear that Livy was deficient in some of the most essential qualifications for producing such a history of Rome as would satisfy the standards of our own day. Neither well informed nor specially interested in politics or the art of war, and lacking even such practical knowledge of constitutional matters as scores of his contemporaries must have gained from participating in the actual business of the state, he undertook to trace the development of the greatest military

---

[1] Quint. *Inst. Or.* x. i. 39; Sen. *Suas.* vi. 17 and 22.

[2] H. D. Naylor, *Latin and English Idiom*, p. 6, says: "If I were asked 'What is *the* great feature of Livy's style?' I would boldly answer: 'His brilliant use of order.'" [3] Norden, *Antike Kunstprosa* i., p. 235.

[4] Quint. *Inst. Or.* x. i. 31. Historia . . . . . est . . . proxima poetis et quodam modo carmen solutum.

INTRODUCTION

power (save one) that the world has ever seen, and the growth of an empire which has taught the principles of organization and government to all succeeding ages. Nor was this lack of technical knowledge the only or indeed the heaviest handicap that Livy was compelled to carry. His mind was fundamentally uncritical, and he was unable to subject his authorities to such a judicial examination as might have made it possible for him to choose the safer guides and reject the less trustworthy. Towards original documents he manifests an almost incredible indifference.[1] As regards the earlier period, he himself remarks that the Gauls in burning Rome had swept away the "pontifical commentaries" and pretty much all the other public and private records,[2] but there is nothing to indicate that he made much use of even such shreds of evidence as survived the fire, or that he referred, in writing of a later period, to so important a source as the *Annales Maximi*, though they had been published in 123 B.C., in eighty books, by P. Mucius Scaevola. He excuses himself from transcribing the expiatory hymn composed by Livius Andronicus, and publicly sung, in the year 207 B.C., by a chorus of girls, as a thing too uncouth for modern taste.[3] He seems never to have bothered

---

[1] Taine says: "On ne trouve pas [chez Tite Live] l'amour infatigable de la science complète et de la vérité absolue. Il n'en a que le goût; il n'en a pas la passion" (*Essai sur Tite Live*, p. 64).

[2] Liv. VI. i. 2.

[3] Liv. XXVII. xxxvii. 13.

INTRODUCTION

to examine the terrain of so important a battle as Cannae, and his account of the operations there shows that he had no very clear notion of the topography of the field. It would be easy to multiply instances. There is an example at II. xli. 10, where he refers to an inscription, but without having himself consulted it, as his contemporary, Dionysius of Halicarnassus, did.[1]

Livy's history supplanted the works of the annalists, which have consequently perished, so that it is impossible to ascertain with exactness his relation to his sources. His own references to them are rather casual. He makes no attempt to indicate his authorities systematically, but cites them in certain cases where they conflict with one another, or where he is sceptical of their statements and does not choose to assume the responsibility for them.[2] Often he does not give names, but contents himself with a phrase like, "men say," or "I find in certain writers." For the first decade he derived his materials from a number of annalists. The oldest were Q. Fabius Pictor and L. Cincius Alimentus. Both men wrote in Greek and lived in the time of the war with Hannibal, in which both men fought. Another was L. Calpurnius Piso Frugi, who opposed the Gracchi and was consul in

[1] Dion. Hal. *Antiq. Rom.* IV. xxvi. and VIII. xxvii. Dionysius and Livy worked independently of each other, though they used common sources.

[2] A. Klotz, "Zu den Quellen der 4ten und 5ten Dekade des Livius" in *Hermes*, l. (1915), pp. 482 and 536.

INTRODUCTION

133.[1] Cato's valuable history, the *Origines*,[2] he seems not to have used until he came to treat of the events in which Cato himself played a part. It was to writers who lived nearer his own day, whose style caused Livy to rank them above their less sophisticated but no doubt far more trustworthy predecessors that he mainly resorted. Such were Valerius Antias, whose seventy-five books were certainly the most abundant source available, and are thought to have covered the history of Rome to the death of Sulla; C. Licinius Macer, tribune of the plebs in 73, who wrote from the democratic standpoint; and Q. Aelius Tubero, who took part in the Civil War on the side of Pompey, and brought down his annals to his own times.

For the third decade Livy used Polybius,[3] though whether directly or through a Roman intermediary, and whether for the whole or only a part of the ten books, are questions still *sub iudice*. For this decade he also drew upon L. Coelius Antipater, a writer whose treatise on the Second Punic War in seven

---

[1] He composed a comprehensive chronicle of Roman events in seven books, written in Latin.

[2] This work, also in seven books, beginning with the Aeneas-legend and coming down to the year of the author's death, 149 B.C., should have been of the greatest use to Livy.

[3] Polybius was born about 210 B.C., in Megalopolis, where he died at the age of 82. His great philosophical history of the Romans, from the outbreak of the Second Punic War to the fall of Corinth, in 146 B.C., contained forty books. Only I.–V. are extant in their entirety, but we have extracts from VI.–XVIII., and some fragments of xix.–xl.

INTRODUCTION

books[1] had introduced into Roman literature the genre of the historical monograph.

In the fourth and fifth decades Livy's main reliance seems to have been Polybius, in describing eastern affairs, and the annalists Q. Claudius Quadrigarius[2] and Valerius Antias, in treating of Italy and Spain. A recent critic[3] has found reason for thinking that Livy used Valerius as his chief authority for western matters (controlling his statements however by those of Claudius) until, coming to the prosecution of Scipio (see Book XXXVIII), he found so much in Valerius that was incredible that his mistrust, which had hitherto been confined to that annalist's reports of numbers (see *e.g.* XXXIII. x. 8.) caused him to take Claudius thenceforth for his principal guide.

This unscientific attitude towards the sources was the product partly of Livy's own characteristics, partly of the conception of history as a means of edification and entertainment prevalent in ancient times.[4] Another shortcoming, which would have to be insisted on if we were criticising him as though he were a contemporary, is his inability to clear his mind of ideas belonging to his own day in considering the men and institutions of the past,—though this again is a limitation which he shares with his age.

---

[1] Written after the death of C. Gracchus, in 121 B.C.

[2] Claudius wrote of the period from the Gallic invasion to his own times, the Sullan age. His work had not fewer than 23 books.   [3] A. Klotz, *op. cit.*, p. 533.

[4] Quint. *Inst. Or.* x. i. 31; Plin. *Ep.* v. viii. 9; Cic. *De Orat.* ii. 59.

INTRODUCTION

It is evident that the student of history must use Livy with caution, especially in those portions of his work where his statements cannot be tested by comparison with those of Polybius. Yet, quite apart from his claims upon our attention as a supreme literary artist, it would be hard to overrate his importance as an historian, which is chiefly of two sorts. In the first place, uncritical though he is, we have no one to put in his place, and his pages are our best authority for long stretches of Roman history. In the second place he possesses a very positive excellence to add to this accidental one, in the fidelity and spirit with which he depicts for us the Roman's own idea of Rome. Any one of half a dozen annalists would have served as well as Livy to tell us what the Romans *did*, but it required genius to make us realize as Livy does what the Romans *were*. No mere critical use of documents could ever make the Roman character live again as it lives for us in his " pictured page." The People and the State are idealized no doubt by the patriotic imagination of this extraordinary writer,—but a people's ideals are surely not the least significant part of their history.[1]

---

[1] See Mr. Duff's excellent remarks in the finely appreciative chapter on Livy in his *Literary History of Rome*.

INTRODUCTION

IV

We have seen that each of the extant decades was handed down in a separate tradition. The manuscripts of the later portions will be briefly described in introductory notes to the volumes in which they are contained. Books I.-X. are preserved in a twofold MS. tradition. One family is represented by a single MS., the Verona palimpsest (V). The portion of this codex which contains the Livy consists of sixty leaves, on which are preserved fragments of Books III.-VI., written in uncial characters of the fourth century. These fragments were deciphered and published by Mommsen in 1868. The other family is the so-called Nichomachean. This edition, as it may be called, of the first decade was produced under the auspices of Q. Aurelius Symmachus, who was consul in 391 A.D. He appears to have commissioned Tascius Victorianus to prepare an amended copy of Books I.-X., and the latter's subscription (*Victorianus emendabam dominis Symmachis*) is found after every book as far as the ninth. In Books VI.-VIII. the subscription of Victorianus is preceded by one of Nichomachus Flavianus, son-in-law of Symmachus (*Nichomachus Flavianus v. c. III. praefect. urbis emendavi apud Hennam*), and in Books III.-V. by one of Nichomachus Dexter, a son of Flavianus (*Titi Livi Nichomachus Dexter v.c. emendavi ab*

INTRODUCTION

urbe condita), who adds the information, in subscribing Book V., that he had used the copy of his kinsman Clementianus. To this origin all the MSS. now extant are referred, with the exception of the *Veronensis*. The most famous member of the family is the *Mediceus*, a minuscule codex of the tenth or eleventh century containing the ten books and written with great fidelity—even in absurdities—to its exemplar. It has been shown to be the work of at least three scribes. The MS. abounds with dittographies and other errors, but is possibly the most valuable of its class, because of its honesty. For a full description of this and the other Nichomachean MSS. the reader should consult the Oxford edition of Livy, Books I.–V., by Conway and Walters. A list of all the MSS. used in that edition is given at the end of this introduction.

The *editio princeps*, edited by Andreas, afterwards Bishop of Aleria, was issued in Rome in 1469. In 1518 came the Aldine edition. The first complete edition of all the books now extant was also brought out at Rome, in 1616, by Lusignanus. Of modern editions may be mentioned those of Gronovius, Leyden, 1645 and 1679; Drakenborch (with notes of Duker and others, and the supplements of Freinsheimius), Leyden, 1738–1746; Alschefski, Berlin, 1841–1846 (critical edition of Books I.–X. and XXI.–XXIII.), and Berlin, 1843–44 (text of Books I.–X. and XXI.–XXX.); Madvig and Ussing, Copenhagen[4], 1886 ff. (Madvig's *Emendationes Livianae*—a

INTRODUCTION

classic of criticism—had appeared at Copenhagen in 1860); Hertz, Leipsic, 1857-1863; Weissenborn (Teubner text, revised by M. Müller and W. Heraeus) Leipsic, 1881 ff.; Luchs, Books XXI.-XXV. and XXVI.-XXX., Berlin, 1888-1889 (best critical apparatus for third decade); Zingerle, Leipsic, 1888-1908; Weissenborn and H. J. Müller, Berlin, 1880-1909 (best explanatory edition of the whole of Livy, with German notes; the several volumes are more or less frequently republished in revised editions); M. Müller, F. Luterbacher, E. Wölfflin, H. J. Müller, and F. Friedersdorff (Books I.-X. and XXI.-XXX., separate volumes, with German notes) Leipsic, various dates; Books I. and II. are in their second edition (II. by W. Heraeus).

Of the numerous editions of parts of the first decade which are provided with English notes may be cited: Book I. by Sir J. Seeley, Oxford, 1874; by H. J. Edwards, Cambridge, 1912; Books I. and II. by J. B. Greenough, Boston, 1891; Book II. by R. S. Conway, Cambridge, 1901; Books II. and III. by H. M. Stephenson, London, 1882; Book III. by P. Thoresby Jones, Oxford, 1914; Book IV. by H. M. Stephenson, Cambridge, 1890; Books V.-VII. by A. R. Cluer and P. E. Matheson, Oxford, 1904[2]; Book IX. by W. B. Anderson, Cambridge, 1909.

For the first decade the critical edition by Conway and Walters, of which the first half was published by the Oxford University Press in 1914, is the standard.

INTRODUCTION

There are translations of the whole of Livy by Philemon Holland, London, 1600; by George Baker, London, 1797; and by Rev. Canon Roberts, now in course of publication in Everyman's Library, London, 1912 ff. Books XXI.–XXV. have been done by A. J. Church and W. J. Brodribb, London, 1890.

Of books concerned wholly or in part with Livy the following may be mentioned: H. Taine, *Essai sur Tite Live*, Paris, 1856; J. Wight Duff, *A Literary History of Rome*, London and New York, 1909; O. Riemann, *Etudes sur la Langue et la Grammaire de Tite-Live*, Paris, 1885; C. Wachsmuth, *Einleitung in das Studium der alten Geschichte*, Leipsic, 1895; H. Darnley Naylor, *Latin and English Idiom, an Object Lesson from Livy's Preface*, and *More Latin and English Idiom*, Cambridge, 1909 and 1915.

For further information about the bibliography of Livy, including the great mass of pamphlets and periodical articles, the student may consult Schanz, *Geschichte der römischen Litteratur* ii. 1^3, Munich, 1911 (in Iwan von Müller's *Handbuch der Klassischen Altertumswissenschaft*) and the various *Jahresberichte*, by H. J. Müller and others, which Schanz lists on p. 418.

See also: Commentary on Books I.–V. by R. M. Ogilvie, Oxford, 1965; Complete Text of Livy by Conway, Walters, Johnson, MacDonald, Oxford, still in progress.

INTRODUCTION

The Manuscripts

V = Veronensis, 4th century.
F = Floriacensis, 9th century.
P = Parisiensis, 10th century.
E = Einsiedlensis, 10th century.
H = Harleianus prior, 10th century.
B = Bambergensis, 10th or 11th century.
M = Mediceus, 10th or 11th century.
Vorm. = Vormatiensis (as reported by Rhenanus).
R = Romanus, 11th century.
U = Upsaliensis, 11th century.
D = Dominicanus, 11th or 12th century.
L = Leidensis, 12th century.
A = Aginnensis, 13th century.
M^1 M^2 etc. denote corrections made by the original scribe or a later corrector. When it is impossible to identify the corrector M^x is employed.
Ω = all or some of the above MSS.
a = later part of *A*, 14th century.
s = one or more of the inferior MSS and early editions.

Abbreviations

Ald. (or ed. Ald.) = the Aldine edition, Venice, 1518.
Cassiod. = Cassiodorius.
Class. Quart. = *The Classical Quarterly*, London, 1907 ff.
C.I.L. = *Corpus Inscriptionum Latinarum*, vol. i.^{2} Berlin, 1893–5.
Diod. = Diodorus Siculus.
Dion. Hal. = Dionysius of Halicarnassus.

LIVY
FROM THE FOUNDING OF THE CITY

BOOK I

T. LIVI
AB URBE CONDITA

LIBER I

Praefatio

Facturusne operae pretium sim,[1] si a primordio urbis res populi Romani perscripserim, nec satis scio, 2 nec, si sciam, dicere ausim, quippe qui cum veterem tum volgatam esse rem videam, dum novi semper scriptores aut in rebus certius aliquid allaturos se aut scribendi arte rudem vetustatem superaturos 3 credunt. Utcumque erit, iuvabit tamen rerum gestarum memoriae principis terrarum populi pro virili parte et ipsum consuluisse; et si in tanta scriptorum turba mea fama in obscuro sit, nobilitate ac magnitudine eorum me qui nomini officient meo 4 consoler. Res est praeterea et immensi operis, ut quae supra septingentesimum annum repetatur, et

---

[1] operae pretium sim *Sabellicus (from Quint.* ix. iv. 74): sim operae pretium Ω.

LIVY

FROM THE FOUNDING OF THE CITY

BOOK I

Preface

WHETHER I am likely to accomplish anything worthy of the labour, if I record the achievements of the Roman people from the foundation of the city, I do not really know, nor if I knew would I dare to avouch it; perceiving as I do that the theme[1] is not only old but hackneyed, through the constant succession of new historians, who believe either that in their facts they can produce more authentic information, or that in their style they will prove better than the rude attempts of the ancients. Yet, however this shall be, it will be a satisfaction to have done myself as much as lies in me to commemorate the deeds of the foremost people of the world; and if in so vast a company of writers my own reputation should be obscure, my consolation would be the fame and greatness of those whose renown will throw mine into the shade. Moreover, my subject involves infinite labour, seeing that it must be traced back

[1] Some scholars take *rem* to mean "the practice," *sc.* of expressing confidence in one's ability.

quae ab exiguis profecta initiis eo creverit ut iam magnitudine laboret sua; et legentium plerisque haud dubito quin primae origines proximaque originibus minus praebitura voluptatis sint, festinantibus ad haec nova, quibus iam pridem praevalentis populi
5 vires se ipsae conficiunt: ego contra hoc quoque laboris praemium petam, ut me a conspectu malorum quae nostra tot per annos vidit aetas, tantisper certe dum prisca illa tota mente repeto, avertam, omnis expers curae quae scribentis animum, etsi non flectere a vero, sollicitum tamen efficere posset.
6 Quae ante conditam condendamve urbem poeticis magis decora fabulis quam incorruptis rerum gestarum monumentis traduntur, ea nec adfirmare nec
7 refellere in animo est. Datur haec venia antiquitati, ut miscendo humana divinis primordia urbium augustiora faciat; et si cui populo licere oportet consecrare origines suas et ad deos referre auctores, ea belli gloria est populo Romano ut cum suum conditorisque sui parentem Martem potissimum ferat tam et hoc gentes humanae patiantur aequo animo
8 quam imperium patiuntur. Sed haec et his similia, utcumque animadversa aut existimata erunt, haud
9 in magno equidem ponam discrimine: ad illa mihi pro se quisque acriter intendat animum, quae vita,

---

[1] Livy refers to the animosities inevitably aroused by writers who dealt with such thorny subjects as the civil wars, during the lifetime of many who had taken part in them.

BOOK I

above seven hundred years, and that proceeding from slender beginnings it has so increased as now to be burdened by its own magnitude; and at the same time I doubt not that to most readers the earliest origins and the period immediately succeeding them will give little pleasure, for they will be in haste to reach these modern times, in which the might of a people which has long been very powerful is working its own undoing. I myself, on the contrary, shall seek in this an additional reward for my toil, that I may avert my gaze from the troubles which our age has been witnessing for so many years, so long at least as I am absorbed in the recollection of the brave days of old, free from every care which, even if it could not divert the historian's mind from the truth, might nevertheless cause it anxiety.[1]

Such traditions as belong to the time before the city was founded, or rather was presently to be founded, and are rather adorned with poetic legends than based upon trustworthy historical proofs, I purpose neither to affirm nor to refute. It is the privilege of antiquity to mingle divine things with human, and so to add dignity to the beginnings of cities; and if any people ought to be allowed to consecrate their origins and refer them to a divine source, so great is the military glory of the Roman People that when they profess that their Father and the Father of their Founder was none other than Mars, the nations of the earth may well submit to this also with as good a grace as they submit to Rome's dominion. But to such legends as these, however they shall be regarded and judged, I shall, for my own part, attach no great importance. Here are the questions to which I would have every reader

LIVY

qui mores fuerint, per quos viros quibusque artibus domi militiaeque et partum et auctum imperium sit; labente deinde paulatim disciplina velut desidentis[1] primo mores sequatur animo, deinde ut magis magisque lapsi sint, tum ire coeperint praecipites, donec ad haec tempora quibus nec vitia nostra nec remedia pati possumus perventum est.

10   Hoc illud est praecipue in cognitione rerum salubre ac frugiferum, omnis te exempli documenta in inlustri posita monumento intueri; inde tibi tuaeque rei publicae quod imitere capias, inde 11 foedum inceptu, foedum exitu, quod vites. Ceterum aut me amor negotii suscepti fallit, aut nulla umquam res publica nec maior nec sanctior nec bonis exemplis ditior fuit, nec in quam civitatem tam serae avaritia luxuriaque inmigraverint, nec ubi tantus ac tam diu paupertati ac parsimoniae honos fuerit. Adeo quanto rerum minus, tanto minus 12 cupiditatis erat; nuper divitiae avaritiam et abundantes voluptates desiderium per luxum atque libidinem pereundi perdendique omnia invexere.

Sed querellae, ne tum quidem gratae futurae cum forsitan necessariae erunt, ab initio certe 13 tantae ordiendae rei absint; cum bonis potius ominibus votisque et precationibus deorum dearumque,

[1] desidentes ς: discidentis *M*: dissidentis (*or* dissidentes) Ω.

---

[1] The metaphor is from a decaying building.
[2] The monument Livy means is the body of a nation's achievements (*cf. res* in § 1), the "history" of a nation, in

BOOK I

give his close attention—what life and morals were like; through what men and by what policies, in peace and in war, empire was established and enlarged; then let him note how, with the gradual relaxation of discipline, morals first gave way, as it were, then sank lower and lower, and finally began the downward plunge[1] which has brought us to the present time, when we can endure neither our vices nor their cure.

What chiefly makes the study of history wholesome and profitable is this, that you behold the lessons of every kind of experience set forth as on a conspicuous monument;[2] from these you may choose for yourself and for your own state what to imitate, from these mark for avoidance what is shameful in the conception and shameful in the result. For the rest, either love of the task I have set myself deceives me, or no state was ever greater, none more righteous or richer in good examples, none ever was where avarice and luxury came into the social order so late, or where humble means and thrift were so highly esteemed and so long held in honour. For true it is that the less men's wealth was, the less was their greed. Of late, riches have brought in avarice, and excessive pleasures the longing to carry wantonness and licence to the point of ruin for oneself and of universal destruction.

But complaints are sure to be disagreeable, even when they shall perhaps be necessary; let the beginning, at all events, of so great an enterprise have none. With good omens rather would we begin, and, if historians had the same custom which poets have,

that objective sense of the word. This he likens to a monument of stone on which men's deeds are recorded.

7

si, ut poetis, nobis quoque mos esset, libentius inciperemus, ut orsis tantum operis successus prosperos darent.

I. Iam primum omnium satis constat Troia capta in ceteros saevitum esse Troianos: duobus, Aeneae Antenorique, et vetusti iure hospitii et quia pacis reddendaeque Helenae semper auctores fuerunt, 2 omne ius belli Achivos abstinuisse; casibus deinde variis Antenorem cum multitudine Enetum, qui seditione ex Paphlagonia pulsi et sedes et ducem rege Pylaemene ad Troiam amisso quaerebant, 3 venisse in intimum maris Hadriatici sinum, Euganeisque, qui inter mare Alpesque incolebant, pulsis, Enetos Troianosque eas tenuisse terras. Et in quem primum egressi sunt locum Troia vocatur, pagoque inde Troiano nomen est: gens universa Veneti 4 appellati. Aeneam ab simili clade domo profugum, sed ad maiora rerum initia ducentibus fatis, primo in Macedoniam venisse, inde in Siciliam quaerentem sedes delatum, ab Sicilia classe ad Laurentem agrum 5 tenuisse. Troia et huic loco nomen est. Ibi egressi Troiani, ut quibus ab inmenso prope errore nihil praeter arma et naves superesset, cum praedam ex agris agerent, Latinus rex Aboriginesque, qui tum ea tenebant loca, ad arcendam vim advenarum 6 armati ex urbe atque agris concurrunt. Duplex inde

---

[1] See the *Iliad*, v. 576.

BOOK I. i. 1-6

with prayers and entreaties to the gods and goddesses, that they might grant us to bring to a successful issue the great task we have undertaken.

I. First of all, then, it is generally agreed that when Troy was taken vengeance was wreaked upon the other Trojans, but that two, Aeneas and Antenor, were spared all the penalties of war by the Achivi, owing to long-standing claims of hospitality, and because they had always advocated peace and the giving back of Helen. They then experienced various vicissitudes. Antenor, with a company of Eneti who had been expelled from Paphlagonia in a revolution and were looking for a home and a leader—for they had lost their king, Pylaemenes, at Troy [1]—came to the inmost bay of the Adriatic. There, driving out the Euganei, who dwelt between the sea and the Alps, the Eneti and Trojans took possession of those lands. And in fact the place where they first landed is called Troy, and the district is therefore known as Trojan, while the people as a whole are called the Veneti. Aeneas, driven from home by a similar misfortune, but guided by fate to undertakings of greater consequence, came first to Macedonia; thence was carried, in his quest of a place of settlement, to Sicily; and from Sicily laid his course towards the land of Laurentum. This place too is called Troy. Landing there, the Trojans, as men who, after their all but immeasurable wanderings, had nothing left but their swords and ships, were driving booty from the fields, when King Latinus and the Aborigines, who then occupied that country, rushed down from their city and their fields to repel with arms the violence of the invaders. From this point the tradition follows two

LIVY

fama est. Alii proelio victum Latinum pacem cum
7 Aenea, deinde affinitatem iunxisse tradunt: alii, cum
instructae acies constitissent, priusquam signa cane-
rent processisse Latinum inter primores ducemque
advenarum evocasse ad conloquium; percunctatum
deinde qui mortales essent, unde aut quo casu profecti domo quidve quaerentes in agrum Laurenti-
8 num[1] exissent, postquam audierit multitudinem
Troianos esse, ducem Aeneam, filium Anchisae et
Veneris, cremata patria domo profugos sedem con-
dendaeque urbi locum quaerere, et nobilitatem
admiratum gentis virique et animum vel bello vel
paci paratum, dextra data fidem futurae amicitiae
9 sanxisse. Inde foedus ictum inter duces, inter exercitus salutationem factam; Aeneam apud Latinum
fuisse in hospitio; ibi Latinum apud penates deos
domesticum publico adiunxisse foedus filia Aeneae
10 in matrimonium data. Ea res utique Troianis spem
adfirmat tandem stabili certaque sede finiendi erroris.
11 Oppidum condunt; Aeneas ab nomine uxoris Lavinium appellat. Brevi stirpis quoque virilis ex novo
matrimonio fuit, cui Ascanium parentes dixere
nomen.

II. Bello deinde Aborigines Troianique simul
petiti. Turnus, rex Rutulorum, cui pacta Lavinia
ante adventum Aeneae fuerat, praelatum sibi adve-

[1] Laurentinum Ω: Laurentem $MO^2DL\varsigma$.

---

[1] This, in a nutshell, is the form of the legend on which Virgil based Books vii.–xii. of the *Aeneid*.

lines. Some say that Latinus, having been defeated in the battle, made a peace with Aeneas, and later an alliance of marriage.[1] Others maintain that when the opposing lines had been drawn up, Latinus did not wait for the charge to sound, but advanced amidst his chieftains and summoned the captain of the strangers to a parley. He then inquired what men they were, whence they had come, what mishap had caused them to leave their home, and what they sought in landing on the coast of Laurentum. He was told that the people were Trojans and their leader Aeneas, son of Anchises and Venus; that their city had been burnt, and that, driven from home, they were looking for a dwelling-place and a site where they might build a city. Filled with wonder at the renown of the race and the hero, and at his spirit, prepared alike for war or peace, he gave him his right hand in solemn pledge of lasting friendship. The commanders then made a treaty, and the armies saluted each other. Aeneas became a guest in the house of Latinus; there the latter, in the presence of his household gods, added a domestic treaty to the public one, by giving his daughter in marriage to Aeneas. This event removed any doubt in the minds of the Trojans that they had brought their wanderings to an end at last in a permanent and settled habitation. They founded a town, which Aeneas named Lavinium, after his wife. In a short time, moreover, there was a male scion of the new marriage, to whom his parents gave the name of Ascanius.

II. War was then made upon Trojans and Aborigines alike. Turnus was king of the Rutulians, and to him Lavinia had been betrothed before the coming

nam aegre patiens simul Aeneae Latinoque bellum
intulerat. Neutra acies laeta ex eo certamine abiit:
victi Rutuli: victores Aborigines Troianique ducem
Latinum amisere. Inde Turnus Rutulique diffisi
rebus ad florentes opes Etruscorum Mezentiumque
regem eorum confugiunt, qui Caere opulento tum
oppido imperitans, iam inde ab initio minime laetus
novae origine urbis, et tum nimio plus quam satis
tutum esset accolis rem Troianam crescere ratus,
haud gravatim socia arma Rutulis iunxit. Aeneas,
adversus tanti belli terrorem ut animos Aboriginum
sibi conciliaret, nec sub eodem iure solum sed etiam
nomine omnes essent, Latinos utramque gentem
appellavit. Nec deinde Aborigines Troianis studio
ac fide erga regem Aeneam cessere. Fretusque his
animis coalescentium in dies magis duorum populorum Aeneas, quamquam tanta opibus Etruria erat
ut iam non terras solum sed mare etiam per totam
Italiae longitudinem ab Alpibus ad fretum Siculum
fama nominis sui inplesset, tamen, cum moenibus
bellum propulsare posset, in aciem copias eduxit.
Secundum inde proelium Latinis, Aeneae etiam
ultimum operum mortalium fuit. Situs est, quem-

---

[1] Virgil makes Jupiter grant, as a favour to Juno, that

of Aeneas. Indignant that a stranger should be preferred before him, he attacked, at the same time, both Aeneas and Latinus. Neither army came off rejoicing from that battle. The Rutulians were beaten: the victorious Aborigines and Trojans lost their leader Latinus. Then Turnus and the Rutulians, discouraged at their situation, fled for succour to the opulent and powerful Etruscans and their king Mezentius, who held sway in Caere, at that time an important town. Mezentius had been, from the very beginning, far from pleased at the birth of the new city; he now felt that the Trojan state was growing much more rapidly than was altogether safe for its neighbours, and readily united his forces with those of the Rutulians. Aeneas, that he might win the goodwill of the Aborigines to confront so formidable an array, and that all might possess not only the same rights but also the same name, called both nations Latins;[1] and from that time on the Aborigines were no less ready and faithful than the Trojans in the service of King Aeneas. Accordingly, trusting to this friendly spirit of the two peoples, which were growing each day more united, and, despite the power of Etruria, which had filled with the glory of her name not only the lands but the sea as well, along the whole extent of Italy from the Alps to the Sicilian Strait, Aeneas declined to defend himself behind his walls, as he might have done, but led out his troops to battle. The fight which ensued was a victory for the Latins: for Aeneas it was, besides, the last of his mortal labours. He lies buried, whether it is fitting and right

the Trojan name shall be sunk in the Latin (*Aen.* xii. 835).

LIVY

cumque eum dici ius fasque est, super Numicum flumen: Iovem indigetem appellant.

III. Nondum maturus imperio Ascanius Aeneae filius erat; tamen id imperium ei ad puberem aetatem incolume mansit; tantisper tutela muliebri—tanta indoles in Lavinia erat—res Latina et regnum avitum paternumque puero stetit. Haud ambigam—quis enim rem tam veterem pro certo adfirmet?—hicine fuerit Ascanius an maior quam hic, Creusa matre Ilio incolumi natus comesque inde paternae fugae, quem Iulum eundem Iulia gens auctorem nominis sui nuncupat. Is Ascanius, ubicumque et quacumque matre genitus—certe natum Aenea constat—abundante Lavini multitudine florentem iam, ut tum res erant, atque opulentam urbem matri seu novercae reliquit: novam ipse aliam sub Albano monte condidit, quae ab situ porrectae in dorso urbis Longa Alba appellata. Inter Lavinium conditum[1] et Albam Longam coloniam deductam triginta ferme interfuere anni. Tantum tamen opes creverant, maxime fusis Etruscis, ut ne morte quidem Aeneae nec deinde inter muliebrem tutelam rudimentumque primum puerilis regni movere arma aut Mezentius Etruscique aut ulli alii accolae ausi sint. Pax ita convenerat ut Etruscis Latinisque fluvius Albula,

[1] Lavinium conditum *Harant*: Lavinium Ω.

---

[1] *Indiges* means "of or belonging to a certain place" (Fowler, *Fest.* p. 192). Dion. Hal. i. 64, says that the Latins made a shrine to Aeneas with an inscription in which

BOOK I. ii. 6–iii. 5

to term him god or man, on the banks of the river Numicus; men, however, call him Jupiter Indiges.[1]

III. Ascanius, Aeneas' son, was not yet ripe for authority; yet the authority was kept for him, unimpaired, until he arrived at manhood. Meanwhile, under a woman's regency, the Latin State and the kingdom of his father and his grandfather stood unshaken—so strong was Lavinia's character—until the boy could claim it. I shall not discuss the question —for who could affirm for certain so ancient a matter? —whether this boy was Ascanius, or an elder brother, born by Creusa while Ilium yet stood, who accompanied his father when he fled from the city, being the same whom the Julian family call Iulus and claim as the author of their name. This Ascanius, no matter where born, or of what mother—it is agreed in any case that he was Aeneas' son—left Lavinium, when its population came to be too large, for it was already a flourishing and wealthy city for those days, to his mother, or stepmother, and founded a new city himself below the Alban Mount. This was known from its position, as it lay stretched out along the ridge, by the name of Alba Longa. From the settlement of Lavinium to the planting of the colony at Alba Longa was an interval of some thirty years. Yet the nation had grown so powerful, in consequence especially of the defeat of the Etruscans, that even when Aeneas died, and even when a woman became its regent and a boy began his apprenticeship as king, neither Mezentius and his Etruscans nor any other neighbours dared to attack them. Peace had been agreed to on these terms, that the River Albula, which men now call the Tiber, should be the boundary

he was called πατὴρ χθόνιος (*Pater Indiges*). He was also called *Deus Indiges* and *Aeneas Indiges*.

LIVY

6 quem nunc Tiberim vocant, finis esset. Silvius deinde regnat, Ascanii filius, casu quodam in silvis 7 natus. Is Aeneam Silvium creat; is deinde Latinum Silvium. Ab eo coloniae aliquot deductae, Prisci 8 Latini appellati. Mansit Silviis postea omnibus cognomen qui Albae regnarunt.[1] Latino Alba ortus, Alba Atys, Atye Capys, Capye Capetus, Capeto Tiberinus, qui in traiectu [2] Albulae amnis submersus 9 celebre ad posteros nomen flumini dedit. Agrippa inde Tiberini filius, post Agrippam Romulus Silvius a patre accepto imperio regnat. Aventino fulmine ipse ictus regnum per manus tradidit. Is sepultus in eo colle, qui nunc pars Romanae est urbis, cogno- 10 men colli fecit. Proca deinde regnat. Is Numitorem atque Amulium procreat; Numitori, qui stirpis maximus erat, regnum vetustum Silviae gentis legat. Plus tamen vis potuit quam voluntas patris aut verecundia aetatis: pulso fratre Amulius regnat. Addit sceleri scelus: stirpem fratris virilem interemit[3]: fratris filiae Reae Silviae per speciem honoris, cum Vestalem eam legisset, perpetua virginitate spem partus adimit.[4]

IV. Sed debebatur, ut opinor, fatis tantae origo urbis maximique secundum deorum opes imperii 2 principium. Vi compressa Vestalis, cum geminum partum edidisset, seu ita rata, seu quia deus auctor culpae honestior erat, Martem incertae stirpis patrem

---

[1] regnarunt Ω : regnaverunt M.
[2] traiectu R²D² (or D¹) : traiecto Ω.
[3] interemit Ω : interimit MO? HR.
[4] adimit Ω : ademit UOE².

BOOK I. iii. 5–iv. 2

between the Etruscans and the Latins. Next Silvius reigned, son of Ascanius, born, as it chanced, in the forest. He begat Aeneas Silvius, and he Latinus Silvius. By him several colonies were planted, and called the Ancient Latins. Thereafter the cognomen Silvius was retained by all who ruled at Alba. From Latinus came Alba, from Alba Atys, from Atys Capys, from Capys Capetus, from Capetus Tiberinus. This last king was drowned in crossing the River Albula, and gave the stream the name which has been current with later generations. Then Agrippa, son of Tiberinus, reigned, and after Agrippa Romulus Silvius was king, having received the power from his father. Upon the death of Romulus by lightning, the kingship passed from him to Aventinus. This king was buried on that hill, which is now a part of the City of Rome, and gave his name to the hill. Proca ruled next. He begat Numitor and Amulius; to Numitor, the elder, he bequeathed the ancient realm of the Silvian family. Yet violence proved more potent than a father's wishes or respect for seniority. Amulius drove out his brother and ruled in his stead. Adding crime to crime, he destroyed Numitor's male issue; and Rhea Silvia, his brother's daughter, he appointed a Vestal under pretence of honouring her, and by consigning her to perpetual virginity, deprived her of the hope of children.

IV. But the Fates were resolved, as I suppose, upon the founding of this great City, and the beginning of the mightiest of empires, next after that of Heaven. The Vestal was ravished, and having given birth to twin sons, named Mars as the father of her doubtful offspring, whether actually so believing, or because it seemed less wrong if a god

LIVY

3 nuncupat. Sed nec dii nec homines aut ipsam aut stirpem a crudelitate regia vindicant: sacerdos vincta in custodiam datur: pueros in profluentem aquam 4 mitti iubet. Forte quadam divinitus super ripas Tiberis effusus lenibus stagnis nec adiri usquam ad iusti cursum poterat amnis et posse quamvis languida 5 mergi aqua infantes spem ferentibus dabat. Ita, velut defuncti regis imperio, in proxima alluvie ubi nunc ficus Ruminalis est—Romularem vocatam ferunt 6 —pueros exponunt. Vastae tum in his locis solitudines erant. Tenet fama, cum fluitantem alveum quo expositi erant pueri tenuis in sicco aqua destituisset, lupam sitientem ex montibus qui circa sunt ad puerilem vagitum cursum flexisse; eam summissas infantibus adeo mitem praebuisse mammas ut lingua lambentem pueros magister regii pecoris invenerit— 7 Faustulo fuisse nomen ferunt. Ab eo ad stabula Larentiae[1] uxori educandos datos. Sunt qui Larentiam[1] vulgato corpore lupam inter pastores vocatam 8 putent: inde locum fabulae ac miraculo datum. Ita geniti itaque educati, cum primum adolevit aetas, nec in stabulis nec ad pecora segnes, venando peragrare 9 saltus. Hinc robore corporibus animisque sumpto

[1] Larentiae (-am) *MDL*: Laurentiae (-am) Ω.

[1] The word *lupa* was sometimes used in the sense of "courtesan."

were the author of her fault. But neither gods nor men protected the mother herself or her babes from the king's cruelty; the priestess he ordered to be manacled and cast into prison, the children to be committed to the river. It happened by singular good fortune that the Tiber having spread beyond its banks into stagnant pools afforded nowhere any access to the regular channel of the river, and the men who brought the twins were led to hope that being infants they might be drowned, no matter how sluggish the stream. So they made shift to discharge the king's command, by exposing the babes at the nearest point of the overflow, where the fig-tree Ruminalis—formerly, they say, called Romularis—now stands. In those days this was a wild and uninhabited region. The story persists that when the floating basket in which the children had been exposed was left high and dry by the receding water, a she-wolf, coming down out of the surrounding hills to slake her thirst, turned her steps towards the cry of the infants, and with her teats gave them suck so gently, that the keeper of the royal flock found her licking them with her tongue. Tradition assigns to this man the name of Faustulus, and adds that he carried the twins to his hut and gave them to his wife Larentia to rear. Some think that Larentia, having been free with her favours, had got the name of "she-wolf" among the shepherds, and that this gave rise to this marvellous story.[1] The boys, thus born and reared, had no sooner attained to youth than they began—yet without neglecting the farmstead or the flocks—to range the glades of the mountains for game. Having in this way gained both strength and resolution, they would now not

iam non feras tantum subsistere, sed in latrones
praeda onustos impetus facere pastoribusque rapta
dividere et cum his crescente in dies grege iuvenum
seria ac iocos celebrare.

V. Iam tum in Palatio monte Lupercal hoc fuisse
ludicrum ferunt et a Pallanteo, urbe Arcadica, Pal-
2 lantium, dein Palatium montem appellatum. Ibi
Euandrum, qui ex eo genere Arcadum multis ante
tempestatibus tenuerit loca, sollemne adlatum ex
Arcadia instituisse ut nudi iuvenes Lycaeum Pana
venerantes per lusum atque lasciviam currerent,
3 quem Romani deinde vocarunt Inuum. Huic deditis
ludicro, cum sollemne notum esset, insidiatos ob iram
praedae amissae latrones, cum Romulus vi se defen-
disset, Remum cepisse, captum regi Amulio tradi-
4 disse ultro accusantes. Crimini maxime dabant in
Numitoris agros ab iis impetus[1] fieri; inde eos
collecta iuvenum manu hostilem in modum praedas
agere. Sic Numitori ad supplicium Remus deditur.
5 Iam inde ab initio Faustulo spes fuerat regiam stirpem apud se educari; nam et expositos iussu regis
infantes sciebat, et tempus quo ipse eos sustulisset
ad id ipsum congruere; sed rem inmaturam nisi aut

[1] impetus *Gronovius*: impetum Ω.

---

[1] The derivation here given is fanciful. The word is probably akin to *palus*, " pale," and meant a " fenced place."

BOOK I. iv. 9–v. 5

only face wild beasts, but would attack robbers laden with their spoils, and divide up what they took from them among the shepherds, with whom they shared their toils and pranks, while their band of young men grew larger every day.

V. They say that the Palatine was even then the scene of the merry festival of the Lupercalia which we have to-day, and that the hill was named Pallantium, from Pallanteum, an Arcadian city, and then Palatium.[1] There Evander, an Arcadian of that stock, who had held the place many ages before the time of which I am writing, is said to have established the yearly rite, derived from Arcadia, that youths should run naked about in playful sport, doing honour to Lycaean Pan, whom the Romans afterwards called Inuus. When the young men were occupied in this celebration, the rite being generally known, some robbers who had been angered by the loss of their plunder laid an ambush for them, and although Romulus successfully defended himself, captured Remus and delivered up their prisoner to King Amulius, even lodging a complaint against him. The main charge was that the brothers made raids on the lands of Numitor, and pillaged them, with a band of young fellows which they had got together, like an invading enemy. So Remus was given up to Numitor to be punished. From the very beginning Faustulus had entertained the suspicion that they were children of the royal blood that he was bringing up in his house; for he was aware both that infants had been exposed by order of the king, and that the time when he had himself taken up the children exactly coincided with that event. But he had been unwilling that the

LIVY

per occasionem aut per necessitatem aperire[1] noluerat. Necessitas prior venit; ita metu subactus Romulo rem aperit. Forte et Numitori, cum in custodia Remum haberet audissetque geminos esse fratres, comparando et aetatem eorum et ipsam minime servilem indolem tetigerat animum memoria nepotum; sciscitandoque eodem pervenit, ut haud procul esset quin Remum agnosceret. Ita undique regi dolus nectitur. Romulus non cum globo iuvenum—nec enim erat ad vim apertam par—sed aliis alio itinere iussis certo tempore ad regiam venire pastoribus ad regem impetum facit, et a domo Numitoris alia comparata manu adiuvat Remus. Ita regem obtruncat.[2] VI. Numitor inter primum tumultum hostis invasisse urbem atque adortos regiam dictitans, cum pubem Albanam in arcem praesidio armisque obtinendam avocasset, postquam iuvenes perpetrata caede pergere ad se gratulantes vidit, extemplo advocato concilio scelera in se fratris, originem nepotum, ut geniti, ut educati, ut cogniti essent, caedem deinceps tyranni seque eius auctorem ostendit. Iuvenes per mediam contionem agmine ingressi cum avum regem salutassent, secuta ex omni multitudine consentiens vox ratum nomen imperiumque regi efficit.

[1] aperire *PFUBOE* : aperiri (app- *H*) *MRDLH*.
[2] obtruncat Ω : obtruncant ς.

BOOK I. v. 5–vi. 2

matter should be disclosed prematurely, until opportunity offered or necessity compelled. Necessity came first; accordingly, driven by fear, he revealed the facts to Romulus. It chanced that Numitor too, having Remus in custody, and hearing that the brothers were twins, had been reminded, upon considering their age and their far from servile nature, of his grandsons. The inquiries he made led him to the same conclusion, so that he was almost ready to acknowledge Remus. Thus on every hand the toils were woven about the king. Romulus did not assemble his company of youths—for he was not equal to open violence—but commanded his shepherds to come to the palace at an appointed time, some by one way, some by another, and so made his attack upon the king; while from the house of Numitor came Remus, with another party which he had got together, to help his brother. So Romulus slew the king. VI. At the beginning of the fray Numitor exclaimed that an enemy had invaded the city and attacked the palace, and drew off the active men of the place to serve as an armed garrison for the defence of the citadel; and when he saw the young men approaching, after they had dispatched the king, to congratulate him, he at once summoned a council, and laid before it his brother's crimes against himself, the parentage of his grandsons, and how they had been born, reared, and recognised. He then announced the tyrant's death, and declared himself to be responsible for it. The brothers advanced with their band through the midst of the crowd, and hailed their grandfather king, whereupon such a shout of assent arose from the entire throng as confirmed the new monarch's title and authority.

LIVY

3 Ita Numitori Albana re permissa Romulum Remumque cupido cepit in iis[1] locis ubi expositi ubique educati erant urbis condendae. Et supererat multitudo Albanorum Latinorumque; ad id pastores quoque accesserant, qui omnes facile spem facerent parvam Albam, parvum Lavinium prae ea urbe quae 4 conderetur fore. Intervenit deinde his cogitationibus avitum malum, regni cupido, atque inde foedum certamen, coortum a satis miti principio. Quoniam gemini essent nec aetatis verecundia discrimen facere posset, ut dii, quorum tutelae ea loca essent, auguriis legerent, qui nomen novae urbi daret, qui conditam imperio regeret, Palatium Romulus, Remus Aventinum ad inaugurandum templa capiunt. VII. Priori Remo augurium venisse fertur, sex vultures, iamque nuntiato augurio cum duplex numerus Romulo se ostendisset, utrumque regem sua multitudo consalu- 2 taverat: tempore illi praecepto, at hi numero avium regnum trahebant. Inde cum altercatione congressi certamine irarum ad caedem vertuntur; ibi in turba ictus Remus cecidit. Vulgatior fama est ludibrio fratris Remum novos transiluisse muros; inde ab irato Romulo, cum verbis quoque increpitans adiecisset "sic deinde, quicumque alius transiliet moenia 3 mea," interfectum. Ita solus potitus imperio Romulus; condita urbs conditoris nomine appellata.

A.U.C. 1

[1] iis ϛ : his Ω.

---

[1] A form of the legend preserved by Dion. Hal. i. 87, and Ovid, *Fasti*, iv. 843, names Celer, whom Romulus had put in charge of the rising wall, as the slayer of Remus.

BOOK I. vi. 3–vii. 3

The Alban state being thus made over to Numitor, Romulus and Remus were seized with the desire to found a city in the region where they had been exposed and brought up. And in fact the population of Albans and Latins was too large; besides, there were the shepherds. All together, their numbers might easily lead men to hope that Alba would be small, and Lavinium small, compared with the city which they should build. These considerations were interrupted by the curse of their grandsires, the greed of kingly power, and by a shameful quarrel which grew out of it, upon an occasion innocent enough. Since the brothers were twins, and respect for their age could not determine between them, it was agreed that the gods who had those places in their protection should choose by augury who should give the new city its name, who should govern it when built. Romulus took the Palatine for his augural quarter, Remus the Aventine. VII. Remus B.C. 753 is said to have been the first to receive an augury, from the flight of six vultures. The omen had been already reported when twice that number appeared to Romulus. Thereupon each was saluted king by his own followers, the one party laying claim to the honour from priority, the other from the number of the birds. They then engaged in a battle of words and, angry taunts leading to bloodshed, Remus was struck down in the affray. The commoner story is that Remus leaped over the new walls in mockery of his brother, whereupon Romulus in great anger slew him, and in menacing wise added these words withal, "So perish whoever else shall leap over my walls!"[1] Thus Romulus acquired sole power, and the city, thus founded, was called by its founder's name.

LIVY

Palatium primum, in quo ipse erat educatus, muniit. Sacra diis aliis Albano ritu, Graeco Herculi, ut ab Euandro instituta erant, facit. Herculem in ea loca Geryone interempto boves mira specie abegisse memorant ac prope Tiberim fluvium, qua prae se armentum agens nando traiecerat, loco herbido, ut quiete et pabulo laeto reficeret boves, et ipsum fessum via procubuisse. Ibi cum eum cibo vinoque gravatum sopor oppressisset, pastor accola eius loci, nomine Cacus, ferox viribus, captus pulchritudine boum cum avertere eam praedam vellet, quia si agendo armentum in speluncam compulisset ipsa vestigia quaerentem dominum eo deductura erant, aversos boves, eximium quemque pulchritudine, caudis in speluncam traxit. Hercules ad primam auroram somno excitus cum gregem perlustrasset oculis et partem abesse numero sensisset, pergit ad proximam speluncam, si forte eo vestigia ferrent. Quae ubi omnia foras versa vidit nec in partem aliam ferre, confusus atque incertus animi ex loco infesto agere porro armentum occepit. Inde cum actae boves quaedam ad desiderium, ut fit, relictarum mugissent, reddita inclusarum ex spelunca boum vox Herculem convertit. Quem cum vadentem ad spel-

BOOK I. VII. 3-7

His first act was to fortify the Palatine, on which B.C. 753
he had himself been reared. To other gods he sacrificed after the Alban custom, but employed the Greek
for Hercules, according to the institution of Evander.
The story is as follows: Hercules, after slaying
Geryones, was driving off his wondrously beautiful
cattle, when, close to the river Tiber, where he had
swum across it with the herd before him, he found a
green spot, where he could let the cattle rest and
refresh themselves with the abundant grass; and
being tired from his journey he lay down himself.
When he had there fallen into a deep sleep, for he
was heavy with food and wine, a shepherd by the
name of Cacus, who dwelt hard by and was insolent
by reason of his strength, was struck with the beauty
of the animals, and wished to drive them off as plunder. But if he had driven the herd into his cave,
their tracks would have been enough to guide their
owner to the place in his search; he therefore chose
out those of the cattle that were most remarkable
for their beauty, and turning them the other way,
dragged them into the cave by their tails. At daybreak Hercules awoke. Glancing over the herd, and
perceiving that a part of their number was lacking,
he proceeded to the nearest cave, in case there might
be foot-prints leading into it. When he saw that they
were all turned outward and yet did not lead to any
other place, he was confused and bewildered, and
made ready to drive his herd away from that uncanny spot. As the cattle were being driven off,
some of them lowed, as usually happens, missing those
which had been left behind. They were answered
with a low by the cattle shut up in the cave, and this
made Hercules turn back. When he came towards the

LIVY

uncam Cacus vi prohibere conatus esset, ictus clava fidem pastorum nequiquam invocans morte occubuit. Euander tum ea profugus ex Peloponneso auctoritate magis quam imperio regebat loca, venerabilis vir miraculo litterarum, rei novae inter rudes artium homines, venerabilior divinitate credita Carmentae matris, quam fatiloquam ante Sibyllae in Italiam adventum miratae eae gentes fuerant. Is tum Euander concursu pastorum trepidantium circa advenam manifestae reum caedis excitus postquam facinus facinorisque causam audivit, habitum formamque viri aliquantum ampliorem augustioremque humana intuens, rogitat qui vir esset. Ubi nomen patremque ac patriam accepit, "Iove nate, Hercules, salve," inquit; "te mihi mater, veridica interpres deum, aucturum caelestium numerum cecinit tibique aram hic dicatum iri quam opulentissima olim in terris gens maximam vocet tuoque ritu colat." Dextra Hercules data accipere se omen inpleturumque fata ara condita ac dicata ait. Ibi tum primum bove eximia capta de grege sacrum Herculi[1] adhibitis ad ministerium dapemque[1] Potitiis ac Pinariis, quae tum familiae maxime inclitae ea loca incolebant,

[1] Herculi ... dapemque *MP²*: *omitted by* Ω.

---

[1] Evander is said to have invented the Roman alphabet.

BOOK I. VII. 7–12

cave, Cacus would have prevented his approach with force, but received a blow from the hero's club, and calling in vain upon the shepherds to protect him, gave up the ghost. Evander, an exile from the Peloponnese, controlled that region in those days, more through personal influence than sovereign power. He was a man revered for his wonderful invention of letters,[1] a new thing to men unacquainted with the arts, and even more revered because of the divinity which men attributed to his mother Carmenta, whom those tribes had admired as a prophetess before the Sibyl's coming into Italy. Now this Evander was then attracted by the concourse of shepherds, who, crowding excitedly about the stranger, were accusing him as a murderer caught red-handed. When he had been told about the deed and the reason for it, and had marked the bearing of the man and his figure, which was somewhat ampler and more august than a mortal's, he inquired who he was. Upon learning his name, his father, and his birth-place, he exclaimed, "Hail, Hercules, son of Jupiter! You are he, of whom my mother, truthful interpreter of Heaven, foretold to me that you should be added to the number of the gods, and that an altar should be dedicated to you here which the nation one day to be the most powerful on earth should call the Greatest Altar, and should serve according to your rite." Hercules gave him his hand, and declared that he accepted the omen, and would fulfil the prophecy by establishing and dedicating an altar. Then and there men took a choice victim from the herd, and for the first time made sacrifice to Hercules. For the ministry and the banquet they employed the Potitii and the Pinarii, being the families

LIVY

A.U.C. 1 13 factum. Forte ita evenit, ut Potitii ad tempus praesto essent iisque exta apponerentur, Pinarii extis adesis ad ceteram venirent dapem. Inde institutum mansit, donec Pinarium genus fuit, ne extis eorum 14 sollemnium[1] vescerentur. Potitii ab Euandro edocti antistites sacri eius per multas aetates fuerunt, donec tradito servis publicis sollemni familiae ministerio 15 genus omne Potitiorum interiit. Haec tum sacra Romulus una ex omnibus peregrina suscepit, iam tum inmortalitatis virtute partae,[2] ad quam eum sua fata ducebant, fautor.

VIII. Rebus divinis rite perpetratis vocataque ad concilium multitudine, quae coalescere in populi unius corpus nulla re praeterquam legibus poterat, iura dedit; quae ita sancta generi hominum agresti fore ratus si se ipse venerabilem insignibus imperii fecisset cum cetero habitu se augustiorem, tum 3 maxime lictoribus duodecim sumptis fecit. Alii ab numero avium quae augurio regnum portenderant eum secutum numerum putant: me haud paenitet eorum sententiae esse quibus et apparitores hoc genus[3] ab Etruscis finitimis, unde sella curulis, unde toga praetexta sumpta est, et numerum[4] quoque ipsum ductum placet, et ita habuisse Etruscos, quod

---

[1] eorum sollemnium *Walters*: eo sollemnium (*or the like*) Ω: sollemnium *M*: sollemnibus (*or* sol- *or* solempn-) *FPUBOE*.
[2] partae *E*: parta Ω.
[3] hoc genus *Gronov.*: et hoc genus Ω.
[4] et numerum *Heumann*: numerum Ω.

---

[1] For the story of Cacus and the origin of the Ara Maxima see also Virgil, *Aen.* viii. 182-279; Prop. iv. 9; Ovid, *Fasti*, i. 543-586.

BOOK I. VII. 12–VIII. 3

of most distinction then living in that region. It so fell out that the Potitii were there at the appointed time, and to them were served the inwards; the Pinarii came after the inwards had been eaten, in season for the remainder of the feast. Thence came the custom, which persisted as long as the Pinarian family endured, that they should not partake of the inwards at that sacrifice. The Potitii, instructed by Evander, were priests of this cult for many generations, until, having delegated to public slaves the solemn function of their family, the entire stock of the Potitii died out. This was the only sacred observance, of all those of foreign origin, which Romulus then adopted, honouring even then the immortality won by worth to which his own destiny was leading him.[1]

VIII. When Romulus had duly attended to the worship of the gods, he called the people together and gave them the rules of law, since nothing else but law could unite them into a single body politic. But these, he was persuaded, would only appear binding in the eyes of a rustic people in case he should invest his own person with majesty, by adopting emblems of authority. He therefore put on a more august state in every way, and especially by the assumption of twelve lictors.[2] Some think the twelve birds which had given him an augury of kingship led him to choose this number. For my part, I am content to share the opinion of those who derive from the neighbouring Etruscans (whence were borrowed the curule chair and purple-bordered toga) not only the type of attendants but their number as well—a number which the Etruscans themselves are thought to have chosen because each

[2] The lictors carried axes in bundles of rods, in readiness to execute the king's sentence of scourging and decapitation.

LIVY

ex duodecim populis communiter creato rege singulos singuli populi lictores dederint.

Crescebat interim urbs munitionibus alia atque alia adpetendo loca, cum in spem magis futurae multitudinis quam ad id quod tum hominum erat munirent. Deinde, ne vana urbis magnitudo esset, adiciendae multitudinis causa vetere consilio condentium urbes, qui obscuram atque humilem conciendo ad se multitudinem natam e terra sibi prolem ementiebantur, locum qui nunc saeptus escendentibus[1] inter duos lucos est, asylum aperit. Eo ex finitimis populis turba omnis, sine discrimine liber an servus esset, avida novarum rerum perfugit, idque primum ad coeptam magnitudinem roboris fuit. Cum iam virium haud paeniteret, consilium deinde viribus parat. Centum creat senatores, sive quia is numerus satis erat, sive quia soli centum erant qui creari patres possent. Patres certe ab honore, patriciique progenies eorum appellati.

IX. Iam res Romana adeo erat valida ut cuilibet finitimarum civitatum bello par esset; sed penuria mulierum hominis aetatem duratura magnitudo erat, quippe quibus nec domi spes prolis nec cum finitimis conubia essent. Tum ex consilio patrum Romulus legatos circa vicinas gentes misit, qui societatem

---

[1] escendentibus *Edwards*: descendentibus Ω.

---

[1] *i.e.* the Capitoline.
[2] As being heads of clans, *patres familiarum.*

of the twelve cities which united to elect the king B.C. 753 contributed one lictor.

Meanwhile the City was expanding and reaching out its walls to include one place after another, for they built their defences with an eye rather to the population which they hoped one day to have than to the numbers they had then. Next, lest his big City should be empty, Romulus resorted to a plan for increasing the inhabitants which had long been employed by the founders of cities, who gather about them an obscure and lowly multitude and pretend that the earth has raised up sons to them. In the place which is now enclosed, between the two groves as you go up the hill,[1] he opened a sanctuary. Thither fled, from the surrounding peoples, a miscellaneous rabble, without distinction of bond or free, eager for new conditions; and these constituted the first advance in power towards that greatness at which Romulus aimed. He had now no reason to be dissatisfied with his strength, and proceeded to add policy to strength. He appointed a hundred senators, whether because this number seemed to him sufficient, or because there were no more than a hundred who could be designated Fathers.[2] At all events, they received the designation of Fathers from their rank, and their descendants were called patricians.

IX. Rome was now strong enough to hold her own B.C. 753–717 in war with any of the adjacent states; but owing to the want of women a single generation was likely to see the end of her greatness, since she had neither prospect of posterity at home nor the right of intermarriage with her neighbours. So, on the advice of the senate, Romulus sent envoys round among all the neighbouring nations to solicit for the new people

LIVY

3 conubiumque novo populo peterent: urbes quoque, ut cetera, ex infimo nasci; dein, quas[1] sua virtus ac di iuvent, magnas opes sibi magnumque
4 nomen facere; satis scire origini Romanae et deos adfuisse et non defuturam virtutem; proinde ne gravarentur homines cum hominibus sanguinem
5 ac genus miscere. Nusquam benigne legatio audita est; adeo simul spernebant, simul tantam in medio crescentem molem sibi ac posteris suis metuebant. A[2] plerisque rogitantibus dimissi, ecquod feminis quoque asylum aperuissent; id enim demum con-
6 par conubium fore. Aegre id Romana pubes passa, et haud dubie ad vim spectare res coepit. Cui tempus locumque aptum ut daret Romulus, aegritudinem animi dissimulans ludos ex industria parat Neptuno equestri sollemnis; Consualia vocat.
7 Indici deinde finitimis spectaculum iubet, quantoque apparatu tum sciebant aut poterant, concelebrant, ut rem claram exspectatamque facerent.
8 Multi mortales convenere, studio etiam videndae novae urbis, maxime proximi quique, Caeninenses,
9 Crustumini, Antemnates; etiam[3] Sabinorum omnis

---

[1] quas *Aldus*: qua Ω.   [2] A ς: ac Ω.
[3] etiam *Scheibe*: iam Ω.

---

[1] The Consualia was a harvest festival, held on August 21. Consus, the true name of the god, is from *condere*, "to store up." From the association of the festival with horses came

an alliance and the privilege of intermarrying. Cities, they argued, as well as all other things, take their rise from the lowliest beginnings. As time goes on, those which are aided by their own worth and by the favour of Heaven achieve great power and renown. They said they were well assured that Rome's origin had been blessed with the favour of Heaven, and that worth would not be lacking; their neighbours should not be reluctant to mingle their stock and their blood with the Romans, who were as truly men as they were. Nowhere did the embassy obtain a friendly hearing. In fact men spurned, at the same time that they feared, both for themselves and their descendants, that great power which was then growing up in their midst; and the envoys were frequently asked, on being dismissed, if they had opened a sanctuary for women as well as for men, for in that way only would they obtain suitable wives. This was a bitter insult to the young Romans, and the matter seemed certain to end in violence. Expressly to afford a fitting time and place for this, Romulus, concealing his resentment, made ready solemn games in honour of the equestrian Neptune, which he called Consualia.[1] He then bade proclaim the spectacle to the surrounding peoples, and his subjects prepared to celebrate it with all the resources within their knowledge and power, that they might cause the occasion to be noised abroad and eagerly expected. Many people—for they were also eager to see the new city—gathered for the festival, especially those who lived nearest, the inhabitants of Caenina, Crustumium, and Antemnae. The Sabines,

the later identification of the god with *Neptunus Equester*. See Fowler, *Fest.* pp. 206-9.

multitudo cum liberis ac coniugibus venit. Invitati hospitaliter per domos cum situm moeniaque et frequentem tectis urbem vidissent, mirantur tam brevi rem Romanam crevisse. Ubi spectaculi tempus venit deditaeque eo mentes cum oculis erant, tum ex composito orta vis, signoque dato iuventus Romana ad rapiendas virgines discurrit. Magna pars forte, in quem quaeque inciderat, raptae: quasdam forma excellentes primoribus patrum destinatas ex plebe homines, quibus datum negotium erat, domos deferebant: unam longe ante alias specie ac pulchritudine insignem a globo Thalassii cuiusdam raptam ferunt, multisque sciscitantibus cuinam eam ferrent, identidem, ne quis violaret, Thalassio ferri clamitatum; inde nuptialem hanc vocem factam. Turbato per metum ludicro maesti parentes virginum profugiunt, incusantes violati hospitii scelus[1] deumque invocantes, cuius ad sollemne ludosque per fas ac fidem decepti venissent. Nec raptis aut spes de se melior aut indignatio est minor. Sed ipse Romulus circumibat docebatque patrum id superbia factum, qui conubium finitimis negassent; illas tamen in matrimonio, in societate fortunarum omnium civitatisque, et quo nihil carius humano generi sit, liberum fore; molli-

[1] scelus *Grunaver*: foedus Ω.

---

[1] Plutarch, *Rom.* 15, also gives the story, and observes that the Romans used "Talasius" as the Greeks did "Hymenaeus." See also Catullus, lxi. 134.

BOOK I. ix. 9-15

too, came with all their people, including their
children and wives. They were hospitably entertained in every house, and when they had looked
at the site of the City, its walls, and its numerous
buildings, they marvelled that Rome had so rapidly
grown great. When the time came for the show,
and people's thoughts and eyes were busy with it,
the preconcerted attack began. At a given signal
the young Romans darted this way and that, to seize
and carry off the maidens. In most cases these were
taken by the men in whose path they chanced to be.
Some, of exceptional beauty, had been marked out
for the chief senators, and were carried off to their
houses by plebeians to whom the office had been
entrusted. One, who far excelled the rest in mien
and loveliness, was seized, the story relates, by the
gang of a certain Thalassius. Being repeatedly asked
for whom they were bearing her off, they kept shouting that no one should touch her, for they were
taking her to Thalassius, and this was the origin of
the wedding-cry.[1] The sports broke up in a panic,
and the parents of the maidens fled sorrowing. They
charged the Romans with the crime of violating
hospitality, and invoked the gods to whose solemn
games they had come, deceived in violation of religion and honour. The stolen maidens were no
more hopeful of their plight, nor less indignant. But
Romulus himself went amongst them and explained
that the pride of their parents had caused this deed,
when they had refused their neighbours the right
to intermarry; nevertheless the daughters should be
wedded and become co-partners in all the possessions of the Romans, in their citizenship and, dearest
privilege of all to the human race, in their children;

rent modo iras et, quibus fors corpora dedisset,[1] darent animos. Saepe ex iniuria postmodum gratiam ortam, eoque melioribus usuras viris, quod adnisurus pro se quisque sit ut, cum suam vicem functus officio sit, parentium etiam patriaeque expleat desiderium. 16 Accedebant blanditiae virorum factum purgantium cupiditate atque amore, quae maxime ad muliebre ingenium efficaces preces sunt.

X. Iam admodum mitigati animi raptis erant; at raptarum parentes tum maxime sordida veste lacrimisque et querellis civitates concitabant. Nec domi tantum indignationes continebant, sed congregabantur undique ad T. Tatium regem Sabinorum, et legationes eo, quod maximum Tatii nomen in iis regioni- 2 bus erat, conveniebant. Caeninenses Crustuminique et Antemnates erant ad quos eius iniuriae pars pertinebat. Lente agere his Tatius Sabinique visi sunt: ipsi inter se tres populi communiter bellum parant. 3 Ne Crustumini quidem atque Antemnates pro ardore iraque Caeninensium satis se impigre movent; ita per se ipsum nomen Caeninum in agrum Romanum 4 impetum facit. Sed effuse vastantibus fit obvius cum exercitu Romulus levique certamine docet vanam sine viribus iram esse. Exercitum fundit fugatque, fusum persequitur: regem in proelio obtruncat et

[1] dedisset *UOD*³: dedissent Ω.

BOOK I. ix. 15–x. 4

only let them moderate their anger, and give their hearts to those to whom fortune had given their persons. A sense of injury had often given place to affection, and they would find their husbands the kinder for this reason, that every man would earnestly endeavour not only to be a good husband, but also to console his wife for the home and parents she had lost. His arguments were seconded by the wooing of the men, who excused their act on the score of passion and love, the most moving of all pleas to a woman's heart.

X. The resentment of the brides was already much diminished at the very moment when their parents, in mourning garb and with tears and lamentations, were attempting to arouse their states to action. Nor did they confine their complaints to their home towns, but thronged from every side to the house of Titus Tatius, king of the Sabines; and thither, too, came official embassies, for the name of Tatius was the greatest in all that country. The men of Caenina, Crustumium, and Antemnae, were those who had had a share in the wrong. It seemed to them that Tatius and the Sabines were procrastinating, and without waiting for them these three tribes arranged for a joint campaign. But even the Crustuminians and Antemnates moved too slowly to satisfy the burning anger of the Caeninenses, and accordingly that nation invaded alone the Roman territory. But while they were dispersed and engaged in pillage, Romulus appeared with his troops and taught them, by an easy victory, how ineffectual is anger without strength. Their army he broke and routed, and pursued it as it fled; their king he killed

spoliat; duce hostium occiso urbem primo impetu
5 capit. Inde exercitu victore reducto, ipse, cum factis
vir magnificus tum factorum ostentator haud minor,
spolia ducis hostium caesi suspensa fabricato ad id
apte ferculo gerens in Capitolium escendit ibique ea
cum ad quercum pastoribus sacram deposuisset, simul
cum dono designavit templo Iovis finis cognomenque
6 addidit deo. "Iuppiter Feretri" inquit, "haec tibi
victor Romulus rex regia arma fero, templumque his
regionibus quas modo animo metatus sum dedico
sedem opimis spoliis, quae regibus ducibusque hostium caesis me auctorem sequentes posteri ferent."
7 Haec templi est origo quod primum omnium Romae
sacratum est. Ita deinde diis visum, nec inritam
conditoris templi vocem esse qua laturos eo spolia
posteros nuncupavit, nec multitudine conpotum eius
doni volgari laudem. Bina postea inter tot annos,
tot bella, opima parta sunt spolia; adeo rara eius
fortuna decoris fuit.

XI. Dum ea ibi Romani gerunt, Antemnatium
exercitus per occasionem ac solitudinem hostiliter
in fines Romanos incursionem facit. Raptim et ad

---

[1] Jupiter Feretrius (etymology unknown) was the pure Italian Jupiter, whose worship was later overshadowed by the Etruscan god of the great temple on the Capitol. See Fowler, *Fest.* p. 229.

[2] The other instances were the victories of Cossus over Tolumnius, king of Veii (iv. 20), and of Marcellus over

BOOK I. x. 4–xi. 1

in battle and despoiled; their city, once their leader was slain, he captured at the first assault. He then led his victorious army back, and being not more splendid in his deeds than willing to display them, he arranged the spoils of the enemy's dead commander upon a frame, suitably fashioned for the purpose, and, carrying it himself, mounted the Capitol. Having there deposited his burden, by an oak which the shepherds held sacred, at the same time as he made his offering he marked out the limits of a temple to Jupiter, and bestowed a title upon him. "Jupiter Feretrius," he said, "to thee I, victorious Romulus, myself a king, bring the panoply of a king, and dedicate a sacred precinct within the bounds which I have even now marked off in my mind, to be a seat for the spoils of honour which men shall bear hither in time to come, following my example, when they have slain kings and commanders of the enemy." This was the origin of the first temple that was consecrated in Rome.[1] It pleased Heaven, in the sequel, that while the founder's words should not be in vain, when he declared that men should bring spoils thither in the after time, yet the glory of that gift should not be staled by a multitude of partakers. Twice only since then, in all these years with their many wars, have the spoils of honour been won; so rarely have men had the good fortune to attain to that distinction.[2]

XI. While the Romans were thus occupied in the City, the army of the Antemnates seized the opportunity afforded by their absence, and made an inroad upon their territory; but so swiftly was the Roman

Virdomarus, king of the Insubrian Gauls. Propertius tells the three stories in iv. 10.

LIVY

hos Romana legio ducta palatos in agris oppressit.
2 Fusi igitur primo impetu et clamore hostes; oppidum captum; duplicique victoria ovantem Romulum Hersilia coniunx precibus raptarum fatigata orat ut parentibus earum det veniam et in civitatem accipiat; ita rem coalescere concordia posse. Facile
3 impetratum. Inde contra Crustuminos profectus bellum inferentes. Ibi minus etiam, quod alienis
4 cladibus ceciderant animi, certaminis fuit. Utroque coloniae missae; plures inventi qui propter ubertatem terrae in Crustuminum nomina darent. Et Romam inde frequenter migratum est, a parentibus maxime ac propinquis raptarum.

5 Novissimum ab Sabinis bellum ortum, multoque id maximum fuit; nihil enim per iram aut cupiditatem actum est, nec ostenderunt bellum prius quam
6 intulerunt. Consilio etiam additus dolus. Sp. Tarpeius Romanae praeerat arci. Huius filiam virginem auro corrumpit Tatius ut armatos in arcem accipiat; aquam forte ea tum sacris extra moenia petitum
7 ierat. Accepti obrutam armis necavere, seu ut vi capta potius arx videretur, seu prodendi exempli
8 causa, ne quid usquam fidum proditori esset. Additur fabula,[1] quod vulgo Sabini aureas armillas magni

---

[1] fabula *Glareanus*: fabulae (*or* -le) Ω.

---

[1] As a vestal, she had to draw water from the spring of the Camenae.

BOOK I. xi. 1-8

levy led against them that they, too, were taken off their guard while scattered about in the fields. They were therefore routed at the first charge and shout, and their town was taken. As Romulus was exulting in his double victory, his wife Hersilia, beset with entreaties by the captive women, begged him to forgive their parents and receive them into the state; which would, in that case, gain in strength by harmony. He readily granted her request. He then set out to meet the Crustuminians, who were marching to attack him. They offered even less resistance than their allies had done, for their ardour had been quenched by the defeats of the others. Colonies were sent out to both places, though most of the colonists preferred to enrol for Crustumium on account of the fertility of its soil. On the other hand, many persons left Crustumium and came to live in Rome, chiefly parents and kinsmen of the captured women.

The last to attack Rome were the Sabines, and this war was by far the gravest of all, for passion and greed were not their motives, nor did they parade war before they made it. To their prudence they even added deception. Spurius Tarpeius commanded the Roman citadel. This man's maiden daughter was bribed with gold by Tatius to admit armed men into the fortress: she happened at that time to have gone outside the walls to fetch water for a sacrifice.[1] Once within, they threw their shields upon her and killed her so, whether to make it appear that the citadel had been taken by assault, or to set an example, that no one might anywhere keep faith with a traitor. There is also a legend that because most of the Sabines wore heavy golden

43

LIVY

ponderis bracchio laevo gemmatosque magna specie anulos habuerint, pepigisse eam quod in sinistris manibus haberent; eo scuta illi pro aureis donis congesta. Sunt qui eam ex pacto tradendi quod in sinistris manibus esset derecto arma petisse dicant, et fraude visam agere, sua ipsam peremptam mercede.

XII. Tenuere tamen arcem Sabini, atque inde postero die, cum Romanus exercitus instructus quod inter Palatinum Capitolinumque collem campi est complesset, non prius descenderunt in aequum quam ira et cupiditate reciperandae arcis stimulante animos in adversum Romani subiere. Principes utrimque pugnam ciebant ab Sabinis Mettius Curtius, ab Romanis Hostius Hostilius. Hic rem Romanam iniquo loco ad prima signa animo atque audacia sustinebat. Ut Hostius cecidit, confestim Romana inclinatur acies fusaque est ad veterem portam Palatii. Romulus et ipse turba fugientium actus arma ad caelum tollens, "Iuppiter, tuis" inquit, "iussus avibus hic in Palatio prima urbi fundamenta ieci. Arcem iam scelere emptam Sabini habent; inde huc armati superata media valle tendunt; at tu, pater deum hominumque, hinc saltem arce hostes, deme terrorem Romanis fugamque foedam siste! Hic ego tibi templum Statori Iovi, quod monumen-

---

[1] According to Dion. Hal. ii. 38, this was the version given by L. Calpurnius Piso. Propertius wrote the best of his aetiological poems (iv. 5) about Tarpeia.

BOOK I. xi. 8–xii. 6

bracelets on their left arms and magnificent jewelled rings, she had stipulated for what they had on their left arms, and that they had therefore heaped their shields upon her, instead of gifts of gold. Some say that, in virtue of the compact that they should give her what they wore on their arms, she flatly demanded their shields and, her treachery being perceived, forfeited her life to the bargain she herself had struck.[1]

XII. Be that as it may, the Sabines held the citadel. Next day the Roman army was drawn up, and covered the ground between the Palatine Hill and the Capitoline, but the Sabines would not come down till rage and eagerness to regain the citadel had goaded their enemy into marching up the slope against them. Two champions led the fighting, the Sabine Mettius Curtius on the one side, and the Roman Hostius Hostilius on the other. Hostius held the Romans firm, despite their disadvantage of position, by the reckless courage he displayed in the thick of the fray. But when he fell, the Roman line gave way at once and fled towards the old gate of the Palatine. Romulus himself was swept along in the crowd of the fugitives, till lifting his sword and shield to heaven, he cried, "O Jupiter, it was thy omen that directed me when I laid here on the Palatine the first foundations of my City. The fortress is already bought by a crime and in the possession of the Sabines, whence they are come, sword in hand, across the valley to seek us here. But do thou, father of gods and men, keep them back from this spot at least; deliver the Romans from their terror, and stay their shameful flight! I here vow to thee, Jupiter the Stayer, a temple, to be a

LIVY

tum sit posteris tua praesenti ope servatam urbem
7 esse, voveo." Haec precatus, veluti[1] sensisset auditas preces, "Hinc" inquit, "Romani, Iuppiter optimus maximus resistere atque iterare pugnam iubet." Restitere Romani tamquam caelesti voce
8 iussi: ipse ad primores Romulus provolat. Mettius Curtius ab Sabinis princeps ab arce decucurrerat et effusos egerat Romanos, toto quantum foro spatium est. Nec procul iam a porta Palati erat clamitans, "Vicimus perfidos hospites, imbelles hostes; iam sciunt longe aliud esse virgines rapere, aliud pugnare cum
9 viris." In eum haec gloriantem cum globo ferocissimorum iuvenum Romulus impetum facit. Ex equo tum forte Mettius pugnabat; eo pelli facilius fuit. Pulsum Romani persequuntur; et alia Romana acies
10 audacia regis accensa fundit Sabinos. Mettius in paludem sese strepitu sequentium trepidante equo coniecit; averteratque ea res etiam Sabinos tanti periculo viri. Et ille quidem adnuentibus ac vocantibus suis favore multorum addito animo evadit: Romani Sabinique in media convalle duorum montium redintegrant proelium. Sed res Romana erat superior.

XIII. Tum Sabinae mulieres, quarum ex iniuria bellum ortum erat, crinibus passis scissaque veste

---

[1] ueluti *BR* : uelutis *M*? *P*?: uelut si *M*¹ς: ueluti si Ω.

BOOK I. xii. 6-xiii. 1

memorial to our descendants how the City was saved by thy present help." Having uttered this prayer he exclaimed, as if he had perceived that it was heard, "Here, Romans, Jupiter Optimus Maximus commands us to stand and renew the fight!" The Romans did stand, as though directed by a voice from Heaven, Romulus himself rushing into the forefront of the battle. Mettius Curtius, on the Sabine side, had led the charge down from the citadel, and driven the Romans in disorder over all that ground which the Forum occupies. He was not now far from the gate of the Palatine, shouting, "We have beaten our faithless hosts, our cowardly enemies! They know now how great is the difference between carrying off maidens and fighting with men!" While he pronounced this boast a band of gallant youths, led on by Romulus, assailed him. It chanced that Mettius was fighting on horseback at the time, and was therefore the more easily put to flight. As he fled, the Romans followed; and the rest of their army, too, fired by the reckless daring of their king, drove the Sabines before them. Mettius plunged into a swamp, his horse becoming unmanageable in the din of the pursuit, and even the Sabines were drawn off from the general engagement by the danger to so great a man. As for Mettius, heartened by the gestures and shouts of his followers and the encouragement of the throng, he made his escape; and the Romans and the Sabines renewed their battle in the valley that lies between the two hills. But the advantage rested with the Romans.

XIII. Then the Sabine women, whose wrong had given rise to the war, with loosened hair and torn

LIVY

victo malis muliebri pavore, ausae se inter tela volantia inferre, ex transverso impetu facto dirimere infestas acies, dirimere iras, hinc patres hinc viros orantes ne se sanguine nefando soceri generique respergerent, ne parricidio macularent partus suos, nepotum illi, hi liberum progeniem. "Si adfinitatis inter vos, si conubii piget, in nos vertite iras; nos causa belli, nos volnerum ac caedium viris ac parentibus sumus; melius peribimus quam sine alteris vestrum viduae aut orbae vivemus." Movet[1] res cum multitudinem tum duces; silentium et repentina fit quies; inde ad foedus faciendum duces prodeunt; nec pacem modo, sed civitatem unam ex duabus faciunt. Regnum consociant: imperium omne conferunt Romam. Ita geminata urbe, ut Sabinis tamen aliquid daretur, Quirites a Curibus appellati. Monumentum eius pugnae, ubi primum ex profunda emersus palude equus Curtium in vado statuit, Curtium lacum appellarunt.

Ex bello tam tristi laeta repente pax cariores Sabinas viris ac parentibus et ante omnes Romulo

---

[1] mouet $M^1\varsigma$: mouit F : moues L : mouent Ω.

---

[1] *Quirites* probably comes not from Cures, nor (as Varro thought) from the Sabine word *quiris* (*curis*), "spear," but from *curia* (*cf.* next section); it would then mean "wardsmen."

[2] For another explanation of the name see vii. 6. Varro, *L. L.* v. 14 ff., assigns this version of the story to Piso, the other to Procilius, adding a third, on the authority of Cornelius and Lutatius, to the effect that the Lacus

BOOK I. XIII. 1-6

garments, their woman's timidity lost in a sense of their misfortune, dared to go amongst the flying missiles, and rushing in from the side, to part the hostile forces and disarm them of their anger, beseeching their fathers on this side, on that their husbands, that fathers-in-law and sons-in-law should not stain themselves with impious bloodshed, nor pollute with parricide the suppliants' children, grandsons to one party and sons to the other. "If you regret," they continued, "the relationship that unites you, if you regret the marriage-tie, turn your anger against us; we are the cause of war, the cause of wounds, and even death to both our husbands and our parents. It will be better for us to perish than to live, lacking either of you, as widows or as orphans." It was a touching plea, not only to the rank and file, but to their leaders as well. A stillness fell on them, and a sudden hush. Then the leaders came forward to make a truce, and not only did they agree on peace, but they made one people out of the two. They shared the sovereignty, but all authority was transferred to Rome. In this way the population was doubled, and that some concession might after all be granted the Sabines, the citizens were named Quirites, from the town of Cures.[1] As a reminder of this battle they gave the name of Curtian Lake to the pool where the horse of Curtius first emerged from the deep swamp and brought his rider to safety.[2]

The sudden exchange of so unhappy a war for a joyful peace endeared the Sabine women even more to their husbands and parents, and above all to

Curtius was a place which had been struck by lightning in the consulship of a Curtius.

LIVY

ipsi fecit. Itaque cum populum in curias triginta divideret, nomina earum curiis inposuit. Id non traditur, cum haud dubie aliquanto numerus maior hoc mulierum fuerit, aetate an dignitatibus suis virorumve an sorte lectae sint quae nomina curiis darent. Eodem tempore et centuriae tres equitum conscriptae sunt. Ramnenses ab Romulo, ab T. Tatio Titienses appellati, Lucerum nominis et originis causa incerta est. Inde non modo commune, sed concors etiam regnum duobus regibus fuit.

XIV. Post aliquot annos propinqui regis Tatii legatos Laurentium pulsant, cumque Laurentes iure gentium agerent, apud Tatium gratia suorum et preces plus poterant. Igitur illorum poenam in se vertit; nam Lavinii, cum ad sollemne sacrificium eo venisset, concursu facto interficitur. Eam rem minus aegre quam dignum erat tulisse Romulum ferunt, seu ob infidam societatem regni, seu quia haud iniuria caesum credebat. Itaque bello quidem abstinuit; ut tamen expiarentur legatorum iniuriae regisque caedes, foedus inter Romam Laviniumque urbes renovatum est.

Et cum his quidem insperata pax erat: aliud multo propius atque in ipsis prope portis bellum ortum. Fidenates nimis vicinas prope se convalescere opes

---

[1] The *curia* was a political unit the members of which had certain religious rites in common.

[2] All three names are obscure, but it is not improbable that they represent a Roman, a Sabine, and an Etruscan element in the population.

BOOK I. xiii. 6–xiv. 4

Romulus himself. And so, when he divided the people into thirty *curiae*, he named these wards after the women.[1] Undoubtedly the number of the women was somewhat greater than this, but tradition does not tell whether it was their age, their own or their husbands' rank, or the casting of lots, that determined which of them should give their names to the wards. At the same time there were formed three centuries of knights: the Ramnenses were named after Romulus; the Titienses after Titus Tatius; the name and origin of the Luceres are alike obscure.[2] From this time forth the two kings ruled not only jointly but in harmony.

XIV. Some years later the kinsmen of King Tatius maltreated the envoys of the Laurentians, and when their fellow-citizens sought redress under the law of nations, Titus yielded to his partiality for his relations and to their entreaties. In consequence of this he drew down their punishment upon himself, for at Lavinium, whither he had gone to the annual sacrifice, a mob came together and killed him. This act is said to have awakened less resentment than was proper in Romulus, whether owing to the disloyalty that attends a divided rule, or because he thought Tatius had been not unjustly slain. He therefore declined to go to war; but yet, in order that he might atone for the insults to the envoys and the murder of the king, he caused the covenant between Rome and Lavinium to be renewed.

Thus with the Laurentians peace was preserved against all expectation; but another war broke out, much nearer, and indeed almost at the city gates. The men of Fidenae, perceiving the growth of a power which they thought too near themselves for

LIVY

rati, priusquam tantum roboris esset quantum futurum apparebat, occupant bellum facere. Iuventute armata immissa vastatur agri quod inter urbem ac 5 Fidenas est. Inde ad laevam versi, quia dextra Tiberis arcebat, cum magna trepidatione agrestium populantur; tumultusque repens ex agris in urbem 6 inlatus pro nuntio fuit. Excitus Romulus—neque enim dilationem pati tam vicinum bellum poterat— exercitum educit, castra a Fidenis mille passuum 7 locat. Ibi modico praesidio relicto egressus omnibus copiis partem militum locis circa densa virgulta [1] obscuris subsidere in insidiis iussit; cum parte maiore atque omni equitatu profectus, id quod quaerebat, tumultuoso et minaci genere pugnae, adequitando ipsis prope portis hostem excivit. Fugae quoque, quae simulanda erat, eadem equestris pugna causam 8 minus mirabilem dedit. Et cum, velut inter pugnae fugaeque consilium trepidante equitatu, pedes quoque referret gradum, plenis repente portis effusi hostes impulsa Romana acie studio instandi sequendique 9 trahuntur ad locum insidiarum. Inde subito exorti Romani transversam invadunt hostium aciem; addunt pavorem mota e castris signa eorum qui in praesidio relicti fuerant; ita multiplici terrore perculsi Fidenates prius paene quam Romulus quique avehi cum eo visi erant [2] circumagerent frenis equos, terga ver-

---

[1] densa uirgulta *H. J. Mueller*: obsita uirgulta *Conway*: densa obsita uirgulta Ω.

[2] quique auehi cum eo uisi erant *Walters*: quique cum eo uisi erant (quisierant *P*: equis ierant *P²FB*) *UOEHPFB*: quique cum eo quique cum equis abierant usi (uisi *DL*) *MDL*: quique cum eo equites erant *D²ς*.

safety, did not wait till its promised strength should
be realized, but began war themselves. Arming the
young men, they sent them to ravage the land between the City and Fidenae. Thence they turned
to the left—for the Tiber stopped them on the right
—and by their devastations struck terror into the
farmers, whose sudden stampede from the fields into
the City brought the first tidings of war. Romulus
led forth his army on the instant, for delay was impossible with the enemy so near, and pitched his
camp a mile from Fidenae. Leaving there a small
guard, he marched out with all his forces. A part
of his men he ordered to lie in ambush, on this side
and on that, where thick underbrush afforded cover;
advancing with the greater part of the infantry and
all the cavalry, and delivering a disorderly and provoking attack, in which the horsemen galloped almost up to the gates, he accomplished his purpose
of drawing out the enemy. For the flight, too, which
had next to be feigned, the cavalry engagement
afforded a favourable pretext. And when not only
the cavalry began to waver, as if undecided whether
to fight or run, but the infantry also fell back, the
city gates were quickly thronged by the enemy, who
poured out and hurled themselves against the Roman
line, and in the ardour of attack and pursuit were
drawn on to the place of ambuscade. There the
Romans suddenly sprang out and assailed the enemy's
flanks, while, to add to their terror, the standards of
the detachment which had been left on guard were
seen advancing from the camp; thus threatened by
so many dangers the men of Fidenae scarcely afforded time for Romulus and those whom they had
seen riding off with him to wheel about, before they

LIVY

10 tunt; multoque effusius, quippe vera fuga, qui simulantes paulo ante secuti erant, oppidum repetebant.
11 Non tamen eripuere se hosti: haerens in tergo Romanus, priusquam fores portarum obicerentur, velut agmine uno inrumpit.

XV. Belli Fidenatis contagione inritati Veientium animi et consanguinitate—nam Fidenates quoque Etrusci fuerunt—et quod ipsa propinquitas loci, si Romana arma omnibus infesta finitimis essent, stimulabat. In fines Romanos excucurrerunt populabundi
2 magis quam iusti more belli. Itaque non castris positis, non exspectato hostium exercitu raptam ex agris praedam portantes Veios rediere. Romanus contra, postquam hostem in agris non invenit, dimicationi ultimae instructus intentusque Tiberim tran-
3 sit. Quem postquam castra ponere et ad urbem accessurum Veientes audivere, obviam egressi, ut potius acie decernerent quam inclusi de tectis moeni-
4 busque dimicarent. Ibi viribus nulla arte[1] adiutis tantum veterani robore exercitus rex Romanus vicit, persecutusque fusos ad moenia hostes urbe valida muris ac situ ipso munita abstinuit: agros rediens

[1] arte $F^3\varsigma$ *Petrus Nannius*: parte Ω.

BOOK I. xiv. 9–xv. 4

broke and ran, and in far greater disorder than that of the pretended fugitives whom they had just been chasing—for the flight was a real one this time—sought to regain the town. But the Fidenates did not escape their foes; the Romans followed close upon their heels, and before the gates could be shut burst into the city, as though they both formed but a single army.

B.C. 753-717

XV. From Fidenae the war-spirit, by a kind of contagion, spread to the Veientes, whose hostility was aroused by their kinship with the Fidenates, Etruscans like themselves, and was intensified by the danger which lay in their very proximity to Rome, if her arms should be directed against all her neighbours. They made an incursion into Roman territory which more resembled a marauding expedition than a regular campaign; and so, without having entrenched a camp or waited for the enemy's army, they carried off their booty from the fields and brought it back to Veii. The Romans, on the contrary, not finding their enemy in the fields, crossed the Tiber, ready and eager for a decisive struggle. When the Veientes heard that they were making a camp, and would be advancing against their city, they went out to meet them, preferring to settle the quarrel in the field of battle rather than to be shut up and compelled to fight for their homes and their town. Without employing strategy to aid his forces, the Roman king won the battle by the sheer strength of his seasoned army, and routing his enemies, pursued them to their walls. But the city was strongly fortified, besides the protection afforded by its site, and he refrained from attacking it. Their fields, indeed, he laid waste as he returned, more in

LIVY

5 vastat, ulciscendi magis quam praedae studio. Eaque clade haud minus quam adversa pugna subacti Veientes pacem petitum oratores Romam mittunt. Agri parte multatis in centum annos induciae datae.

6 Haec ferme Romulo regnante domi militiaeque gesta, quorum nihil absonum fidei divinae originis divinitatisque post mortem creditae fuit, non animus in regno avito reciperando, non condendae urbis 7 consilium, non bello ac pace firmandae. Ab illo enim profecto viribus datis tantum valuit ut in quad- 8 raginta deinde annos tutam pacem haberet. Multitudini tamen gratior fuit quam patribus, longe ante alios acceptissimus militum animis; trecentosque armatos ad custodiam corporis, quos Celeres appellavit, non in bello solum sed etiam in pace habuit.

XVI. His inmortalibus editis operibus cum ad exercitum recensendum contionem in campo ad Caprae paludem haberet, subito coorta tempestas cum magno fragore tonitribusque tam denso regem operuit nimbo ut conspectum eius contioni abstu- 2 lerit; nec deinde in terris Romulus fuit. Romana pubes sedato tandem pavore, postquam ex tam turbido die serena et tranquilla lux rediit, ubi vacuam sedem regiam vidit, etsi satis credebat patribus, qui

---

[1] Literally, "the Swift."
[2] For the deification *cf.* Cic. *de Rep.* ii. 17; Dion. Hal. ii. 56; Plut. *Rom.* xxvii. Ovid also tells the story in *Fasti*, ii. 491 ff., and *Met.* xiv. 806 ff.

BOOK I. xv. 4–xvi. 2

revenge than from a desire for booty, and this disaster, following upon their defeat, induced the Veientes to send envoys to Rome and sue for peace. They were deprived of a part of their land, and a truce was granted them for a hundred years.

Such were the principal achievements of the reign of Romulus, at home and in the field, nor is any of them incompatible with the belief in his divine origin and the divinity which was ascribed to the king after his death, whether one considers his spirit in recovering the kingdom of his ancestors, or his wisdom in founding the City and in strengthening it by warlike and peaceful measures. For it was to him, assuredly, that Rome owed the vigour which enabled her to enjoy an untroubled peace for the next forty years. Nevertheless, he was more liked by the commons than by the senate, and was preeminently dear to the hearts of his soldiers. Of these he had three hundred for a bodyguard, to whom he gave the name of Celeres,[1] and kept them by him, not only in war, but also in time of peace.

XVI. When these deathless deeds had been done, as the king was holding a muster in the Campus Martius, near the swamp of Capra, for the purpose of reviewing the army, suddenly a storm came up, with loud claps of thunder, and enveloped him in a cloud so thick as to hide him from the sight of the assembly; and from that moment Romulus was no more on earth.[2] The Roman soldiers at length recovered from their panic, when this hour of wild confusion had been succeeded by a sunny calm; but when they saw that the royal seat was empty, although they readily believed the assertion of the senators, who had been standing next to Romulus,

LIVY

<small>A.U.C.
38</small>

proximi steterant, sublimem raptum procella, tamen velut orbitatis metu icta maestum aliquamdiu silen- 3 tium obtinuit. Deinde a paucis initio facto deum deo natum, regem parentemque urbis Romanae salvere universi Romulum iubent; pacem precibus exposcunt, uti volens propitius suam semper sospitet 4 progeniem. Fuisse credo tum quoque aliquos qui discerptum regem patrum manibus taciti arguerent; manavit enim haec quoque sed perobscura fama; illam alteram admiratio viri et pavor praesens nobili- 5 tavit. Et consilio etiam unius hominis addita rei dicitur fides. Namque Proculus Iulius, sollicita civitate desiderio regis et infensa patribus, gravis, ut traditur, quamvis magnae rei auctor, in contionem 6 prodit. "Romulus" inquit, "Quirites, parens urbis huius, prima hodierna luce caelo repente delapsus se mihi obvium dedit. Cum perfusus horrore venerabundus[1] adstitissem, petens precibus ut contra in- 7 tueri fas esset, 'Abi, nuntia,' inquit 'Romanis caelestes ita velle ut mea Roma caput orbis terrarum sit; proinde rem militarem colant, sciantque et ita posteris tradant nullas opes humanas armis Romanis resistere posse.' Haec," inquit, "locutus 8 sublimis abiit." Mirum quantum illi viro nuntianti haec fides fuerit, quamque desiderium Romuli

[1] uenerabundus *Mς* : uenerabundusque Ω.

---

[1] The Romans regularly prayed with the head cloaked.

BOOK I. XVI. 2–8

that he had been caught up on high in the blast, they nevertheless remained for some time sorrowful and silent, as if filled with the fear of orphanhood. Then, when a few men had taken the initiative, they all with one accord hailed Romulus as a god and a god's son, the King and Father of the Roman City, and with prayers besought his favour that he would graciously be pleased forever to protect his children. There were some, I believe, even then who secretly asserted that the king had been rent in pieces by the hands of the senators, for this rumour, too, got abroad, but in very obscure terms; the other version obtained currency, owing to men's admiration for the hero and the intensity of their panic. And the shrewd device of one man is also said to have gained new credit for the story. This was Proculus Julius, who, when the people were distracted with the loss of their king and in no friendly mood towards the senate, being, as tradition tells, weighty in council, were the matter never so important, addressed the assembly as follows: "Quirites, the Father of this City, Romulus, descended suddenly from the sky at dawn this morning and appeared to me. Covered with confusion, I stood reverently before him, praying that it might be vouchsafed me to look upon his face without sin.[1] 'Go,' said he, 'and declare to the Romans the will of Heaven that my Rome shall be the capital of the world; so let them cherish the art of war, and let them know and teach their children that no human strength can resist Roman arms.' So saying," he concluded, "Romulus departed on high." It is wonderful what credence the people placed in that man's tale, and how the grief for the loss of Romulus, which the plebeians

apud plebem exercitumque facta fide inmortalitatis lenitum sit.

XVII. Patrum interim animos certamen regni ac cupido versabat. Necdum ad singulos,[1] quia nemo magnopere eminebat in novo populo, pervenerat: 2 factionibus inter ordines certabatur. Oriundi ab Sabinis, ne, quia post Tati mortem ab sua parte non erat regnatum, in societate aequa possessionem imperii amitterent, sui corporis creari regem volebant; Romani veteres peregrinum regem aspernabantur. 3 In variis voluntatibus regnari[2] tamen omnes volebant 4 libertatis dulcedine nondum experta. Timor deinde patres incessit, ne civitatem sine imperio, exercitum sine duce multarum circa civitatium inritatis animis vis aliqua externa adoriretur. Et esse igitur aliquod caput placebat, et nemo alteri concedere in animum 5 inducebat. Ita rem inter se centum patres, decem decuriis factis singulisque in singulas decurias creatis qui summae rerum praeessent, consociant. Decem imperitabant: unus cum insignibus imperii et lictori- 6 bus erat; quinque dierum spatio finiebatur imperium ac per omnes in orbem ibat; annuumque intervallum regni fuit. Id ab re, quod nunc quoque tenet nomen, 7 interregnum appellatum. Fremere deinde plebs multiplicatam servitutem, centum pro uno dominos

[1] ad singulos *Graevius*: a singulis Ω.
[2] regnari ς: regnare Ω.

and the army felt, was quieted by the assurance of his immortality.   B.C. 716

XVII. The senators meanwhile were engaged in a struggle for the coveted kingship. So far it had not come to a question of any one person, for nobody stood out with special prominence in the new nation; instead, a strife of factions was waging between the two stocks. Those of Sabine origin, having had no king on their side since the death of Tatius, feared that despite their equal rights they might lose their hold upon the sovereign power, and hence desired that the king should be chosen from their own body. The original Romans spurned the idea of an alien king. Various, however, as were men's inclinations, to be ruled by a king was their universal wish, for they had not yet tasted the sweetness of liberty. Then the senators became alarmed, lest the state wanting a ruler and the army a leader, and many neighbouring states being disaffected, some violence might be offered from without. All therefore were agreed that there should be some head, but nobody could make up his mind to yield to his fellow. And so the hundred senators shared the power among themselves, establishing ten decuries and appointing one man for each decury to preside over the administration. Ten men exercised authority; only one had its insignia and lictors. Five days was the period of his power, which passed in rotation to all; and for a year the monarchy lapsed. This interval was called, as it was, an interregnum, a name which even yet obtains. Murmurs then arose among the plebs that their servitude had been multiplied; that a hundred masters had been given them instead of

LIVY

factos; nec ultra nisi regem et ab ipsis creatum videbantur passuri. Cum sensissent ea moveri patres, offerendum ultro rati quod amissuri erant, ita gratiam ineunt summa potestate populo permissa ut non plus darent iuris quam retinerent.[1] Decreverunt enim ut cum populus regem iussisset, id sic ratum[2] esset, si patres auctores fierent. Hodie quoque in legibus magistratibusque rogandis usurpatur idem[3] ius vi adempta; priusquam populus suffragium ineat, in incertum comitiorum eventum patres auctores fiunt. Tum interrex contione advocata, "Quod bonum, faustum felixque sit" inquit, "Quirites, regem create; ita patribus visum est. Patres deinde, si dignum qui secundus ab Romulo numeretur crearitis, auctores fient." Adeo id gratum plebi fuit ut, ne victi beneficio viderentur, id modo sciscerent iuberentque, ut senatus decerneret qui Romae regnaret.

XVIII. Inclita iustitia religioque ea tempestate Numae Pompili erat. Curibus Sabinis habitabat, consultissimus vir, ut in illa quisquam esse aetate poterat, omnis divini atque humani iuris. Auctorem doctrinae eius, quia non exstat alius, falso Samium Pythagoram edunt, quem Servio Tullio regnante Romae, centum amplius post annos, in ultima Italiae

---

[1] retinerent *Gronov.*: detinerent Ω.
[2] sic ratum $F^3D^4\varsigma$: si (sic *U*) gratum Ω.
[3] idem $F^3\varsigma$: id enim Ω.

one. No longer, it seemed, would they endure anything short of a king, and a king, too, of their own choosing. Perceiving that such ideas were in the wind, the senators thought it would be well to proffer spontaneously a thing which they were on the verge of losing, and obtained the favour of the people by granting them supreme power on such terms as to part with no greater prerogative than they retained. For they decreed that when the people should have named a king, their act should only be valid in case the senators ratified it. Even now, in voting for laws and magistrates, the same right is exercised, but is robbed of its significance; before the people can begin to vote, and when the result of the election is undetermined, the Fathers ratify it. On the present occasion the interrex summoned the assembly and spoke as follows: "May prosperity, favour, and fortune attend our action! Quirites, choose your king. Such is the pleasure of the Fathers, who, in their turn, if your choice fall upon one worthy to be called Romulus' successor, will confirm your election." This so pleased the plebs, that, unwilling to appear outdone in generosity, they merely resolved and ordered that the senate should decree who should be king in Rome.

B.C. 716

XVIII. A great reputation for justice and piety was enjoyed in those days by Numa Pompilius. Cures, a town of the Sabines, was his home, and he was deeply versed, so far as anyone could be in that age, in all law, divine and human. The teacher to whom he owed his learning was not, as men say, in default of another name, the Samian Pythagoras; for it is well established that Servius Tullius was king at Rome, more than a hundred years after this

LIVY

ora circa Metapontum Heracleamque et Crotona iuvenum aemulantium studia coetus habuisse constat. Ex quibus locis, etsi eiusdem aetatis fuisset, quae fama in Sabinos? Aut quo linguae commercio quemquam ad cupiditatem discendi excivisset? Quove praesidio unus per tot gentes dissonas sermone moribusque pervenisset? Suopte igitur ingenio temperatum animum virtutibus fuisse opinor magis instructumque non tam peregrinis artibus quam disciplina tetrica ac tristi veterum Sabinorum, quo genere nullum quondam incorruptius fuit. Audito nomine Numae patres Romani, quamquam inclinari opes ad Sabinos rege inde sumpto videbantur, tamen neque se quisquam nec factionis suae alium nec denique patrum aut civium quemquam praeferre illi viro ausi ad unum omnes Numae Pompilio regnum deferendum decernunt. Accitus, sicut Romulus augurato urbe condenda regnum adeptus est, de se quoque deos consuli iussit. Inde ab augure, cui deinde honoris ergo publicum id perpetuumque sacerdotium fuit, deductus in arcem in lapide[1] ad meridiem versus consedit. Augur ad laevam eius capite velato sedem cepit, dextra manu baculum sine nodo aduncum tenens, quem lituum appellarunt.

[1] in lapide R_ς: in lapidem (or lapidem) Ω.

---

[1] It was about 530 B.C. when Pythagoras settled in Croton.

BOOK I. XVIII. 2–7

time, when Pythagoras gathered about him, on the farthest coasts of Italy, in the neighbourhood of Metapontum, Heraclea, and Croton, young men eager to share his studies.[1] And from that country, even if he had been contemporary, how could his fame have reached the Sabines? Again, in what common language could he have induced anyone to seek instruction of him? Or under whose protection could a solitary man have made his way through so many nations differing in speech and customs? It was Numa's native disposition, then, as I incline to believe, that tempered his soul with noble qualities, and his training was not in foreign studies, but in the stern and austere discipline of the ancient Sabines, a race incorruptible as any race of the olden time. When Numa's name had been proposed, the Roman senators perceived that the Sabines would gain the ascendancy if a king were to be chosen from that nation; yet nobody ventured to urge his own claims in preference to those of such a man, nor the claim of any other of his faction, nor those, in short, of any of the senators or citizens. And so they unanimously voted to offer the sovereignty to Numa Pompilius. Being summoned to Rome he commanded that, just as Romulus had obeyed the augural omens in building his city and assuming regal power, so too in his own case the gods should be consulted. Accordingly an augur (who thereafter, as a mark of honour, was made a priest of the state in permanent charge of that function) conducted him to the citadel and caused him to sit down on a stone, facing the south. The augur seated himself on Numa's left, having his head covered, and holding his in right hand the crooked staff without a knot

B.C. 716

65

LIVY

A.U.C. 38

Inde ubi prospectu in urbem agrumque capto deos precatus regiones ab oriente ad occasum determinavit, dextras ad meridiem partes, laevas ad septentrionem esse dixit; signum contra, quoad[1] ongissime conspectum oculi ferebant, animo finivit; tum lituo in laevam manum translato dextra in caput Numae imposita ita precatus est,[2] "Iuppiter pater, si est fas hunc Numam Pompilium, cuius ego caput teneo, regem Romae esse, uti tu signa nobis certa adclarassis inter eos fines quos feci." Tum peregit verbis auspicia quae mitti vellet. Quibus missis declaratus rex Numa de templo descendit.

A.U.C. 39-82

XIX. Qui regno ita potitus urbem novam, conditam vi et armis, iure eam legibusque ac moribus de integro condere parat. Quibus cum inter bella adsuescere videret non posse, quippe efferari militia animos, mitigandum ferocem populum armorum desuetudine ratus, Ianum ad infimum Argiletum indicem pacis bellique fecit, apertus ut in armis esse civitatem, clausus pacatos circa omnes populos significaret. Bis deinde post Numae regnum clausus fuit, semel T. Manlio consule post Punicum primum perfectum bellum, iterum, quod nostrae aetati di dederunt ut videremus, post bellum Actiacum ab imperatore Caesare Augusto pace terra marique

---

[1] quoad *Weissenborn*: quod Ω: quo $P^2\varsigma$: quo *M*.
[2] ita precatus est *Walters*: precatus est ita *ORDL*: precatus ita est *MPFUBEH*.

BOOK I. XVIII. 7–XIX. 3

which they call a *lituus*. Then, looking out over the City and the country beyond, he prayed to the gods, and marked off the heavens by a line from east to west, designating as 'right' the regions to the south, as 'left' those to the north, and fixing in his mind a landmark opposite to him and as far away as the eye could reach; next shifting the crook to his left hand and, laying his right hand on Numa's head, he uttered the following prayer: "Father Jupiter, if it is Heaven's will that this man Numa Pompilius, whose head I am touching, be king in Rome, do thou exhibit to us unmistakable signs within those limits which I have set." He then specified the auspices which he desired should be sent, and upon their appearance Numa was declared king, and so descended from the augural station.

B.C. 716

XIX. When he had thus obtained the kingship, he prepared to give the new City, founded by force of arms, a new foundation in law, statutes, and observances. And perceiving that men could not grow used to these things in the midst of wars, since their natures grew wild and savage through warfare, he thought it needful that his warlike people should be softened by the disuse of arms, and built the temple of Janus at the bottom of the Argiletum, as an index of peace and war, that when open it might signify that the nation was in arms, when closed that all the peoples round about were pacified. Twice since Numa's reign has it been closed: once in the consulship of Titus Manlius, after the conclusion of the First Punic War; the second time, which the gods permitted our own generation to witness, was after the battle of Actium, when the emperor Caesar Augustus had brought about peace on land and

B.C. 715–672

LIVY

A.U.C.
39–82

4 parta. Clauso eo cum omnium circa finitimorum societate ac foederibus iunxisset animos, positis externorum periculorum curis ne luxuriarent otio animi, quos metus hostium disciplinaque militaris continuerat, omnium primum, rem ad multitudinem imperitam et illis saeculis rudem efficacissimam, deorum

5 metum iniciendum ratus est. Qui cum descendere ad animos sine aliquo commento miraculi non posset, simulat sibi cum dea Egeria congressus nocturnos esse; eius se monitu, quae acceptissima diis essent sacra instituere, sacerdotes suos cuique deorum praeficere.

6 Atque omnium primum ad cursus lunae in duodecim menses discribit[1] annum; quem, quia tricenos dies singulis mensibus luna non explet, desuntque undecim dies[2] solido anno qui solstitiali circumagitur orbe, intercalariis[3] mensibus interponendis ita dispensavit, ut vicesimo anno ad metam eandem solis unde orsi essent, plenis omnium annorum

7 spatiis, dies congruerent. Idem nefastos dies fastosque fecit, quia aliquando nihil cum populo agi utile futurum erat.

---

[1] discribit *Buecheler*: describit Ω.
[2] desuntque undecim dies *J. S. Reid* (*who, however, prefers to assume that Livy did not commit himself to any definite number of days. See Jour. Rom. Stud. V. p.* 144): desͦ (= desunt) qui (*for* que ui) dies B, *whence Conway proposes* desuntque sex dies (*but* ui = VI *may be a corruption of* XI): desuntque dies Ω.
[3] intercalariis *Heerwagen*: intercalares Ω.

sea.¹ Numa closed the temple after first securing the good will of all the neighbouring tribes by alliances and treaties. And fearing lest relief from anxiety on the score of foreign perils might lead men who had hitherto been held back by fear of their enemies and by military discipline into extravagance and idleness, he thought the very first thing to do, as being the most efficacious with a populace which was ignorant and, in those early days, uncivilized, was to imbue them with the fear of Heaven. As he could not instil this into their hearts without inventing some marvellous story, he pretended to have nocturnal meetings with the goddess Egeria, and that hers was the advice which guided him in the establishment of rites most approved by the gods, and in the appointment of special priests for the service of each.

And first of all he divided the year into twelve months, according to the revolutions of the moon. But since the moon does not give months of quite thirty days each, and eleven days are wanting to the full complement of a year as marked by the sun's revolution, he inserted intercalary months in such a way that in the twentieth year the days should fall in with the same position of the sun from which they had started, and the period of twenty years be rounded out. He also appointed days when public business might not be carried on, and others when it might, since it would sometimes be desirable that nothing should be brought before the people.

¹ This was evidently written before 25 B.C., when the temple was again closed by Augustus. But it was not written before 27, for it was not until that year that the title of Augustus was conferred upon the emperor. We thus arrive at an approximate date for the beginning of Livy's history.

LIVY

XX. Tum sacerdotibus creandis animum adiecit, quamquam ipse plurima sacra obibat, ea maxime quae nunc ad Dialem flaminem pertinent. Sed quia in civitate bellicosa plures Romuli quam Numae similes reges putabat fore iturosque ipsos ad bella, ne sacra regiae vicis desererentur, flaminem Iovi adsiduum sacerdotem creavit insignique eum veste et curuli regia sella adornavit. Huic duos flamines adiecit, Marti unum, alterum Quirino; virginesque Vestae legit, Alba oriundum sacerdotium et genti conditoris haud alienum. Iis, ut adsiduae templi antistites essent, stipendium de publico statuit, virginitate aliisque caerimoniis venerabiles ac sanctas fecit. Salios item duodecim Marti Gradivo legit tunicaeque pictae insigne dedit et super tunicam aeneum pectori tegumen caelestiaque arma, quae ancilia appellantur, ferre ac per urbem ire canentes carmina cum tripudiis sollemnique saltatu iussit. Pontificem deinde Numam Marcium Marci filium ex patribus legit eique sacra omnia exscripta exsignataque attribuit, quibus hostiis, quibus diebus, ad quae templa sacra fierent atque unde in eos sumptus pecunia erogaretur. Cetera quoque omnia publica privataque sacra pontificis scitis subiecit, ut esset

---

[1] The original *ancile* was a shield fabled to have fallen from heaven. To lessen the chance of its being stolen, eleven others were made exactly like it. It was of a peculiar shape, something like a violin. See Fowler, *Fest.* p.42.

BOOK I. xx. 1-6

XX. He then turned his attention to the appointment of priests, although he performed very many priestly duties himself, especially those which now belong to the Flamen Dialis. But inasmuch as he thought that in a warlike nation there would be more kings like Romulus than like Numa, and that they would take the field in person, he did not wish the sacrificial duties of the kingly office to be neglected, and so appointed a flamen for Jupiter, as his perpetual priest, and provided him with a conspicuous dress and the royal curule chair. To him he added two other flamens, one for Mars, the other for Quirinus. In like manner he designated virgins for Vesta's service—a priesthood, this, that derived from Alba and so was not unsuited to the founder's stock. That they might be perpetual priestesses of the temple, he assigned them a stipend from the public treasury, and by the rule of virginity and other observances invested them with awe and sanctity. He likewise chose twelve Salii for Mars Gradivus, and granted them the distinction of wearing the embroidered tunic and over it a bronze breastplate, and of bearing the divine shields which men call *ancilia*,[1] while they proceeded through the City, chanting their hymns to the triple beat of their solemn dance. He next chose as pontifex Numa Marcius, son of Marcus, one of the senators, and to him he intrusted written directions, full and accurate, for performing the rites of worship; with what victims, on what days, in what temple, sacrifices should be offered, and from what sources money was to be disbursed to pay their costs. All other public and private sacrifices he likewise made subject to the decrees of the pontifex, that there

LIVY

quo consultum plebes veniret, ne quid divini iuris neglegendo patrios ritus peregrinosque adsciscendo turbaretur; nec caelestes modo caerimonias, sed iusta quoque funebria placandosque manes ut idem pontifex edoceret, quaeque prodigia fulminibus aliove quo visu missa susciperentur atque curarentur. Ad ea elicienda ex mentibus divinis Iovi Elicio aram in Aventino dicavit deumque consuluit auguriis, quae suscipienda essent.

XXI. Ad haec consultanda procurandaque multitudine omni a vi et armis conversa, et animi aliquid agendo occupati erant, et deorum adsidua insidens cura, cum interesse rebus humanis caeleste numen videretur, ea pietate omnium pectora imbuerat, ut fides ac ius iurandum pro[1] legum ac poenarum metu civitatem regerent. Et cum ipsi se homines in regis velut unici exempli mores formarent, tum finitimi etiam populi, qui antea[2] castra, non urbem positam in medio ad sollicitandam omnium pacem crediderant, in eam verecundiam adducti sunt ut civitatem totam in cultum versam deorum violare[3] ducerent nefas. Lucus erat, quem medium ex opaco specu fons perenni rigabat aqua. Quo quia se per-

---

[1] pro *Novák*: pro nimio *Walters*: proximo Ω.
[2] antea *M*: ante Ω.
[3] uiolare *PFUB*: uiolari Ω.

BOOK I. xx. 6–xxi. 3

might be someone to whom the commons could come for advice, lest any confusion should arise in the religious law through the neglect of ancestral rites and the adoption of strange ones. And not merely ceremonies relating to the gods above, but also proper funeral observances and the propitiation of the spirits of the dead were to be taught by the pontifex as well, and also what prodigies manifested by lightning or other visible sign were to be taken in hand and averted. With the purpose of eliciting this knowledge from the minds of the gods, Numa dedicated an altar on the Aventine to Jupiter Elicius, and consulted the god by augury, that he might learn what portents were to be regarded.

XXI. The consideration and disposal of these matters diverted the thoughts of the whole people from violence and arms. Not only had they something to occupy their minds, but their constant preoccupation with the gods, now that it seemed to them that concern for human affairs was felt by the heavenly powers, had so tinged the hearts of all with piety, that the nation was governed by its regard for promises and oaths, rather than by the dread of laws and penalties. And while Numa's subjects were spontaneously imitating the character of their king, as their unique exemplar, the neighbouring peoples also, who had hitherto considered that it was no city but a camp that had been set up in their midst, as a menace to the general peace, came to feel such reverence for them, that they thought it sacrilege to injure a nation so wholly bent upon the worship of the gods. There was a grove watered by a perennial spring which flowed through the midst of it, out of a dark cave. Thither

LIVY

saepe Numa sine arbitris velut ad congressum deae inferebat, Camenis eum lucum sacravit, quod earum ibi[1] concilia cum coniuge sua Egeria essent, et Fidei[2] 4 sollemne instituit. Ad id sacrarium flamines bigis curru arcuato vehi iussit, manuque ad digitos usque involuta rem divinam facere, significantes fidem tutandam sedemque eius etiam in dexteris sacratam 5 esse. Multa alia sacrificia locaque sacris faciendis, quae Argeos pontifices vocant, dedicavit. Omnium tamen maximum eius operum fuit tutela per omne regni tempus haud minor pacis quam regni. Ita duo deinceps reges, alius alia via, ille bello, hic pace, civitatem auxerunt. Romulus septem et triginta regnavit annos, Numa tres et quadraginta. Cum valida tum temperata et belli et pacis artibus erat civitas.

XXII. Numae morte ad interregnum res rediit. Inde Tullum Hostilium nepotem Hostili, cuius in infima arce clara pugna adversus Sabinos fuerat, 2 regem populus iussit; patres auctores facti. Hic non solum proximo regi dissimilis, sed ferocior etiam quam Romulus fuit. Cum aetas viresque, tum avita quoque gloria animum stimulabat. Senescere igitur civitatem otio ratus undique materiam excitandi belli 3 quaerebat. Forte evenit ut agrestes Romani ex

---

[1] ibi ς: sibi Ω.   [2] Fidei *Sigonius*: soli Fidei Ω.

---

[1] There were six of these shrines or chapels in each of the four regions of the Servian city. A procession made the round of the *Argei* on March 17; and on May 15 rush puppets, also called *Argei*, and probably corresponding to

BOOK I. xxi. 3–xxii. 3

Numa would often withdraw, without witnesses, as if to meet the goddess; so he dedicated the grove to the Camenae, alleging that they held counsel there with his wife Egeria. He also established an annual worship of Faith, to whose chapel he ordered that the flamens should proceed in a two-horse hooded carriage, and should wrap up their arms as far as the fingers before sacrificing, as a sign that faith must be kept, and that even in men's clasped hands her seat is sacred. He established many other rites, as well as places of sacrifice, which the pontiffs called *Argei*.[1] But of all his services the greatest was this, that throughout his reign he guarded peace no less jealously than his kingdom. Thus two successive kings in different ways, one by war, the other by peace, promoted the nation's welfare. Romulus ruled thirty-seven years, Numa forty-three. The state was not only strong, but was also well organized in the arts both of war and of peace.

XXII. At Numa's death the state reverted to an interregnum. Then Tullus Hostilius, grandson of that Hostilius who had distinguished himself in the battle with the Sabines at the foot of the citadel, was declared king by the people, and the senate confirmed their choice. This monarch was not only unlike the last, but was actually more warlike than Romulus had been. Besides his youth and strength, the glory of his grandfather was also an incentive to him. So, thinking that the nation was growing decrepit from inaction, he everywhere sought excuses for stirring up war. It happened that the Roman rustics were

B.C. 715-672

B.C. 672-640

the shrines in number, were thrown into the Tiber by the Vestal Virgins, in the presence of the priestess of Jupiter, who was dressed in mourning. The meaning of both ceremonies is obscure. See Fowler, *Fest.* pp. 54 and 111.

LIVY

Albano agro, Albani ex Romano praedas in vicem agerent. Imperitabat tum C. Cluilius[1] Albae. Utrimque legati fere sub idem tempus ad res repetendas missi. Tullus praeceperat suis ne quid prius quam mandata agerent; satis sciebat negaturum Albanum; ita pie bellum indici posse. Ab Albanis socordius res acta; excepti hospitio ab Tullo blande ac benigne, comiter regis convivium celebrant. Tantisper Romani et res repetiverant priores et neganti Albano bellum in tricesimum diem indixerant. Haec renuntiant Tullo. Tum legatis Tullus dicendi potestatem, quid petentes venerint, facit. Illi omnium ignari primum purgando terunt tempus: se invitos quicquam quod minus placeat Tullo dicturos, sed imperio subigi; res repetitum se venisse; ni reddantur bellum indicere iussos. Ad haec Tullus "Nuntiate," inquit, "regi vestro regem Romanum deos facere testes uter prius populus res repetentes legatos aspernatus dimiserit, ut in eum omnes expetant huiusce clades belli."

XXIII. Haec nuntiant domum Albani. Et bellum utrimque summa ope parabatur, civili simillimum bello, prope inter parentes natosque, Troianam

---

[1] Cluilius *Glareanus* (*cf.* i. 23. 7): cluilius (*or* ciuilius *or* ciiiilius *or* ciuibus) Ω.

driving off cattle from Alban territory, while the Albans were treating the Romans in the same way. The man who was then in power in Alba was Gaius Cluilius. Each side, at about the same time, sent envoys to demand restitution. Tullus had commanded his envoys to do nothing else till they had carried out his orders; he felt convinced that the Albans would refuse his demands, in which case he could declare war with a good conscience. The Alban representatives proceeded rather laxly. Received by Tullus with gracious and kindly hospitality, they attended in a friendly spirit the banquet which he gave in their honour. Meanwhile the Romans had been beforehand with them in seeking redress, and, being denied it by the Alban leader, had made a declaration of war, to take effect in thirty days. Returning, they reported these things to Tullus, who thereupon invited the Alban envoys to inform him of the object of their mission. They, knowing nothing of what had happened, at first spent some time in apologies. They said they should be sorry to utter anything which might give offence to Tullus, but that they were compelled to do so by their orders; they had come to seek restitution; if it should be denied them they were commanded to declare war. To this Tullus replied: "Tell your king the Roman king calls the gods to witness which people first spurned the other's demand for redress and dismissed its envoys, that they may call down upon the guilty nation all the disasters of this war."

XXIII. With this answer the Albans returned to their city, and both sides prepared for war with the greatest energy—a civil war, to all intents and purposes, almost as if fathers were arrayed against sons;

B.C. 672-640

LIVY

utramque prolem, cum Lavinium ab Troia, ab Lavinio Alba, ab Albanorum stirpe regum oriundi Romani essent. Eventus tamen belli minus miserabilem dimicationem fecit, quod nec acie certatum est et tectis modo dirutis alterius urbis duo populi in unum confusi sunt. Albani priores ingenti exercitu in agrum Romanum impetum fecere. Castra ab urbe haud plus quinque milia passuum locant; fossa circumdant; fossa Cluilia[1] ab nomine ducis per aliquot saecula appellata est, donec cum re nomen quoque vetustate[2] abolevit. In his castris Cluilius[3] Albanus rex moritur; dictatorem Albani Mettium Fufetium creant. Interim Tullus ferox, praecipue morte regis, magnumque deorum numen ab ipso capite orsum in omne nomen Albanum expetiturum poenas ob bellum impium dictitans, nocte praeteritis hostium castris infesto exercitu in agrum Albanum pergit. Ea res ab stativis excivit Mettium. Ducit quam proxume ad hostem potest. Inde legatum praemissum nuntiare Tullo iubet priusquam dimicent opus esse conloquio; si secum congressus sit, satis scire ea se allaturum quae nihilo minus ad rem Romanam quam ad Albanam pertineant. Haud aspernatus Tullus tamen, si vana adferantur,[4] in aciem educit. Exeunt contra et Albani. Postquam structi utrimque sta-

---

[1] Cluilia *Glareanus* (*cf*. i. 22. 4) : cliuli, ciuilia, *etc*. Ω.

[2] uetustate *M* : cum uetustate Ω.

[3] Cluilius *Glareanus* : cluiuilius (*or* ciuilius) Ω.

[4] tamen si uana adferantur *I. H. Voss* : tametsi uana adferebantur Ω.

BOOK I. XXIII. 1-6

for both were of Trojan ancestry, since Lavinium had been planted from Troy, Alba from Lavinium, and from the line of the Alban kings had come the Romans. Still, the issue of the war made the struggle less deplorable, for no battle was fought, and when only the buildings of one of the cities had been destroyed, the two peoples were fused into one. The Albans were first in the field, and with a great army invaded the Roman territory. Their camp they pitched not more than five miles from the City, and surrounded it with a trench. (This was known for some centuries as the Cluilian Trench, from the name of the general, until in the course of time both trench and name disappeared.) In this camp Cluilius the Alban king died, and the Albans chose as dictator Mettius Fufetius. Meantime Tullus, emboldened principally by the death of the king, and asserting that Heaven's great powers would take vengeance upon all of the Alban name, beginning with their king himself, for their unscrupulous war, made a night march past the enemy's camp and led his army into the country of the Albans. This move drew Mettius out from his fortifications. Leading his troops the shortest way towards the enemy, he sent an envoy on ahead to say to Tullus that before they fought it was well that they should confer together; if Tullus would meet him he was confident he had that to say which would be of no less moment to the Roman state than to the Alban. Without rejecting this suggestion, Tullus nevertheless drew up his men in line of battle, in case the proposals should prove impracticable. On the other side the Albans also formed up. When both armies had been marshalled, the leaders,

LIVY

bant, cum paucis procerum in medium duces prodeunt. Ibi infit Albanus:

7 "Iniurias et non redditas res ex foedere quae repetitae sint et ego regem nostrum Cluilium causam huiusce esse belli audisse videor nec te dubito, Tulle, eadem prae te ferre; sed si vera potius quam dictu speciosa dicenda sunt, cupido imperii duos cognatos vicinosque populos ad arma
8 stimulat. Neque recte an perperam interpretor; fuerit ista eius deliberatio qui bellum suscepit; me Albani gerendo bello ducem creavere. Illud te, Tulle, monitum velim. Etrusca res quanta circa nos teque maxime sit, quo propior es,[1] hoc magis scis. Multum illi terra, plurimum mari pollent.
9 Memor esto, iam cum signum pugnae dabis, has duas acies spectaculo fore, ut fessos confectosque, simul victorem ac victum, adgrediantur. Itaque, si nos di amant, quoniam non contenti libertate certa in dubiam imperii servitiique aleam imus, ineamus aliquam viam qua utri utris imperent, sine magna clade, sine multo sanguine utriusque populi decerni possit."
10 Haud displicet res Tullo, quamquam cum indole animi tum spe victoriae ferocior erat. Quaerentibus utrimque ratio initur cui et Fortuna ipsa praebuit materiam.

[1] es *Voss*: es Volscis Ω: es Tuscis *Strothius*.

BOOK I. xxiii. 6-10

attended by a few of their nobles, advanced to the middle of the field. Then the Alban began as follows:

"Pillage and failure to make the amends demanded in accordance with our treaty I think I have myself heard named by our king, Cluilius, as the occasion of this war, and I doubt not, Tullus, but you make the same contention. But if truth is to be spoken, rather than sophistries, it is greed for dominion that is goading two kindred and neighbouring peoples into war. Whether rightly or wrongly I do not attempt to determine; that is a question that may well have been considered by him who undertook the war; I am only the general appointed by the Albans to prosecute that war. But this is the point, Tullus, which I wish to suggest to you: Of the magnitude of the Etruscan power which encompasses us, and you especially, you are better aware than we, in proportion as you are nearer to that people. Great is their strength on land, exceedingly great on the sea. You must consider that the instant you give the signal for battle, the Tuscans will be watching our two armies, so that, when we have become tired and exhausted, they may attack at once the victor and the vanquished. In Heaven's name, therefore, since we are not content with unquestioned liberty, but are proceeding to the doubtful hazard of dominion or enslavement, let us adopt some plan by which we may decide the question which nation shall rule the other, without a great disaster and much carnage on both sides."

Tullus made no objection, though inclined to war by nature no less than by his anticipation of victory. While both parties were considering what to do, a plan was hit upon for the execution of which Fortune herself supplied the means.

LIVY

XXIV. Forte in duobus tum exercitibus erant trigemini fratres nec aetate nec viribus dispares. Horatios Curiatiosque fuisse satis constat, nec ferme res antiqua alia est nobilior; tamen in re tam clara nominum error manet, utrius populi Horatii, utrius Curiatii fuerint. Auctores utroque trahunt; plures tamen invenio qui Romanos Horatios vocent; hos ut 2 sequar inclinat animus. Cum trigeminis agunt reges, ut pro sua quisque patria dimicent ferro: ibi imperium fore unde victoria fuerit. Nihil recusatur; 3 tempus et locus convenit. Priusquam dimicarent, foedus ictum inter Romanos et Albanos est his legibus, ut cuiusque populi cives eo certamine vicissent, is alteri populo cum bona pace imperitaret. Foedera alia aliis legibus, ceterum eodem modo omnia fiunt. 4 Tum ita factum accepimus, nec ullius vetustior foederis memoria est. Fetialis regem Tullum ita rogavit: "Iubesne me, rex, cum patre patrato populi Albani foedus ferire?" Iubente rege "Sagmina," 5 inquit, "te, rex, posco." Rex ait: "Puram tollito." Fetialis ex arce graminis herbam puram attulit. Postea regem ita rogavit: "Rex, facisne me tu regium nuntium populi Romani Quiritium, vasa comi-

---

[1] The *fetiales* (related to *facio*, "do") were a college of priests whose duties were to represent the state in declaring war, making peace, entering into treaties, etc. The *pater*

BOOK I. XXIV. 1-5

XXIV. It chanced that there were in each of these armies triplet brothers, not ill-matched either in age or in physical prowess. That they were Horatii and Curiatii is generally allowed, and scarcely any other ancient tradition is better known; yet, in spite of the celebrity of the affair, an uncertainty persists in regard to the names—to which people, that is, the Horatii belonged, and to which the Curiatii. The writers of history are divided. Still, the majority, I find, call the Roman brothers Horatii, and theirs is the opinion I incline to adopt. To these young men the kings proposed a combat in which each should fight for his own city, the dominion to belong with that side where the victory should rest. No objection was raised, and time and place were agreed on. Before proceeding with the battle, a treaty was made between the Romans and the Albans, providing that the nation whose citizens should triumph in this contest should hold undisputed sway over the other nation. One treaty differs from another in its terms, but the same procedure is always employed. On the present occasion we are told that they did as follows, nor has tradition preserved the memory of any more ancient compact. The fetial[1] asked King Tullus, "Dost thou command me, King, to make a treaty with the *pater patratus* of the Alban People?" Being so commanded by the king, he said, "I demand of thee, King, the sacred herb." The king replied, "Thou shalt take it untainted." The fetial brought from the citadel an untainted plant. After this he asked the king, "Dost thou grant me, King, with my emblems and my companions, the royal sanction, to

patratus (from *patro*, "accomplish" or "bring about") was the spokesman of the deputation.

LIVY

tesque meos?" Rex respondit: "Quod sine fraude mea populique Romani Quiritium fiat, facio." Fetialis erat M. Valerius; is patrem[1] patratum Sp. Fusium fecit verbena caput capillosque tangens. Pater patratus ad ius iurandum patrandum, id est sanciendum fit foedus; multisque id verbis, quae longo effata carmine non operae est referre, peragit. Legibus deinde recitatis "Audi," inquit, "Iuppiter, audi, pater patrate populi Albani, audi tu, populus Albanus. Ut illa palam prima postrema ex illis tabulis cerave recitata sunt sine dolo malo utique ea hic hodie rectissime intellecta sunt, illis legibus populus Romanus prior non deficiet. Si prior defexit publico consilio dolo malo, tum tu ille Diespiter[2] populum Romanum sic ferito ut ego hunc porcum hic hodie feriam; tantoque magis ferito quanto magis potes pollesque." Id ubi dixit, porcum saxo silice percussit. Sua item carmina Albani suumque ius iurandum per suum dictatorem suosque sacerdotes peregerunt.

XXV. Foedere icto trigemini, sicut convenerat, arma capiunt. Cum sui utrosque adhortarentur, deos patrios, patriam ac parentes, quicquid civium domi, quicquid in exercitu sit, illorum tunc arma, illorum intueri manus, feroces et suopte ingenio et pleni

---

[1] is patrem *VM* : patrem Ω.
[2] tum tu (*Crevier*) ille Diespiter *Turnebus and Duker*: tum ille dies iuppiter Ω.

speak for the Roman People of the Quirites?" The king made answer, "So far as may be without prejudice to myself and the Roman People of the Quirites, I grant it." The fetial was Marcus Valerius; he made Spurius Fusius *pater patratus,* touching his head and hair with the sacred sprig. The *pater patratus* is appointed to pronounce the oath, that is, to solemnize the pact; and this he accomplishes with many words, expressed in a long metrical formula which it is not worth while to quote. The conditions being then recited, he cries, "Hear, Jupiter; hear, *pater patratus* of the Alban People: hear ye, People of Alba: From these terms, as they have been publicly rehearsed from beginning to end, without fraud, from these tablets, or this wax, and as they have been this day clearly understood, the Roman People will not be the first to depart. If it shall first depart from them, by general consent, with malice aforethought, then on that day do thou, great Diespiter, so smite the Roman People as I shall here to-day smite this pig: and so much the harder smite them as thy power and thy strength are greater." When Spurius had said these words, he struck the pig with a flint. In like manner the Albans pronounced their own forms and their own oath, by the mouth of their own dictator and priests.

XXV. When the treaty had been established, the brothers armed themselves, in accordance with the agreement. On either side the soldiers urged on their champions. They reminded them that their fathers' gods, their native land, their parents, and all their countrymen, whether at home or with the army, had their eye only on their swords and their right hands. Eager for the combat, as well owing to their

LIVY

adhortantium vocibus in medium inter duas acies
procedunt. Consederant utrimque pro castris duo
exercitus periculi magis praesentis quam curae expertes;
quippe imperium agebatur in tam paucorum
virtute atque fortuna positum. Itaque ergo erecti
suspensique in minime gratum spectaculum animos
intendunt.[1] Datur signum infestisque armis velut
acies terni iuvenes magnorum exercituum animos
gerentes concurrunt. Nec his nec illis periculum
suum, publicum imperium servitiumque obversatur
animo futuraque ea deinde patriae fortuna quam ipsi
fecissent. Ut primo statim concursu concrepuere[2]
arma micantesque fulsere gladii, horror ingens spectantis
perstringit; et neutro inclinata spe torpebat
vox spiritusque. Consertis deinde manibus cum iam
non motus tantum corporum agitatioque anceps telorum
armorumque sed vulnera quoque et sanguis
spectaculo essent, duo Romani, super alium alius,
vulneratis tribus Albanis exspirantes corruerunt. Ad
quorum casum cum conclamasset gaudio Albanus
exercitus, Romanas legiones iam spes tota, nondum
tamen cura deseruerat, exanimes vice unius quem
tres Curiatii circumsteterant. Forte is integer fuit,
ut universis solus nequaquam par, sic adversus singulos
ferox. Ergo, ut segregaret pugnam eorum,

[1] animos intendunt *H. J. Mueller*: animo incenduntur Ω.
[2] concrepuere *H. J. Mueller*: increpuere Ω.

BOOK I. xxv. 1–7

native spirit as to the shouts of encouragement which filled their ears, the brothers advanced into the space between the two lines of battle. The two armies were drawn up, each in front of its own camp, no longer in any immediate danger, but their concern as great as ever; and no wonder, since empire was staked on those few men's valour and good fortune! Alert, therefore, and in suspense, they concentrated their attention upon this unpleasing spectacle. The signal was given, and with drawn steel, like advancing battle-lines, the six young men rushed to the charge, breathing the courage of great armies. Neither side thought of its own danger, but of the nation's sovereignty or servitude, and how from that day forward their country must experience the fortune they should themselves create. The instant they encountered, there was a clash of shields and a flash of glittering blades, while a deep shudder ran through the onlookers, who, as long as neither side had the advantage, remained powerless to speak or breathe. Then, in the hand-to-hand fight which followed, wherein were soon exhibited to men's eyes not only struggling bodies and the play of the sword and shield, but also bloody wounds, two of the Romans fell, fatally wounded, one upon the other, while all three of the Albans were wounded. At the fall of the Romans a shout of joy burst from the Alban army, while the Roman levies now bade farewell to all their hopes; but not to their anxiety, for they were horror-stricken at the plight of the single warrior whom the three Curiatii had surrounded. He happened to have got no hurt, and though no match for his enemies together, was ready to fight them one at a time. So, to divide their attack, he

LIVY

capessit fugam, ita ratus secuturos ut quemque vul-
8 nere adfectum corpus sineret. Iam aliquantum spatii
ex eo loco ubi pugnatum est aufugerat, cum respi-
ciens videt magnis intervallis sequentes; unum haud
9 procul ab sese abesse. In eum magno impetu rediit,
et dum Albanus exercitus inclamat Curiatiis uti opem
ferant fratri, iam Horatius caeso hoste victor secundam pugnam petebat. Tunc clamore, qualis ex insperato faventium solet, Romani adiuvant militem
10 suum; et ille defungi proelio festinat. Prius itaque
quam alter—nec[1] procul aberat—consequi posset, et
11 alterum Curiatium conficit; iamque aequato Marte
singuli supererant, sed nec spe nec viribus pares.
Alterum intactum ferro corpus et geminata victoria
ferocem in certamen tertium dabat: alter fessum
vulnere fessum cursu trahens corpus, victusque fra-
12 trum ante se strage victori obicitur hosti. Nec illud
proelium fuit. Romanus exsultans "Duos," inquit,
"fratrum Manibus dedi: tertium causae[2] belli
huiusce, ut Romanus Albano imperet, dabo." Male
sustinenti arma gladium superne iugulo defigit;
13 iacentem spoliat. Romani ovantes ac gratulantes
Horatium accipiunt eo maiore cum gaudio quo
prope metum res fuerat. Ad sepulturam inde suo-

---

[1] nec M: qui nec Ω.   [2] causae $M\varsigma$: causam Ω.

fled, thinking that each of them would pursue him with what speed his wounds permitted. He had already run some little distance from the spot where they had fought, when, looking back, he saw that they were following at wide intervals and that one of them had nearly overtaken him. Facing about, he ran swiftly up to his man, and while the Alban host were calling out to the Curiatii to help their brother, Horatius had already slain him, and was hastening, flushed with victory, to meet his second antagonist. Then with a cheer, such as is often drawn from partisans by a sudden turn in a contest, the Romans encouraged their champion, and he pressed on to end the battle. And so, before the third Curiatius could come up—and he was not far off—Horatius dispatched the second. They were now on even terms, one soldier surviving on each side, but in hope and vigour they were far from equal. The one, unscathed and elated by his double victory, was eager for a third encounter. The other dragged himself along, faint from his wound and exhausted with running; he thought how his brothers had been slaughtered before him, and was a beaten man when he faced his triumphant foe. What followed was no combat. The Roman cried exultantly, "Two victims I have given to the shades of my brothers: the third I will offer up to the cause of this war, that Roman may rule Alban." His adversary could barely hold up his shield. With a downward thrust Horatius buried his sword in the Alban's throat, and despoiled him where he lay. The Romans welcomed their hero with jubilations and thanksgivings, and their joy was all the greater that they had come near despairing. The burial of their dead then claimed the attention

LIVY

rum nequaquam paribus animis vertuntur, quippe imperio alteri aucti, alteri dicionis alienae facti. 14 Sepulcra exstant, quo quisque loco cecidit, duo Romana uno loco propius Albam, tria Albana Romam versus, sed distantia locis, ut et pugnatum est.

XXVI. Priusquam inde digrederentur, roganti Mettio, ex foedere icto, quid imperaret, imperat Tullus uti iuventutem in armis habeat: usurum se eorum opera, si bellum cum Veientibus foret. Ita 2 exercitus inde domos abducti. Princeps Horatius ibat trigemina spolia prae se gerens; cui soror virgo, quae desponsa uni ex Curiatiis fuerat, obvia ante portam Capenam fuit; cognitoque super umeros fratris paludamento sponsi, quod ipsa confecerat, solvit crines et flebiliter nomine sponsum mortuum appel- 3 lat. Movet feroci iuveni animum conploratio sororis in victoria sua tantoque gaudio publico. Stricto itaque gladio simul verbis increpans transfigit 4 puellam. "Abi hinc cum immaturo amore ad sponsum" inquit, "oblita fratrum mortuorum vi- 5 vique, oblita patriae. Sic eat quaecumque Romana lugebit hostem."

Atrox visum id facinus patribus plebique, sed recens meritum facto obstabat. Tamen raptus in ius ad regem. Rex, ne ipse tam tristis ingratique ad volgus iudicii ac[1] secundum iudicium supplicii auctor

---

[1] ac *Rhenanus F³*: ad Ω.

BOOK I. xxv. 13–xxvi. 5

of the two armies,—with widely different feelings, since one nation was exalted with imperial power, the other made subject to a foreign sway. The graves may still be seen where each soldier fell: two Roman graves in one spot, nearer Alba; those of the three Albans towards Rome, but separated, just as they had fought.

XXVI. Before they left the field Mettius asked, in pursuance of the compact, what Tullus commanded him to do, and the Roman ordered him to hold his young men under arms, saying that he should employ their services, if war broke out with the Veientes. The armies then marched home. In the van of the Romans came Horatius, displaying his triple spoils. As he drew near the Porta Capena he was met by his unwedded sister, who had been promised in marriage to one of the Curiatii. When she recognized on her brother's shoulders the military cloak of her betrothed, which she herself had woven, she loosed her hair and, weeping, called on her dead lover's name. It enraged the fiery youth to hear his sister's lamentations in the hour of his own victory and the nation's great rejoicing. And so, drawing his sword and at the same time angrily upbraiding her, he ran her through the body. "Begone" he cried, "to your betrothed, with your ill-timed love, since you have forgot your brothers, both the dead and the living, and forgot your country! So perish every Roman woman who mourns a foe!"

Horrid as this deed seemed to the Fathers and the people, his recent service was an off-set to it; nevertheless he was seized and brought before the king for trial. The king, that he might not take upon himself the responsibility for so stern and unpopular a judgement, and for the punishment which must follow

B.C. 672-640

LIVY

A.U.C.
82-114

esset, concilio populi advocato "Duumviros," inquit, "qui Horatio perduellionem iudicent, secundum
6 legem facio." Lex horrendi carminis erat: duumviri perduellionem iudicent; si a duumviris provocarit, provocatione certato; si vincent, caput obnubito; infelici arbori reste suspendito; verberato vel
7 intra pomerium vel extra pomerium. Hac lege duumviri creati. Qui se absolvere non rebantur ea lege ne innoxium quidem posse, cum condemnassent, tum alter ex iis[1] " P. Horati, tibi perduellionem
8 iudico," inquit; "i, lictor,[2] colliga manus." Accesserat lictor iniciebatque laqueum. Tum Horatius auctore Tullo, clemente legis interprete, " Provoco," inquit. Itaque[3] provocatione certatum ad populum
9 est. Moti homines sunt in eo iudicio maxime P. Horatio patre proclamante se filiam iure caesam iudicare: ni ita esset, patrio iure in filium[4] animadversurum fuisse. Orabat deinde, ne se, quem paulo ante cum egregia stirpe conspexissent, orbum liberis
10 facerent. Inter haec senex iuvenem amplexus, spolia Curiatiorum fixa eo loco qui nunc pila Horatia appellatur ostentans, " Huncine" aiebat, "quem modo

---

[1] iis *Madvig*: his Ω.
[2] inquit i, lictor ς *Modius*: inqui i lictor *M*: inquit lictor Ω.
[3] itaque *Tan. Faber*: ita de Ω.   [4] filium ς : filiam Ω.

---

[1] By taking it upon himself to punish his sister, Horatius had usurped a function of the state, and so was guilty of treason.
[2] I have adopted the view of Oldfather (*T.A.P.A.* xxxix. pp. 49 ff.) that neither hanging nor crucifixion is meant, but

BOOK I. xxvi. 5-10

sentence, called together the council of the people and said: "In accordance with the law I appoint duumvirs to pass judgement upon Horatius for treason."[1] The dread formula of the law ran thus: "Let the duumvirs pronounce him guilty of treason; if he shall appeal from the duumvirs, let the appeal be tried; if the duumvirs win, let the lictor veil his head; let him bind him with a rope to a barren tree; let him scourge him either within or without the pomerium."[2] By the terms of this law duumvirs were appointed. They considered that they might not acquit, under that act, even one who was innocent, and having given a verdict of guilty, one of them pronounced the words, "Publius Horatius, I adjudge you a traitor; go, lictor, bind his hands." The lictor had approached and was about to fit the noose. Then Horatius, at the prompting of Tullus, who put a merciful construction upon the law, cried, "I appeal!" And so the appeal was tried before the people. What influenced men most of all in that trial was the assertion of Publius Horatius, the father, that his daughter had been justly slain; otherwise he should have used a father's authority and have punished his son, himself. He then implored them not to make him childless whom they had beheld a little while before surrounded by a goodly offspring. So saying, the old man embraced the youth, and pointing to the spoils of the Curiatii set up in the place which is now called "the Horatian Spears,"[3] he exclaimed, "This man you saw but lately advancing

that the culprit was fastened to the tree and scourged to death.

[3] The name of the place which commemorated the spoils reflects the tradition, rejected above by Livy, that the Horatii were Albans, the Curiatii Romans.

LIVY

decoratum ovantemque victoria incedentem vidistis, Quirites, eum sub furca vinctum inter verbera et cruciatus videre potestis? Quod vix Albanorum oculi 11 tam deforme spectaculum ferre possent. I, lictor, colliga manus, quae paulo ante armatae imperium populo Romano pepererunt. I, caput obnube liberatoris urbis huius; arbore infelici suspende; verbera vel intra pomerium, modo inter illa pila et spolia hostium, vel extra pomerium, modo inter sepulcra Curiatiorum. Quo enim ducere hunc iuvenem potestis, ubi non sua decora eum a tanta foeditate 12 supplicii vindicent?" Non tulit populus nec patris lacrimas nec ipsius parem in omni periculo animum, absolveruntque admiratione magis virtutis quam iure causae. Itaque, ut caedes manifesta aliquo tamen piaculo lueretur, imperatum patri ut filium expiaret 13 pecunia publica. Is quibusdam piacularibus sacrificiis factis, quae deinde genti Horatiae tradita sunt, transmisso per viam tigillo capite adoperto velut sub iugum misit iuvenem. Id hodie quoque publice semper refectum manet: sororium tigillum vocant. 14 Horatiae sepulcrum, quo loco corruerat icta, constructum est saxo quadrato.

XXVII. Nec diu pax Albana mansit. Invidia volgi, quod tribus militibus fortuna publica commissa fuerit,[1] vanum ingenium dictatoris corrupit, et, quoniam recta consilia haud bene evenerant, pravis

[1] fuerit Ω: fuerat *HR*²: foret *Madvig*.

decked with spoils and triumphing in his victory; can you bear, Quirites, to see him bound beneath a fork and scourged and tortured? Hardly could Alban eyes endure so hideous a sight. Go, lictor, bind the hands which but now, with sword and shield, brought imperial power to the Roman People! Go, veil the head of the liberator of this city! Bind him to a barren tree! Scourge him within the pomerium, if you will—so it be amidst yonder spears and trophies of our enemies—or outside the pomerium —so it be amongst the graves of the Curiatii! For whither can you lead this youth where his own honours will not vindicate him from so foul a punishment?" The people could not withstand the father's tears, or the courage of Horatius himself, steadfast in every peril; and they acquitted him, more in admiration of his valour than from the justice of his cause. And so, that the flagrant murder might yet be cleansed away, by some kind of expiatory rite, the father was commanded to make atonement for his son at the public cost. He therefore offered certain piacular sacrifices, which were thenceforward handed down in the Horatian family, and, erecting a beam across the street, to typify a yoke, he made his son pass under it, with covered head. It remains to this day, being restored from time to time at the state's expense, and is known as "the Sister's Beam." Horatia's tomb, of hewn stone, was built on the place where she had been struck down.

XXVII. But the peace with Alba did not last long. The discontent of the people, who criticized the dictator for having confided the nation's welfare to three soldiers, broke down his weak character, and since honest measures had proved unsuccessful,

LIVY

A.U.C. 82-114

2 reconciliare popularium animos coepit. Igitur, ut prius in bello pacem, sic in pace bellum quaerens, quia suae civitati animorum plus quam virium cernebat esse, ad bellum palam atque ex edicto gerundum alios concitat populos, suis per speciem societatis 3 proditionem reservat. Fidenates colonia Romana Veientibus sociis consilii adsumptis pacto transitionis 4 Albanorum ad bellum atque arma incitantur. Cum Fidenae aperte descissent, Tullus Mettio exercituque eius ab Alba accito contra hostes ducit. Ubi Anienem transiit,[1] ad confluentis conlocat castra. Inter eum locum et Fidenas Veientium exercitus Tiberim 5 transierat. Hi in[2] acie prope flumen tenuere dextrum cornu: in sinistro Fidenates propius montes consistunt. Tullus adversus Veientem hostem derigit[3] suos, Albanos contra legionem Fidenatium conlocat. Albano non plus animi erat quam fidei. Nec manere ergo nec transire aperte ausus sensim ad 6 montes succedit; inde, ubi satis subisse sese ratus est, erigit totam aciem, fluctuansque animo ut tereret tempus ordines explicat. Consilium erat, qua fortuna rem daret ea inclinare vires. Miraculo primo esse Romanis qui proximi steterant, ut nudari latera sua sociorum digressu senserunt; inde eques citato

[1] transiit $D^2\varsigma$: transierat $U\varsigma$: transit Ω.
[2] hi in *Weissenborn*: hi (*or* hii *or* hic) et in Ω.
[3] derigit PL: dirigit Ω.

BOOK I. XXVII. 1-7

he resorted to evil ones to regain the favour of his countrymen. Accordingly, just as in war he had sought peace, so now in time of peace he desired war. But seeing that his own state was richer in courage than in strength, he stirred up other tribes to make war openly after due declaration; while for his own people he reserved the part of the traitor under the disguise of friendship. The men of Fidenae, a Roman colony, and the Veientes, whom they admitted to a share in their designs, were induced to commence hostilities by a promise that the Albans would go over to their side. Fidenae having openly revolted, Tullus summoned Mettius and his army from Alba, and led his forces against the enemy. Crossing the Anio, he pitched his camp at the confluence of the rivers. The Veientine army had crossed the Tiber between that place and Fidenae. These troops, drawn up next the river, formed the right wing; on the left the Fidenates were posted, nearer the mountains. Tullus marshalled his own men against the Veientine enemy; the Albans he posted opposite the army of Fidenae. The Alban commander was as wanting in courage as in loyalty. Not daring, therefore, either to hold his ground or openly to desert, he drew off by imperceptible degrees in the direction of the mountains. Then, when he thought he had got near enough to them, he brought up his whole battle-line to an elevated position, and still irresolute, deployed his ranks with the object of consuming time. His purpose was to swing his forces to the side which fortune favoured. At first the Romans posted next to the Albans were amazed when they perceived that their flank was being uncovered by the withdrawal of their allies; then a

LIVY

equo nuntiat regi abire Albanos. Tullus in re trepida duodecim vovit Salios fanaque Pallori ac Pavori. 8 Equitem clara increpans voce, ut hostes exaudirent, redire in proelium iubet: nihil trepidatione opus esse; suo iussu circumduci Albanum exercitum, ut Fidenatium nuda terga invadant; idem imperat ut 9 hastas equites erigerent.[1] Id factum magnae parti peditum Romanorum conspectum abeuntis Albani exercitus intersaepsit: qui viderant, id quod ab rege auditum erat rati, eo acrius pugnant. Terror ad hostes transit; et audiverant clara voce dictum, et magna pars Fidenatium, ut quibus coloni additi Romani[2] essent, Latine sciebant. Itaque, ne subito ex collibus decursu Albanorum intercluderentur ab oppido, terga vertunt. Instat Tullus fusoque Fidenatium cornu in Veientem alieno pavore perculsum ferocior redit. Nec illi tulere impetum, sed ab effusa 11 fuga flumen obiectum ab tergo arcebat. Quo postquam fuga inclinavit, alii arma foede iactantes in aquam caeci ruebant, alii, dum cunctantur in ripis, inter fugae pugnaeque consilium oppressi. Non alia ante Romana pugna atrocior fuit.

---

[1] erigerent ϛ: erigere erigerent iubeat *M*: erigerent iubeat (*or* erigere iubeat, *or* eriere iubeat, *or* erigere erigerent iubet, *or* erigere iubet) Ω.

[2] ut quibus ... Romani *Walters* (*following Tan. Faber's* ut queis ... Romani): ut qui (et qui *DL*) ... Romanis Ω.

BOOK I. XXVII. 7-11

horseman galloped up to the king, and told him that the Albans were marching off. In this crisis Tullus vowed to establish twelve Salian priests,[1] and to build shrines to Pallor and Panic. The horseman he reprimanded in a loud voice, that the enemy might overhear him, and ordered him to go back and fight; there was no occasion for alarm; it was by his own command that the Alban army was marching round, that they might attack the unprotected rear of the Fidenates. He also ordered the cavalry to raise their spears. This manœuvre hid the retreat of the Alban army from a large part of the Roman foot-soldiers; those who had seen it, believing what the king had been heard to say, fought all the more impetuously. The enemy in their turn now became alarmed; they had heard Tullus's loud assertion, and many of the Fidenates, having had Romans among them as colonists, knew Latin. And so, lest the Albans should suddenly charge down from the hills and cut them off from their town, they beat a retreat. Tullus pressed them hard, and having routed the wing composed of the Fidenates, returned, bolder than ever, to the Veientes, who were demoralized by the panic of their neighbours. They, too, failed to withstand his attack, but their rout was stopped by the river in their rear. When they had fled thus far, some basely threw away their arms and rushed blindly into the water, others hesitated on the bank and were overtaken before they had made up their minds whether to flee or resist. Never before had the Romans fought a bloodier battle.

B.C. 672-640

[1] These were the so-called *Collini*, or *Agonales*, and were associated with Quirinus, as the *Palatini* (chap. xx.) were with Mars Gradivus. See also v. lii. 7.

LIVY

XXVIII. Tum Albanus exercitus, spectator certaminis, deductus in campos. Mettius Tullo devictos hostes gratulatur; contra Tullus Mettium benigne adloquitur. Quod bene vertat, castra Albanos Romanis castris iungere iubet; sacrificium lustrale in 2 diem posterum parat. Ubi inluxit, paratis omnibus, ut adsolet, vocari ad contionem utrumque exercitum iubet. Praecones ab extremo orsi primos excivere Albanos. Hi novitate etiam rei moti, ut regem Romanum contionantem audirent proximi consti- 3 tere. Ex conposito armata circumdatur Romana legio; centurionibus datum negotium erat ut sine 4 mora imperia exsequerentur. Tum ita Tullus infit:

"Romani, si umquam ante alias ullo in bello fuit quod primum dis immortalibus gratias ageretis, deinde vestrae ipsorum virtuti, hesternum id proelium fuit. Dimicatum est enim non magis cum hostibus quam, quae dimicatio maior atque periculosior est, 5 cum proditione ac perfidia sociorum. Nam, ne vos falsa opinio teneat, iniussu meo Albani subiere ad montes, nec imperium illud meum sed consilium et imperii simulatio fuit, ut nec vobis ignorantibus deseri vos averteretur a certamine animus et hostibus circumveniri[1] se ab tergo ratis terror ac fuga 6 iniceretur. Nec ea culpa quam arguo omnium Albanorum est: ducem secuti sunt, ut et vos, si quo ego

[1] circumveniri *F? Dς*: circumuenire Ω.

BOOK I. XXVIII. 1-6

XXVIII. Then the Alban army, which had been a spectator of the battle, was led down into the plain. Mettius congratulated Tullus on the conquest of his enemies; Tullus replied kindly to Mettius, and commanded the Albans in a good hour to join their camp to that of the Romans. He then made preparations to perform, on the morrow, a sacrifice of purification. At dawn, when all things were in readiness, he issued to both armies the customary order, convoking them to an assembly. The heralds, beginning at the outskirts of the camp, called out the Albans first, who being moved by the very novelty of the occasion, took their stand close to the Roman king, that they might hear him harangue his army. The Roman troops, by previous arrangement, were armed and disposed around them, and the centurions were bidden to execute orders promptly. Then Tullus began as follows:

"Romans, if ever anywhere in any war you have had reason to give thanks, first to the immortal gods and then to your own valour, it was in the battle of yesterday. For you fought not only against your enemies, but a harder and more dangerous fight — against the treachery and the perfidy of your allies. For, to undeceive you, I gave no orders that the Albans should draw off towards the mountains. What you heard was not my command, but a trick and a pretended command, devised in order that you might not know you were being deserted, and so be distracted from the fight; and that the enemy, thinking that they were being hemmed in on the rear, might be panic-stricken and flee. And yet this guilt which I am charging does not attach to all the Albans; they but followed

B.C.
672-640

LIVY

inde agmen declinare voluissem, fecissetis. Mettius ille est ductor itineris huius, Mettius idem huius machinator belli, Mettius foederis Romani Albanique ruptor. Audeat deinde talia alius, nisi in hunc insigne iam documentum mortalibus dedero."

7 Centuriones armati Mettium circumsistunt; rex cetera, ut orsus erat, peragit: "Quod bonum faustum felixque sit populo Romano ac mihi vobisque, Albani, populum omnem Albanum Romam traducere in animo est, civitatem dare plebi, primores in patres legere, unam urbem, unam rem publicam facere. Ut ex uno quondam in duos populos divisa Albana res est, sic 8 nunc in unum redeat.[1]" Ad haec Albana pubes inermis ab armatis saepta in variis voluntatibus com9 muni tamen metu cogente silentium tenet. Tum Tullus "Metti Fufeti," inquit, "si ipse discere posses fidem ac foedera servare, vivo tibi ea disciplina a me adhibita esset; nunc, quoniam tuum insanabile ingenium est, at tu tuo supplicio doce humanum genus ea sancta credere quae a te violata sunt. Ut igitur paulo ante animum inter Fidenatem Romanamque rem ancipitem gessisti, ita iam corpus passim distra10 hendum dabis." Exinde duabus admotis quadrigis in currus earum distentum inligat Mettium, deinde in diversum iter equi concitati lacerum in utroque

[1] redeat Ω: redeant MO.

their general, as you, too, would have done, had I desired to lead you off anywhere. It is Mettius yonder who led this march; Mettius, too, who contrived this war; Mettius who broke the treaty between Roman and Alban. Let another dare such a deed hereafter if I do not speedily visit such a punishment on him as shall be a conspicuous warning to all mankind."

Thereupon the centurions, sword in hand, surrounded Mettius, while the king proceeded: "May prosperity, favour, and fortune be with the Roman people and myself, and with you, men of Alba! I purpose to bring all the Alban people over to Rome, to grant citizenship to their commons, to enroll the nobles in the senate, to make one city and one state. As formerly from one people the Alban nation was divided into two, so now let it be reunited into one." Hearing these words the Alban soldiers, themselves unarmed and fenced in by armed men, were constrained, however their wishes might differ, by a common fear, and held their peace. Then Tullus said: "Mettius Fufetius, if you were capable of learning, yourself, to keep faith and abide by treaties, you should have lived that I might teach you this; as it is, since your disposition is incurable, you shall yet by your punishment teach the human race to hold sacred the obligations you have violated. Accordingly, just as a little while ago your heart was divided between the states of Fidenae and Rome, so now you shall give up your body to be torn two ways." He then brought up two four-horse chariots, and caused Mettius to be stretched out and made fast to them, after which the horses were whipped up in opposite directions, and bore off in

LIVY

curru corpus, qua inhaeserant vinculis membra, por-
11 tantes.   Avertere omnes ab tanta foeditate spectaculi oculos.   Primum ultimumque illud supplicium
apud Romanos exempli parum memoris legum huma-
narum fuit : in aliis gloriari licet nulli gentium miti-
ores placuisse poenas.

XXIX. Inter haec iam praemissi Albam erant
equites qui multitudinem traducerent Romam.   Le-
2 giones deinde ductae ad diruendam urbem.   Quae
ubi intravere portas, non quidem fuit tumultus ille
nec pavor, qualis captarum esse urbium solet, cum
effractis portis stratisve ariete muris aut arce vi capta
clamor hostilis et cursus per urbem armatorum om-
3 nia ferro flammaque miscet; sed silentium triste ac
tacita maestitia ita defixit omnium animos ut prae
metu quid[1] relinquerent, quid secum ferrent deficiente consilio rogitantesque alii alios nunc in limi-
nibus starent, nunc errabundi domos suas ultimum
4 illud visuri pervagarentur.   Ut vero iam equitum
clamor exire iubentium instabat, iam fragor tectorum
quae diruebantur ultimis urbis partibus audiebatur,
pulvisque ex distantibus locis ortus velut nube in-
ducta omnia impleverat, raptim quibus quisque poterat elatis, cum larem ac penates tectaque in quibus
natus quisque educatusque esset relinquentes exirent,
5 iam continens agmen migrantium impleverat vias, et

[1] quid *Madvig* : obliti quid Ω.

---

[1] Each family had its *lar,* a special deity who protected the household, and its *penates,* guardians of the *penus* (the family store of provisions).

each of the cars fragments of the mangled body, where the limbs held to their fastenings. All eyes were turned away from so dreadful a sight. Such was the first and last punishment among the Romans of a kind that disregards the laws of humanity. In other cases we may boast that with no nation have milder punishments found favour.

XXIX. While this was going on, horsemen had already been sent on to Alba to fetch the inhabitants to Rome, and afterwards the legions were marched over to demolish the city. When they entered the gates there was not, indeed, the tumult and panic which usually follow the capture of a city, when its gates have been forced or its walls breached with a ram or its stronghold stormed, when the shouts of the enemy and the rush of armed men through the streets throw the whole town into a wild confusion of blood and fire. But at Alba oppressive silence and grief that found no words quite overwhelmed the spirits of all the people; too dismayed to think what they should take with them and what leave behind, they would ask each other's advice again and again, now standing on their thresholds, and now roaming aimlessly through the houses they were to look upon for that last time. But when at length the horsemen began to be urgent, and clamorously commanded them to come out; when they could now hear the crash of the buildings which were being pulled down in the outskirts of the city; when the dust rising in different quarters had overcast the sky like a gathering cloud; then everybody made haste to carry out what he could, and forth they went, abandoning their lares and penates,[1] and the houses where they had been born and brought up. And now the streets were filled with an unbroken

LIVY

conspectus aliorum mutua miseratione integrabat lacrimas, vocesque etiam miserabiles exaudiebantur mulierum praecipue, cum obsessa ab armatis templa augusta praeterirent ac velut captos relinquerent 6 deos. Egressis urbe[1] Albanis Romanus passim publica privataque omnia tecta adaequat solo, unaque hora quadringentorum annorum opus quibus Alba steterat excidio ac ruinis dedit; templis tamen deum —ita enim edictum ab rege fuerat—temperatum est.

XXX. Roma interim crescit Albae ruinis. Duplicatur civium numerus; Caelius additur urbi mons, et quo frequentius habitaretur, eam sedem Tullus regiae 2 capit ibique deinde[2] habitavit. Principes Albanorum in patres, ut ea quoque pars rei publicae cresceret, legit, Iulios,[3] Servilios, Quinctios, Geganios, Curiatios, Cloelios; templumque ordini ab se aucto curiam fecit quae Hostilia usque ad patrum nostro- 3 rum aetatem appellata est. Et ut omnium ordinum viribus aliquid ex novo populo adiceretur equitum decem turmas ex Albanis legit, legiones et veteres eodem supplemento explevit et novas scripsit.

4 Hac fiducia virium Tullus Sabinis bellum indicit,

[1] urbe ς : urbem Ω.   [2] ibique deinde *VM* : ibique Ω.
[3] Iulios *Sabellicus* (*cf. Dion. Hal.* 1. 70. *and* 2. 79): Tullios Ω.

---

[1] When Clodius was murdered, in 52 B.C., the mob burnt his body in the Curia Hostilia, which caught fire and was destroyed.

BOOK I. xxix. 5–xxx. 4

procession of emigrants, whose mutual pity, as they gazed at one another, caused their tears to start afresh; plaintive cries too began to be heard, proceeding chiefly from the women, when they passed the venerable temples beset by armed men, and left in captivity, as it seemed to them, their gods. When the Albans had quitted the city, the Romans everywhere levelled with the ground all buildings, both public and private, and a single hour gave over to destruction and desolation the work of the four hundred years during which Alba had stood. But the temples of the gods were spared, for so the king had decreed.

XXX. Rome, meanwhile, was increased by Alba's downfall. The number of citizens was doubled, the Caelian Hill was added to the City, and, that it might be more thickly settled, Tullus chose it for the site of the king's house and from that time onwards resided there. The chief men of the Albans he made senators, that this branch of the nation might grow too. Such were the Julii, the Servilii, the Quinctii, the Geganii, the Curiatii, and the Cloelii. He also built, as a consecrated place for the order he had enlarged, a senate-house, which continued to be called the Curia Hostilia as late as the time of our own fathers.[1] And that all the orders might gain some strength from the new people, he enrolled ten squadrons of knights[2] from among the Albans, and from the same source filled up the old legions and enlisted new ones.

Confiding in these forces, Tullus declared war on

---

[2] Each squadron contained thirty men. The total number was, therefore, the same as that of the three centuries of Romulus.

LIVY

genti ea tempestate secundum Etruscos opulentissimae viris armisque. Utrimque iniuriae factae ac res nequiquam erant repetitae. Tullus ad Feroniae fanum mercatu frequenti negotiatores Romanos comprehensos querebatur, Sabini suos prius in lucum confugisse ac Romae retentos. Hae causae belli ferebantur. Sabini, haud parum memores et suarum virium partem Romae ab Tatio locatam et Romanam rem nuper etiam adiectione populi Albani auctam, circumspicere et ipsi externa auxilia. Etruria erat vicina, proximi Etruscorum Veientes. Inde ob residuas bellorum iras maxime sollicitatis ad defectionem animis voluntarios traxere, et apud vagos quosdam ex inopi plebe etiam merces valuit. Publico auxilio nullo adiuti sunt, valuitque apud Veientes—nam de ceteris minus mirum est—pacta cum Romulo indutiarum fides. Cum bellum utrimque summa ope pararent, vertique in eo res videretur, utri prius arma inferrent, occupat Tullus in agrum Sabinum transire. Pugna atrox ad silvam Malitiosam fuit, ubi et peditum quidem robore, ceterum equitatu aucto nuper plurimum Romana acies valuit. Ab equitibus repente invectis turbati ordines sunt Sabinorum; nec pugna deinde illis constare nec fuga explicari sine magna caede potuit.

---

[1] *i.e.* "Guileful Wood."

BOOK I. xxx. 4-10

the Sabines, a nation second only at that time to the Etruscans in its wealth of men and arms. On either side there had been aggressions and refusals to grant satisfaction. Tullus complained that at the shrine of Feronia, in a crowded fair, Roman traders had been seized; the Sabines alleged that, before this, refugees from their country had fled to the grove of sanctuary, and had been detained in Rome. These were put forward as the causes of war. The Sabines, not forgetting that a portion of their own forces had been settled in Rome by Tatius and that the Roman state had recently been further strengthened by the addition of the Alban people, began themselves to look about for outside help. Etruria was close by, and the nearest of the Etruscans were the Veientes. There the resentment left over from the wars was the strongest incentive to revolt, and procured them some volunteers; while with certain vagrant and poverty-stricken plebeians even the prospect of pay was effectual. Official aid there was none, and the Veientes (for there is less to surprise us in the others) held firmly to the truce they had agreed upon with Romulus. While preparations for war were making on both sides with the greatest energy, and success appeared to hinge upon which should first take the field, Tullus anticipated his enemies and invaded the Sabine country. A desperate battle was fought near the Silva Malitiosa,[1] where, owing partly, it is true, to the strength of their infantry, but most of all to their newly augmented cavalry, the Roman army gained the mastery. The cavalry made a sudden charge; the ranks of the Sabines were thrown into disorder, and from that moment were unable, without heavy loss, either to hold their own in the fight or to extricate themselves by a retreat.

LIVY

XXXI. Devictis Sabinis cum in magna gloria magnisque opibus regnum Tulli ac tota res Romana esset, nuntiatum regi patribusque est in monte Albano 2 lapidibus pluvisse. Quod cum credi vix posset, missis ad id visendum prodigium, in conspectu haud aliter quam cum grandinem venti glomeratam in terras 3 agunt, crebri cecidere caelo lapides. Visi etiam audire vocem ingentem ex summi cacuminis luco, ut patrio ritu sacra Albani facerent, quae velut dis quoque simul cum patria relictis oblivioni dederant, et aut Romana sacra susceperant aut fortunae, ut fit, 4 obirati cultum reliquerant deum. Romanis quoque ab eodem prodigio novendiale sacrum publice susceptum est, seu voce caelesti ex Albano monte missa —nam id quoque traditur—seu haruspicum monitu; mansit certe sollemne, ut quandoque idem prodigium nuntiaretur, feriae per novem dies agerentur.

5 Haud ita multo post pestilentia laboratum est. Unde cum pigritia militandi oreretur, nulla tamen ab armis quies dabatur a bellicoso rege, salubriora etiam credente militiae quam domi iuvenum corpora esse, donec ipse quoque longinquo morbo est impli-6 citus. Tunc adeo fracti simul cum corpore sunt spiritus illi feroces, ut qui nihil ante ratus esset minus regium quam sacris dedere animum, repente omnibus magnis parvisque superstitionibus obnoxius

BOOK I. XXXI. 1-6

XXXI. After the defeat of the Sabines, when King Tullus and the entire Roman state were at a high pitch of glory and prosperity, it was reported to the king and senators that there had been a rain of stones on the Alban Mount. As this could scarce be credited, envoys were dispatched to examine the prodigy, and in their sight there fell from the sky, like hail-stones which the wind piles in drifts upon the ground, a shower of pebbles. They thought too that they heard a mighty voice issuing from the grove on the mountain-top, which commanded the Albans to celebrate, according to the fashion of their fathers, the sacrifices, which as though they had forsaken their gods along with their city, they had given over to oblivion, either adopting Roman rites, or in anger at their fortune, such as men sometimes feel, abandoning the worship of the gods. The Romans also, in consequence of the same portent, undertook an official nine days' celebration, whether so commanded by the divine utterance from the Alban Mount—for this too is handed down—or on the advice of soothsayers. At all events it remained a regular custom that whenever the same prodigy was reported there should be a nine days' observance.

Not very long after this Rome was afflicted with a pestilence. This caused a reluctance to bear arms, yet no respite from service was allowed by the warlike king (who believed, besides, that the young men were healthier in the field than at home) until he himself contracted a lingering illness. Then that haughty spirit was so broken, with the breaking of his health, that he who had hitherto thought nothing less worthy of a king than to devote his mind to sacred rites, suddenly became a prey to all sorts of

B.C. 672-640

111

LIVY

degeret religionibusque etiam populum impleret.
7 Vulgo iam homines eum statum rerum qui sub
Numa rege fuerat requirentes, unam opem aegris
corporibus relictam, si pax veniaque ab dis impetrata
8 esset, credebant. Ipsum regem tradunt volventem
commentarios Numae, cum ibi quaedam occulta sollemnia sacrificia Iovi Elicio facta invenisset, operatum iis[1] sacris se abdidisse; sed non rite initum aut
curatum id sacrum esse, nec solum nullam ei oblatam
caelestium speciem, sed ira Iovis sollicitati prava
religione fulmine ictum cum domo conflagrasse.
Tullus magna gloria belli regnavit annos duos et
triginta.

XXXII. Mortuo Tullo res, ut institutum iam inde
ab initio erat, ad patres redierat, hique interregem
nominaverant. Quo comitia habente Ancum Marcium regem populus creavit; patres fuere auctores.
Numae Pompili regis nepos, filia ortus, Ancus Mar-
2 cius erat. Qui ut regnare coepit, et avitae gloriae
memor et quia proximum regnum, cetera egregium,
ab una parte haud satis prosperum fuerat, aut neglectis religionibus aut prave cultis, longe[2] antiquissimum ratus sacra publica ut ab Numa instituta erant
facere, omnia ea ex commentariis regis pontificem in
album relata[3] proponere in publico iubet. Inde et

---

[1] iis ϛ: is *or* his Ω.   [2] longe ϛ *Gronov.*: longeque Ω.
[3] relata *Sabellicus*: elata (elatam *M³*) Ω.

BOOK I. XXXI. 6–XXXII. 2

superstitions great and small, and filled even the minds of the people with religious scruples. Men were now agreed in wishing to recall the conditions which had obtained under King Numa, believing that the only remedy left for their ailing bodies was to procure peace and forgiveness from the gods. The king himself, so tradition tells, in turning over the commentaries of Numa discovered there certain occult sacrifices performed in honour of Jupiter Elicius, and devoted himself in secret to those rites; but the ceremony was improperly undertaken or performed, and not only was no divine manifestation vouchsafed him, but in consequence of the wrath of Jupiter, who was provoked by his faulty observance, he was struck by a thunderbolt and consumed in the flames of his house. Tullus was greatly renowned in war and reigned thirty-two years.

XXXII. On the death of Tullus, the government reverted, in accordance with the custom established in the beginning, to the senators, who named an interrex. This official called together the comitia, and the people elected Ancus Marcius king, a choice which the Fathers ratified. Ancus Marcius was a grandson, on the mother's side, of King Numa Pompilius. When he began to rule he was mindful of his grandfather's glory, and considered that the last reign, excellent in all else, had failed to prosper in one respect, owing to neglect or misconduct of religious observances. Deeming it therefore a matter of the utmost consequence to perform the state sacrifices as Numa had established them, he bade the pontifex copy out all these from the commentaries of the king and display them in public on a whitened table. This act led the citizens, who were eager for peace,

civibus otii cupidis et finitimis civitatibus facta spes in avi mores atque instituta regem abiturum. Igitur Latini, cum quibus Tullo regnante ictum foedus erat, sustulerant animos, et cum incursionem in agrum Romanum fecissent, repetentibus res Romanis superbe responsum reddunt, desidem Romanum regem inter sacella et aras acturum esse regnum rati. Medium erat in Anco ingenium, et Numae et Romuli memor; et praeterquam quod avi regno magis necessariam fuisse pacem credebat cum in novo tum feroci populo, etiam quod illi contigisset otium sine iniuria, id se haud facile habiturum; temptari patientiam et temptatam contemni, temporaque esse Tullo regi aptiora quam Numae. Ut tamen, quoniam Numa in pace religiones instituisset, a se bellicae caerimoniae proderentur, nec gererentur solum sed etiam indicerentur bella aliquo ritu, ius ab antiqua gente Aequicolis, quod nunc fetiales habent, descripsit quo res repetuntur.

Legatus ubi ad fines eorum venit unde res repetuntur, capite velato filo—lanae velamen est— "Audi, Iuppiter," inquit; "audite, fines"—cuiuscumque gentis sunt nominat;—"audiat fas. Ego sum publicus nuntius populi Romani; iuste pieque legatus venio verbisque meis fides sit." Peragit

---

[1] The institution of the fetials was ascribed in chap. xxiv. to Tullus (so also Cic. *Rep.* ii. 31). Livy is here following another authority, without taking the trouble to remove the discrepancy. Other writers (Dion. ii. 72; Plut. *Numa* xii.) credit Numa with the institution.

BOOK I. XXXII. 2-6

and also the neighbouring nations, to hope that he would adopt the character and institutions of his grandfather. Hence the Latins, with whom a treaty had been made in the time of Tullus, plucked up courage, and raided Roman territory, and when called on by the Romans to make restitution, returned an arrogant answer, persuaded that the Roman king would spend his reign in inactivity amid shrines and altars. But the character of Ancus was well balanced, and he honoured the memory of Romulus, as well as Numa. And besides having a conviction that peace had been more necessary to his grandfather's reign, when the nation had been both young and mettlesome, he also believed that the tranquillity, so free of attack, which had fallen to the lot of Numa would be no easy thing for himself to compass; his patience was being tried, and when proved would be regarded with contempt, and in short the times were better suited to the rule of a Tullus than a Numa. In order however that, as Numa had instituted religious practices in time of peace, he might himself give out a ceremonial of war, and that wars might not only be waged but also declared with some sort of formality, he copied from the ancient tribe of the Aequicoli the law, which the fetials now have,[1] by which redress is demanded.

When the envoy has arrived at the frontiers of the people from whom satisfaction is sought, he covers his head with a bonnet—the covering is of wool—and says: "Hear, Jupiter; hear, ye boundaries of"—naming whatever nation they belong to;—"let righteousness hear! I am the public herald of the Roman People; I come duly and religiously commissioned; let my words be credited." Then he

LIVY

7 deinde postulata. Inde Iovem testem facit: "Si ego iniuste impieque illos homines illasque res dedier mihi[1] exposco, tum patriae compotem me numquam
8 siris esse." Haec cum fines suprascandit, haec quicumque ei primus vir obvius fuerit, haec portam ingrediens, haec forum ingressus, paucis verbis carminis concipiendique iuris iurandi mutatis, peragit.
9 Si non deduntur quos exposcit diebus tribus et triginta—tot enim sollemnes sunt—peractis bellum ita
10 indicit: "Audi, Iuppiter, et tu, Iane[2] Quirine, dique omnes caelestes vosque, terrestres, vosque, inferni, audite. Ego vos testor populum illum"—quicumque est nominat—"iniustum esse neque ius persolvere. Sed de istis rebus in patria maiores natu consulemus quo pacto ius nostrum adipiscamur." Tum[3] nuntius Romam ad consulendum redit. Confestim rex his[4]
11 ferme verbis patres consulebat: "Quarum rerum, litium, causarum condixit pater patratus populi Romani Quiritium patri patrato Priscorum Latinorum hominibusque Priscis Latinis,[5] quas res nec dederunt nec solverunt nec fecerunt, quas res dari, solvi, fieri[6] oportuit, dic," inquit ei[7] quem primum sententiam
12 rogabat, "quid censes?" Tum ille: "Puro pioque duello quaerendas censeo itaque consentio consciscoque." Inde ordine alii rogabantur; quandoque

[1] mihi *MV*: p. r. (*or* Po R *or* populi romani *or* nuntio populi Romani) mihi (michi *O*) Ω.
[2] Iane *Perizonius*: iuno Ω.
[3] tum *Hachtmann*: cum *R*: cum his (*or* iis *or* is) Ω.
[4] rex his *Gruter*: rex ex his (exis *D*) Ω.
[5] Priscis Latinis *O*₅: priscis uel latinis Ω.
[6] solvi fieri *Ald.*: fieri solui (solui *F*) Ω.
[7] ei *M*¹ (*or* *M*²) *R*²₅ : et Ω.

recites his demands, after which he takes Jupiter to witness: "If I demand unduly and against religion that these men and these things be surrendered to me, then let me never enjoy my native land." These words he rehearses when he crosses the boundary line, the same to what man soever first meets him, the same when he enters the city gates, the same when he has come into the market-place, with only a few changes in the form and wording of the oath. If those whom he demands are not surrendered, at the end of three and thirty days—for such is the conventional number—he declares war thus: "Hear, Jupiter, and thou, Janus Quirinus, and hear all heavenly gods, and ye, gods of earth, and ye of the lower world; I call you to witness that this people"—naming whatever people it is—"is unjust, and does not make just reparation. But of these matters we will take counsel of the elders in our country, how we may obtain our right." Then the messenger returns to Rome for the consultation. Immediately the king would consult the Fathers, in some such words as these: "Touching the things, the suits, the causes, concerning which the *pater patratus* of the Roman People of the Quirites has made demands on the *pater patratus* of the Ancient Latins, and upon the men of the Ancient Latins, which things they have not delivered, nor fulfilled, nor satisfied, being things which ought to have been delivered, fulfilled, and satisfied, speak,"—turning to the man whose opinion he was wont to ask first,—"what think you?" Then the other would reply: "I hold that those things ought to be sought in warfare just and righteous; and so I consent and vote." The others were then asked the question, in their order, and when the majority

LIVY

pars maior eorum qui aderant in eandem sententiam ibat, bellum erat consensum. Fieri solitum ut fetialis hastam ferratam aut praeustam sanguineam[1] ad fines eorum ferret et non minus tribus puberibus praesen- 13 tibus diceret: "Quod populi Priscorum Latinorum hominesque[2] Prisci Latini adversus populum Romanum Quiritium fecerunt, deliquerunt, quod populus Romanus Quiritium bellum cum Priscis Latinis iussit esse senatusque[3] populi Romani Quiritium censuit, consensit, conscivit, ut bellum cum Priscis Latinis fieret, ob eam rem ego populusque Romanus populis Priscorum Latinorum hominibusque Priscis Latinis bellum indico facioque." Id ubi dixisset, hastam in 14 fines eorum emittebat. Hoc tum modo ab Latinis repetitae res ac bellum indictum, moremque eum posteri acceperunt.

XXXIII. Ancus demandata cura sacrorum flaminibus sacerdotibusque aliis, exercitu novo conscripto profectus, Politorium, urbem Latinorum, vi cepit, secutusque morem regum priorum, qui rem Romanam auxerant hostibus in civitatem accipiendis, multitu- 2 dinem omnem Romam traduxit, et cum circa Palatium, sedem veterum[4] Romanorum, Sabini Capitolium atque arcem, Caelium montem Albani implessent, Aventinum novae multitudini datum. Additi eodem haud ita multo post, Tellenis Ficanaque captis, novi 3 cives. Politorium inde rursus bello repetitum, quod

[1] praeustam sanguineam *Madvig*: sanguineam praeustam Ω.
[2] hominesque *Sigonius*: hominesue (homines *M*) Ω.
[3] senatusque ϛ: senatusue Ω.
[4] veterum *MP²OH*: veterem Ω.

BOOK I. XXXII. 12–XXXIII. 3

of those present went over to the same opinion, war had been agreed upon. It was customary for the fetial to carry to the bounds of the other nation a cornet-wood spear, iron-pointed or hardened in the fire, and in the presence of not less than three grown men to say: "Whereas the tribes of the Ancient Latins and men of the Ancient Latins have been guilty of acts and offences against the Roman People of the Quirites; and whereas the Roman People of the Quirites has commanded that war be made on the Ancient Latins, and the Senate of the Roman People has approved, agreed, and voted a war with the Ancient Latins; I therefore and the Roman People declare and make war on the tribes of the Ancient Latins and the men of the Ancient Latins." Having said this, he would hurl his spear into their territory. This is the manner in which at that time redress was sought from the Latins and war was declared, and the custom has been received by later generations.

B.C. 640-616

XXXIII. Ancus delegated the care of the sacrifices to the flamens and other priests, and having enlisted a new army proceeded to Politorium, one of the Latin cities. He took this place by storm, and adopting the plan of former kings, who had enlarged the state by making her enemies citizens, transferred the whole population to Rome. The Palatine was the quarter of the original Romans; on the one hand were the Sabines, who had the Capitol and the Citadel; on the other lay the Caelian, occupied by the Albans. The Aventine was therefore assigned to the new-comers, and thither too were sent shortly afterwards the citizens recruited from the captured towns of Tellenae and Ficana. Politorium was then attacked

LIVY

vacuum occupaverant Prisci Latini; eaque causa diruendae urbis eius fuit Romanis, ne hostium semper receptaculum esset. Postremo omni bello Latino Medulliam compulso aliquamdiu ibi Marte incerto, varia victoria pugnatum est; nam et urbs tuta munitionibus praesidioque firmata valido erat, et castris in aperto positis aliquotiens exercitus Latinus comminus cum Romanis signa contulerat. Ad ultimum omnibus copiis conisus Ancus acie primum vincit; inde ingenti praeda potens Romam redit, tum quoque multis milibus Latinorum in civitatem acceptis, quibus, ut iungeretur Palatio Aventinum, ad Murciae datae sedes. Ianiculum quoque adiectum, non inopia loci, sed ne quando ea arx hostium esset. Id non muniri[1] solum sed etiam ob commoditatem itineris ponte sublicio, tum primum in Tiberi facto, coniungi urbi placuit. Quiritium quoque fossa, haud parvum munimentum a planioribus aditu locis, Anci regis opus est.

Ingenti incremento rebus auctis cum in tanta multitudine hominum, discrimine recte an perperam facti confuso, facinora clandestina fierent, carcer ad terrorem increscentis audaciae media urbe

[1] muniri *H. J. Mueller*: muro Ω.

---

[1] This was the famous Pons Sublicius, "Pile Bridge," made of wood, without metal of any sort.

a second time, for having been left empty it had been seized by the Ancient Latins, and this gave the Romans an excuse for razing the town, lest it should serve continually as a refuge for their enemies. In the end the Latin levies were all forced back upon Medullia, where for some time the fighting was indecisive and victory shifted from one side to the other; for the city was protected by fortifications and was defended by a strong garrison, and from their camp in the open plain the Latin army several times came to close quarters with the Romans. At last, throwing all his troops into the struggle, Ancus succeeded first in defeating the enemy's army, and then in capturing the town, whence he returned to Rome enriched with immense spoils. On this occasion also many thousands of Latins were granted citizenship. These people, in order that the Aventine might be connected with the Palatine, were made to settle in the region of the Altar of Murcia. Janiculum was also annexed to the city, not from any lack of room, but lest it might some day become a stronghold of Rome's enemies. It was decided not only to fortify it, but also to connect it with the City, for greater ease in passing to and fro, by a bridge of piles, the first bridge ever built over the Tiber.[1] The Quirites' Ditch also, no small protection on the more level and accessible side of town, was the work of King Ancus.

When these enormous additions to the community had been effected, it was found that in so great a multitude the distinction between right and wrong had become obscured, and crimes were being secretly committed. Accordingly, to overawe men's growing lawlessness, a prison was built in

LIVY

9 inminens foro aedificatur. Nec urbs tantum hoc rege crevit, sed etiam ager finesque. Silva Maesia Veientibus adempta usque ad mare imperium prolatum et in ore Tiberis Ostia urbs condita, salinae circa factae, egregieque rebus bello gestis aedis Iovis Feretri amplificata.

XXXIV. Anco regnante Lucumo, vir impiger ac divitiis potens, Romam commigravit, cupidine maxime ac spe magni honoris, cuius adipiscendi Tarquiniis —nam ibi quoque peregrina stirpe oriundus erat— 2 facultas non fuerat. Demarati Corinthii filius erat, qui ob seditiones domo profugus cum Tarquiniis forte consedisset, uxore ibi ducta duos filios genuit. Nomina his Lucumo atque Arruns fuerunt. Lucumo superfuit patri bonorum omnium heres: Arruns prior 3 quam pater moritur uxore gravida relicta. Nec diu manet superstes filio pater; qui cum, ignorans nurum ventrem ferre, immemor in testando nepotis decessisset, puero post avi mortem in nullam sortem bonorum nato ab inopia Egerio inditum nomen. Lucumoni contra omnium heredi bonorum cum divi-4 tiae iam animos facerent, auxit ducta in matrimonium Tanaquil summo loco nata, et quae haud facile iis in quibus nata erat humiliora sineret ea quo

---

[1] This prison, *the* Carcer, may still be seen at the foot of the Capitoline, between the Temple of Concord and the Curia. It is thought to be as old as any structure in Rome. It was used as a place of detention and execution for condemned criminals. [2] *i.e.* "Necessitous."

BOOK I. XXXIII. 8–XXXIV. 4

the midst of the city, above the Forum.¹ And this reign was a period of growth, not only for the City, but also for her lands and boundaries. The Maesian Forest was taken from the Veientes, extending Rome's dominion clear to the sea; at the Tiber's mouth the city of Ostia was founded, and salt-works were established near-by; while in recognition of signal success in war the temple of Jupiter Feretrius was enlarged.

XXXIV. In the reign of Ancus one Lucumo, a man of energy and wealth, took up his residence in Rome, chiefly from ambition and the hope that he might there achieve a station such as he had found no opportunity of attaining in Tarquinii; for though he had been born there himself, his race was alien to that place also. He was the son of Demaratus of Corinth, who had been driven from home by a political upheaval. Happening to settle in Tarquinii, he had married there and had two sons, named Lucumo and Arruns. Lucumo survived his father and inherited all his property; Arruns died before his father, leaving his wife with child. Demaratus did not long survive Arruns, and, unaware that his son's wife was to become a mother, he died without making provision for his grandson in his will. When the babe was born his grandfather was dead, and having no share in the inheritance, he was given the name of Egerius,² in consequence of his penniless condition. Lucumo, on the other hand, was heir to the whole estate. The self-confidence implanted in his bosom by his wealth was heightened by his marriage with Tanaquil, who was a woman of the most exalted birth, and not of a character lightly to endure a humbler rank in her new environment than she had

LIVY

5 innupsisset.[1] Spernentibus Etruscis Lucumonem exsule[2] advena ortum, ferre indignitatem non potuit oblitaque ingenitae erga patriam caritatis, dummodo virum honoratum videret, consilium migrandi ab 6 Tarquiniis cepit. Roma est ad id potissima[3] visa: in novo populo, ubi omnis repentina atque ex virtute nobilitas sit, futurum locum forti ac strenuo viro; regnasse Tatium Sabinum, arcessitum in regnum Numam a Curibus, et Ancum Sabina matre ortum 7 nobilemque una imagine Numae esse. Facile persuadet ut cupido honorum et cui Tarquinii materna tantum patria esset. Sublatis itaque rebus amigrant 8 Romam. Ad Ianiculum forte ventum erat. Ibi ei carpento sedenti cum uxore aquila suspensis demissa leniter[4] alis pilleum aufert, superque carpentum cum magno clangore volitans, rursus velut ministerio divinitus missa capiti apte reponit; inde sublimis 9 abiit. Accepisse id augurium laeta dicitur Tanaquil, perita, ut volgo Etrusci, caelestium prodigiorum mulier. Excelsa et alta sperare conplexa virum iubet: eam alitem, ea regione caeli et eius dei nuntiam venisse, circa summum culmen hominis auspicium fecisse, levasse humano superpositum capiti

---

[1] ea quo innupsisset *Weissenborn*: ac cum (*or* hec cum *or* ea cum) innupsisset Ω.   [2] exsule R^2F^3 ς: exulem Ω.
[3] potissima *Gronov.*: potissimum Ω.
[4] leniter ς: leuiter Ω.

BOOK I. XXXIV. 4-9

enjoyed in the condition to which she had been born. The Etruscans looked with disdain on Lucumo, the son of a banished man and a stranger. She could not endure this indignity, and forgetting the love she owed her native land, if she could only see her husband honoured, she formed the project of emigrating from Tarquinii. Rome appeared to be the most suitable place for her purpose; amongst a new people, where all rank was of sudden growth and founded on worth, there would be room for a brave and strenuous man; the City had been ruled by Tatius the Sabine, it had summoned Numa to the sovereignty from Cures, even Ancus was the son of a Sabine mother, and could point to no noble ancestor but Numa. She had no trouble in persuading a man who was eager for distinction, to whom Tarquinii was only his mother's birthplace. They therefore gathered their possessions together and removed to Rome. They had come, as it happened, as far as Janiculum, when, as they were sitting in their covered waggon, an eagle poised on its wings gently descended upon them and plucked off Lucumo's cap, after which, rising noisily above the car and again stooping, as if sent from heaven for that service, it deftly replaced the cap upon his head, and departed on high. This augury was joyfully accepted, it is said, by Tanaquil, who was a woman skilled in celestial prodigies, as was the case with most Etruscans. Embracing her husband, she bade him expect transcendent greatness: such was the meaning of that bird, appearing from that quarter of the sky, and bringing tidings from that god; the highest part of the man had been concerned in the omen; the eagle had removed the adornment placed upon a mortal's head that it might

LIVY

10 decus, ut divinitus eidem redderet. Has spes cogitationesque secum portantes urbem ingressi sunt, domicilioque ibi comparato L. Tarquinium Priscum
11 edidere nomen. Romanis conspicuum eum novitas divitiaeque faciebant; et ipse fortunam benigno adloquio, comitate invitandi beneficiisque quos poterat sibi conciliando adiuvabat, donec in regiam quoque
12 de eo fama perlata est. Notitiamque eam brevi apud regem liberaliter dextereque obeundo officia in familiaris amicitiae adduxerat iura, ut publicis pariter ac privatis consiliis bello domique interesset et per omnia expertus postremo tutor etiam liberis regis testamento institueretur.

XXXV. Regnavit Ancus annos quattuor et viginti, cuilibet superiorum regum belli pacisque et artibus et gloria par. Iam filii prope puberem aetatem erant. Eo magis Tarquinius instare ut quam pri-
2 mum comitia regi creando fierent; quibus indictis sub tempus pueros venatum ablegavit. Isque primus et petisse ambitiose regnum et orationem dicitur habuisse ad conciliandos plebis animos compositam:
3 se[1] non rem novam petere, quippe qui non primus, quod quisquam indignari mirarive posset, sed tertius Romae peregrinus regnum adfectet; et Tatium non ex peregrino solum, sed etiam ex hoste regem factum, et Numam ignarum urbis non petentem in

[1] se *Duker*: cum (tum F^1) se Ω.

restore it with the divine approbation. Such were their hopes and their reflections as they entered the City. Having obtained a house, they gave out the name of Lucius Tarquinius Priscus. The Romans regarded him with special interest, as a stranger and a man of wealth, and he steadily pushed his fortune by his own exertions, making friends wherever possible, by kind words, courteous hospitality, and benefactions, until his reputation extended even to the palace. He had not long been known in this way to the king before the liberality and adroitness of his services procured him the footing of an intimate friend. He was now consulted in matters both of public and private importance, in time of war and in time of peace, and having been tested in every way was eventually even named in the king's will as guardian of his children.

XXXV. Ancus reigned four and twenty years, a king inferior to none of his predecessors in the arts of peace and war and in the reputation they conferred. By this time his sons were nearly grown. Tarquinius was therefore all the more insistent in urging that the comitia should be held without delay to choose a king. When the meeting had been proclaimed, and the day drew near, he sent the boys away on a hunting expedition. Tarquinius was the first, they say, to canvass votes for the kingship and to deliver a speech designed to win the favour of the commons. He pointed out that it was no new thing he sought; he was not the first outsider to aim at the sovereignty in Rome—a thing which might have occasioned indignation and astonishment,—but the third. Tatius indeed, had been not merely an alien but an enemy when he was made king; while Numa was a stranger

LIVY

A.U.C. 138-176

4 regnum ultro accitum: se, ex quo sui potens fuerit, Romam cum coniuge ac fortunis omnibus commigrasse; maiorem partem aetatis eius qua civilibus officiis fungantur homines, Romae se quam in vetere
5 patria vixisse; domi militiaeque sub haud paenitendo magistro, ipso Anco rege, Romana se iura, Romanos ritus didicisse; obsequio et observantia in regem cum omnibus, benignitate erga alios cum rege ipso
6 certasse. Haec eum haud falsa memorantem ingenti consensu populus Romanus regnare iussit. Ergo virum cetera egregium secuta quam in petendo habuerat etiam regnantem ambitio est; nec minus regni sui firmandi quam augendae rei publicae memor centum in patres legit, qui deinde minorum gentium sunt appellati, factio haud dubia regis, cuius beneficio in curiam venerant.

7 Bellum primum cum Latinis gessit, et oppidum ibi Apiolas vi cepit, praedaque inde maiore quam quanta belli fama fuerat revecta, ludos opulentius
8 instructiusque quam priores reges fecit. Tum primum circo qui nunc maximus dicitur designatus locus est. Loca divisa patribus equitibusque ubi spectacula sibi quisque facerent; fori appellati.

---

[1] The senate had doubtless shown its disapproval of the accession of Tarquinius, who now sought to render its opposition futile by doubling the membership and appointing none but his own supporters.

to the City, and, far from seeking the kingship, had actually been invited to come and take it. As for himself, he had no sooner become his own master than he had removed to Rome with his wife and all his property. For the greater part of that period of life during which men serve the state he had lived in Rome, and not in the city of his birth. Both in civil life and in war he had had no mean instructor—King Ancus himself had taught him Roman laws and Roman rites. In subordination and deference to the king he had vied, he said, with all his hearers; in generosity to his fellow-subjects he had emulated the king himself. Hearing him advance these not unwarranted claims, the people, with striking unanimity, named him king. The result was that the man, so admirable in all other respects, continued even after he had obtained the sovereignty to manifest the same spirit of intrigue which had governed him in seeking it; and being no less concerned to strengthen his own power than to enlarge the state, he added a hundred members to the senate, who were known thenceforward as Fathers of the "lesser families," and formed a party of unwavering loyalty to the king, to whom they owed their admission to the Curia.[1]

His first war was with the Latins, whose town of Apiolae he took by storm. Returning thence with more booty than the rumours about the war had led people to expect, he exhibited games on a more splendid and elaborate scale than former kings had done. It was then that the ground was first marked out for the circus now called Maximus. Places were divided amongst the Fathers and the knights where they might each make seats for themselves; these were called 'rows.' They got their view from seats

LIVY

9 Spectavere furcis duodenos ab terra spectacula alta sustinentibus pedes. Ludicrum fuit equi pugilesque, ex Etruria maxime acciti. Sollemnes deinde annui mansere ludi, Romani magnique varie appel-
10 lati. Ab eodem rege et circa forum privatis aedificanda divisa sunt loca; porticus tabernaeque factae.

XXXVI. Muro quoque lapideo circumdare urbem parabat, cum Sabinum bellum coeptis intervenit. Adeoque ea subita res fuit, ut prius Anienem transirent hostes quam obviam ire ac prohibere exercitus
2 Romanus posset. Itaque trepidatum Romae est, et primo dubia victoria magna utrimque caede pugnatum est. Reductis deinde in castra hostium copiis datoque spatio Romanis ad comparandum de integro bellum, Tarquinius, equitem maxime suis deesse viribus ratus, ad Ramnes, Titienses, Luceres, quas centurias Romulus scripserat, addere alias constituit
3 suoque insignes relinquere nomine. Id quia inaugurato Romulus fecerat, negare Attus Navius, inclitus ea tempestate augur, neque mutari neque novum
4 constitui, nisi aves addixissent, posse. Ex eo ira regi mota, eludensque artem, ut ferunt, "Age dum," inquit, "divine tu, inaugura fierine possit, quod nunc ego mente concipio." Cum ille augurio[1] rem expertus profecto futuram dixisset, "Atqui hoc animo

---

[1] augurio *Tan. Faber*: in augurio Ω.

BOOK I. xxxv. 9–xxxvi. 4

raised on props to a height of twelve feet from the ground. The entertainment was furnished by horses and boxers, imported for the most part from Etruria. From that time the Games continued to be a regular annual show, and were called indifferently the Roman and the Great Games. It was the same king, too, who apportioned building sites about the Forum among private citizens, and erected covered walks and booths.

XXXVI. He was also preparing to build a stone wall around the City, when a Sabine war interrupted his plans. And so sudden was the invasion, that they had crossed the Anio before the Roman army was able to march out and stop them, so that the City was thrown into a panic. The first battle was indecisive, with heavy losses on both sides. The enemy then withdrew into their camp, affording the Romans an opportunity to renew their preparations for the war. Tarquinius believed that cavalry was what he chiefly lacked. To the Ramnes, Titienses, and Luceres, the centuries which Romulus had enrolled, he therefore determined to add others, and to give them his own name as a permanent distinction. But since this was a matter in which Romulus had obtained the sanction of augury before acting, it was asserted by Attus Navius, a famous augur of those days, that no change or innovation could be introduced unless the birds had signified their approval. The king's ire was aroused by this, and he is reported to have said, in derision of the science, "Come now, divine seer! Inquire of your augury if that of which I am now thinking can come to pass." When Attus, having taken the auspices, replied that it would surely come to pass, the king said, "Nay, but this is

LIVY

agitavi," inquit, "te novacula cotem discissurum; cape haec et perage quod aves tuae fieri posse portendunt." Tum illum haud cunctanter discidisse 5 cotem ferunt. Statua Atti capite velato, quo in loco res acta est, in comitio in gradibus ipsis ad laevam curiae fuit; cotem quoque eodem loco sitam fuisse memorant, ut esset ad posteros miraculi eius monu- 6 mentum. Auguriis certe sacerdotioque augurum tantus honos accessit ut nihil belli domique postea nisi auspicato gereretur, concilia populi, exercitus vocati, summa rerum, ubi aves non admisissent, diri- 7 merentur. Neque tum Tarquinius de equitum centuriis quicquam mutavit; numero alterum tantum[1] adiecit, ut mille et octingenti equites in tribus cen- 8 turiis essent. Posteriores modo sub iisdem nominibus, qui additi erant, appellati sunt; quas nunc, quia geminatae sunt, sex vocant centurias.

XXXVII. Hac parte copiarum aucta iterum cum Sabinis confligitur. Sed praeterquam quod viribus creverat Romanus exercitus, ex occulto etiam additur dolus, missis qui magnam vim lignorum, in Anienis ripa iacentem, ardentem in flumen conicerent; ventoque iuvante accensa ligna et pleraque ratibus[2] inpacta sublicisque[3] cum haererent, pontem incendunt

[1] alterum tantum *Lipsius*: tantum alterum Ω.
[2] ratibus *M¹Gronov.*: in ratibus Ω.
[3] sublicisque *Gronov.*: sublicis (*or* -iis) Ω.

BOOK I. xxxvi. 4–xxxvii. 1

what I was thinking of, that you should cleave a whetstone with a razor. Take them, and accomplish what your birds declare is possible!" Whereupon, they say, the augur, without a sign of hesitation, cut the whetstone in two. There was a statue of Attus standing, with his head covered, on the spot where the thing was done, in the comitium, even at the steps on the left of the senate-house; tradition adds that the whetstone also was deposited in the same place, to be a memorial of that miracle to posterity. However this may be, auguries and the augural priesthood so increased in honour that nothing was afterwards done, in the field or at home, unless the auspices had first been taken: popular assemblies, musterings of the army, acts of supreme importance —all were put off when the birds refused their consent. Neither did Tarquinius at that time make any change in the organization of the centuries of knights. Their numerical strength he doubled, so that there were now eighteen hundred knights, in three centuries. But though enrolled under the old names, the new men were called the "secondary knights," and the centuries are now, because doubled, known as the "six centuries."

XXXVII. When this arm of the service had been enlarged, a second battle was fought with the Sabines. And in this, besides being increased in strength, the Roman army was further helped by a stratagem, for men were secretly dispatched to light a great quantity of firewood lying on the bank of the Anio, and throw it into the river. A favouring wind set the wood in a blaze, and the greater part of it lodged against the boats and piles, where it stuck fast and

LIVY

2 Ea quoque res in pugna terrorem attulit Sabinis, et fusis[1] eadem fugam impedit; multique mortales, cum hostem effugissent, in flumine ipso periere; quorum fluitantia arma ad urbem cognita in Tiberi prius paene quam nuntiari posset insignem victoriam 3 fecere. Eo proelio praecipua equitum gloria fuit; utrimque ab cornibus positos, cum iam pelleretur media peditum suorum acies, ita incurrisse ab lateribus ferunt, ut non sisterent modo Sabinas legiones ferociter instantes cedentibus, sed subito in fugam 4 averterent. Montes effuso cursu Sabini petebant, et pauci tenuere; maxima pars, ut ante dictum est, ab 5 equitibus in flumen acti sunt. Tarquinius instandum perterritis ratus, praeda captivisque Romam missis, spoliis hostium—id votum Volcano erat—ingenti cumulo accensis, pergit porro in agrum Sabinum 6 exercitum inducere; et quamquam male gesta res erat nec gesturos melius sperare poterant, tamen, quia consulendi res non dabat spatium, ire obviam Sabini tumultuario milite; iterumque ibi fusi perditis iam prope rebus pacem petiere.

XXXVIII. Collatia et quidquid citra Collatiam agri erat Sabinis ademptum; Egerius—fratris hic

[1] et fusis *Jac. Gronov.*: effusis Ω.

BOOK I. XXXVII. 2–XXXVIII. 1

set the bridge on fire. This was another source of alarm to the Sabines during the battle, and upon their being routed the same thing hindered their flight, so that many of them escaped the Romans only to perish in the stream ; while their shields floated down the Tiber toward the City, and, being recognized, gave assurance that a victory had been won almost sooner than the news of it could be brought. In this battle the cavalry particularly distinguished themselves. They were posted on either flank of the Romans, and when the centre, composed of infantry, was already in retreat, they are said to have charged from both sides, with such effect that they not only checked the Sabine forces, which were pressing hotly forward as their enemy gave way, but suddenly put them to flight. The Sabines made for the mountains in a scattered rout, and indeed a few gained that refuge. Most of them, as has been said before, were driven by the cavalry into the river. Tarquinius thought it proper to follow up his victory while the other side was panic-stricken ; he therefore sent the booty and the prisoners to Rome, and after making a huge pile of the captured arms and setting fire to it, in fulfilment of a vow to Vulcan, pushed forward at the head of his army into the enemy's country. Although defeat had been the portion of the Sabines, and another battle could not be expected to result in better success, still, as the situation allowed no room for deliberation, they took the field with what soldiers they could hastily muster, and being then routed a second time and fairly reduced to extremities, they sued for peace.

XXXVIII. Collatia, and what land the Sabines had on the hither side of Collatia, was taken from

B.C. 616–578

LIVY

filius erat regis—Collatiae in praesidio relictus.
Deditosque Collatinos ita accipio eamque deditionis formulam esse; rex interrogavit: "Estisne vos legati oratoresque missi a populo Collatino, ut vos populumque Collatinum dederetis?" "Sumus." "Estne populus Collatinus in sua potestate?" "Est." "Deditisne vos populumque Collatinum, urbem, agros, aquam, terminos, delubra, utensilia, divina humanaque omnia in meam populique Romani dicionem?" "Dedimus." "At ego recipio."
Bello Sabino perfecto Tarquinius triumphans Romam redit. Inde Priscis Latinis bellum fecit. Ubi nusquam ad universae rei dimicationem ventum est, ad singula oppida circumferendo arma omne nomen Latinum domuit. Corniculum, Ficulea Vetus, Cameria, Crustumerium, Ameriola, Medullia,[1] Nomentum—haec de Priscis Latinis aut qui ad Latinos defecerant capta oppida. Pax deinde est facta.

Maiore inde animo pacis opera incohata quam quanta mole gesserat bella, ut non quietior populus domi esset quam militiae fuisset; nam et muro lapideo, cuius exordium operis Sabino bello turbatum erat, urbem qua nondum munierat cingere parat, et infima urbis loca circa forum aliasque interiectas collibus convalles, quia ex planis locis haud facile evehebant aquas, cloacis[2] fastigio in Tiberim ductis

---

[1] Medullia *Ald.*: medulla Ω.
[2] aquas cloacis *RD*²ς: aqua se (*or* aquā se *or* aquas e cloacis Ω.

BOOK I. xxxviii. 1-6

them, and Egerius, the son of the king's brother, was left in the town with a garrison. The surrender of the Collatini took place, I understand, in accordance with this formula: the king asked, "Are you the legates and spokesmen sent by the People of Collatia to surrender yourselves and the People of Collatia?" "We are." "Is the People of Collatia its own master?" "It is." "Do you surrender yourselves and the People of Collatia, city, lands, water, boundary marks, shrines, utensils, all appurtenances, divine and human, into my power and that of the Roman People?" "We do." "I receive the surrender." Upon the conclusion of the Sabine war Tarquinius returned to Rome and triumphed. He then made war against the Ancient Latins. In this campaign there was no general engagement at any point, but the king led his army from one town to another until he had subdued the entire Latin race. Corniculum, Ficulea Vetus, Cameria, Crustumerium, Ameriola, Medullia, and Nomentum—these were the towns which were captured from the Ancient Latins, or from those who had gone over to the Latins. Peace was then made.

From that moment the king devoted himself to peaceful undertakings with an enthusiasm which was even greater than the efforts he had expended in waging war, so that there was no more rest for the people at home than there had been in the field. For he set to work to encircle the hitherto unfortified parts of the City with a stone wall, a task which had been interrupted by the Sabine war; and he drained the lowest parts of the City, about the Forum, and the other valleys between the hills, which were too flat to carry off the flood-waters easily, by means of sewers so made as to slope down toward the Tiber.

LIVY

A.U.C.
138-176

7 siccat, et aream ad aedem in Capitolio Iovis, quam voverat bello Sabino, iam praesagiente animo futuram olim amplitudinem loci occupat fundamentis.

XXXIX. Eo tempore in regia prodigium visu[1] eventuque mirabile fuit. Puero dormienti, cui Servio Tullio fuit nomen,[2] caput arsisse ferunt multorum in 2 conspectu. Plurimo igitur clamore inde ad tantae rei miraculum orto excitos reges, et cum quidam familiarium aquam ad restinguendum ferret, ab regina retentum, sedatoque eam tumultu moveri vetuisse puerum donec sua sponte experrectus esset. 3 Mox cum somno et flammam abisse. Tum abducto in secretum viro Tanaquil, "Viden[3] tu puerum hunc," inquit, "quem tam humili cultu educamus? Scire licet hunc lumen quondam rebus nostris dubiis futurum praesidiumque regiae adflictae; proinde materiam ingentis publice privatimque decoris omni 4 indulgentia nostra nutriamus." Inde puerum liberum loco coeptum haberi, erudirique artibus, quibus ingenia ad magnae fortunae cultum excitantur. Evenit facile quod dis cordi esset. Iuvenis evasit vere indolis regiae, nec, cum quaereretur gener Tarquinio, quisquam Romanae iuventutis ulla arte conferri 5 potuit, filiamque ei suam rex despondit. Hic quacumque de causa tantus illi honos habitus credere

[1] visu O_{ς} : uisum Ω.
[2] puero dormienti, cui Servio Tullio fuit nomen M_{ς} : *these words are missing or corrupted in the other MSS.*
[3] viden M^2_{ς} : uidene D^2 : uidesne Ω.

138

BOOK I. xxxviii. 6–xxxix. 5

Finally, with prophetic anticipation of the splendour which the place was one day to possess, he laid foundations for the temple of Jupiter on the Capitol, which he had vowed in the Sabine war.

XXXIX. At this time there happened in the house of the king a portent which was remarkable alike in its manifestation and in its outcome. The story is that while a child named Servius Tullius lay sleeping, his head burst into flames in the sight of many. The general outcry which so great a miracle called forth brought the king and queen to the place. One of the servants fetched water to quench the fire, but was checked by the queen, who stilled the uproar and commanded that the boy should not be disturbed until he awoke of himself. Soon afterwards sleep left him, and with it disappeared the flames. Then, taking her husband aside, Tanaquil said: "Do you see this child whom we are bringing up in so humble a fashion? Be assured he will one day be a lamp to our dubious fortunes, and a protector to the royal house in the day of its distress. Let us therefore rear with all solicitude one who will lend high renown to the state and to our family." It is said that from that moment the boy began to be looked upon as a son, and to be trained in the studies by which men are inspired to bear themselves greatly. It was a thing easily accomplished, being the will of Heaven. The youth turned out to be of a truly royal nature, and when Tarquinius sought a son-in-law there was no other young Roman who could be at all compared to Servius; and the king accordingly betrothed his daughter to him. This great honour, for whatever cause conferred on him, forbids us to suppose that

prohibet serva natum eum parvumque ipsum servisse. Eorum magis sententiae sum qui Corniculo capto Ser. Tulli, qui princeps in illa urbe fuerat, gravidam viro occiso uxorem, cum inter reliquas captivas cognita esset, ob unicam nobilitatem ab regina Romana prohibitam ferunt servitio partum Romae edidisse
6 Prisci Tarquini in domo[1]; inde tanto beneficio et inter mulieris familiaritatem auctam et puerum, ut in domo a parvo eductum, in caritate atque honore fuisse; fortunam matris, quod capta patria in hostium manus venerit, ut serva natus crederetur fecisse.

XL. Duodequadragesimo ferme anno, ex quo regnare coeperat Tarquinius, non apud regem modo sed apud patres plebemque longe maximo honore
2 Ser. Tullius erat. Tum Anci filii duo, etsi antea semper pro indignissimo habuerant se patrio regno tutoris fraude pulsos, regnare Romae advenam non modo vicinae, sed ne Italicae quidem stirpis, tum impensius iis indignitas crescere, si ne ab Tarquinio
3 quidem ad se rediret regnum, sed praeceps inde porro ad servitia caderet, ut in eadem civitate post centesimum fere annum quod[2] Romulus, deo prognatus deus ipse, tenuerit regnum donec in terris

---

[1] in domo ϛ: domo Ω.
[2] quod *Madvig*: quam Ω.

BOOK I. XXXIX. 5–XL. 3

his mother was a slave and that he himself had been in a state of servitude as a child. I am rather of the opinion of those who say, that on the capture of Corniculum, when Servius Tullius, the chief man of that city, had been slain, his wife, who was great with child, had been recognized amongst the other captive women, and on the score of her unique nobility had been rescued from slavery by the Roman queen, and had brought forth her child at Rome in the house of Priscus Tarquinius; in the sequel this act of generosity led to a growing intimacy between the women, and the boy, as one reared from childhood in the palace, was held in affection and esteem; it was his mother's misfortune, who by the capture of her native town came into the power of its enemies, which gave rise to the belief that Servius was born of a slave woman.

XL. It was now about thirty-eight years since Tarquinius had begun to reign, and not only the king, but the Fathers and the commons too, held Servius Tullius in the very highest honour. Now the two sons of Ancus had always considered it a great outrage that they had been ousted from their father's kingship by the crime of their guardian, and that Rome should be ruled by a stranger whose descent was derived from a race not only remote but actually not even Italian. But their indignation was vastly increased by the prospect that even after Tarquinius' death the sovereignty would not revert to them, but, plunging down to yet baser depths, would fall into the hands of slaves; so that where, a hundred years before, Romulus, a god's son and himself a god, had borne sway, so long as he remained on earth, in that self-same state a slave and

B.C. 616–578

fuerit, id servus serva natus possideat. Cum commune Romani nominis tum praecipue id domus suae dedecus fore, si Anci regis virili stirpe salva non modo advenis, sed servis etiam regnum Romae pateret. Ferro igitur eam arcere contumeliam statuunt. Sed et iniuriae dolor in Tarquinium ipsum magis quam in Servium eos stimulabat, et quia gravior ultor caedis, si superesset, rex futurus erat quam privatus, tum Servio occiso quemcumque alium generum delegisset eundem regni heredem facturus videbatur, ob haec ipsi regi insidiae parantur. Ex pastoribus duo ferocissimi delecti ad facinus, quibus consueti erant uterque agrestibus ferramentis, in vestibulo regiae quam potuere tumultuosissime specie rixae in se omnes apparitores regios convertunt; inde, cum ambo regem appellarent clamorque eorum penitus in regiam pervenisset, vocati ad regem pergunt. Primo uterque vociferari et certatim alter alteri obstrepere; coerciti ab lictore et iussi in vicem dicere tandem obloqui desistunt; unus rem ex composito orditur. Dum intentus in eum se rex totus averteret, alter elatam securim in caput deiecit, relictoque in volnere telo ambo se foras eiciunt.

XLI. Tarquinium moribundum cum qui circa erant

BOOK I. xl. 3–xli. 1

the son of a slave woman would be king. It would be not only a general disgrace to the Roman name, but particularly to their own house, if during the lifetime of Ancus' sons it should be open not only to strangers, but even to slaves to rule over the Romans. They therefore determined to repel that insult with the sword. But resentment at their wrong urged them rather against Tarquinius himself than against Servius, not only because the king, if he survived, would be more formidable to avenge the murder than a subject would be, but because if Servius should be dispatched it seemed probable that the kingdom would be inherited by whomsoever else Tarquinius might choose to be his son-in-law. For these reasons they laid their plot against the king himself. Two very desperate shepherds were selected to do the deed. Armed with the rustic implements to which they were both accustomed, they feigned a brawl in the entrance-court of the palace and, making as much noise as possible, attracted the attention of all the royal attendants; then they appealed to the king, until their shouts were heard inside the palace and they were sent for and came before him. At first each raised his voice and tried to shout the other down. Being repressed by the lictor and bidden to speak in turn, they finally ceased to interrupt each other, and one of them began to state his case, as they had planned beforehand. While the king, intent upon the speaker, turned quite away from the other shepherd, the latter lifted his axe and brought it down upon his head. Then, leaving the weapon in the wound, they both ran out of doors.

XLI. The dying Tarquinius had hardly been caught

LIVY

excepissent, illos fugientes lictores comprehendunt. Clamor inde concursusque populi, mirantium[1] quid rei esset. Tanaquil inter tumultum claudi regiam iubet, arbitros eicit.[2] Simul quae curando volneri opus sunt, tamquam spes subesset, sedulo conparat, 2 simul, si destituat spes, alia praesidia molitur. Servio propere accito cum paene exsanguem virum ostendisset, dextram tenens orat ne inultam mortem soceri, ne socrum inimicis ludibrio esse sinat. 3 "Tuum est," inquit, "Servi, si vir es, regnum, non eorum qui alienis manibus pessimum facinus fecere. Erige te deosque duces sequere, qui clarum hoc fore caput divino quondam circumfuso igni portenderunt. Nunc te illa caelestis excitet flamma, nunc expergiscere vere. Et nos peregrini regnavimus; qui sis, non unde natus sis, reputa. Si tua re subita consilia 4 torpent, at tu mea consilia sequere." Cum clamor impetusque multitudinis vix sustineri posset, ex superiore parte aedium per fenestras in Novam viam versas[3]—habitabat enim rex ad Iovis Statoris—popu- 5 lum Tanaquil adloquitur. Iubet bono animo esse: sopitum fuisse regem subito ictu; ferrum haud alte in corpus descendisse; iam ad se redisse; inspectum

---

[1] mirantium ς: mirantum (*or* mirandum) Ω.
[2] eicit $R\varsigma$: eiecit Ω.   [3] versas ς: uersus Ω.

up in the arms of the bystanders when the fugitives were seized by the lictors. Then there was an uproar, as crowds hurried to the scene, asking one another in amazement what the matter was. In the midst of the tumult Tanaquil gave orders to close the palace, and ejected all witnesses. She busily got together the remedies needful for healing a wound, as if there were still hope, taking at the same time other measures to protect herself in case her hope should fail her. Having hastily summoned Servius, she showed him her husband's nearly lifeless body, and grasping his right hand, besought him not to suffer the death of his father-in-law to go unpunished, nor his mother-in-law to become a jest to her enemies. "To you, Servius," she cried, "if you are a man, belongs this kingdom, not to those who by the hands of others have committed a dastardly crime. Arouse yourself and follow the guidance of the gods, who once declared by the token of divine fire poured out upon this head that you should be a famous man. Now is the time for that heaven-sent flame to quicken you! Now wake in earnest! We, too, were foreigners, yet we reigned. Consider what you are, not whence you were born. If your own counsels are benumbed in this sudden crisis, at least use mine." When the shouting and pushing of the crowd could hardly be withstood, Tanaquil went up into the upper storey of the house, and through a window looking out upon the Nova Via—for the king lived near the temple of Jupiter the Stayer—addressed the populace. She bade them be of good cheer: the king had been stunned by a sudden blow; the steel had not sunk deep into his body; he had already recovered consciousness; the blood had been

LIVY

volnus absterso cruore; omnia salubria esse; confidere prope diem ipsum eos visuros; interim Ser. Tullio iubere populum dicto audientem esse; eum iura redditurum obiturumque alia regis munia esse. 6 Servius cum trabea et lictoribus prodit ac sede regia sedens alia decernit, de aliis consulturum se regem esse simulat. Itaque per aliquot dies, cum iam exspirasset Tarquinius, celata morte per speciem alienae fungendae vicis suas opes firmavit. Tum demum palam factum est[1] comploratione in regia orta. Servius praesidio firmo munitus primus iniussu populi 7 voluntate patrum regnavit. Anci liberi iam tum, comprensis[2] sceleris ministris ut vivere regem et tantas esse opes Servi nuntiatum est, Suessam Pometiam exsulatum ierant.

XLII. Nec iam publicis magis consiliis Servius quam privatis munire opes, et ne, qualis Anci liberum animus adversus Tarquinium fuerat, talis adversus se Tarquini liberum esset, duas filias iuvenibus 2 regiis, Lucio atque Arrunti Tarquiniis, iungit; nec rupit tamen fati necessitatem humanis consiliis, quin invidia regni etiam inter domesticos infida omnia atque infesta faceret. Peropportune ad praesentis

[1] est ς : et Ω.
[2] comprensis ς-*Ald.*: com (*or* con-) pressis *or* cum com (*or* con-) prensis (*or* -pressis) *or* cum comprehensis Ω.

BOOK I. XLI. 5–XLII. 2

wiped away and the wound examined; all the symptoms were favourable; she trusted that they would soon see Tarquinius himself; meanwhile she commanded that the people should obey Servius Tullius, who would dispense justice and perform the other duties of the king. Servius went forth in the royal robe, accompanied by lictors, and sitting in the king's seat rendered judgment in some cases, while in regard to others he gave out that he would consult the king. In this way for several days after Tarquinius had breathed his last he concealed his death, pretending that he was merely doing another's work, while he was really strengthening his own position; then at last the truth was allowed to be known, from the lamentations which arose within the palace. Servius surrounded himself with a strong guard, and ruled at first without the authorization of the people, but with the consent of the Fathers. The sons of Ancus, upon the arrest of the agents of their crime and the report that the king was alive and that Servius was so strong, had already gone into voluntary exile at Suessa Pometia.

XLII. Servius now took steps to assure his position by private as well as public measures. In order that the sons of Tarquinius might not show the same animosity towards himself which the sons of Ancus had felt towards Tarquinius, he married his two daughters to the young princes, Lucius and Arruns Tarquinius. But he could not break the force of destiny by human wisdom; and jealousy of his power, even among the members of his household, created an atmosphere of treachery and hostility. Most opportune for the tranquil preservation

LIVY

quietem status bellum cum Veientibus—iam enim indutiae exierant—aliisque Etruscis sumptum. In eo bello et virtus et fortuna enituit Tulli; fusoque ingenti hostium exercitu haud dubius rex seu patrum seu plebis animos periclitaretur, Romam rediit. Adgrediturque inde ad pacis longe maximum opus, ut quemadmodum Numa divini auctor iuris fuisset, ita Servium conditorem omnis in civitate discriminis ordinumque quibus inter gradus dignitatis fortunaeque aliquid interlucet, posteri fama ferrent. Censum enim instituit, rem saluberrimam tanto futuro imperio, ex quo belli pacisque munia non viritim, ut ante, sed pro habitu pecuniarum fierent; tum classes centuriasque et hunc ordinem ex censu discripsit,[1] vel paci decorum vel bello. XLIII. Ex iis,[2] qui centum milium aeris aut maiorem censum haberent

[1] discripsit *R*: descripsit Ω.   [2] iis *Ald.*: his Ω.

---

[1] Perhaps a reference to the hundred years' truce with Romulus (xv. 5), for Livy has not mentioned any war with Veii in the interval, though one is implied in the statement (xxxiii. 9) that the Veientes surrendered the Maesian Forest, in the reign of Ancus.

[2] The organisation now to be described was primarily designed to increase the fighting strength of Rome. Formerly the right to bear arms had belonged solely to the patricians. Now plebeians were to be given a place in the army, which was to be reclassified according to every man's property, *i.e.* his ability to provide himself a more or less complete equipment for the field. See Dion. Hal. iv. 16-21; Cic. *Rep.* ii. 39.

of the existing state of things was a war which was undertaken against the people of Veii—for the truce[1] had now run out—and the other Etruscans. In this war the bravery and good fortune of Tullius were conspicuous; and when he had utterly defeated the vast army of his enemies, he found on returning to Rome that his title to the kingship was no longer questioned, whether he tested the feeling of the Fathers or that of the commons. He then addressed himself to what is by far the most important work of peace: as Numa had established religious law, so Servius intended that posterity should celebrate himself as the originator of all distinctions among the citizens, and of the orders which clearly differentiate the various grades of rank and fortune. For he instituted the census,[2] a most useful thing for a government destined to such wide dominion, since it would enable the burdens of war and peace to be borne not indiscriminately, as heretofore, but in proportion to men's wealth. He then distributed the people into classes and centuries according to the following scale, which was based upon the census and was suitable either for peace or war: XLIII. Out of those who had a rating of a hundred thousand asses[3] or more he made eighty

[3] Capital, not income. The *as* was originally a rod of copper a foot long and divided into twelve inches (*unciae*). Some time during the regal period weight was substituted for measure in appraising the *as*, and it began to be stamped with the figure of an ox, which was the source of the Latin name for money, viz. *pecunia*. From being a full pound the *as* was gradually reduced, till, in the Second Punic War, it came to weigh only one ounce. What its value may have been in the time of Servius is a highly speculative question. See the note in the edition of Book I. by H. J. Edwards (pp. 179 ff.).

LIVY

octoginta confecit centurias, quadragenas seniorum
2 ac iuniorum; prima[1] classis omnes appellati; seniores
ad urbis custodiam ut praesto essent, iuvenes ut foris
bella gererent. Arma his imperata galea, clipeum,
ocreae, lorica, omnia ex aere, haec ut tegumenta
corporis essent; tela in hostem hastaque et gladius.
3 Additae huic classi duae fabrum centuriae, quae sine
armis stipendia facerent; datum munus ut machinas
4 in bello facerent.[2] Secunda classis intra centum
usque ad quinque et septuaginta milium censum
instituta, et ex iis, senioribus iunioribusque, viginti
conscriptae centuriae. Arma imperata scutum pro
5 clipeo et praeter loricam omnia eadem. Tertiae
classis[3] quinquaginta[4] milium censum esse voluit;
totidem centuriae et hae[5] eodemque discrimine
aetatium factae. Nec de armis quicquam mutatum,
6 ocreae tantum ademptae. In quarta classe census
quinque et viginti milium; totidem centuriae factae;
arma mutata, nihil praeter hastam et verutum da-
7 tum. Quinta classis aucta; centuriae triginta factae;
fundas lapidesque missiles hi secum gerebant. His[6]
accensi cornicines tubicinesque,[7] in duas[8] centurias
distributi. Undecim milibus haec classis censebatur.
8 Hoc minor census reliquam multitudinem habuit;
inde una centuria facta est immunis militia. Ita

---

[1] prima ς F³R² : prime R? : primo Ω.
[2] facerent *Lipsius* : ferrent Ω.
[3] tertiae classis ς : tertia classis Ω.
[4] quinquaginta *Sobius* : in quinquaginta Ω.
[5] hae ς : haec Ω.   [6] his *Iac. Perizonius* : in his Ω.
[7] tubicinesque ς : tibicinesque Ω.
[8] duas *Sigonius* (*cf. Dion. Hal.* iv. 17, 3) : tres Ω.

centuries, forty each of seniors and of juniors; these were all known as the first class; the seniors were to be ready to guard the city, the juniors to wage war abroad. The armour which these men were required to provide consisted of helmet, round shield, greaves, and breast-plate, all of bronze, for the protection of their bodies; their offensive weapons were a spear and a sword. There were added to this class two centuries of mechanics, who were to serve without arms; to them was entrusted the duty of fashioning siege-engines in war. The second class was drawn up out of those whose rating was between a hundred thousand and seventy-five thousand; of these, seniors and juniors, twenty centuries were enrolled. The arms prescribed for them were an oblong shield in place of the round one, and everything else, save for the breast-plate, as in the class above. He fixed the rating of the third class at fifty thousand; a like number of centuries was formed in this class as in the second, and with the same distinction of ages; neither was any change made in their arms, except that the greaves were omitted. In the fourth class the rating was twenty-five thousand; the same number of centuries was formed, but their equipment was changed, nothing being given them but a spear and a javelin. The fifth class was made larger, and thirty centuries were formed. These men carried slings, with stones for missiles. Rated with them were the horn-blowers and trumpeters, divided into two centuries. Eleven thousand was the rating of this class. Those who were assessed at less than this amount, being all the rest of the population, were made into a single century, exempt from military service. When the

LIVY

pedestri exercitu ornato distributoque equitum ex
9 primoribus civitatis duodecim scripsit centurias. Sex
item alias centurias, tribus ab Romulo institutis, sub
iisdem quibus inauguratae erant nominibus fecit. Ad
equos emendos dena milia aeris ex publico data, et
quibus equos alerent, viduae attributae, quae bina
milia aeris in annos singulos penderent. Haec omnia
10 in dites a pauperibus inclinata onera. Deinde est
honos additus; non enim, ut ab Romulo traditum
ceteri servaverant reges, viritim suffragium eadem vi
eodemque iure promisce omnibus datum est, sed
gradus facti, ut neque exclusus quisquam suffragio
videretur et vis omnis penes primores civitatis esset.
11 Equites enim vocabantur primi; octoginta inde primae classis centuriae; ibi[1] si variaret, quod raro incidebat, institutum ut[2] secundae classis vocarentur,
nec fere unquam infra ita descenderunt,[3] ut ad infi-
12 mos pervenirent. Nec mirari oportet hunc ordinem,
qui nunc est post expletas quinque et triginta tribus
duplicato earum numero centuriis iuniorum seniorumque, ad[4] institutam ab Ser. Tullio summam non
13 convenire. Quadrifariam enim urbe divisa regionibus collibusque qui habitabantur, partes eas tribus

[1] centuriae; ibi ϛ: centuriae primum peditum uocabantur ibi Ω.
[2] incidebat, institutum ut *Novák*: incidebat ut Ω.
[3] descenderunt ϛ: descenderent Ω.
[4] ad ϛ: se (*or* sese, *or* sed) ad Ω.

BOOK I. XLIII. 8-13

equipment and distribution of the infantry had been thus provided for, Servius enrolled twelve centuries of knights out of the leading men of the state. He likewise formed six other centuries—three had been instituted by Romulus—employing the same names which had been hallowed to their use by augury. For the purchase of horses they were allowed ten thousand asses each from the state treasury, and for the maintenance of these horses unmarried women were designated, who had to pay two thousand asses each, every year. All these burdens were shifted from the shoulders of the poor to those of the rich. The latter were then granted special privileges: for manhood suffrage, implying equality of power and of rights, was no longer given promiscuously to all, as had been the practice handed down by Romulus and observed by all the other kings; but gradations were introduced, so that ostensibly no one should be excluded from the suffrage, and yet the power should rest with the leading citizens. For the knights were called upon to vote first; then the eighty centuries of the first class: if there were any disagreement there, which rarely happened, it was provided that the centuries of the second class should be called; and they almost never descended so far as to reach the lowest citizens. Nor ought it to cause any surprise that the present organization, which exists since the increase of the tribes to thirty-five, and the doubling of their number in the matter of the junior and senior centuries, does not correspond with the total established by Servius Tullius. For, having divided the City according to its inhabited regions and hills into four parts, he named them "tribes," a word

B.C. 578-534

LIVY

appellavit, ut ego arbitror, ab tributo; nam eius quoque aequaliter ex censu conferendi ab eodem inita ratio est; neque eae tribus ad centuriarum distributionem numerumque quicquam pertinuere.

XLIV. Censu perfecto, quem maturaverat metu legis de incensis latae cum vinculorum minis mortisque, edixit, ut omnes cives Romani, equites peditesque, in suis quisque centuriis in campo Martio prima luce adessent. Ibi instructum exercitum omnem suovetaurilibus[1] lustravit; idque conditum lustrum appellatum, quia is[2] censendo finis factus est. Milia octoginta eo lustro civium censa dicuntur; adicit scriptorum antiquissimus Fabius Pictor eorum qui arma ferre possent eum numerum fuisse. Ad eam multitudinem urbs quoque amplificanda visa est. Addit duos colles, Quirinalem Viminalemque; inde deinceps auget Esquilias, ibique ipse, ut loco dignitas fieret, habitat. Aggere et fossis et muro circumdat urbem; ita pomerium profert. Pomerium, verbi vim solam intuentes, postmoerium interpretantur esse; est autem magis circamoerium, locus quem in condendis urbibus quondam Etrusci, qua murum

[1] suovetaurilibus *Rhenanus*: sue oue taurilibus (*or other corruptions*) Ω.
[2] is *Gronovius* "*ex cod. Mureti*": in Ω.

---

[1] *Tributum* comes from *tribus* (not *vice versa*, as Livy has it), which meant originally "third part," but lost the numerical force and became simply "part," "district," like the French "*quartier*," which Walde compares.

[2] Dion. iv. 13, and Strabo, v. 3, 7, make Servius the first to include the Esquiline in the City. Livy appears to have

BOOK I. XLIII. 13–XLIV. 4

derived, I suppose, from "tribute";[1] for this likewise the same king planned to have apportioned equitably, on the basis of the census; nor had these tribes anything whatever to do with the distribution or the number of the centuries.

XLIV. Upon the completion of the census, which had been expedited by fear of a law that threatened with death and imprisonment those who failed to register, Servius issued a proclamation calling on all Roman citizens, both horse and foot, to assemble at daybreak, each in his own century, in the Campus Martius. There the whole army was drawn up, and a sacrifice of a pig, a sheep, and a bull was offered by the king for its purification. This was termed the "closing of the lustrum," because it was the last act in the enrolment. Eighty thousand citizens are said to have been registered in that census; the most ancient of the historians, Fabius Pictor, adds that this was the number of those capable of bearing arms. To meet the wants of this population it was apparent that the City must expand, and so the king added two hills, the Quirinal and the Viminal, after which he proceeded to enlarge the Esquiline,[2] going there to live himself, that the place might obtain a good reputation. He surrounded the City with a rampart, trenches, and a wall, and so extended the "pomerium." This word is interpreted by those who look only at its etymology as meaning "the tract behind the wall," but it signifies rather "the tract on both sides of the wall," the space which the Etruscans used formerly to consecrate with augural

thought of him as merely increasing the extent of that district. Conway and Walters adopt O's *Viminalemque, Viminalem*, and Gronov's *Esquiliis*, thus reconciling Livy with Dion. and Strabo.

155

ducturi erant, certis circa terminis inaugurato consecrabant, ut neque interiore parte aedificia moenibus continuarentur, quae nunc volgo etiam coniungunt, et extrinsecus puri aliquid ab humano cultu pateret soli. Hoc spatium, quod neque habitari neque arari fas erat, non magis quod post murum esset quam quod murus post id, pomerium Romani appellarunt; et in urbis incremento semper, quantum moenia processura erant tantum termini hi consecrati proferebantur.

XLV. Aucta civitate magnitudine urbis, formatis omnibus domi et ad belli et ad pacis usus, ne semper armis opes adquirerentur, consilio augere imperium conatus est, simul et aliquod addere urbi decus. Iam tum erat inclitum Dianae Ephesiae fanum; id communiter a civitatibus Asiae factum fama ferebat. Eum consensum deosque consociatos laudare mire Servius inter proceres Latinorum, cum quibus publice privatimque hospitia amicitiasque de industria iunxerat. Saepe iterando eadem perpulit tandem, ut Romae fanum Dianae populi Latini cum populo Romano facerent. Ea erat confessio caput rerum Romam esse, de quo totiens armis certatum fuerat.

---

[1] *Pomerium* at first meant the boundary-line itself, then the strip of land left free within the wall, and finally was loosely used of the strip on both sides of the wall.

ceremonies, where they proposed to erect their wall, establishing definite limits on either side of it, so that they might at the same time keep the walls free on their inward face from contact with buildings, which now, as a rule, are actually joined to them, and on the outside keep a certain area free from human uses. This space, which the gods forbade men to inhabit or to till, was called "pomerium" by the Romans, quite as much because the wall stood behind it as because it stood behind the wall; and as the city grew, these consecrated limits were always pushed out for as great a distance as the walls themselves were to be advanced.[1]

XLV. When the king had promoted the grandeur of the state by enlarging the City, and had shaped all his domestic policy to suit the demands of peace as well as those of war, he was unwilling that arms should always be the means employed for strengthening Rome's power, and sought to increase her sway by diplomacy, and at the same time to add something to the splendour of the City. Even at that early date the temple of Diana at Ephesus enjoyed great renown. It was reputed to have been built through the co-operation of the cities of Asia, and this harmony and community of worship Servius praised in superlative terms to the Latin nobles, with whom, both officially and in private, he had taken pains to establish a footing of hospitality and friendship. By dint of reiterating the same arguments he finally carried his point, and a shrine of Diana was built in Rome by the nations of Latium conjointly with the Roman People. This was an admission that Rome was the capital—a point which had so often been disputed

LIVY

Id quamquam omissum iam ex omnium cura Latinorum ob rem totiens infeliciter temptatam armis videbatur, uni se ex Sabinis fors dare visa est privato 4 consilio imperii reciperandi. Bos in Sabinis nata cuidam patri familiae dicitur miranda magnitudine ac specie; fixa per multas aetates cornua in vestibulo templi Dianae monumentum ei fuere miraculo. 5 Habita, ut erat, res prodigii loco est; et cecinere vates, cuius civitatis eam civis Dianae immolasset,[1] ibi fore imperium; idque carmen pervenerat ad anti- 6 stitem fani Dianae Sabinusque, ut prima apta dies sacrificio visa est, bovem Romam actam deducit ad fanum Dianae et ante aram statuit. Ibi antistes Romanus, cum eum magnitudo victimae celebrata fama movisset, memor responsi Sabinum ita adloquitur: "Quidnam tu, hospes, paras?" inquit, "inceste sacrificium Dianae facere? Quin tu ante vivo perfunderis flumine? Infima valle praefluit Tiberis." 7 Religione tactus hospes, qui omnia, ut prodigio responderet eventus, cuperet rite facta, extemplo descendit ad Tiberim. Interea Romanus immolat Dianae bovem. Id mire gratum regi atque civitati fuit.

XLVI. Servius quamquam iam usu haud dubie[2] regnum possederat, tamen quia interdum iactari

[1] immolasset *Rhenan.*: immolassent Ω.
[2] dubie *M*¹ (*or M*²): dubiae (*or* dubiem *or* dubium) Ω.

BOOK I. XLV. 3-XLVI. 1

with force of arms. But though it seemed that the Latins had lost all interest in this contention after the repeated failure of their appeals to war, there was one man amongst the Sabines who thought that he saw an opportunity to recover the empire by a shrewd plan of his own. In the Sabine country, on the farm of a certain head of a family, there was born a heifer of extraordinary size and beauty; a marvel to which the horns afterwards bore testimony, for they were fastened up for many generations in the vestibule of Diana's temple. This heifer was regarded as a prodigy, as indeed it was; soothsayers prophesied that the state whose citizens should sacrifice the animal to Diana would be the seat of empire, and this prediction had reached the ears of the priest of Diana's shrine. On the earliest day which seemed suitable for the sacrifice, the Sabine drove the heifer to Rome, and bringing her to the shrine of Diana, led her up to the altar. There the Roman priest, moved by the great size of the victim, which had been much talked of, and recalling the prophecy, asked the Sabine, "What is this that you are doing, stranger? Would you sacrifice, unpurified, to Diana? Not so! First bathe in a running stream; the Tiber flows by in the bottom of the valley." The stranger, touched by a scruple and wishing to do everything according to ritual, that the prodigy might be answered by the event, at once descended to the Tiber. Meanwhile the Roman offered the heifer to Diana, an act which was exceedingly acceptable to the king and the citizens.

XLVI. Servius had by this time a definite prescriptive right to the supreme power. Still, hearing

voces a iuvene Tarquinio audiebat se iniussu populi regnare, conciliata prius voluntate plebis agro capto ex hostibus viritim diviso ausus est ferre ad populum, vellent iuberentne se regnare; tantoque consensu quanto haud quisquam alius ante rex est declaratus.
2 Neque ea res Tarquinio spem adfectandi regni minuit; immo eo impensius, quia de agro plebis adversa[1] patrum voluntate[2] senserat agi, criminandi Servi apud patres crescendique in curia sibi occasionem datam ratus est, et ipse iuvenis ardentis animi et domi uxore Tullia inquietum animum stimulante.
3 Tulit enim et Romana regia sceleris tragici exemplum, ut taedio regum maturior veniret libertas ultimumque regnum esset quod scelere partum foret.
4 Hic L. Tarquinius—Prisci Tarquini regis filius neposne fuerit parum liquet; pluribus tamen auctoribus filium ediderim—fratrem habuerat Arruntem
5 Tarquinium, mitis ingenii iuvenem. His duobus, ut ante dictum est, duae Tulliae regis filiae nupserant, et ipsae longe dispares moribus. Forte ita inciderat ne duo violenta ingenia matrimonio iungerentur fortuna, credo, populi Romani, quo diuturnius Servi regnum esset constituique civitatis mores possent.

[1] adversa $M^2PO?$: adversam (*or* -um) Ω.
[2] voluntate ς: uoluntatem Ω.

---

[1] The reference is to the stories of Atreus and Oedipus.

BOOK I. XLVI. 1-5

that the young Tarquinius now and then threw out a hint that he was reigning without the consent of the people, he proceeded to gain the goodwill of the commons by dividing among all the citizens the land obtained by conquest from the enemy; after which he made bold to call upon the people to vote whether he should be their ruler, and was declared king with such unanimity as none of his predecessors had experienced. Yet the circumstance did not lessen Tarquinius's hopes of obtaining the kingship. On the contrary, perceiving that the bestowal of land on the plebeians was in opposition to the wishes of the senate, he felt that he had got the better opportunity of vilifying Servius to the Fathers and of increasing his own influence in the senate-house. He was a hot-headed youth himself, and he had at hand, in the person of Tullia his wife, one who goaded on his restless spirit. For the royal house of Rome produced an example of tragic guilt, as others had done,[1] in order that loathing of kings might hasten the coming of liberty, and that the end of reigning might come in that reign which was the fruit of crime. This Lucius Tarquinius—whether he was the son or the grandson of King Tarquinius Priscus is uncertain; but, following the majority of historians, I would designate him son—had a brother, Arruns Tarquinius, a youth of a gentle disposition. These two, as has been said before, had married the two Tullias, daughters of the king, themselves of widely different characters. Chance had so ordered matters that the two violent natures should not be united in wedlock, thanks doubtless to the good fortune of the Roman People, that the reign of Servius might be prolonged and the traditions of

LIVY

6 Angebatur ferox Tullia nihil materiae in viro neque ad cupiditatem neque ad audaciam esse; tota in alterum aversa[1] Tarquinium eum mirari, eum virum dicere ac regio sanguine ortum: spernere sororem, 7 quod virum nacta muliebri cessaret audacia. Contrahit celeriter similitudo eos, ut fere fit: malum malo aptissimum; sed initium turbandi omnia a femina ortum est. Ea secretis viri alieni adsuefacta sermonibus nullis verborum contumeliis parcere de viro ad fratrem, de sorore ad virum; et se rectius viduam et illum caelibem futurum fuisse contendere, quam cum inpari iungi, ut elanguescendum aliena 8 ignavia esset. Si sibi eum, quo digna esset, di dedissent virum, domi se propediem visuram regnum fuisse, quod apud patrem videat. Celeriter adules-9 centem suae temeritatis implet.[2] Prope continuatis funeribus cum domos vacuas novo matrimonio fecissent, iunguntur nuptiis magis non prohibente Servio quam adprobante.

XLVII. Tum vero in dies infestior Tulli senectus, infestius coepit regnum esse. Iam enim ab scelere ad aliud spectare mulier scelus, nec nocte nec interdiu virum conquiescere pati, ne gratuita praeterita 2 parricidia essent: non sibi defuisse cui nupta dice-

---

[1] aversa *ς* : adversa *D* ? : versa (*or* versam *or* adversa) Ω.
[2] *Between* implet *and* prope *the MSS. give the words* Arruns Tarquinius et Tullia minor *which Walters brackets.*

the state become established. It was distressing to the headstrong Tullia that her husband should be destitute of ambition and enterprise. With her whole soul she turned from him to his brother; him she admired, him she called a man and a prince: she despised her sister because, having got a man for a mate, she lacked a woman's daring. Their similarity soon brought these two together, as is generally the case, for evil is strongly drawn to evil; but it was the woman who took the lead in all the mischief. Having become addicted to clandestine meetings with another's husband, she spared no terms of insult when speaking of her own husband to his brother, or of her sister to that sister's husband. She urged that it would have been juster for her to be unmarried and for him to lack a wife than for them to be united to their inferiors and be compelled to languish through the cowardice of others. If the gods had given her the man she deserved she would soon have seen in her own house the royal power which she now saw in her father's. It was not long before she had inspired the young man with her own temerity, and, having made room in their respective houses for a new marriage, by deaths which followed closely upon one another, they were joined together in nuptials which Servius rather tolerated than approved.

XLVII. From that moment the insecurity of the aged Tullius and the menace to his authority increased with each succeeding day. For the woman was already looking forward from one crime to another, nor would she allow her husband any rest by night or day, lest the murders they had done before should be without effect. She had not wanted a

LIVY

retur, nec cum quo tacita serviret; defuisse qui se regno dignum putaret, qui meminisset se esse Prisci Tarquini filium, qui habere quam sperare regnum 3 mallet. "Si tu is es cui nuptam esse me arbitror, et virum et regem appello; sin minus, eo nunc peius mutata res est quod istic cum ignavia est scelus. 4 Quin accingeris? Non tibi ab Corintho nec ab Tarquiniis, ut patri tuo, peregrina regna moliri necesse est: di te penates patriique et patris imago et domus regia et in domo regale solium et nomen 5 Tarquinium creat vocatque regem. Aut si ad haec parum est animi, quid frustraris civitatem? Quid te ut regium iuvenem conspici sinis? Facesse hinc Tarquinios aut Corinthum, devolvere retro ad stir- 6 pem, fratris similior quam patris." His aliisque increpando iuvenem instigat, nec conquiescere ipsa potest, si, cum Tanaquil peregrina mulier tantum moliri potuisset animo ut duo continua regna viro ac deinceps genero dedisset, ipsa regio semine orta nullum momentum[1] in dando adimendoque regno 7 faceret. His muliebribus instinctus furiis Tarquinius circumire et prensare minorum maxime gentium patres; admonere paterni beneficii ac pro eo gratiam repetere; allicere donis iuvenes; cum de se ingentia

[1] momentum $D^2R^2\varsigma$: momenmentum D: monumentum Ω.

man just to be called a wife, just to endure servitude with him in silence; she had wanted one who should deem himself worthy of the sovereignty, who bethought him that he was the son of Tarquinius Priscus, who preferred the possession of the kingship to the hope of it. "If you are he," she cried, "whom I thought I was marrying, I call you both man and king; if not, then I have so far changed for the worse, in that crime is added, in your case, to cowardice. Come, rouse yourself! You are not come, like your father, from Corinth or Tarquinii, that you must make yourself king in a strange land; the gods of your family and your ancestors, your father's image, the royal palace, with its throne, and the name of Tarquinius create and proclaim you king. Else, if you have no courage for this, why do you cheat the citizens? why do you suffer yourself to be looked on as a prince? Away with you to Tarquinii or Corinth! Sink back into the rank of your family, more like your brother than your father!" With these and other taunts she excited the young man's ambition. Nor could she herself submit with patience to the thought that Tanaquil, a foreign woman, had exerted her spirit to such purpose as twice in succession to confer the royal power—upon her husband first, and again upon her son-in-law—if Tullia, the daughter of a king, were to count for nothing in bestowing and withdrawing a throne. Inspired by this woman's frenzy Tarquinius began to go about and solicit support, especially among the heads of the lesser families, whom he reminded of his father's kindness to them, and desired their favour in return; the young men he attracted by gifts; both by the great things he promised to do

LIVY

pollicendo tum regis criminibus omnibus locis crescere. Postremo, ut iam agendae rei tempus visum est, stipatus agmine armatorum in forum inrupit. Inde omnibus perculsis pavore in regia sede pro curia sedens patres in curiam per praeconem ad regem Tarquinium citari iussit. Convenere extemplo, alii iam ante ad hoc praeparati, alii metu ne non venisse fraudi esset, novitate ac miraculo attoniti et iam de Servio actum rati. Ibi Tarquinius maledicta ab stirpe ultima orsus: servum servaque natum post mortem indignam parentis sui, non interregno, ut antea, inito, non comitiis habitis, non per suffragium populi, non auctoribus patribus, muliebri dono regnum occupasse. Ita natum, ita creatum regem, fautorem infimi generis hominum, ex quo ipse sit, odio alienae honestatis ereptum primoribus agrum sordidissimo cuique divisisse; omnia onera quae communia quondam fuerint, inclinasse in primores civitatis; instituisse censum, ut insignis ad invidiam locupletiorum fortuna esset, et parata unde, ubi[1] vellet, egentissimis largiretur.

[1] unde ubi *M* : ubi Ω.

BOOK I. XLVII. 7-12

himself, and by slandering the king as well, he everywhere strengthened his interest. At length, when it seemed that the time for action was now come, he surrounded himself with a body of armed men and burst into the Forum. Then, amidst the general consternation which ensued, he seated himself on the throne in front of the Curia, and commanded, by the mouth of a herald, that the senators should come to King Tarquinius at the senate-house. They at once assembled: some of them already prepared beforehand, others afraid that they might be made to suffer for it if they did not come; for they were astounded at this strange and wonderful sight, and supposed that Servius was utterly undone. Tarquinius then went back to the very beginning of Servius's family and abused the king for a slave and a slave-woman's son who, after the shameful death of his own father, Tarquinius Priscus, had seized the power; there had been no observance of the interregnum, as on former occasions; there had been no election held; not by the votes of the people had sovereignty come to him, not with the confirmation of the Fathers, but by a woman's gift. Such having been his birth, and such his appointment to the kingship, he had been an abettor of the lowest class of society, to which he himself belonged, and his hatred of the nobility possessed by others had led him to plunder the leading citizens of their land and divide it amongst the dregs of the populace. All the burdens which had before been borne in common he had laid upon the nation's foremost men. He had instituted the census that he might hold up to envy the fortunes of the wealthy, and make them available, when he chose to draw upon them, for largesses to the destitute.

XLVIII. Huic orationi Servius cum intervenisset trepido nuntio excitatus, extemplo a vestibulo curiae magna voce "Quid hoc," inquit, "Tarquini, rei est? Qua tu audacia me vivo vocare ausus es patres aut in 2 sede considere mea?" Cum ille ferociter ad haec, se patris sui tenere sedem, multo quam servum potiorem filium regis regni heredem, satis illum diu per licentiam eludentem insultasse dominis, clamor ab utriusque fautoribus oritur, et concursus populi fiebat in curiam, apparebatque regnaturum qui vicisset. 3 Tum Tarquinius necessitate iam etiam ipsa cogente ultima audere, multo et aetate et viribus validior, medium arripit Servium elatumque e curia in inferiorem partem per gradus deiecit; inde ad 4 cogendum senatum in curiam rediit. Fit fuga regis apparitorum atque comitum: ipse prope exsanguis cum sine regio comitatu domum se reciperet ab iis,[1] qui missi ab Tarquinio fugientem consecuti erant 5 interficitur. Creditur, quia non abhorret a cetero scelere, admonitu Tulliae id factum. Carpento certe, id quod satis constat, in forum invecta, nec reverita coetum virorum, evocavit virum e curia regemque 6 prima appellavit. A quo facessere iussa ex tanto tumultu, cum se domum reciperet pervenissetque ad summum Cyprium vicum, ubi Dianium nuper fuit,

[1] cum sine regio comitatu domum se reciperet ab iis *Alschefski*: cum semianimis (*or* -mes) regio comitatu domum se reciperet pervenissetque ad summum cōs primum vicum Ω.

BOOK I. XLVIII. 1-6

XLVIII. In the midst of this harangue Servius, who had been aroused by the alarming news, came up and immediately called out in a loud voice from the vestibule of the Curia: "What means this, Tarquinius? With what assurance have you dared, while I live, to convene the Fathers or to sit in my chair?" Tarquinius answered truculently that it was his own father's seat he occupied; that the king's son was a fitter successor to his kingdom than a slave was; that Tullius had long enough been suffered to mock his masters and insult them. Shouts arose from the partisans of each, and the people began to rush into the senate-house; it was clear that he would be king who won the day. Tarquinius was now compelled by sheer necessity to go on boldly to the end. Being much superior to Servius in youth and strength, he seized him by the middle, and bearing him out of the senate-house, flung him down the steps. He then went back into the Curia to hold the senate together. The king's servitors and companions fled. The king himself, half fainting, was making his way home without the royal attendants, when the men whom Tarquinius had sent in pursuit of the fugitive came up with him and killed him. It is believed, inasmuch as it is not inconsistent with the rest of her wickedness, that this deed was suggested by Tullia. It is agreed, at all events, that she was driven in her carriage into the Forum, and nothing abashed at the crowd of men, summoned her husband from the Curia and was the first to hail him king. Tarquinius bade her withdraw from so turbulent a scene. On her way home she had got to the top of the Vicus Cyprius, where the shrine of Diana recently stood, and was bidding her driver

LIVY

flectenti carpentum dextra in Urbium clivum ut in collem Esquiliarum eveheretur, restitit pavidus atque inhibuit frenos is qui iumenta agebat, iacentemque 7 dominae Servium trucidatum ostendit. Foedum inhumanumque inde traditur scelus, monumentoque locus est—Sceleratum vicum vocant—quo amens agitantibus furiis sororis ac viri, Tullia per patris corpus carpentum egisse fertur, partemque sanguinis ac caedis paternae cruento vehiculo, contaminata ipsa respersaque, tulisse[1] ad penates suos virique sui, quibus iratis malo regni principio similes propediem exitus sequerentur.

8 Ser. Tullius regnavit annos quattuor et quadraginta ita ut bono etiam moderatoque succedenti regi difficilis aemulatio esset. Ceterum id quoque ad gloriam accessit quod cum illo simul iusta ac legi- 9 tima regna occiderunt. Id ipsum tam mite ac tam moderatum imperium tamen, quia unius esset, deponere eum in animo habuisse quidam auctores sunt, ni scelus intestinum liberandae patriae consilia agitanti[2] intervenisset.

XLIX. Inde L. Tarquinius regnare occepit, cui Superbo cognomen facta indiderunt, quia socerum gener sepultura prohibuit, Romulum quoque inse- 2 pultum perisse dictitans, primoresque patrum, quos Servi rebus favisse credebat, interfecit; conscius deinde male quaerendi regni ab se ipso adversus se exemplum capi posse, armatis corpus circumsaepsit;

[1] tulisse $\Omega^2\varsigma$: tulisset Ω.
[2] agitanti $R\varsigma$: agitanci M? : agitandi Ω.

170

BOOK I. XLVIII. 6–XLIX. 2

turn to the right into the Clivus Urbius, to take her to the Esquiline Hill, when the man gave a start of terror, and pulling up the reins pointed out to his mistress the prostrate form of the murdered Servius. Horrible and inhuman was the crime that is said to have ensued, which the place commemorates—men call it the Street of Crime—for there, crazed by the avenging spirits of her sister and her former husband, they say that Tullia drove her carriage over her father's corpse, and, herself contaminated and defiled, carried away on her vehicle some of her murdered father's blood to her own and her husband's penates, whose anger was the cause that the evil beginning of this reign was, at no long date, followed by a similar end.

Servius Tullius had ruled forty-four years, so well that even a good and moderate successor would have found it hard to emulate him. But there was this to enhance his renown, that just and lawful kingship perished with him. Yet, mild and moderate though his sway was, some writers state that he had intended to resign it, as being a government by one man, had not the crime of one of his family interrupted his plans for the liberation of his country.

XLIX. Now began the reign of Lucius Tarquinius, whose conduct procured him the surname of Superbus, or the Proud. For he denied the rites of sepulture to his own father-in-law, asserting that Romulus had also perished without burial. He put to death the leading senators, whom he believed to have favoured the cause of Servius and, conscious that a precedent for gaining the kingship by crime might be found in his own career and turned against himself, he

171

LIVY

A.U.C.
220-244

3 neque enim ad ius regni quicquam praeter vim habebat, ut qui neque populi iussu neque auctoribus
4 patribus regnaret. Eo accedebat ut in caritate civium nihil spei reponenti metu regnum tutandum esset. Quem ut pluribus incuteret, cognitiones capitalium rerum sine consiliis per se solus exercebat,
5 perque eam causam occidere, in exsilium agere, bonis multare poterat non suspectos modo aut invisos sed
6 unde nihil aliud quam praedam sperare posset. Praecipue ita patrum numero imminuto statuit nullos in patres legere, quo contemptior paucitate ipsa ordo
7 esset, minusque per se nihil agi indignarentur. Hic enim regum primus traditum[1] a prioribus morem de omnibus senatum consulendi solvit, domesticis consiliis rem publicam administravit; bellum, pacem, foedera, societates per se ipse, cum quibus voluit,
8 iniussu populi ac senatus, fecit diremitque. Latinorum sibi maxime gentem conciliabat, ut peregrinis quoque opibus tutior inter cives esset, neque hospitia modo cum primoribus eorum, sed adfinitates quoque
9 iungebat. Octavio Mamilio Tusculano—is longe princeps Latini nominis erat, si famae credimus, ab Ulixe deaque Circa oriundus—ei Mamilio filiam nuptum dat perque eas nuptias multos sibi cognatos amicosque eius conciliat.

---

[1] traditum *Grynaeus* ϛ : ut traditur Ω.

---

[1] *i.e.* causes affecting the *caput* (which might mean either "life" or "civic rights") of the accused.
[2] Circe bore to Ulysses a son, Telegonus, who founded Tusculum.

BOOK I. xlix. 3-9

assumed a body-guard. He had indeed no right to the throne but might, since he was ruling neither by popular decree nor senatorial sanction. Moreover, as he put no trust in the affection of his people, he was compelled to safeguard his authority by fear. To inspire terror therefore in many persons, he adopted the practice of trying capital causes[1] by himself, without advisers; and, under the pretext thus afforded, was able to inflict death, exile, and forfeiture of property, not only upon persons whom he suspected and disliked, but also in cases where he could have nothing to gain but plunder. It was chiefly the senators whose numbers were reduced by this procedure, and Tarquinius determined to make no new appointments to the order, that it might be the more despised for its very paucity, and might chafe less at being ignored in all business of state. For this king was the first to break with the custom handed down by his predecessors, of consulting the senate on all occasions, and governed the nation without other advice than that of his own household. War, peace, treaties, and alliances were entered upon or broken off by the monarch himself, with whatever states he wished, and without the decree of people or senate. The Latin race he strove particularly to make his friends, that his strength abroad might contribute to his security at home. He contracted with their nobles not only relations of hospitality but also matrimonial connections. To Octavius Mamilius of Tusculum, a man by long odds the most important of the Latin name, and descended, if we may believe report, from Ulysses and the goddess Circe,[2] he gave his daughter in marriage, and in this way attached to himself the numerous kinsmen and friends of the man.

LIVY

L. Iam magna Tarquini auctoritas inter Latinorum proceres erat, cum in diem certam ut ad lucum Ferentinae conveniant indicit: esse quae agere de 2 rebus communibus velit. Conveniunt frequentes prima luce: ipse Tarquinius diem quidem servavit, sed paulo ante quam sol occideret venit. Multa ibi toto die in concilio variis iactata sermonibus erant. 3 Turnus Herdonius ab Aricia ferociter in absentem Tarquinium erat invectus: haud mirum esse Superbo inditum Romae cognomen—iam enim ita clam quidem mussitantes, volgo tamen eum appellabant. An quicquam superbius esse quam ludificari sic omne 4 nomen Latinum? Principibus longe[1] ab domo excitis, ipsum qui concilium indixerit non adesse. Temptari profecto patientiam ut, si iugum acceperint, obnoxios premat. Cui enim non apparere adfectare 5 eum imperium in Latinos? Quod si sui bene crediderint cives, aut si creditum illud et non raptum parricidio sit, credere et Latinos, quamquam ne sic 6 quidem alienigenae, debere[2]; sin suos eius paeniteat, quippe qui alii super alios trucidentur, exsulatum eant, bona amittant, quid spei melioris Latinis portendi? Si se audiant, domum suam quemque inde abituros, neque magis observaturos diem concilii 7 quam ipse qui indixerit observet. Haec atque alia

[1] Principibus (principibui *O*) longe Ω: principibus enim *U*: longe *M*.   [2] debere *M*: deberet (*or* -ent) Ω.

BOOK I. L. 1-7

L. Tarquinius had already won great influence with the Latin nobles, when he gave notice that they should assemble on a certain day at the grove of Ferentina, saying that there were matters of common interest which he wished to discuss. The Latins gathered at daybreak in large numbers; Tarquinius himself, though he did indeed keep the day, arrived but a little while before sundown. There had been much talk in the council all day about various subjects. Turnus Herdonius of Aricia had inveighed violently against the absent Tarquinius. He said it was no wonder he had been given the name of Superbus at Rome—for that was the name by which they already called him, secretly and in whispers, but still quite generally;—could anything be more overbearing than to flout the whole Latin race as he was doing then? Their leaders had been summoned from distant homes, and the very man who had called the council was not there. He was evidently trying their patience, intending, if they submitted to the yoke, to use them as his vassals. For who could fail to see that he was aiming at sovereignty over the Latins? If his own people had done well to intrust this to him, if indeed it had been intrusted to him at all, and had not been ravished by foul murder, then it was right that the Latins also should intrust it to him—nay, not even then, for he was of foreign birth; but if his own subjects were weary of him, as men who, one after another, were being made to suffer death, exile, confiscation, what better prospect was held out to the Latins? If they were guided by the speaker they would depart every man to his own home, nor observe the day of meeting more than he who had proclaimed it was observing it. As these

LIVY

eodem pertinentia seditiosus facinerosusque homo hisque artibus opes domi nactus cum maxime dissereret, intervenit Tarquinius. Is finis orationi fuit; aversi omnes ad Tarquinium salutandum. Qui silentio facto monitus a proximis ut purgaret se, quod id temporis venisset, disceptatorem ait se sumptum inter patrem et filium, cura reconciliandi eos in gratiam moratum esse, et quia ea res exemisset illum diem, postero die acturum quae constituisset. Ne id quidem ab Turno tulisse tacitum ferunt; dixisse enim nullam breviorem esse cognitionem quam inter patrem et filium, paucisque transigi verbis posse: ni pareat patri, habiturum infortunium esse.

LI. Haec Aricinus in regem Romanum increpans ex concilio abiit. Quam rem Tarquinius aliquanto quam videbatur aegrius ferens confestim Turno necem machinatur, ut eundem terrorem quo civium animos domi oppresserat Latinis iniceret. Et quia pro imperio palam interfici non poterat, oblato falso crimine insontem oppressit. Per adversae factionis quosdam Aricinos servum Turni auro corrupit, ut in[1] deversorium eius vim magnam gladiorum inferri clam sineret. Ea cum una nocte perfecta essent, Tarquinius paulo ante lucem accitis ad se principibus

---

[1] ut in *MR²Ald.*: in (ten *O*) Ω.

words and others of the same import were being uttered by the factious and turbulent Latin, who owed to these qualities his influence amongst his own people, Tarquinius came up. This was the end of the speech; all turned to salute Tarquinius. Silence was commanded, and the king, being advised by those nearest him to excuse himself for having come so late, declared that he had been chosen arbiter between a father and his son, and had been delayed by his anxiety to reconcile them. He added that since this business had used up that day, he would take up on the morrow the matters which he had meant to bring before them. They say that Turnus would not suffer even this to go unchallenged, asserting that there was no question more quickly settled than one betwixt father and son, for these few words were enough to end it: "Unless you obey your father it will be the worse for you."

LI. Girding thus against the Roman king, the Arician quitted the council. Tarquinius was considerably more vexed than he appeared to be, and at once looked about him for the means of destroying Turnus, that he might inspire in the Latins the same terror with which he had broken the spirit of the Romans. And since he could not openly put his man to death by virtue of sovereign right, he charged him with a crime of which he was innocent, and so destroyed him. Through the agency of certain men of the opposite party in Aricia, he bribed a slave of Turnus with gold to allow a large quantity of swords to be brought secretly into his master's lodging. Having accomplished this in a single night, Tarquinius, shortly before dawn, summoned the chief men of the Latins to his quarters, pretending to

LIVY

Latinorum quasi re nova perturbatus, moram suam hesternam, velut deorum quadam providentia inla-
4 tam, ait saluti sibi atque illis fuisse. Ab Turno dici sibi et primoribus populorum parari necem ut Latinorum solus imperium teneat. Adgressurum fuisse hesterno die in concilio; dilatam rem esse, quod
5 auctor concilii afuerit, quem maxime peteret. Inde illam absentis insectationem esse natam, quod morando spem destituerit. Non dubitare, si vera deferantur, quin prima luce, ubi ventum in concilium sit, instructus cum coniuratorum manu armatusque
6 venturus sit. Dici gladiorum ingentem esse numerum ad eum convectum. Id vanum[1] necne sit extemplo sciri posse. Rogare eos ut inde secum ad
7 Turnum veniant. Suspectam fecit rem et ingenium Turni ferox et oratio hesterna et mora Tarquini, quod videbatur ob eam differri caedes potuisse. Eunt inclinatis quidem ad credendum animis, tamen nisi
8 gladiis deprehensis cetera vana existimaturi. Ubi est eo ventum, Turnum ex somno excitatum circumsistunt custodes; comprehensisque servis, qui caritate domini vim parabant, cum gladii abditi ex omnibus locis deverticuli protraherentur, enimvero manifesta

---

[1] vanum Ω : uarum *R* ; uerum *R²L*.

have received alarming news, and informed them
that his tardiness on the preceding day, as though
somehow providentially occasioned, had been the
means of saving himself and them. For he was
told that Turnus was plotting his murder and that
of the chief men of the different cities, that he might
be sole ruler over the Latins. He would have attacked them the day before in the council, but had
postponed the attempt because the summoner of the
council, whom he chiefly aimed at, was not there.
That was the reason Turnus had railed at him in his
absence, for his delay had balked the Arician's expectation. Tarquinius said that he had no doubt, if
his information was true, that Turnus would come at
dawn, when they had assembled in the council, and
would be armed and attended by a band of conspirators. It was said that a great quantity of swords
had been carried to his lodging; the falsity or truth
of this could be ascertained immediately, and he
asked them to go with him to Turnus's quarters.
The charge was made plausible both by the aggressive spirit of Turnus and his speech of the day
before, and by Tarquinius's delay, since it seemed
that the massacre might have been postponed on
that account. The nobles went therefore with a disposition to believe the story, but still, if the swords
should not be found, they were prepared to conclude
the other charges false. As soon as they reached the
place they wakened Turnus from his sleep and surrounded him with guards; and having overpowered
the slaves, who out of affection for their master
would have resorted to force, they proceeded to
pull out the hidden swords from every corner of
the inn. There was now no doubt that Turnus was

LIVY

res visa, iniectaeque Turno catenae; et confestim Latinorum concilium magno cum tumultu advocatur. 9 Ibi tam atrox invidia orta est gladiis in medio positis ut indicta causa, novo genere leti, deiectus ad caput aquae Ferentinae crate superne iniecta saxisque congestis mergeretur.

LII. Revocatis deinde ad concilium Latinis Tarquinius conlaudatisque qui Turnum novantem res pro manifesto parricidio merita poena adfecissent, 2 ita verba fecit: posse quidem se vetusto iure agere, quod, cum omnes Latini ab Alba oriundi sint, eo foedere[1] teneantur quo[2] ab Tullo res omnis Albana cum coloniis[3] suis in Romanum cesserit 3 imperium; ceterum se utilitatis id magis omnium causa censere ut renovetur id foedus, secundaque potius fortuna populi Romani ut participes Latini fruantur quam urbium excidia vastationesque agrorum, quas Anco prius, patre deinde suo regnante perpessi sint, semper aut exspectent aut patiantur. 4 Haud difficulter persuasum Latinis, quamquam in eo foedere superior Romana res erat; ceterum et capita nominis Latini stare ac sentire cum rege videbant, et sui[4] cuique periculi, si adversatus esset, recens erat 5 documentum. Ita renovatum foedus indictumque

---

[1] eo foedere *Perizonius*: in eo foedere Ω.
[2] quo ς: quod Ω. [3] coloniis ς: colonis Ω.
[4] sui *M*: Turnus sui Ω.

---

[1] In the account of this treaty at xxiv. 3 no Alban colonies are mentioned, nor do we know of any. Conway and Walters, therefore, keep *colonis* of the MSS., but we should rather expect *civibus* in this context.

BOOK I. LI. 8–LII. 5

caught in the act, and he was cast into chains, while the summons was instantly sent out, amidst intense excitement, for a council of the Latins. There such bitter resentment was aroused by the public display of the swords, that the accused was not permitted to plead his cause, but suffered a new kind of death, being plunged into the source of the Ferentine Water and sunk beneath a wicker crate heaped up with stones.

LII. Tarquinius then called the Latins again to the place of council, and praised them for the punishment which they had justly meted out to the rebellious attempt of Turnus, in view of the treason in which he had just been taken. The king then went on to say that it was in his power to proceed according to an ancient right, since all the Latins, having sprung from Alba, were included in that treaty by which, from the time of Tullus, the whole Alban state, with its colonies, had come under Rome's dominion.[1] But the advantage of all would be better served, he thought, if that treaty were renewed and the good fortune of the Roman people were thrown open to the participation of the Latins, than if they were always to be dreading or enduring the razing of their cities and the devastation of their lands which they had suffered first in Ancus's reign and afterward in that of the speaker's father. It was not difficult to persuade the Latins, although the Roman interest preponderated in this treaty. For the rest, they saw that the chiefs of the Latin name stood with the king and took his view of the matter, and they had just been given a demonstration of the danger they would each incur if they opposed the project. So the treaty was renewed, and the Latin

LIVY

iunioribus Latinorum ut ex foedere die certa ad lucum Ferentinae armati frequentes adessent. Qui ubi ad edictum Romani regis ex omnibus populis convenere, ne ducem suum neve secretum imperium propriave signa haberent, miscuit manipulos ex Latinis Romanisque ut ex binis singulos faceret binosque ex singulis; ita geminatis manipulis centuriones imposuit.

LIII. Nec ut iniustus in pace rex, ita dux belli pravus fuit; quin ea arte aequasset superiores reges, ni degeneratum in aliis huic quoque decori offecisset. Is primus Volscis bellum in ducentos amplius post suam aetatem annos movit, Suessamque Pometiam ex iis vi cepit. Ubi cum divendita[1] praeda quadraginta talenta argenti refecisset,[2] concepit animo eam amplitudinem Iovis templi quae digna deum hominumque rege, quae Romano imperio, quae ipsius etiam loci maiestate esset. Captivam pecuniam in aedificationem eius templi seposuit.

Excepit deinde eum[3] lentius spe bellum, quo Gabios, propinquam urbem, nequiquam vi adortus, cum obsidendi quoque urbem spes pulso a moenibus adempta esset, postremo minime arte Romana, fraude

[1] divendita ς : dividenta *M* : dividenda Ω.
[2] refecisset *Gronov.* P¹ *or* P² *marg.*: refecisset coepisset (*or* r. ac recepisset) *MRDL* : reque cepisset (*or* reccepisset *or* cepisset) Ω.   [3] deinde eum Ω : deinde *M*.

---

[1] A Roman maniple was divided into halves, and each half was combined with the half of a Latin maniple, similarly divided, to form a new unit. The maniples were not, strictly speaking, doubled.

BOOK I. LII. 5–LIII. 4

juniors were commanded to present themselves at the grove of Ferentina on a certain day, armed and in full force, as the treaty prescribed. When they had assembled, agreeably to the king's edict, from the different districts, Tarquinius was unwilling that they should have their own leaders, or a separate command, or their own standards; he therefore mingled Latins and Romans in the maniples, making one maniple of two and two of one, and over the maniples thus doubled he put centurions.[1]

LIII. But if the king was unjust in peace, yet he was not a bad general in war. Indeed, he would have equalled in this art the kings who had gone before him, if his degeneracy in other things had not also dimmed his glory here. It was he who began the war with the Volsci which was to last more than two hundred years after his time, and took Suessa Pometia from them by storm. There, having sold oft the booty and raised forty talents of silver,[2] he conceived the project of a temple of Jupiter so magnificent that it should be worthy of the king of gods and men, the Roman empire, and the majesty of the site itself. The money from the captured city he put aside to build this temple.

He then engaged in an unexpectedly tedious war with Gabii, a neighbouring town. After first assaulting the place in vain, he laid siege to it, but this attempt was as unsuccessful as the other, for he was driven off from the walls; and he finally resorted to the policy, so unlike a Roman, of deceit

[2] As Livy gives the sum in talents, it has been suggested that he may here be following Fabius Pictor, whose history was written in Greek. The Euboic talent was worth roughly £220 or $1,060.

LIVY

5 ac dolo, adgressus est. Nam cum velut posito bello fundamentis templi iaciendis[1] aliisque urbanis operibus intentum se esse simularet, Sextus filius eius, qui minimus ex tribus erat, transfugit ex composito Gabios, patris in se saevitiam intolerabilem conque-
6 rens: iam ab alienis in suos vertisse superbiam, et liberorum quoque eum frequentiae taedere, ut quam in curia solitudinem fecerit domi quoque faciat, ne quam stirpem, ne quem heredem regni relinquat.
7 Se quidem inter tela et gladios patris elapsum nihil usquam sibi tutum nisi apud hostes L. Tarquini credidisse. Nam ne errarent, manere iis bellum quod positum simuletur, et per occasionem eum incautos
8 invasurum. Quod si apud eos supplicibus locus non sit, pererraturum se omne Latium, Volscosque inde[2] et Aequos et Hernicos petiturum, donec ad eos perveniat qui a patrum crudelibus atque impiis suppli-
9 ciis tegere liberos sciant. Forsitan etiam ardoris aliquid ad bellum armaque se adversus superbissimum regem ac ferocissimum populum inventurum.
10 Cum, si nihil morarentur, infensus ira porro inde abiturus videretur, benigne ab Gabinis excipitur. Vetant mirari si, qualis in cives, qualis in socios,
11 talis ad ultimum in liberos esset; in se ipsum post-

[1] iaciendis *Vacosanus* ϛ: faciendis Ω.
[2] inde *Gronov.*: se inde Ω.

BOOK I. LIII. 4-11

and trickery. For he pretended to have given up the war and to be engrossed in laying the foundations of his temple and in other city works, arranging meanwhile to let Sextus, who was the youngest of his three sons, desert to Gabii, and there complain that his father was intolerably cruel to him. His father's pride, he said, was now diverted from strangers upon his own family. Even his children were too many to please him, and the solitude which he had caused in the senate-house he wished to bring to pass in his own home also, that he might leave no descendant, no heir to his kingdom. The young man said that he had himself escaped from amidst the swords and javelins of his father, and had made up his mind that there was no safety for him anywhere save with the enemies of Lucius Tarquinius. Let them not delude themselves, he said; the war which the king pretended to have abandoned was still awaiting them, and when the chance offered he would attack them unawares. But if they had no room for suppliants, he was prepared to wander all over Latium, and thence seek out the Volsci and the Aequi and the Hernici, till at last he should come to people who knew how to protect a son from the cruel and wicked tortures inflicted on him by a father. Possibly he might even discover some enthusiasm for war and arms against the haughtiest of kings and the most insolent of nations. When it appeared that if they were indifferent he would leave them in anger and continue his flight, the Gabini bade him welcome. They told him not to be surprised if the king had been the same to his children that he had been to his subjects, to his allies; he would end by venting his cruelty upon

B.C. 534–510

LIVY

remo saeviturum, si alia desint. Sibi vero gratum adventum eius esse, futurumque credere brevi ut illo adiuvante a portis Gabinis sub Romana moenia bellum transferatur.

LIV. Inde in consilia publica adhiberi. Ubi cum de aliis rebus adsentiri se veteribus Gabinis diceret, quibus eae notiores essent, ipse identidem belli auctor esse et in[1] eo sibi praecipuam prudentiam adsumere, quod utriusque populi vires nosset sciretque invisam profecto superbiam regiam civibus esse, quam ferre ne liberi quidem potuis-
2 sent. Ita cum sensim ad rebellandum primores Gabinorum incitaret, ipse cum promptissimis iuvenum praedatum atque in expeditiones iret, et dictis factisque omnibus ad fallendum instructis vana ad-
3 cresceret fides, dux ad ultimum belli legitur. Ibi cum inscia multitudine quid ageretur proelia parva inter Romam Gabiosque fierent, quibus plerumque Gabina res superior esset, tum certatim summi infimique Gabinorum Sex. Tarquinium dono deum sibi
4 missum ducem credere. Apud milites vero obeundo pericula ac labores pariter, praedam munifice largiendo, tanta caritate esse ut non pater Tarquinius

esse et in *Alschefski*: esset in Ω.

himself if other objects failed him. But for their own part, they said, they were glad of his coming, and they believed that in a short time, with his help, the seat of war would be shifted from the gates of Gabii to the walls of Rome.

LIV. Sextus next obtained admission to the Gabian councils of state, where, on all subjects but one, he professed a deference for the opinion of those who had long been citizens of Gabii and were better acquainted with the facts. War, however, he did take it upon himself to urge, again and again; and in so doing he assumed a special competence, as one who was acquainted with the strength of both nations, and knew that the king's pride must necessarily be hateful to all the citizens, since even his children had not been able to put up with it. In this way, little by little, he stirred up the leaders of the Gabini to reopen the war. He would himself take the boldest of the young men and go upon raids and forays. All his words and acts were calculated to deceive, and their ill-grounded confidence so increased that in the end he was chosen commander-in-chief. The war began, and the people had no suspicion of what was going forward. Skirmishes took place between Rome and Gabii, in which, as a rule, the Gabini had the best of it. Thereupon their citizens, both high and low, contended who should be loudest in expressing the belief that in Sextus Tarquinius they had a heaven-sent leader. And the soldiers, seeing him ever ready to share in their dangers and hardships, and ever lavish in distributing the plunder, came to love him so devotedly that the elder Tarquinius was not more truly master

5 potentior Romae quam filius Gabiis esset. Itaque
postquam satis virium conlectum ad omnes conatus
videbat, tum ex suis unum sciscitatum Romam ad
patrem mittit quidnam se facere vellet, quandoqui-
dem ut omnia unus publice Gabiis[1] posset ei di
6 dedissent. Huic nuntio quia, credo, dubiae fidei
videbatur, nihil voce responsum est; rex velut deli-
berabundus in hortum aedium transit sequente nuntio filii; ibi inambulans tacitus summa papaverum
7 capita dicitur baculo decussisse. Interrogando ex-
spectandoque responsum nuntius fessus, ut re imper-
fecta, redit Gabios; quae dixerit ipse quaeque viderit
refert: seu ira, seu odio, seu superbia insita ingenio
8 nullam eum vocem emisisse. Sexto ubi quid vellet
parens quidve praeciperet tacitis ambagibus patuit,
primores civitatis criminando alios apud populum,
9 alios sua ipsos invidia opportunos interemit. Multi
palam, quidam, in quibus minus speciosa criminatio
erat futura, clam interfecti. Patuit quibusdam volen-
tibus fuga, aut in exsilium acti sunt, absentiumque
10 bona iuxta atque interemptorum divisui fuere. Lar-
gitiones inde praedaeque; et dulcedine privati commodi sensus malorum publicorum adimi, donec orba
consilio auxilioque Gabina res regi Romano sine ulla
dimicatione in manum traditur.

[1] publice Gabiis *Heerwagen*: $\bar{\text{P}}$ (*or* $\bar{\text{p}}$ *or* prae) Gabiis Ω:
p. Gabinis *PBFO*: populis Gabinis facere *U*.

in Rome than was his son in Gabii. And so, when Sextus saw that he had acquired strength enough for any enterprise, he despatched one of his own followers to his father in Rome, to ask what the king might please to have him do, since the gods had granted that at Gabii all power in the state should rest with him alone. To this messenger, I suppose because he seemed not quite to be trusted, no verbal reply was given. The king, as if absorbed in meditation, passed into the garden of his house, followed by his son's envoy. There, walking up and down without a word, he is said to have struck off the heads of the tallest poppies with his stick. Tired of asking questions and waiting for an answer, the messenger returned to Gabii, his mission, as he thought, unaccomplished. He reported what he had said himself and what he had seen. Whether from anger, or hatred, or native pride, the king, he said, had not pronounced a single word. As soon as it was clear to Sextus what his father meant and what was the purport of his silent hints, he rid himself of the chief men of the state. Some he accused before the people; against others he took advantage of the odium they had themselves incurred. Many were openly executed; some, whom it would not have looked well to accuse, were put to death in secret. Some were permitted, if they chose, to leave the country; or they were driven into banishment, and once out of the way, their property was forfeited, just as in the case of those who had been put to death. Thence came largesses and spoils, and in the sweetness of private gain men lost their feeling for the wrongs of the nation, until, deprived of counsel and aid, the state of Gabii was handed over unresisting to the Roman king.

LIVY

LV. Gabiis receptis Tarquinius pacem cum Aequorum gente fecit, foedus cum Tuscis renovavit. Inde ad negotia urbana animum convertit; quorum erat primum ut Iovis templum in monte Tarpeio monumentum regni sui nominisque relinqueret: Tarquinios 2 reges ambos patrem vovisse, filium perfecisse. Et ut libera a ceteris religionibus area esset tota Iovis templique eius quod inaedificaretur, exaugurare fana sacellaque statuit, quae aliquot ibi, a Tatio rege primum in ipso discrimine adversus Romulum pugnae 3 vota, consecrata inaugurataque postea fuerant. Inter principia condendi huius operis movisse numen ad indicandam tanti imperii molem traditur deos. Nam cum omnium sacellorum exaugurationes admitterent 4 aves, in Termini fano non addixere; idque omen auguriumque ita acceptum est, non motam Termini sedem unumque eum deorum non evocatum sacratis 5 sibi finibus firma stabiliaque cuncta portendere. Hoc perpetuitatis auspicio accepto secutum aliud magnitudinem imperii portendens prodigium est: caput humanum integra facie aperientibus fundamenta 6 templi dicitur apparuisse. Quae visa species haud per ambages arcem eam imperii caputque rerum fore portendebat, idque ita cecinere vates, quique in urbe

---

[1] *i.e.* the Capitoline. So Propertius calls the Capitoline Jupiter "Tarpeius Pater" (IV. i. 7).

BOOK I. LV. 1-6

LV. Having got possession of Gabii, Tarquinius made peace with the Aequian nation and renewed the treaty with the Etruscans. He next turned his attention to affairs in the city. Here his first concern was to build a temple of Jupiter on the Tarpeian Mount[1] to stand as a memorial of his reign and of his name, testifying that of the two Tarquinii, both kings, the father had made the vow and the son had fulfilled it. And that the site might be free from all other religious claims and belong wholly to Jupiter and his temple, which was building there, he determined to annul the consecration of several fanes and shrines which had been first vowed by King Tatius at the crisis of the battle against Romulus, and had afterwards been consecrated and inaugurated. At the very time when he began this task the gods are said to have exerted their power to show the magnitude of this mighty empire. For whereas the birds permitted that the consecrations of all the other shrines should be rescinded, they refused their consent for the shrine of Terminus. This omen and augury was thus construed: the fact that the seat of Terminus was not moved, and that of all the gods he alone was not called away from the place consecrated to him, meant that the whole kingdom would be firm and steadfast. When this auspice of permanence had been received, there followed another prodigy foretelling the grandeur of their empire. A human head, its features intact, was found, so it is said, by the men who were digging for the foundations of the temple. This appearance plainly foreshowed that here was to be the citadel of the empire and the head of the world, and such was the interpretation of the soothsayers, both those who were in

LIVY

erant quosque ad eam rem consultandam ex Etruria
acciverant. Augebatur ad impensas regis animus.
Itaque Pometinae[1] manubiae, quae perducendo ad
culmen operi destinatae erant, vix in fundamenta
suppeditavere. Eo magis Fabio, praeterquam quod
antiquior est, crediderim quadraginta ea sola talenta
fuisse, quam Pisoni, qui quadraginta milia pondo
argenti seposita in eam rem scribit, summam[2] pecuniae neque ex unius tum urbis praeda sperandam et
nullius ne horum quidem[3] operum fundamenta non
exsuperaturam.

LVI. Intentus perficiendo templo fabris undique
ex Etruria accitis non pecunia solum ad id publica
est usus, sed operis etiam ex plebe. Qui cum
haud parvus et ipse militiae adderetur labor, minus
tamen plebs gravabatur se templa deum exaedificare manibus suis quam[4] postquam et ad alia ut
specie minora, sic laboris aliquanto maioris traducebantur opera, foros in circo faciendos cloacamque
maximam, receptaculum omnium purgamentorum
urbis, sub terra agendam; quibus duobus operibus
vix nova haec magnificentia quicquam adaequare
potuit. His laboribus exercita plebe, quia et urbi
multitudinem, ubi usus non esset, oneri rebatur esse,
et colonis mittendis occupari latius imperii fines vole-

---

[1] Pometinae *D³Sabellicus* (*cf.* liii. 2): Pomptinae (*or* Promptinae *or* Pontinae) Ω.

[2] summam *Glareanus*: quia summam Ω: quippe summam *Bekker*.

[3] *After* quidem Ω *have* magnificentiae (-a *M*), *which Frigell expelled as a gloss from* lvi. 2.

[4] quam *Bekker*: quae (quem *O*: que *D*) Ω.

192

the City and those who were called in from Etruria to consider the matter. This made the king all the more ready to spend money on the work. Hence the Pometian spoils, which had been destined to carry the building up to the roof, barely sufficed for the foundations. This disposes me to believe the statement of Fabius (who is, besides, the earlier writer) that the spoils were only forty talents, rather than Piso's, who writes that forty thousand pounds of silver were put aside for this work. So great a sum of money could not be expected from the booty of a single city of that time, and there is no building, even among those of our own day, for the foundations of which it would not be more than enough.

LVI. Being intent upon completing the temple, the king called in workmen from every quarter of Etruria, and used for this purpose not only the state funds but labourers drawn from the commons. This work was far from light in itself, and was added to their military service. Yet the plebeians felt less abused at having to build with their own hands the temples of the gods, than they did when they came to be transferred to other tasks also, which, while less in show, were yet rather more laborious. I mean the erection of seats in the circus, and the construction underground of the Great Sewer, as a receptacle for all the offscourings of the City,—two works for which the new splendour of these days has scarcely been able to produce a match. After making the plebeians toil at these hard tasks, the king felt that a populace which had now no work to do was only a burden to the City; he wished, moreover, by sending out settlers, to extend the frontiers of his dominions.

LIVY

bat, Signiam Circeiosque colonos misit, praesidia urbi futura terra marique.

4 Haec agenti portentum terribile visum: anguis ex columna lignea elapsus cum terrorem fugamque in regia[1] fecisset, ipsius regis non tam subito pavore 5 perculit pectus, quam anxiis implevit curis. Itaque cum ad publica prodigia Etrusci tantum vates adhiberentur, hoc velut domestico exterritus visu Delphos ad maxime inclitum in terris oraculum mittere 6 statuit; neque responsa sortium ulli alii committere ausus duos filios per ignotas ea tempestate terras, 7 ignotiora maria in Graeciam misit. Titus et Arruns profecti. Comes iis additus L. Iunius Brutus Tarquinia sorore regis natus, iuvenis longe alius ingenii,[2] quam cuius simulationem induerat. Is cum primores civitatis, in quibus fratrem suum, ab avunculo interfectum audisset, neque in animo suo quicquam regi timendum neque in fortuna concupiscendum relinquere statuit, contemptuque tutus esse ubi in iure 8 parum praesidii esset. Ergo ex industria factus ad imitationem stultitiae, cum se suaque praedae esse regi sineret, Bruti quoque haud abnuit cognomen, ut sub eius obtentu cognominis liberator ille populi 9 Romani animus latens opperiretur tempora sua. Is tum[3] ab Tarquiniis ductus Delphos, ludibrium verius quam comes, aureum baculum inclusum corneo cavato

[1] regia *Bauer D*?: regiam Ω.
[2] ingenii *Madvig*: ingenio Ω.   [3] tum D_ς: cum Ω.

---

[1] Literally "Dullard."

194

He therefore sent colonists to Signia and Circei, to safeguard the City by land and sea.

While he was thus occupied, a terrible portent appeared. A snake glided out of a wooden pillar, causing fright and commotion in the palace. As for the king himself, his heart was not so much struck with sudden terror as filled with anxious forebodings. Now for public prodigies none but Etruscan soothsayers were wont to be employed, but this domestic apparition, as he regarded it, so thoroughly alarmed him that he determined to send to Delphi, the most famous oracle in the world; and, not daring to trust the oracle's reply to anybody else, he sent two of his sons, through strange lands, as they were then, and over stranger seas, to Greece. Titus and Arruns were the ones who went; and, to bear them company, Lucius Junius Brutus was sent too, the son of Tarquinia, sister of the king, a young man of a very different mind from that which he pretended to bear. Having heard that the leading men of the state, and among them his own brother, had been put to death by his uncle, he determined to leave nothing in his disposition which the king might justly fear, nor anything in his fortune to covet, resolving to find safety in contempt, where justice afforded no protection. He therefore deliberately assumed the appearance of stupidity, and permitted himself and his property to become the spoil of the king; he even accepted the surname Brutus,[1] that behind the screen afforded by this title the great soul which was to free the Roman People might bide its time unseen. He it was who was then taken by the Tarquinii to Delphi, more as a butt than as a comrade; and he is said to have carried a golden staff inclosed within one

LIVY

ad id baculo tulisse donum Apollini dicitur, per ambages effigiem ingenii sui. Quo postquam ventum est, perfectis patris mandatis cupido incessit animos iuvenum sciscitandi, ad quem eorum regnum Romanum esset venturum. Ex infimo specu vocem redditam ferunt, "Imperium summum Romae habebit, qui vestrum primus, o iuvenes, osculum matri tulerit." Tarquinii, ut[1] Sextus, qui Romae relictus fuerat, ignarus responsi expersque imperii esset, rem summa ope taceri iubent; ipsi inter se uter prior, cum Romam redisset, matri osculum daret, sorti permittunt. Brutus alio ratus spectare Pythicam vocem velut si prolapsus cecidisset terram osculo contigit, scilicet quod ea communis mater omnium mortalium esset. Reditum inde Romam, ubi adversus Rutulos bellum summa vi parabatur.

LVII. Ardeam Rutuli habebant, gens ut in ea regione atque in ea aetate divitiis praepollens. Eaque ipsa causa belli fuit, quod rex Romanus cum ipse ditari, exhaustus magnificentia publicorum operum, tum praeda delenire popularium animos studebat, praeter aliam superbiam regno infestos etiam quod se in fabrorum ministeriis ac servili tam diu habitos opere ab rege indignabantur. Temptata res est si primo impetu capi Ardea posset. Ubi id parum pro-

---

[1] Tarquinii, ut ς : Tarquinius Ω : Tarquinius SEX O.

BOOK I. LVI. 9–LVII. 3

of cornel wood, hollowed out to receive it, as a gift to Apollo, and a roundabout indication of his own character. When they came there, and had carried out their father's instructions, a desire sprang up in the hearts of the youths to find out which one of them should be king at Rome. From the depths of the cavern this answer, they say, was returned: "The highest power at Rome shall be his, young men, who shall be first among you to kiss his mother." The Tarquinii, anxious that Sextus, who had been left in Rome, might know nothing of the answer and have no share in the rule, gave orders that the incident should be kept strictly secret; as between themselves, they decided by lot which should be first, upon their return to Rome, to give their mother a kiss. Brutus thought the Pythian utterance had another meaning; pretending to stumble, he fell and touched his lips to Earth, evidently regarding her as the common mother of all mortals. They then returned to Rome, where preparations for war with the Rutuli were being pushed with the greatest vigour.

LVII. Ardea belonged to the Rutuli, who were a nation of commanding wealth, for that place and period. This very fact was the cause of the war, since the Roman king was eager not only to enrich himself, impoverished as he was by the splendour of his public works, but also to appease with booty the feeling of the common people; who, besides the enmity they bore the monarch for other acts of pride, were especially resentful that the king should have kept them employed so long as artisans and doing the work of slaves. An attempt was made to capture Ardea by assault. Having failed in this, the Romans invested

LIVY

A.U.C.
229-244

cessit, obsidione munitionibusque coepti premi hostes.
4 In his stativis, ut fit longo magis quam acri bello,
satis liberi commeatus erant, primoribus tamen magis
5 quam militibus; regii quidem iuvenes interdum
otium conviviis comisationibusque inter se terebant.
6 Forte potantibus his apud Sex. Tarquinium, ubi et
Collatinus cenabat Tarquinius Egerii filius, incidit de
uxoribus mentio; suam quisque laudare miris modis.
7 Inde certamine accenso Collatinus negat verbis opus
esse, paucis id quidem horis posse sciri, quantum
ceteris praestet Lucretia sua. "Quin, si vigor iuventae inest, conscendimus equos invisimusque prae-
sentes nostrarum ingenia? Id cuique spectatissimum
sit quod necopinato [1] viri adventu occurrerit oculis."
8 Incaluerant vino; "Age sane!" omnes; citatis
equis avolant Romam. Quo cum primis se inten-
9 dentibus tenebris pervenissent, pergunt inde Collatiam, ubi Lucretiam haudquaquam ut regias nurus,
quas in convivio luxuque cum aequalibus viderant
tempus terentes, sed nocte sera deditam lanae inter
lucubrantes ancillas in medio aedium sedentem inveniunt. Muliebris certaminis laus penes Lucretiam
10 fuit. Adveniens vir Tarquiniique excepti benigne;
victor maritus comiter invitat regios iuvenes. Ibi

[1] necopinato $R^2 \varsigma$: necinopinato (nec inopinato P) Ω : in
necopinato *Heerwagen*.

---

[1] A similar scene is imagined by Tibullus, I. iii. 83 ff.
(p. 211 of the volume in this series).

BOOK I. LVII. 3-10

the place with intrenchments, and began to beleaguer the enemy. Here in their permanent camp, as is usual with a war not sharp but long drawn out, furlough was rather freely granted, more freely however to the leaders than to the soldiers; the young princes for their part passed their idle hours together at dinners and drinking bouts. It chanced, as they were drinking in the quarters of Sextus Tarquinius, where Tarquinius Collatinus, son of Egerius, was also a guest, that the subject of wives came up. Every man fell to praising his own wife with enthusiasm, and, as their rivalry grew hot, Collatinus said that there was no need to talk about it, for it was in their power to know, in a few hours' time, how far the rest were excelled by his own Lucretia. "Come! If the vigour of youth is in us let us mount our horses and see for ourselves the disposition of our wives. Let every man regard as the surest test what meets his eyes when the woman's husband enters unexpected." They were heated with wine. "Agreed!" they all cried, and clapping spurs to their horses were off for Rome. Arriving there at early dusk, they thence proceeded to Collatia, where Lucretia was discovered very differently employed from the daughters-in-law of the king. These they had seen at a luxurious banquet, whiling away the time with their young friends; but Lucretia, though it was late at night, was busily engaged upon her wool, while her maidens toiled about her in the lamplight as she sat in the hall of her house.[1] The prize of this contest in womanly virtues fell to Lucretia. As Collatinus and the Tarquinii approached, they were graciously received, and the victorious husband courteously invited the young princes to his table. It was there

LIVY

Sex. Tarquinium mala libido Lucretiae per vim stuprandae capit; cum forma tum spectata castitas 11 incitat. Et tum quidem ab nocturno iuvenali ludo in castra redeunt.

LVIII. Paucis interiectis diebus Sex. Tarquinius inscio Collatino cum comite uno Collatiam venit 2 Ubi exceptus benigne ab ignaris consilii cum post cenam in hospitale cubiculum deductus esset, amore ardens, postquam satis tuta circa sopitique omnes videbantur, stricto gladio ad dormientem Lucretiam venit sinistraque manu mulieris pectore oppresso "Tace, Lucretia," inquit; "Sex. Tarquinius sum; ferrum in manu est; moriere, si emiseris vocem." 3 Cum pavida ex somno mulier nullam opem, prope mortem imminentem videret, tum Tarquinius fateri amorem, orare, miscere precibus minas, versare in 4 omnes partes muliebrem animum. Ubi obstinatam videbat et ne mortis quidem metu inclinari, addit ad metum dedecus: cum mortua iugulatum servum nudum positurum ait, ut in sordido adulterio necata 5 dicatur. Quo terrore cum vicisset obstinatam pudicitiam velut vi victrix[1] libido, profectusque inde Tarquinius ferox expugnato decore muliebri esset, Lucretia maesta tanto malo nuntium Romam eundem ad patrem Ardeamque ad virum mittit, ut cum sin-

---

[1] velut vi victrix *M. Mueller*: uelut uictrix Ω.

BOOK I. LVII. 10–LVIII. 5

that Sextus Tarquinius was seized with a wicked desire to debauch Lucretia by force; not only her beauty, but her proved chastity as well, provoked him. However, for the present they ended the boyish prank of the night and returned to the camp.

LVIII. When a few days had gone by, Sextus Tarquinius, without letting Collatinus know, took a single attendant and went to Collatia. Being kindly welcomed, for no one suspected his purpose, he was brought after dinner to a guest-chamber. Burning with passion, he waited till it seemed to him that all about him was secure and everybody fast asleep; then, drawing his sword, he came to the sleeping Lucretia. Holding the woman down with his left hand on her breast, he said, "Be still, Lucretia! I am Sextus Tarquinius. My sword is in my hand. Utter a sound, and you die!" In affright the woman started out of her sleep. No help was in sight, but only imminent death. Then Tarquinius began to declare his love, to plead, to mingle threats with prayers, to bring every resource to bear upon her woman's heart. When he found her obdurate and not to be moved even by fear of death, he went farther and threatened her with disgrace, saying that when she was dead he would kill his slave and lay him naked by her side, that she might be said to have been put to death in adultery with a man of base condition. At this dreadful prospect her resolute modesty was overcome, as if with force, by his victorious lust; and Tarquinius departed, exulting in his conquest of a woman's honour. Lucretia, grieving at her great disaster, dispatched the same message to her father in Rome and to her husband at Ardea:

LIVY

gulis fidelibus amicis veniant; ita facto maturatoque 6 opus esse; rem atrocem incidisse. Sp. Lucretius cum P. Valerio Volesi filio, Collatinus cum L. Iunio Bruto venit, cum quo forte Romam rediens ab nuntio uxoris erat conventus. Lucretiam sedentem maes- 7 tam in cubiculo inveniunt. Adventu suorum lacrimae obortae, quaerentique viro "Satin salve?"[1] "Minime," inquit; "quid enim salvi est mulieri amissa pudicitia? Vestigia viri alieni, Collatine, in lecto sunt tuo; ceterum corpus est tantum violatum, animus insons; mors testis erit. Sed date dextras 8 fidemque haud inpune adultero fore. Sex. est Tarquinius, qui hostis pro hospite priore nocte vi armatus mihi sibique, si vos viri estis, pestiferum hinc 9 abstulit gaudium." Dant ordine omnes fidem; consolantur aegram animi avertendo noxam ab coacta in auctorem delicti: mentem peccare, non corpus, et 10 unde consilium afuerit, culpam abesse. "Vos," inquit, "videritis, quid illi debeatur: ego me etsi peccato absolvo, supplicio non libero; nec ulla deinde 11 inpudica Lucretiae exemplo vivet." Cultrum, quem sub veste abditum habebat, eum in corde defigit pro- 12 lapsaque in volnus moribunda cecidit. Conclamat vir paterque.

[1] salve Ω : saluae R.

BOOK I. LVIII. 5-12

that they should each take a trusty friend and come; that they must do this and do it quickly, for a frightful thing had happened. Spurius Lucretius came with Publius Valerius, Volesus' son. Collatinus brought Lucius Junius Brutus, with whom he chanced to be returning to Rome when he was met by the messenger from his wife. Lucretia they found sitting sadly in her chamber. The entrance of her friends brought the tears to her eyes, and to her husband's question, "Is all well?" she replied, "Far from it; for what can be well with a woman when she has lost her honour? The print of a strange man, Collatinus, is in your bed. Yet my body only has been violated; my heart is guiltless, as death shall be my witness. But pledge your right hands and your words that the adulterer shall not go unpunished. Sextus Tarquinius is he that last night returned hostility for hospitality, and armed with force brought ruin on me, and on himself no less—if you are men—when he worked his pleasure with me." They give their pledges, every man in turn. They seek to comfort her, sick at heart as she is, by diverting the blame from her who was forced to the doer of the wrong. They tell her it is the mind that sins, not the body; and that where purpose has been wanting there is no guilt. "It is for you to determine," she answers, "what is due to him; for my own part, though I acquit myself of the sin, I do not absolve myself from punishment; not in time to come shall ever unchaste woman live through the example of Lucretia." Taking a knife which she had concealed beneath her dress, she plunged it into her heart, and sinking forward upon the wound, died as she fell. The wail for the dead was raised by her husband and her father.

LIVY

LIX. Brutus illis luctu occupatis cultrum ex volnere Lucretiae extractum manantem[1] cruore prae se tenens, "Per hunc," inquit, "castissimum ante regiam iniuriam sanguinem iuro, vosque, di, testes facio, me L. Tarquinium Superbum cum scelerata coniuge et omni liberorum stirpe ferro, igni, quacumque denique[2] vi possim, exsecuturum nec illos nec alium quemquam regnare Romae passurum."
2 Cultrum deinde Collatino tradit, inde Lucretio ac Valerio, stupentibus miraculo rei, unde novum in Bruti pectore ingenium. Ut praeceptum erat iurant; totique ab luctu versi in iram, Brutum iam inde ad expugnandum regnum vocantem sequuntur ducem.
3 Elatum domo Lucretiae corpus in forum deferunt concientque miraculo, ut fit, rei novae atque indigni-
4 tate homines. Pro se quisque scelus regium ac vim queruntur. Movet cum patris[3] maestitia, tum Brutus castigator lacrimarum atque inertium querellarum auctorque quod viros, quod Romanos deceret, arma
5 capiendi adversus hostilia ausos. Ferocissimus quisque iuvenum cum armis voluntarius adest; sequitur et cetera iuventus. Inde patre praeside relicto Collatiae[4] custodibusque datis, ne quis eum motum regibus nuntiaret, ceteri armati duce Bruto Romam
6 profecti. Ubi eo ventum est, quacumque incedit

[1] manantem *O𝑆* : manante Ω.
[2] denique *Madvig* : dehinc (die hinc *O*) Ω.
[3] patris *R²𝑆* : patres (patre *R*) Ω.
[4] patre praeside relicto Collatiae [ad portas] *Walters*: patri paris (*or* pari *or* pars *or* paris) praesidio relicto Collatiae ad portas Ω.

204

LIX. Brutus, while the others were absorbed in grief, drew out the knife from Lucretia's wound, and holding it up, dripping with gore, exclaimed, "By this blood, most chaste until a prince wronged it, I swear, and I take you, gods, to witness, that I will pursue Lucius Tarquinius Superbus and his wicked wife and all his children, with sword, with fire, aye with whatsoever violence I may; and that I will suffer neither them nor any other to be king in Rome!" The knife he then passed to Collatinus, and from him to Lucretius and Valerius. They were dumbfounded at this miracle. Whence came this new spirit in the breast of Brutus? As he bade them, so they swore. Grief was swallowed up in anger; and when Brutus summoned them to make war from that very moment on the power of the kings, they followed his lead. They carried out Lucretia's corpse from the house and bore it to the market-place, where men crowded about them, attracted, as they were bound to be, by the amazing character of the strange event and its heinousness. Every man had his own complaint to make of the prince's crime and his violence. They were moved, not only by the father's sorrow, but by the fact that it was Brutus who chid their tears and idle lamentations and urged them to take up the sword, as befitted men and Romans, against those who had dared to treat them as enemies. The boldest of the young men seized their weapons and offered themselves for service, and the others followed their example. Then, leaving Lucretia's father to guard Collatia, and posting sentinels so that no one might announce the rising to the royal family, the rest, equipped for battle and with Brutus in command, set out for Rome. Once there, wherever their armed

LIVY

armata multitudo pavorem ac tumultum facit; rursus ubi anteire primores civitatis vident, quidquid sit haud temere esse rentur. Nec minorem motum animorum Romae tam atrox res facit quam Collatiae fecerat. Ergo ex omnibus locis urbis in forum curritur. Quo simul ventum est, praeco ad tribunum celerum, in quo tum magistratu forte Brutus erat, populum advocavit. Ibi oratio habita nequaquam eius pectoris ingeniique quod simulatum ad eam diem fuerat, de vi ac libidine Sex. Tarquini, de stupro infando Lucretiae et miserabili caede, de orbitate Tricipitini, cui morte filiae causa mortis indignior ac miserabilior esset. Addita superbia ipsius regis miseriaeque et labores plebis in fossas cloacasque exhauriendas demersae; Romanos homines, victores omnium circa populorum, opifices ac lapicidas pro bellatoribus factos. Indigna Ser. Tulli regis memorata caedes et invecta corpori patris nefando vehiculo filia, invocatique ultores parentum di. His atrocioribusque, credo, aliis, quae praesens rerum indignitas haudquaquam relatu scriptoribus facilia subicit, memoratis incensam multitudinem perpulit ut imperium regi abrogaret exsulesque esse iuberet L. Tarquinium cum coniuge ac liberis. Ipse iunio-

---

[1] For the *Celeres*, see xv. 8 and note. H. J. Edwards (*ad loc.*) thinks that the office comprised both military and civil functions—the command of the cavalry (*cf.* the *Magister Equitum* in republican times) and the presidency (as deputy of the king) of comitia and senate.

band advanced it brought terror and confusion; but again, when people saw that in the van were the chief men of the state, they concluded that whatever it was it could be no meaningless disturbance. And in fact there was no less resentment at Rome when this dreadful story was known than there had been at Collatia. So from every quarter of the City men came running to the Forum. No sooner were they there than a crier summoned the people before the Tribune of the Celeres,[1] which office Brutus then happened to be holding. There he made a speech by no means like what might have been expected of the mind and the spirit which he had feigned up to that day. He spoke of the violence and lust of Sextus Tarquinius, of the shameful defilement of Lucretia and her deplorable death, of the bereavement of Tricipitinus, in whose eyes the death of his daughter was not so outrageous and deplorable as was the cause of her death. He reminded them, besides, of the pride of the king himself and the wretched state of the commons, who were plunged into ditches and sewers and made to clear them out. The men of Rome, he said, the conquerors of all the nations round about, had been transformed from warriors into artisans and stone-cutters. He spoke of the shameful murder of King Tullius, and how his daughter had driven her accursed chariot over her father's body, and he invoked the gods who punish crimes against parents. With these and, I fancy, even fiercer reproaches, such as occur to a man in the very presence of an outrage, but are far from easy for an historian to reproduce, he inflamed the people, and brought them to abrogate the king's authority and to exile Lucius Tarquinius, together with his wife and children. Brutus himself then enrolled the juniors, who

LIVY

ribus, qui ultro nomina dabant, lectis armatisque ad concitandum inde adversus regem exercitum Ardeam in castra est profectus: imperium in urbe Lucretio, praefecto urbis iam ante ab rege instituto, relinquit. 13 Inter hunc tumultum Tullia domo profugit exsecrantibus, quacumque incedebat, invocantibusque parentum furias viris mulieribusque.

LX. Harum rerum nuntiis in castra perlatis cum re nova trepidus rex pergeret Romam ad comprimendos motus, flexit viam Brutus—senserat enim adventum—ne obvius fieret; eodemque fere tempore diversis itineribus Brutus Ardeam, Tarquinius Romam 2 venerunt. Tarquinio clausae portae exsiliumque indictum: liberatorem urbis laeta castra accepere, exactique inde liberi regis. Duo patrem secuti sunt, qui exsulatum Caere in Etruscos ierunt. Sex. Tarquinius Gabios tamquam in suum regnum profectus ab ultoribus veterum simultatium, quas sibi ipse caedibus rapinisque concierat,[1] est interfectus.

3 L. Tarquinius Superbus regnavit annos quinque et viginti.[2] Regnatum Romae ab condita urbe ad 4 liberatam annos ducentos quadraginta quattuor. Duo consules inde comitiis centuriatis a praefecto urbis ex commentariis Ser. Tulli creati sunt, L. Iunius Brutus et L. Tarquinius Collatinus.

[1] concierat *M* : conciuerat *HRDL* : concitauerat Ω.
[2] quinque et viginti *M* : V et XL Ω.

---

[1] The "consuls," as they were called from the time of the Decemvirate, were originally designated "praetors"; Livy is anachronistic. The "centuriate comitia" was the assembly of the people by centuries, as classified by Servius, primarily for military ends. It is more likely that Lucretius presided

208

BOOK I. LIX. 12–LX. 4

voluntarily gave in their names, and arming them set out for the camp at Ardea to arouse the troops against the king. The command at Rome he left with Lucretius, who had been appointed Prefect of the City by the king, some time before. During this confusion Tullia fled from her house, cursed wherever she went by men and women, who called down upon her the furies that avenge the wrongs of kindred.

LX. When the news of these events reached the camp, the king, in alarm at the unexpected danger, set out for Rome to put down the revolt. Brutus, who had perceived the king's approach, made a circuit to avoid meeting him, and at almost the same moment, though by different roads, Brutus reached Ardea and Tarquinius Rome. Against Tarquinius the gates were closed and exile was pronounced. The liberator of the City was received with rejoicings in the camp, and the sons of the king were driven out of it. Two of them followed their father, and went into exile at Caere, in Etruria. Sextus Tarquinius departed for Gabii, as though it had been his own kingdom, and there the revengers of old quarrels, which he had brought upon himself by murder and rapine, slew him.

Lucius Tarquinius Superbus ruled for five and twenty years. The rule of the kings at Rome, from its foundation to its liberation, lasted two hundred and forty-four years. Two consuls were then chosen in the centuriate comitia, under the presidency of the Prefect of the City, in accordance with the commentaries of Servius Tullius.[1] These were Lucius Junius Brutus and Lucius Tarquinius Collatinus.

over the election in the capacity of interrex (to which office Dion. iv. 84 says Lucretius was appointed by Brutus) than in that of prefect.

LIBRI I PERIOCHA

A. ADVENTUS Aeneae in Italiam et res gestae. Ascani regnum Albae et deinceps Silviorum. Numitoris filia a Marte compressa nati Romulus et Remus. Amulius obtruncatus. Urbs a Romulo condita. Senatus lectus. Cum Sabinis bellatum. Spolia opima Feretrio Iovi lata. In curias[1] populus divisus. Fidenates, Veientes victi. Romulus consecratus.

Numa Pompilius ritus sacrorum tradidit. Porta Iani clausa.

Tullus Hostilius Albanos diripuit. Trigeminorum pugna. Metti Fufeti supplicium. Tullus fulmine consumptus.

Ancus Marcius Latinos devicit, Ostiam condidit.

Tarquinius Priscus Latinos superavit, circum fecit, finitimos devicit, muros et cloacas fecit.

Servio Tullio caput arsit. Servius Tullius Veientes devicit et populum in classes divisit, aedem Dianae dedicavit.

Tarquinius Superbus occiso Tullio regnum invasit. Tulliae scelus in patrem. Turnus Herdonius per Tarquinium occisus. Bellum cum Vulscis. Fraude Sex. Tarquini Gabi direpti.[2] Capitolium inchoatum. Termonis[3] et Iuventae arae moveri non potuerunt. Lucretia se occidit. Superbi expulsio. Regnatum est annis CCLV.

---

[1] curias *Sigonius*: centurias *MSS.*
[2] direpti *MSS.*: (Gabini) recepti *Kornemann.*
[3] Termonis *Pithoeus* (*cf. Ennius, An.* 479 *f.* ; *Plut. Numa,* 16 ; *Dion. Hal.* iii. 69): cremonae *MSS.* (*over which* in *C is written* vel termine).

SUMMARY OF BOOK I

A. Arrival of Aeneas in Italy and his deeds. Reign of Ascanius, and after him of the Silvii, at Alba. Romulus and Remus born to Mars by the daughter of Numitor. Amulius killed. The City founded by Romulus. The senate chosen. War with the Sabines. *Spolia opima* dedicated to Jupiter Feretrius. The people divided into wards. The Fidenates and Veientes conquered. Romulus deified.

Numa Pompilius handed on religious rites. The door of Janus's temple closed.

Tullus Hostilius ravaged the country of the Albans. Battle of the triplets. Punishment of Mettius Fufetius. Tullus slain by a thunderbolt.

Ancus Martius conquered the Latins; founded Ostia.

Tarquinius Priscus defeated the Latins; made a circus; conquered the neighbouring peoples; built walls and sewers.

The head of Servius Tullius gave forth flames. Servius Tullius conquered the Veientes and divided the people into classes; dedicated a temple to Diana.

Tarquinius Superbus slew Tullius and seized the kingship. Tullia's crime against her father. Turnus Herdonius killed by the machinations of Tarquinius. War with the Volsci. Gabii sacked,[1] in consequence of the fraud of Sextus Tarquinius. The Capitol commenced. The altars of Termo and Juventa could not be moved.[2] Lucretia slew herself. Expulsion of Superbus. The kings reigned 255 years.[3]

---

[1] According to Livy (liv. 10), Gabii was not sacked, but passed peacefully into the hands of Tarquinius. See critical note.

[2] In Livy (lv. 3) Juventa is not mentioned, and Termo appears in the form Terminus.

[3] Livy (lx. 3) says 244 years.

LIVY

B. Latinis victis montem Aventinum adsignavit, fines protulit, Hostiam coloniam deduxit, caerimonias a Numa institutas renovavit.

Hic temptandae scientiae Atti Navi auguris causa fertur consuluisse eum, an id de quo cogitaret effici posset; quod cum ille fieri posse dixisset, iussisse eum novacula cotem praecidere, idque ab Atto protinus factum.

Regnavit annis XXIIII. Eo regnante Lucumo, Demarati Corinthi filius, a Tarquinis, Etrusca civitate, Romam venit et in amicitiam Anci receptus Tarquini Prisci nomen ferre coepit et post mortem Anci regnum excepit. Centum in patres allegit, Latinos subegit, ludos in circo edidit, equitum centurias ampliavit, urbem muro circumdedit, cloacas fecit.[1] Occisus est ab Anci filiis, cum regnasset annis XXXVIII.

Successit ei Servius Tullius, natus ex captiva nobili Corniculana, cui puero athuc in cunis posito caput arsisse traditum erat. Is censum primum egit, lustrum condidit, quo censa LXXX milia esse dicuntur, pomerium protulit, colles urbi adiecit Quirinalem, Viminalem, Aesquilinum, templum Dianae cum Latinis in Aventino fecit. Interfectus est a Lucio Tarquinio, Prisci filio, consilio filiae uae Tulliae, cum regnasset annis XLIIII.

Post hunc L. Tarquinius Superbus neque patrum neque populi iussu regnum invasit. Is armatos circa se in custodiam sui habuit. Bellum cum Vulscis gessit et ex spoliis eorum templum in Capitolio Iovi fecit. Gabios dolo in potestatem suam[2] redegit. Huius filiis Delphos profectis et consulentibus quis eorum Romae regnaturus

---

[1] Rossbach brackets this paragraph from *Regnavit* to *fecit.*
[2] potestatem suam *edd.*: potestate sua *MSS.*

SUMMARY OF BOOK I

B. Having beaten the Latins,[1] he assigned them the Aventine Hill; planted a colony at Ostia; extended the boundaries and revived the ceremonies established by Numa.

It was he who is said to have asked the augur, Attus Navius, to test his skill, whether the thing he was thinking of could be accomplished and, when Attus replied that it could, to have bid him cut a whetstone in two with a razor. Attus is said forthwith to have done.

He reigned 24 years. In his reign Lucumo, son of the Corinthian Demaratus, came from Tarquinii, an Etruscan city, to Rome, and being received into the friendship of Ancus began to bear the name of Tarquinius Priscus, and after the death of Ancus succeeded to the kingship. He added a hundred members to the senate; subjugated the Latins; gave games in the circus; increased the centuries of knights; surrounded the city with a wall; made sewers. He was killed by the sons of Ancus after ruling 38 years.

His successor was Servius Tullius, son of a noblewoman, a captive from Corniculum. It is related that when he was still a babe, lying in the cradle, his head burst into flames. He conducted the first census and closed the lustrum, and it is said that 80,000 were assessed. He enlarged the pomerium; added to the city the Quirinal, Viminal, and Esquiline Hills; and with the Latins erected a temple to Diana on the Aventine. He was killed by Lucius Tarquinius, son of Priscus, on the advice of his own daughter Tullia, after reigning 44 years.

After him Lucius Tarquinius Superbus seized the kingdom, without the authorization of either Fathers or People. He kept armed men about him to protect him. He waged war with the Volsci, and out of their spoils built a temple to Jupiter on the Capitol. He brought Gabii under his sway by guile. When his sons had gone to Delphi and were consulting the oracle as to which of

---

[1] *i.e.* Ancus.

LIVY

esset, dictum est eum regnaturum qui primum matrem osculatus esset. Quod responsum cum ipsi aliter interpretarentur, Iunius Brutus, qui cum his profectus erat, prolapsum se simulavit et terram osculatus est; idque factum eius eventus conprobavit. Nam cum inpotenter se gerendo Tarquinius Superbus omnes in odium sui adduxisset, ad ultimum propter expugnatam nocturna vi a Sexto filio eius Lucretiae pudicitiam, quae ad se vocato patre Tricipitino et viro Collatino obtestata ne inulta mors eius esset cultro se interfecit, Bruti opera maxime expulsus est, cum regnasset annos XXV. Tum consules primi creati sunt L. Iunius Brutus L. Tarquinius Collatinus.

SUMMARY OF BOOK I

them should be king in Rome, answer was made that he should reign who should first kiss his mother. This response the princes themselves explained otherwise, but Junius Brutus, who had accompanied them, pretended to fall upon his face, and kissed the earth. And the outcome sanctioned his act. For when Tarquinius Superbus had brought all men to hate him by the violence of his behaviour, and finally Lucretia, whose chastity had been violated at night by the king's son Sextus, summoned her father Tricipitinus and her husband Collatinus and, adjuring them not to leave her death unavenged, killed herself with a knife, Tarquinius was expelled, chiefly through the efforts of Brutus, after a reign of 25 years. Then the first consuls were chosen, **Lucius Junius Brutus** and **Lucius Tarquinius Collatinus.**

BOOK II

LIBER II

I. Liberi iam hinc populi Romani res pace belloque gestas, annuos magistratus, imperiaque legum potentiora quam hominum peragam. Quae libertas ut laetior esset proxumi regis superbia fecerat. Nam priores ita regnarunt ut haud immerito omnes deinceps conditores partium certe urbis, quas novas ipsi sedes ab se auctae multitudinis addiderunt, numerentur. Neque ambigitur quin Brutus idem qui tantum gloriae Superbo exacto rege meruit pessimo publico id facturus fuerit, si libertatis immaturae cupidine priorum regum alicui regnum extorsisset. Quid enim futurum fuit, si illa pastorum convenarumque plebs, transfuga ex suis populis, sub tutela inviolati templi aut libertatem aut certe impunitatem adepta, soluta regio metu, agitari coepta esset tribuniciis procellis et in aliena urbe cum patribus serere certamina, priusquam pignera coniugum ac liberorum caritasque ipsius soli, cui longo tempore adsuescitur, animos eorum consociasset? Dissipatae res nondum adultae discordia forent, quas fovit tranquilla moderatio imperii, eoque nutriendo perduxit

---

[1] This statement is too sweeping, for Livy nowhere attributes any enlargement of the City to Numa.

BOOK II

I. The new liberty enjoyed by the Roman people, their achievements in peace and war, annual magistracies, and laws superior in authority to men will henceforth be my theme. This liberty was the more grateful as the last king had been so great a tyrant. For his predecessors so ruled that there is good reason to regard them all as successive founders of parts, at least, of the City, which they added to serve as new homes for the numbers they had themselves recruited.[1] Nor is there any doubt that the same Brutus who earned such honour by expelling the haughty Tarquinius, would have acted in an evil hour for the commonwealth had a premature eagerness for liberty led him to wrest the power from any of the earlier kings. For what would have happened if that rabble of shepherds and vagrants, having deserted their own peoples, and under the protection of inviolable sanctuary having possessed themselves of liberty, or at least impunity, had thrown off their fear of kings only to be stirred by the ruffling storms of tribunician demagogues, breeding quarrels with the senators of a city not their own, before ever the pledges of wife and children and love of the very place and soil (an affection of slow growth) had firmly united their aspirations? The nation would have crumbled away with dissension before it had matured. But it was favoured by the mild restraint of the government, which nursed it up to the point

LIVY

ut bonam frugem libertatis maturis iam viribus ferre
possent. Libertatis autem originem inde magis quia
annuum imperium consulare factum est quam quod
deminutum quicquam sit ex regia potestate, numeres.
Omnia iura, omnia insignia primi consules tenuere;
id modo cautum est ne, si ambo fasces haberent,
duplicatus terror videretur. Brutus prior concedente
collega fasces habuit; qui non acrior vindex libertatis
fuerat quam deinde custos fuit. Omnium primum
avidum novae libertatis populum, ne postmodum
flecti precibus aut donis regiis posset, iure iurando
adegit neminem Romae passuros regnare. Deinde,
quo plus virium in senatu frequentia etiam ordinis
faceret, caedibus regis deminutum patrum numerum
primoribus equestris gradus lectis ad trecentorum
summam explevit; traditumque inde fertur ut in
senatum vocarentur qui patres quique conscripti
essent: conscriptos, videlicet novum senatum, appellabant lectos. Id mirum quantum profuit ad
concordiam civitatis iungendosque patribus plebis
animos.

II. Rerum deinde divinarum habita cura; et quia
quaedam publica sacra per ipsos reges factitata erant,

---

[1] Later any senator might be called *pater conscriptus*, and
it is possible that Livy and Festus (p. 254 M) were misled in
supposing that originally the *patres* were one class of senators and the *conscripti* another. See Conway's note.

[2] Livy appears to have assumed that the new senators
were plebeians, but this is almost certainly wrong. The first

BOOK II. i. 6–ii. 1

where its ripened powers enabled it to bear good fruit of liberty. Moreover you may reckon the beginning of liberty as proceeding rather from the limitation of the consuls' authority to a year than from any diminution of their power compared with that which the kings had exercised. All the rights of the kings and all their insignia were possessed by the earliest consuls; only one thing was guarded against—that the terror they inspired should not be doubled by permitting both to have the rods. Brutus was the first to have them, with his colleague's consent, and he proved as determined in guarding liberty as he had been in asserting it. To begin with, when the people were still jealous of their new freedom, he obliged them to swear an oath that they would suffer no man to be king in Rome, lest they might later be turned from their purpose by the entreaties or the gifts of princes. In the next place, that the strength of the senate might receive an added augmentation from the numbers of that order, he filled up the list of the Fathers, which had been abridged by the late king's butcheries, drawing upon the foremost men of equestrian rank until he had brought the total up to three hundred. From that time, it is said, was handed down the custom of summoning to the senate the Fathers and the Enrolled, the latter being the designation of the new senators, who were appointed.[1] This measure was wonderfully effective in promoting harmony in the state and attaching the plebs to the Fathers.[2]

II. Matters of worship then received attention. Certain public sacrifices had habitually been performed by the kings in person, and that their

definite notice of a plebeian senator occurs at v. xii. 11 (400 B.C.).

LIVY

necubi regum desiderium esset, regem sacrificolum
2 creant. Id sacerdotium pontifici subiecere, ne additus nomini honos aliquid libertati, cuius tunc prima erat cura, officeret. Ac nescio an nimis undique eam minimisque rebus muniendo modum excesserint.
3 Consulis enim alterius, cum nihil aliud offenderet,[1] nomen invisum civitati fuit: nimium Tarquinios regno adsuesse; initium a Prisco factum: regnasse dein Ser. Tullium; ne intervallo quidem facto oblitum, tamquam alieni, regni Superbum Tarquinium velut hereditatem gentis scelere ac vi repetisse; pulso Superbo penes Collatinum imperium esse; nescire
4 Tarquinios privatos vivere. Non placere nomen, periculosum libertati esse. Hic[2] primo sensim temptantium animos sermo per totam civitatem est datus, sollicitamque suspicione plebem Brutus ad contionem
5 vocat. Ibi omnium primum ius iurandum populi recitat neminem regnare passuros nec esse Romae unde periculum libertati foret. Id summa ope tuendum esse neque ullam rem quae eo pertineat contemnendam. Invitum se dicere, hominis causa, nec dicturum fuisse ni caritas rei publicae vinceret: non
6 credere populum Romanum solidam libertatem reciperatam esse; regium genus, regium nomen non

[1] offenderet *Bauer*: offenderit Ω.   [2] hic *Gruter*: hinc Ω.

BOOK II. ii. 1-6

absence might nowhere be regretted, a "king of sacrifices" was appointed. This priesthood they made subordinate to the pontifex, lest the office, in conjunction with the title, might somehow prove an obstacle to liberty, which was at that time their chief concern. Perhaps the pains they took to safeguard it, even in trivial details, may have been excessive. For the name of one of the consuls, though he gave no other offence, was hateful to the citizens. "The Tarquinii had become too used to sovereignty. It had begun with Priscus; Servius Tullius had then been king; but not even this interruption had caused Tarquinius Superbus to forget the throne or regard it as another's; as though it had been the heritage of his family, he had used crime and violence to get it back; Superbus was now expelled, but the supreme power was in the hands of Collatinus. The Tarquinii knew not how to live as private citizens. Their name was irksome and a menace to liberty." Beginning in this way, with a cautious sounding of sentiment, the talk spread through the entire nation, and the plebs had become anxious and suspicious, when Brutus summoned them to an assembly. There he first of all recited the oath which the people had taken, that they would suffer no king in Rome, nor any man who might be dangerous to liberty. This oath they must uphold, he said, with all their might, nor make light of anything which bore upon it. He spoke with reluctance, on the man's account, nor would he have broken silence unless he had been forced to do so by his love of country. The Roman people did not believe that they had recovered absolute freedom. The royal family, the royal name

LIVY

solum in civitate sed etiam in imperio esse; id offi-
cere, id obstare libertati. "Hunc tu," inquit, "tua
voluntate, L. Tarquini, remove metum. Memini-
mus, fatemur, eiecisti reges; absolve beneficium
tuum, aufer hinc regium nomen. Res tuas tibi non
solum reddent cives tui auctore me, sed, si quid
deest, munifice augebunt. Amicus abi; exonera
civitatem vano forsitan metu; ita persuasum est
animis, cum gente Tarquinia regnum hinc abiturum." Consuli primo tam novae rei ac subitae
admiratio incluserat vocem; dicere deinde incipien-
tem primores civitatis circumsistunt, eadem multis
precibus orant. Et ceteri quidem movebant minus:
postquam Sp. Lucretius, maior aetate ac dignitate,
socer praeterea ipsius, agere varie rogando alternis
suadendoque coepit, ut vinci se consensu civitatis
pateretur, timens consul ne postmodum privato sibi
eadem illa cum bonorum amissione additaque alia
insuper ignominia acciderent, abdicavit se consulatu
rebusque suis omnibus Lavinium translatis civitate
cessit. Brutus ex senatus consulto ad populum
tulit ut omnes Tarquiniae gentis exsules essent.
Collegam sibi comitiis centuriatis creavit P. Valerium, quo adiutore reges eiecerat.

were not only present in the state, but were actually in authority, an obstacle and a stumbling-block in the way of liberty. "This fear," he cried, "do you yourself remove, Lucius Tarquinius, of your own free will! We are mindful—we confess it—that you drove out the kings; complete the good work you have begun, and rid us of the royal name. Your possessions shall not only be granted you by the citizens, at my instance, but if they are in any way inadequate they shall be generously increased. Depart our friend, and relieve the state of what is, perhaps, an idle fear. The people are persuaded that with the family of Tarquinius the kingship will vanish from amongst us." The consul was at first prevented from uttering a word by his astonishment at this strange and unexpected turn; then, when he tried to speak, the chief men of the state surrounded him, and with many entreaties made the same request. The others had little influence over him, but when Spurius Lucretius, his superior in years and dignity, and his father-in-law besides, began to urge him, with mingled entreaty and advice, to permit himself to yield to the unanimous wish of his fellow-citizens, Collatinus became alarmed lest when his year of office should have ended, his misfortunes might be increased by the confiscation of his property and the addition of yet other ignominies. He therefore resigned the consulship, and transferring all his possessions to Lavinium, withdrew from the Roman state. In pursuance of a resolution of the senate, Brutus proposed to the people a measure which decreed the exile of all the Tarquinian race. To be his colleague the centuriate comitia, under his presidency, elected Publius Valerius, who had helped him to expel the kings.

LIVY

III. Cum haud cuiquam in dubio esset bellum ab Tarquiniis imminere, id quidem spe omnium serius fuit; ceterum, id quod non timebant, per dolum ac 2 proditionem prope libertas amissa est. Erant in Romana iuventute adulescentes aliquot, nec ii tenui loco orti, quorum in regno libido solutior fuerat, aequales sodalesque adulescentium Tarquiniorum, 3 adsueti more regio vivere. Eam tum aequato iure omnium licentiam quaerentes, libertatem aliorum in suam vertisse servitutem inter se conquerebantur: regem hominem esse, a quo impetres, ubi ius, ubi iniuria opus sit; esse gratiae locum, esse beneficio, et irasci et ignoscere posse, inter amicum atque 4 inimicum discrimen nosse; leges rem surdam, inexorabilem esse, salubriorem melioremque inopi quam potenti, nihil laxamenti nec veniae habere, si modum excesseris; periculosum esse in tot humanis erroribus 5 sola innocentia vivere. Ita iam sua sponte aegris animis legati ab regibus superveniunt sine mentione reditus bona tantum repetentes. Eorum verba postquam in senatu audita sunt, per aliquot dies ea consultatio tenuit, ne non reddita belli causa, reddita 6 belli materia et adiumentum essent. Interim legati

BOOK II. III. 1-6

III. Although no one doubted that the Tarquinii B.C. 509 would presently go to war, their attack was delayed beyond all expectation; while a thing men did not fear at all, to wit a treasonable plot, almost cost Rome her liberty. There were among the young men a number of youths, the sons of families not unimportant, whose pleasures had been less confined under the monarchy, who, being of the same age as the young Tarquinii, and their cronies, had grown used to the untrammelled life of princes. This licence they missed, now that all enjoyed equal rights, and they had got into the way of complaining to each other that the liberty of the rest had resulted in their own enslavement. A king was a man, from whom one could obtain a boon, whether it were just or unjust; there was room for countenance and favour; a king could be angry, could forgive, could distinguish between friend and enemy. The law was a thing without ears, inexorable, more salutary and serviceable to the pauper than to the great man; it knew no relaxation or indulgence, if one exceeded bounds; and, inasmuch as man is so prone to blunder, it was dangerous to rely on innocence alone. Thanks to such reflections, they were already infected with disloyalty when envoys from the royal family appeared, who without saying anything about the return of the Tarquinii, sought merely to recover their property. The senate, having given them a hearing, debated the question for several days; for they feared that if they refused to make restitution it would be a pretext for war, if they consented it would be to furnish means and assistance for its prosecution. Meantime the envoys were

A.U.C. 245

alia[1] moliri, aperte bona repetentes clam reciperandi regni consilia struere, et tamquam ad id quod agi videbatur ambientes, nobilium adulescentium animos 7 pertemptant. A quibus placide oratio accepta est, iis litteras ab Tarquiniis reddunt et de accipiendis clam nocte in urbem regibus conloquuntur. IV. Vitelliis Aquiliisque fratribus primo commissa res est. Vitelliorum soror consuli nupta Bruto erat, iamque ex eo matrimonio adulescentes erant liberi, Titus Tiberiusque; eos quoque in societatem consilii avun- 2 culi adsumunt. Praeterea aliquot nobiles adulescentes conscii adsumpti, quorum vetustate memoria 3 abiit. Interim cum in senatu vicisset sententia quae censebat reddenda bona, eamque ipsam causam morae in urbe haberent legati, quod spatium ad vehicula comparanda a consulibus sumpsissent quibus regum asportarent res, omne id tempus cum coniuratis consultando absumunt, evincuntque instando ut 4 litterae sibi ad Tarquinios darentur: nam aliter qui credituros eos non vana ab legatis super rebus tantis adferri? Datae litterae, ut pignus fidei essent, mani- 5 festum facinus fecerunt. Nam cum pridie quam legati ad Tarquinios proficiscerentur cenatum[2] forte apud Vitellios esset, coniuratique ibi remotis arbitris multa inter se de novo, ut fit, consilio egissent, ser-

[1] alia *Crevier*: alia alia *P*: alii alia Ω.
[2] cenatum ϛ *Duker*: et cenatum (*or* cae-) Ω.

BOOK II. III. 6–IV. 5

exerting themselves to a different purpose. Ostensibly B.C. 509
seeking to recover the property, they secretly laid
their plans for winning back the kingdom; and, as
if in furtherance of their apparent object, they went
about sounding the disposition of the youthful nobles.
To those who gave them a friendly hearing they delivered letters from the Tarquinii, and plotted with
them to admit the royal family secretly by night into
the City. IV. The brothers Vitellii and Aquilii were
the first to be entrusted with the project. A sister
of the Vitellii had married the consul Brutus, and
there were sons of this marriage who were now young
men, Titus and Tiberius; these were also admitted
by their uncles to a share in the design. There were
besides several other young nobles taken into the
secret, but their names are lost in antiquity. The
senate meantime had acquiesced in the opinion of
those who were in favour of giving back the property.
This very fact gave the agents of the exiles an excuse
for lingering in the City, for the consuls had granted
them time for obtaining vehicles with which to
carry away the belongings of the royal family. All
this time they spent in consultation with the conspirators, whom they urged and at length persuaded
to give them letters for the Tarquinii: for otherwise
how could the princes be convinced that the statements of their agents regarding matters of such
importance were to be relied on? These letters,
being given as a pledge of sincerity, furnished clear
proof of the crime, For on the eve of the envoys'
setting out to rejoin their masters it happened that
they were dining at the house of the Vitellii, where
the conspirators, having dismissed all witnesses, had
much talk together, naturally enough, about their

LIVY

A.U.C. 245

monem eorum ex servis unus excepit, qui iam antea
6 id senserat agi, sed eam occasionem, ut litterae
legatis darentur quae deprehensae rem coarguere
possent, exspectabat. Postquam datas sensit, rem ad
7 consules detulit. Consules ad deprehendendos legatos coniuratosque profecti domo sine tumultu rem
omnem oppressere; litterarum in primis habita cura
ne interciderent. Proditoribus extemplo in vincla
coniectis, de legatis paululum addubitatum est, et
quamquam visi sunt commisisse ut hostium loco
essent, ius tamen gentium valuit. V. De bonis
regiis,[1] quae reddi ante censuerant, res integra re-
fertur ad patres. Ibi victi ira[2] vetuere reddi, vetuere
2 in publicum redigi: diripienda plebi sunt data, ut
contacta regia praeda spem in perpetuum cum iis
pacis amitteret. Ager Tarquiniorum, qui inter urbem ac Tiberim fuit, consecratus Marti Martius
3 deinde campus fuit. Forte ibi tum seges farris
dicitur fuisse matura messi. Quem campi fructum
quia religiosum erat consumere, desectam cum stra-
mento segetem magna vis hominum simul immissa
corbibus fudere in Tiberim tenui fluentem aqua, ut
mediis caloribus solet. Ita in vadis haesitantis fru-

[1] regiis *Gruter*: regis Ω.
[2] Ibi victi ira (ibi victā ra *M*) Ω: ii victi ira *Weissenborn*: ibi vicit ira *Frey*.

[1] Ordinarily the Roman farmer cut the stalk close to the ear, but this time it was cut near the ground, that the crop might be completely destroyed.

new design. This conversation one of the slaves over- B.C. 509
heard. He had for some time perceived what was in
the wind, but was waiting for the opportunity which
the delivery of the letters to the envoys would
provide, that their seizure might make good his accusation. When he saw that the letters had been
given, he laid the matter before the consuls. The
consuls left their houses, arrested the agents and
the conspirators, and, without making any disturbance, completely crushed the plot, being especially
careful not to lose the letters. The traitors were
thrown into prison forthwith. As for the envoys, it
was uncertain for a little while what would be done
with them, but, notwithstanding they appeared to
have deserved no less than to be treated as enemies,
the law of nations nevertheless prevailed. V. The
question of the royal property, which they had before
voted to return, was laid before the Fathers for fresh
consideration. This time anger won the day. They
refused to return it, and refused to confiscate it to
the state, but gave it up to the plebeians to plunder,
that having had their fingers in the spoils of the
princes they might for ever relinquish hope of making
their peace with them. The land of the Tarquinii,
lying between the City and the Tiber, was consecrated
to Mars and became the Campus Martius. It happened, they say, that there was then standing upon
it a crop of spelt, ripe for the harvest. Since this
produce of the land might not, for religious reasons,
be consumed, the grain was cut, straw and all,[1] by a
large body of men, who were set to work upon it
simultaneously, and was carried in baskets and thrown
into the Tiber, then flowing with a feeble current,
as is usually the case in midsummer. So the heaps

LIVY

4 menti acervos sedisse inlitos limo; insulam inde paulatim, et aliis quae fert temere flumen eodem invectis, factam. Postea credo additas moles manuque adiutum, ut tam eminens area firmaque templis 5 quoque ac porticibus sustinendis esset. Direptis bonis regum damnati proditores sumptumque supplicium, conspectius eo quod poenae capiendae ministerium patri de liberis consulatus imposuit, et qui spectator erat amovendus, eum ipsum fortuna ex- 6 actorem supplicii dedit. Stabant deligati ad palum nobilissimi iuvenes; sed a ceteris, velut ab ignotis capitibus, consulis liberi omnium in se averterant oculos, miserebatque non poenae magis homines 7 quam sceleris quo poenam meriti essent: illos eo potissimum anno patriam liberatam, patrem liberatorem, consulatum ortum ex domo Iunia, patres, plebem, quidquid deorum hominumque Romanorum esset, induxisse in animum ut superbo quondam regi, 8 tum infesto exsuli proderent. Consules in sedem processere suam, missique lictores ad sumendum supplicium. Nudatos virgis caedunt securique feriunt, cum inter omne tempus pater voltusque et os eius spectaculo esset eminente animo patrio inter 9 publicae poenae ministerium. Secundum poenam

of grain, caught in the shallow water, settled down B.C. 509
in the mud, and out of these and the accumulation
of other chance materials such as a river brings
down, there was gradually formed an island. Later,
I suppose, embankments were added, and work was
done, to raise the surface so high above the water
and make it strong enough to sustain even temples
and porticoes. When the chattels of the princes had
been pillaged, sentence was pronounced and punishment inflicted upon the traitors—a punishment the
more conspicuous because the office of consul imposed upon a father the duty of exacting the penalty
from his sons, and he who ought to have been spared
even the sight of their suffering was the very man
whom Fortune appointed to enforce it. Bound to
the stake stood youths of the highest birth. But
the rest were ignored as if they had been of the
rabble: the consul's sons drew all eyes upon themselves. Men pitied them for their punishment not
more than for the crime by which they had deserved
that punishment. To think that those young men,
in that year of all others, when their country was
liberated and her liberator their own father, and
when the consulship had begun with the Junian
family, could have brought themselves to betray all
—the senate, the plebs, and all the gods and men of
Rome—to one who had formerly been a tyrannical
king and was then an enemy exile! The consuls
advanced to their tribunal and dispatched the lictors
to execute the sentence. The culprits were stripped,
scourged with rods, and beheaded, while through it
all men gazed at the expression on the father's face,
where they might clearly read a father's anguish, as
he administered the nation's retribution. When the

LIVY

nocentium, ut in utramque partem arcendis sceleribus exemplum nobile esset, praemium indici pecunia ex aerario, libertas et civitas data. Ille primum 10 dicitur vindicta liberatus. Quidam vindictae quoque nomen tractum ab illo putant; Vindicio ipsi nomen fuisse. Post illum observatum ut qui ita liberati essent in civitatem accepti viderentur.

VI. His sicut acta erant nuntiatis incensus Tarquinius non dolore solum tantae ad inritum cadentis spei sed etiam odio iraque, postquam dolo viam obsaeptam vidit, bellum aperte moliendum ratus 2 circumire supplex Etruriae urbes; orare maxime Veientes Tarquiniensesque, ne ex se[1] ortum, eiusdem sanguinis, extorrem, egentem ex tanto modo regno cum liberis adulescentibus ante oculos suos perire sinerent. Alios peregre in regnum Romam accitos: se regem, augentem bello Romanum imperium a proximis scelerata coniuratione pulsum. 3 Eos inter se, quia nemo unus satis dignus regno visus sit, partes regni rapuisse; bona sua diripienda populo dedisse, ne quis expers sceleris esset. Patriam se regnumque suum repetere et persequi ingratos

[1] ne ex se *Drakenborch*: ni (*or* ne) se Ω.

[1] A staff with which the slave was touched in the ceremony of manumission. The etymology suggested in the next sentence is wrong; *Vindicius*, like *vindicta*, is derived from *vindex*.

BOOK II. v. 9–vi. 3

guilty had suffered, that the example might be in both respects a notable deterrent from crime, the informer was rewarded with money from the treasury, emancipation, and citizenship. He is said to have been the first to be freed by the *vindicta*.[1] Some think that even the word *vindicta* was derived from his name, which they suppose to have been Vindicius. From his time onwards it was customary to regard those who had been freed by this form as admitted to citizenship.

VI. When these occurrences had been faithfully reported to Tarquinius, he was stirred not only by disappointment at the collapse of so great hopes, but also by hatred and anger. He saw that the way was now closed against trickery, and believed it was time to contrive an open war. He therefore went about as a suppliant amongst the cities of Etruria, directing his prayers chiefly to the Veientes and the Tarquinienses. Reminding them that he had come from them and was of the same blood as themselves, and that exile and poverty had followed hard upon his loss of what had been but now great power, he besought them not to let him perish, with his youthful sons, before their very eyes. Others had been called in from abroad to be kings in Rome: he himself, while actually king, and enlarging Rome's sway by war, had been driven out by his next-of-kin in a wicked conspiracy. His enemies, perceiving that no single claimant was fit to be king, had seized and usurped the power amongst themselves, and had given up his goods to be plundered by the people, that none might be without a share in the guilt. He wished to regain his country and his sovereignty, and to punish the ungrateful Romans. Let them

B.C. 509

LIVY

cives velle. Ferrent opem, adiuvarent; suas quoque veteres iniurias ultum irent, totiens caesas legiones, 4 agrum ademptum. Haec moverunt Veientes, ac pro se quisque Romano saltem duce ignominias demendas belloque amissa repetenda minaciter fremunt. Tarquinienses nomen ac cognatio movet: pulchrum 5 videbatur suos Romae regnare. Ita duo duarum civitatium exercitus ad repetendum regnum belloque persequendos Romanos secuti Tarquinium. Postquam in agrum Romanum ventum est, obviam hosti 6 consules eunt: Valerius quadrato agmine peditem ducit; Brutus ad explorandum cum equitatu antecessit. Eodem modo primus eques hostium agminis fuit; praeerat Arruns Tarquinius, filius regis; rex 7 ipse cum legionibus sequebatur. Arruns ubi ex lictoribus procul consulem esse, deinde iam propius ac certius facie quoque Brutum cognovit, inflammatus ira "Ille est vir," inquit, "qui nos extorres expulit patria. Ipse en ille nostris decoratus insignibus 8 magnifice incedit. Di regum ultores adeste." Concitat calcaribus equum atque in ipsum infestus consulem derigit. Sensit in se iri Brutus. Decorum erat tum ipsis capessere pugnam ducibus; avide 9 itaque se certamini offert, adeoque infestis animis concurrerunt, neuter, dum hostem volneraret, sui protegendi corporis memor, ut contrario ictu per

succour and support him, and avenge, as well, their own long-standing grievances, the oft-repeated destruction of their armies, and seizure of their lands. This last plea moved the men of Veii, and they cried out with threatenings that they ought, at all events with a Roman for their commander, to wipe out their disgraces and recover what they had lost in war. The Tarquinienses were influenced by his name and kinship: it seemed a fine thing to them that one of their blood should be king in Rome. So it came about that two armies, representing two nations, followed Tarquinius, to regain his kingdom for him and to chastise the Romans. When they had come into Roman territory the consuls went out to meet the enemy: Valerius led the foot in defensive formation; Brutus, with the cavalry, went ahead to scout. In the same fashion the enemy's horse headed their march, commanded by Arruns Tarquinius, the king's son, while the king himself followed with the legions. Arruns, perceiving a long way off by the consul's lictors that it was he, and then, as they drew nearer together, recognizing Brutus more unmistakably by his countenance, blazed with resentment. "Yonder," he cried, "is the man who drove us into exile from our native land. Look! He is himself decked out with our trappings, as he comes proudly on! O gods, avengers of kings, be with us!" Spurring his horse, he charged straight at the consul. Brutus saw that he was the object of the man's attack. In those days it was to a general's credit to take part in the actual fighting, so he eagerly accepted the challenge, and they rushed at one another with such desperation, neither of them taking thought for his own defence if only he might wound his adversary, that

B.C. 509

LIVY

parmam uterque transfixus duabus haerentes hastis
10 moribundi ex equis lapsi sint. Simul et cetera
equestris pugna coepit, neque ita multo post et
pedites superveniunt. Ibi varia victoria et velut
aequo Marte pugnatum est: dextera utrimque cor-
11 nua vicere, laeva superata. Veientes, vinci ab Romano milite adsueti, fusi fugatique; Tarquiniensis,
novus hostis, non stetit solum, sed etiam ab sua
parte Romanum pepulit. VII. Ita cum pugnatum
esset, tantus terror Tarquinium atque Etruscos incessit ut omissa inrita re, nocte ambo exercitus,
Veiens Tarquiniensisque, suas quisque abirent domos.
2 Adiciunt miracula huic pugnae: silentio proximae
noctis ex silva Arsia ingentem editam vocem; Silvani
vocem eam creditam; haec dicta: uno plus Tusco-
3 rum cecidisse in acie; vincere bello Romanum. Ita
certe inde abiere Romani ut victores, Etrusci pro
victis. Nam postquam inluxit nec quisquam hostium
in conspectu erat, P. Valerius consul spolia legit
4 triumphansque inde Romam rediit. Collegae funus
quanto tum potuit apparatu fecit; sed multo maius
morti decus publica fuit maestitia, eo ante omnia
insignis quia matronae annum ut parentem eum

BOOK II. vi. 9–vii. 4

each was pierced right through his shield by the other's thrust, and, impaled upon the two spears, they fell dying from their horses. At the same time the rest of the cavalry as well began to fight, and not long after the infantry also appeared. In this battle the advantage was divided, and the fortune of war seemed equally balanced: the right wing on each side was victorious, while the left was defeated. The Veientes, used to being beaten by the Roman troops, were routed and dispersed; the men of Tarquinii, a new enemy, not only stood their ground, but drove back the Roman forces which opposed them. VII. Yet despite the indecisive character of the battle, so great a panic came over Tarquinius and the Etruscans that they gave up the enterprise for lost, and that same night both armies, the Veientine and the Tarquiniensian, marched off every man to his own home. To the story of this fight common report adds a prodigy: that in the silence of the following night a loud voice was heard coming out of the Arsian forest, which was believed to be the voice of Silvanus, and that this was what he said: "The Tuscans have lost one more man in the battle-line; the Romans are conquerors in the war." At all events the Romans left the field like victors, and the Etruscans like an army that has been defeated. For when it grew light and not a single enemy was to be seen, Publius Valerius the consul gathered up the spoils and returned in triumph to Rome. His colleague's funeral he celebrated with all the pomp then possible; but a far greater honour to the dead man was the general grief, which was particularly conspicuous inasmuch as the matrons mourned a year for him, as for a father, because

B.C. 509

LIVY

luxerunt, quod tam acer ultor violatae pudicitiae fuisset.

5 Consuli deinde qui superfuerat, ut sunt mutabiles volgi animi, ex favore non invidia modo sed suspicio 6 etiam cum atroci crimine orta. Regnum eum adfectare fama ferebat, quia nec collegam subrogaverat in locum Bruti et aedificabat in summa Velia: ibi alto atque munito loco arcem inexpugnabilem fieri.[1]
7 Haec dicta volgo creditaque cum indignitate angerent consulis animum, vocato ad concilium populo submissis fascibus in contionem escendit. Gratum id multitudini spectaculum fuit, submissa sibi esse imperii insignia confessionemque factam populi quam 8 consulis maiestatem vimque maiorem esse. Ibi audire iussis consul laudare fortunam collegae, quod liberata patria, in summo honore, pro re publica dimicans, matura gloria necdum se vertente in invidiam, mortem occubuisset: se superstitem gloriae suae ad crimen atque invidiam superesse, ex liberatore patriae ad Aquilios se Vitelliosque recidisse.
9 "Numquamne ergo," inquit, "ulla adeo vobis[2] spectata virtus erit, ut suspicione violari nequeat? Ego me, illum acerrimum regum hostem, ipsum cupidi-

---

[1] fieri *Conway and Walters*; fieri fore Ω; fore D^1 *or* D^2, *Weissenborn-Müller*.
[2] vobis *Gron.* Lς: a vobis Ω.

---

[1] Bundles of rods which symbolized the magistrate's authority to scourge, as the axes (*secures*) did his right to put to death.

BOOK II. vii. 4–9

he had been so spirited an avenger of outraged modesty.   B.C. 509

Soon after this the surviving consul, so fickle are the affections of the mob, became unpopular; not only did the people dislike him, but they actually suspected him and made cruel charges against him. It was noised about that he was aspiring to the power of a king, since he had not caused a colleague to be elected in the place of Brutus, and was building a house on the highest part of the Velia, an elevated position of natural strength, men said, which he was converting into an impregnable citadel. The frequency of these remarks and the general acceptance they met with, shamefully unjust as they were, distressed the consul. He summoned the people to a council, and with lowered fasces[1] mounted the speaker's platform. It was a welcome spectacle to the multitude when they beheld the emblems of authority there abased before them, in acknowledgment that the people's majesty and power were superior to the consul's. Then, bidding them attend, the consul extolled the good fortune of his colleague, who, after his country had thrown off the yoke, had held the highest office in her gift, and, fighting for the state, at the height of a reputation as yet untarnished by envy, had met his death. He had himself outlived his glory, and survived to face accusations and ill-will. From being the saviour of his country he had sunk to the level of the Aquilii and Vitellii. "Will there never be worth and merit, then," he exclaimed, "so established in your minds that suspicion cannot wrong it? Could I possibly have feared that I, well known as the bitterest enemy of kings, should myself incur the charge of

241

LIVY

10 tatis regni crimen subiturum timerem? Ego si in ipsa arce Capitolioque habitarem, metui me crederem posse a civibus meis? Tam levi momento mea apud vos fama pendet? Adeone est fundata leviter fides
11 ut ubi sim quam qui sim magis referat? Non obstabunt P. Valeri aedes libertati vestrae, Quirites; tuta erit vobis Velia. Deferam non in planum modo aedes, sed colli etiam subiciam, ut vos supra suspectum me civem habitetis; in Velia aedificent quibus
12 melius quam P. Valerio creditur libertas." Delata confestim materia omnis infra Veliam et, ubi nunc Vicae Potae[1] est, domus in infimo clivo aedificata.

VIII. Latae deinde leges, non solum quae regni suspicione consulem absolverent, sed quae adeo in contrarium verterent ut popularem etiam facerent.
2 Inde cognomen factum Publicolae est. Ante omnes de provocatione adversus magistratus ad populum sacrandoque cum bonis capite eius qui regni occupandi consilia inisset gratae in volgus leges fuere.
3 Quas cum solus pertulisset, ut sua unius in his gratia esset, tum demum[2] comitia collegae subrogando
4 habuit. Creatus Sp. Lucretius consul, qui magno natu non sufficientibus iam viribus ad consularia munera obeunda intra paucos dies moritur. Suffec-
5 tus in Lucreti locum M. Horatius Pulvillus. Apud

---

[1] Vicae Potae *Lipsius and Klock*: vice (*or* -ae) pocae (*or* -e) Ω: Vicae Pocae aedes *Siesebye*.
[2] demum *Alschefski*: deinde Ω.

BOOK II. vii. 9–viii. 5

seeking kingly power? Could I have believed that, though I dwelt in the very Citadel and on the Capitol itself, I could be feared by my fellow-citizens? Can so trivial a cause ruin my reputation with you? Does your confidence rest on so slight a foundation that it makes more difference where I am than who I am? There shall be no menace in the house of Publius Valerius to your liberties, Quirites; your Velia shall be safe. I will not only bring my house down on to level ground, but will even place it under a hill, that you may live above me, the citizen whom you suspect. Let those build on the Velia who can better be trusted with men's liberty than can Publius Valerius!" Immediately the materials were all brought down below the Velia, and the house was erected where the temple of Vica Pota is now, at the bottom of the slope.

VIII. Laws were then proposed which not only cleared the consul from the suspicion of seeking kingly power, but took such an opposite turn that they even made him popular and caused him to be styled Publicola, the People's Friend. Above all, the law about appealing from the magistrates to the people, and the one that pronounced a curse on the life and property of a man who should plot to make himself king, were welcome to the commons. When he had carried through these measures alone, that he might enjoy without a rival all the favour arising out of them, he finally held an election to choose a colleague for the unexpired term. The choice fell upon Spurius Lucretius, who by reason of his great age was no longer strong enough for the duties of the consulship, and died within a few days. They elected in Lucretius's place Marcus Horatius

LIVY

quosdam veteres auctores non invenio Lucretium consulem; Bruto statim Horatium suggerunt; credo quia nulla gesta res insignem fecerit consulatum memoriam[1] intercidisse.

6 Nondum dedicata erat in Capitolio Iovis aedes. Valerius Horatiusque consules sortiti uter dedicaret. Horatio sorte evenit: Publicola ad Veientium bellum 7 profectus. Aegrius quam dignum erat tulere Valeri necessarii dedicationem tam incliti templi Horatio dari. Id omnibus modis impedire conati, postquam alia frustra temptata erant, postem iam tenenti consuli foedum inter precationem deum nuntium incutiunt mortuum eius filium esse, funestaque familia 8 dedicare eum templum non posse. Non crediderit factum, an tantum animo roboris fuerit, nec traditur certum nec interpretatio est facilis; nihil aliud ad eum nuntium a proposito aversus, quam ut cadaver efferri iuberet, tenens postem precationem peragit et dedicat templum.

9 Haec post exactos reges domi militiaeque gesta primo anno.

IX. Inde P. Valerius iterum T. Lucretius consules facti. Iam Tarquinii ad Lartem Porsinnam,[2] Clusi-

[1] memoriam ς: memoria Ω.
[2] *This name has everywhere in this edition been spelled with an* i, *though here and in some other places* Ω *read* Porsennam, *etc. Probably Livy's own usage varied. cf. Conway and Walters ad loc.*

---

[1] Dion. Hal. (v. 21) says that Valerius was consul for the *third* time, and Horatius for the second time, when the war with Porsinna came. Mommsen thought the MSS. had lost

BOOK II. viii. 5–ix. 1

Pulvillus. In some ancient authorities I do not find Lucretius given as consul, but Brutus is followed immediately by Horatius; I suppose that because no exploit lent distinction to Lucretius's consulship men forgot it.

The temple of Jupiter on the Capitol had not yet been dedicated. Valerius and Horatius the consuls drew lots to determine which should do it. Horatius received the lot, and Publicola set out to conduct the war against the Veientes. With more bitterness than was reasonable, the friends of Valerius resented that the dedication of so famous a temple should be given to Horatius. They tried in all sorts of ways to hinder it, but their schemes all came to naught. Finally, when the consul's hand was on the door-post and he was in the midst of his prayers to the gods, they broke in upon the ceremony with the evil tidings that his son was dead, averring that whilst the shadow of death was over his house he could not dedicate a temple. Whether he did not believe the news to be true, or possessed great fortitude, we are not informed with certainty, nor is it easy to decide. Without permitting himself to be diverted from his purpose by the message, further than to order that the body should be buried, he kept his hand upon the doorpost, finished his prayer, and dedicated the temple.

Such were the achievements, at home and in the field, of the first year after the expulsion of the kings.

IX. Next Publius Valerius (for the second time) and Titus Lucretius were made consuls.[1] By this time the Tarquinii had sought refuge with Lars

B.C. 509

B.C. 508

these names, and proposed to insert them directly after those in the text. But in chap. xi. 8, T. Lucretius is still the colleague of Valerius.

num regem, perfugerant. Ibi miscendo consilium precesque nunc orabant ne se, oriundos ex Etruscis, eiusdem sanguinis nominisque, egentes exsulare pateretur, nunc monebant etiam ne orientem morem pellendi reges inultum sineret. Satis libertatem ipsam habere dulcedinis. Nisi quanta vi civitates eam expetant, tanta regna reges defendant, aequari summa infimis; nihil excelsum, nihil quod supra cetera emineat in civitatibus fore; adesse finem regnis, rei inter deos hominesque pulcherrimae. Porsinna cum regem esse Romae tutum, tum[1] Etruscae gentis regem amplum Tuscis ratus, Romam infesto exercitu venit. Non unquam alias ante tantus terror senatum invasit; adeo valida res tum Clusina erat magnumque Porsinnae nomen. Nec hostes modo timebant, sed suosmet ipsi cives, ne Romana plebs, metu perculsa receptis in urbem regibus, vel cum servitute pacem acciperet. Multa igitur blandimenta plebi per id tempus ab senatu data. Annonae in primis habita cura, et ad frumentum comparandum missi alii in Volscos, alii Cumas. Salis quoque vendendi arbitrium, quia impenso pretio venibat,[2] in publicum omne sumptum,[3] ademptum privatis; portoriisque et tributo plebes[4] liberata, ut divites conferrent, qui oneri ferendo essent: pauperes satis stipendii pendere si liberos educent. Itaque haec

[1] tutum tum *Conway* : tum Ω : fateretur tum *DL*.
[2] venibat $R^2\varsigma$: veniebat (-bant *M*) Ω.
[3] omne sumptum *Gronov.* : omni sumptum *B* : omni sumptu Ω.   [4] plebes *Gronov.*: plebe Ω.

Porsinna, king of Clusium. There they mingled advice B.C. 508
and entreaty, now imploring him not to permit them,
Etruscans by birth and of the same blood and the
same name as himself, to suffer the privations of
exile, and again even warning him not to allow the
growing custom of expelling kings to go unpunished.
Liberty was sweet enough in itself. Unless the
energy with which nations sought to obtain it were
matched by the efforts which kings put forth to
defend their power, the highest would be reduced
to the level of the lowest; there would be nothing
lofty, nothing that stood out above the rest of the
state; there was the end of monarchy, the noblest
institution known to gods or men. Porsinna, believing that it was not only a safe thing for the Etruscans
that there should be a king at Rome, but an honour
to have that king of Etruscan stock, invaded Roman
territory with a hostile army. Never before had such
fear seized the senate, so powerful was Clusium in
those days, and so great Porsinna's fame. And they
feared not only the enemy but their own citizens,
lest the plebs should be terror-stricken and, admitting the princes into the City, should even submit to
enslavement, for the sake of peace. Hence the senate
at this time granted many favours to the plebs. The
question of subsistence received special attention,
and some were sent to the Volsci and others to
Cumae to buy up corn. Again, the monopoly of
salt, the price of which was very high, was taken
out of the hands of individuals and wholly assumed
by the government. Imposts and taxes were removed
from the plebs that they might be borne by the well-
to-do, who were equal to the burden: the poor paid
dues enough if they reared children. Thanks to this

indulgentia patrum asperis postmodum rebus in obsidione ac fame adeo concordem civitatem tenuit ut regium nomen non summi magis quam infimi horre- 8 rent, nec quisquam unus malis artibus postea tam popularis esset quam tum bene imperando universus senatus fuit.

X. Cum hostes adessent, pro se quisque in urbem ex agris demigrant, urbem ipsam saepiunt praesidiis. 2 Alia muris, alia Tiberi obiecto videbantur tuta: pons sublicius iter paene hostibus dedit, ni unus vir fuisset, Horatius Cocles; id munimentum illo die fortuna 3 urbis Romanae habuit. Qui positus forte in statione pontis, cum captum repentino impetu Ianiculum atque inde citatos decurrere hostes vidisset trepidamque turbam suorum arma ordinesque relinquere, reprehensans singulos, obsistens obtestansque deum 4 et hominum fidem testabatur nequiquam deserto praesidio eos fugere; si transitum ponte[1] a tergo reliquissent, iam plus hostium in Palatio Capitolioque quam in Ianiculo fore. Itaque monere, praedicere ut pontem ferro, igni, quacumque vi possint, interrumpant: se impetum hostium, quantum corpore 5 uno posset obsisti, excepturum. Vadit inde in pri-

[1] ponte *Postgate*: pontem Ω.

BOOK II. ix. 7-x. 5

liberality on the part of the Fathers, the distress B.C. 508 which attended the subsequent blockade and famine was powerless to destroy the harmony of the state, which was such that the name of king was not more abhorrent to the highest than to the lowest; nor was there ever a man in after years whose demagogic arts made him so popular as its wise governing at that time made the whole senate.

X. When the enemy appeared, the Romans all, with one accord, withdrew from their fields into the City, which they surrounded with guards. Some parts appeared to be rendered safe by their walls, others by the barrier formed by the river Tiber. The bridge of piles almost afforded an entrance to the enemy, had it not been for one man, Horatius Cocles; he was the bulwark of defence on which that day depended the fortune of the City of Rome. He chanced to be on guard at the bridge when Janiculum was captured by a sudden attack of the enemy. He saw them as they charged down on the run from Janiculum, while his own people behaved like a frightened mob, throwing away their arms and quitting their ranks. Catching hold first of one and then of another, blocking their way and conjuring them to listen, he called on gods and men to witness that if they forsook their post it was vain to flee; once they had left a passage in their rear by the bridge, there would soon be more of the enemy on the Palatine and the Capitol than on Janiculum. He therefore warned and commanded them to break down the bridge with steel, with fire, with any instrument at their disposal; and promised that he would himself receive the onset of the enemy, so far as it could be withstood by a single body. Then, striding to the

LIVY

mum aditum pontis, insignisque inter conspecta cedentium pugnae terga obversis comminus ad ineundum proelium armis ipso miraculo audaciae obstupefecit hostis. Duos tamen cum eo pudor tenuit, Sp. Larcium[1] ac T. Herminium, ambos claros genere factisque. Cum his primam periculi procellam et quod tumultuosissimum pugnae erat parumper sustinuit; deinde eos quoque ipsos exigua parte pontis relicta revocantibus qui rescindebant cedere in tutum coegit. Circumferens inde truces minaciter oculos ad proceres Etruscorum nunc singulos provocare, nunc increpare omnes: servitia regum superborum, suae libertatis immemores alienam oppugnatum venire. Cunctati aliquamdiu sunt, dum alius alium, ut proelium incipiant, circumspectant. Pudor deinde commovit aciem, et clamore sublato undique in unum hostem tela coniciunt. Quae cum in obiecto cuncta scuto haesissent, neque ille minus obstinatus ingenti pontem obtineret gradu, iam impetu conabantur detrudere virum, cum simul fragor rupti pontis, simul clamor Romanorum alacritate perfecti operis sublatus, pavore subito impetum sustinuit. Tum Cocles "Tiberine pater," inquit, "te sancte precor, haec arma et hunc militem propitio flumine accipias." Ita sic armatus in Tiberim desiluit multisque superincidentibus telis incolumis ad suos tranavit,

---

[1] Larcium Ω (and Dion. Hal. v. 23, 2): Lartium O¹ (or O) RDLς: Largium F²ς.

BOOK II. x. 5-11

head of the bridge, conspicuous amongst the fugitives who were clearly seen to be shirking the fight, he covered himself with his sword and buckler and made ready to do battle at close quarters, confounding the Etruscans with amazement at his audacity. Yet were there two who were prevented by shame from leaving him. These were Spurius Larcius and Titus Herminius, both famous for their birth and their deeds. With these he endured the peril of the first rush and the stormiest moment of the battle. But after a while he forced even these two to leave him and save themselves, for there was scarcely anything left of the bridge, and those who were cutting it down called to them to come back. Then, darting glances of defiance around at the Etruscan nobles, he now challenged them in turn to fight, now railed at them collectively as slaves of haughty kings, who, heedless of their own liberty, were come to overthrow the liberty of others. They hesitated for a moment, each looking to his neighbour to begin the fight. Then shame made them attack, and with a shout they cast their javelins from every side against their solitary foe. But he caught them all upon his shield, and, resolute as ever, bestrode the bridge and held his ground; and now they were trying to dislodge him by a charge, when the crash of the falling bridge and the cheer which burst from the throats of the Romans, exulting in the completion of their task, checked them in mid-career with a sudden dismay. Then Cocles cried, "O Father Tiberinus, I solemnly invoke thee; receive these arms and this soldier with propitious stream!" So praying, all armed as he was, he leaped down into the river, and under a shower of missiles swam across unhurt

rem ausus plus famae habituram ad posteros quam
12 fidei. Grata erga tantam virtutem civitas fuit: statua
in comitio posita; agri quantum uno die circumaravit
13 datum. Privata quoque inter publicos honores studia
eminebant; nam in magna inopia pro domesticis
copiis unusquisque ei aliquid, fraudans se ipse victu
suo, contulit.

XI. Porsinna primo conatu repulsus, consiliis ab
oppugnanda urbe ad obsidendam versis, praesidio in
Ianiculo locato ipse in plano ripisque Tiberis castra
2 posuit, navibus undique accitis et ad custodiam, ne
quid Romam frumenti subvehi sineret, et ut praedatum milites trans flumen per occasiones aliis atque
3 aliis locis traiceret[1]; brevique adeo infestum omnem
Romanum agrum reddidit, ut non cetera solum ex
agris sed pecus quoque omne in urbem compelleretur, neque quisquam extra portas propellere aude-
4 ret. Hoc tantum licentiae Etruscis non metu magis
quam consilio concessum. Namque Valerius consul,
intentus in occasionem multos simul et effusos improviso adoriundi, in parvis rebus neglegens ultor,
5 gravem se ad maiora vindicem servabat. Itaque ut
eliceret praedatores, edicit suis, postero die fre-

[1] traiceret *Gronov.*: traicerent Ω.

to his fellows, having given a proof of valour which was destined to obtain more fame than credence with posterity. The state was grateful for so brave a deed: a statue of Cocles was set up in the comitium, and he was given as much land as he could plough around in one day. Private citizens showed their gratitude in a striking fashion, in the midst of his official honours, for notwithstanding their great distress everybody made him some gift proportionate to his means, though he robbed himself of his own ration.

XI. Porsinna, repulsed in his first attempt, gave up the plan of storming the City, and determined to lay siege to it. Placing a garrison on Janiculum, he pitched his camp in the plain by the banks of the Tiber. He collected ships from every quarter, both for guarding the river, to prevent any corn from being brought into the City, and also to send his troops across for plundering, as the opportunity might present itself at one point or another; and in a short time he made all the territory of the Romans so unsafe that not only were they forced to bring all their other property inside the walls, but even their flocks too, nor did anybody dare to drive them outside the gates. This great degree of licence was permitted to the Etruscans not so much from timidity as design. For Valerius the consul, who was eager for an opportunity of assailing a large number at once, when they should be scattered about and not expecting an attack, cared little to avenge small aggressions, and reserved his punishment for a heavier blow. Accordingly, to lure forth plunderers, he issued orders to his people that on the following day a large number of them should drive out their flocks by the

LIVY

quentes porta Esquilina, quae aversissima ab hoste erat, expellerent pecus, scituros id hostes ratus, quod in obsidione et fame servitia infida transfugerent. 6 Et sciere perfugae indicio, multoque plures, ut in 7 spem universae praedae, flumen traiciunt. P. Valerius inde[1] T. Herminium cum modicis copiis ad secundum lapidem Gabina via occultum considere iubet, Sp. Larcium cum expedita iuventute ad portam Collinam stare donec hostis praetereat, inde se 8 obicere ne sit ad flumen reditus. Consulum alter T. Lucretius porta Naevia cum aliquot manipulis militum egressus, ipse Valerius Caelio monte co-9 hortes delectas educit, hique primi apparuere hosti. Herminius ubi tumultum sensit, concurrit ex insidiis versisque in Lucretium Etruscis terga caedit; dextra laevaque, hinc a porta Collina, illinc ab Naevia, red-10 ditus clamor: ita caesi in medio praedatores, neque ad pugnam viribus pares et ad fugam saeptis omnibus viis. Finisque ille tam effuse evagandi[2] Etruscis fuit.

XII. Obsidio erat nihilo minus, et frumenti cum summa caritate inopia, sedendoque expugnaturum se 2 urbem spem Porsinna habebat, cum C. Mucius, adulescens nobilis, cui indignum videbatur populum

[1] inde *Sobius*: m̄ Ω : iñ *R*.
[2] evagandi Ω : auagandi *P* : uagandi ϛ.

---

[1] Where there was a gate called *Porta Caelimontana*, south of the *Porta Esquilina*.
[2] From the standpoint of the inhabitants of the city, looking eastward from the walls.

Esquiline Gate, which was the most remote from the   B.C. 508
enemy, believing that they would hear of it, since
the blockade and famine were causing desertions on
the part of faithless slaves. And in fact the enemy
did hear of it from a deserter's report, and crossed
the river in much greater force than usual, in the
hope of making a clean sweep of the booty. Consequently Publius Valerius directed Titus Herminius
to lie in ambush with a small force two miles out on
the Gabinian Way, and Spurius Larcius with a body
of light-armed youths to take post at the Colline
Gate, until the enemy should pass, and then to throw
themselves between him and the river, cutting off
his retreat. Of the two consuls, Titus Lucretius
went out by the Naevian Gate with several maniples
of soldiers, Valerius himself led out some picked
cohorts by way of the Caelian Mount.[1] These last
were the first to be seen by the enemy. Herminius
had no sooner perceived that the skirmish was begun
than he rushed in from his ambush and fell upon the
rear of the Etruscans, who had turned to meet Valerius. On the right hand and on the left,[2] from the
Naevian Gate and from the Colline, an answering
shout was returned. Thus the raiders were hemmed
in and cut to pieces, for they were no match for the
Romans in fighting strength, and were shut off from
every line of retreat. This was the last time the
Etruscans roamed so far afield.

XII. The blockade went on notwithstanding. The
corn was giving out, and what there was cost a very
high price, and Porsinna was beginning to have hopes
that he would take the City by sitting still, when
Gaius Mucius, a young Roman noble, thinking it a
shame that although the Roman People had not, in

255

LIVY

Romanum servientem cum sub regibus esset nullo bello nec ab hostibus ullis obsessum esse, liberum 3 eundem populum ab iisdem Etruscis obsideri quorum saepe exercitus fuderit,—itaque magno audacique aliquo facinore eam indignitatem vindicandam ratus, primo sua sponte penetrare in hostium castra con- 4 stituit; dein metuens ne, si consulum iniussu et ignaris omnibus iret, forte deprehensus a custodibus Romanis retraheretur ut transfuga, fortuna tum urbis 5 crimen adfirmante, senatum adit. "Transire Tiberim," inquit, "patres, et intrare, si possim, castra hostium volo, non praedo nec populationum in vicem ultor: maius, si di iuvant, in animo est facinus." Adprobant patres. Abdito intra vestem ferro profi- 6 ciscitur. Ubi eo venit, in confertissima turba prope 7 regium tribunal constitit. Ibi cum stipendium militibus forte daretur, et scriba cum rege sedens pari fere ornatu multa ageret eumque milites[1] volgo adirent, timens sciscitari uter Porsinna esset, ne ignorando regem semet ipse aperiret quis esset, quo temere traxit fortuna facinus, scribam pro rege ob- 8 truncat. Vadentem inde, qua per trepidam turbam cruento mucrone sibi ipse fecerat viam, cum concursu ad clamorem facto conprehensum regii satellites retraxissent, ante tribunal regis destitutus, tum quo-

[1] eumque milites *Ald.*: eumue milites *R*: eum nomilites *D*: eum nemilites *L*: eum milites Ω.

the days of their servitude when they lived under kings, been blockaded in a war by any enemies, they should now, when free, be besieged by those same Etruscans whose armies they had so often routed, made up his mind that this indignity must be avenged by some great and daring deed. At first he intended to make his way to the enemy's camp on his own account. Afterwards, fearing that if he should go unbidden by the consuls and without anyone's knowing it, he might chance to be arrested by the Roman sentries and brought back as a deserter—a charge which the state of the City would confirm— he went before the senate. "I wish," said he, "to cross the river, senators, and enter, if I can, the enemy's camp—not to plunder or exact reprisals for their devastations: I have in mind to do a greater deed, if the gods grant me their help." The Fathers approved. Hiding a sword under his dress, he set out. Arrived at the camp, he took up his stand in the thick of the crowd near the royal tribunal. It happened that at that moment the soldiers were being paid; a secretary who sat beside the king, and wore nearly the same costume, was very busy, and to him the soldiers for the most part addressed themselves. Mucius was afraid to ask which was Porsinna, lest his ignorance of the king's identity should betray his own, and following the blind guidance of Fortune, slew the secretary instead of the king. As he strode off through the frightened crowd, making a way for himself with his bloody blade, there was an outcry, and thereat the royal guards came running in from every side, seized him and dragged him back before the tribunal of the king. But friendless as he was, even then, when

LIVY

que inter tantas fortunae minas metuendus magis
9 quam metuens, "Romanus sum," inquit, "civis;
C. Mucium vocant. Hostis hostem occidere volui,
nec ad mortem minus animi est quam fuit ad cae-
10 dem: et facere et pati fortia Romanum est. Nec
unus in te ego hos animos gessi; longus post me
ordo est idem petentium decus. Proinde in hoc discrimen, si iuvat, accingere, ut in singulas horas capite dimices tuo, ferrum hostemque in vestibulo habeas
11 regiae. Hoc tibi iuventus Romana indicimus bellum.
Nullam aciem, nullum proelium timueris; uni tibi et
12 cum singulis res erit." Cum rex simul ira infensus periculoque conterritus circumdari ignes minitabundus iuberet nisi expromeret propere quas insidiarum
13 sibi minas per ambages iaceret, "En tibi," inquit,
"ut sentias quam vile corpus sit iis qui magnam gloriam vident," dextramque accenso ad sacrificium foculo inicit. Quam cum velut alienato ab sensu torreret animo, prope attonitus miraculo rex cum ab sede sua prosiluisset amoverique ab altaribus iuvenem
14 iussisset, "Tu[1] vero abi," inquit, "in te magis quam in me hostilia ausus. Iuberem macte virtute esse, si pro mea patria ista virtus staret; nunc iure belli liberum te intactum inviolatumque hinc dimitto."
15 Tunc Mucius quasi remunerans meritum "Quando

[1] tu M_ς : tum $\Omega\varsigma$.

258

BOOK II. xii. 8–15

Fortune wore so menacing an aspect, yet as one more to be feared than fearing, "I am a Roman citizen," he cried; "men call me Gaius Mucius. I am your enemy, and as an enemy I would have slain you; I can die as resolutely as I could kill: both to do and to endure valiantly is the Roman way. Nor am I the only one to carry this resolution against you: behind me is a long line of men who are seeking the same honour. Gird yourself therefore, if you think it worth your while, for a struggle in which you must fight for your life from hour to hour with an armed foe always at your door. Such is the war we, the Roman youths, declare on you. Fear no serried ranks, no battle; it will be between yourself alone and a single enemy at a time." The king, at once hot with resentment and aghast at his danger, angrily ordered the prisoner to be flung into the flames unless he should at once divulge the plot with which he so obscurely threatened him. Whereupon Mucius, exclaiming, "Look, that you may see how cheap they hold their bodies whose eyes are fixed upon renown!" thrust his hand into the fire that was kindled for the sacrifice. When he allowed his hand to burn as if his spirit were unconscious of sensation, the king was almost beside himself with wonder. He bounded from his seat and bade them remove the young man from the altar. "Do you go free," he said, "who have dared to harm yourself more than me. I would invoke success upon your valour, were that valour exerted for my country; since that may not be, I release you from the penalties of war and dismiss you scathless and uninjured." Then Mucius, as if to requite his generosity, answered, "Since you hold bravery

LIVY

quidem," inquit, "est apud te virtuti honos, ut beneficio tuleris a me quod minis nequisti: trecenti coniuravimus principes iuventutis Romanae, ut in te hac via grassaremur. Mea prima sors fuit; ceteri, ut cuiusque[1] ceciderit primi, quoad te opportunum fortuna dederit, suo quisque tempore aderunt."

XIII. Mucium dimissum, cui postea Scaevolae a clade dextrae manus cognomen inditum, legati a Porsinna Romam secuti sunt; adeo moverat eum et primi periculi casus, a quo[2] nihil se praeter errorem insidiatoris texisset, et subeunda dimicatio totiens quot coniurati superessent, ut pacis condiciones ultro ferret Romanis. Iactatum in condicionibus nequiquam de Tarquiniis in regnum restituendis, magis quia id negare ipse nequiverat Tarquiniis quam quod negatum iri sibi ab Romanis ignoraret. De agro Veientibus restituendo impetratum, expressaque necessitas obsides dandi Romanis, si Ianiculo praesidium deduci vellent. His condicionibus composita pace exercitum ab Ianiculo deduxit Porsinna et agro Romano excessit. Patres C. Mucio virtutis causa trans Tiberim agrum dono dedere quae postea sunt Mucia prata appellata.

Ergo ita honorata virtute feminae quoque ad publica decora excitatae, et Cloelia virgo, una ex obsi-

---

[1] ut cuiusque *Madvig* : utcumque Ω.
[2] a quo *Heumann* : quo Ω.

---

[1] *i.e.* "Left-handed."

BOOK II. xii. 15–xiii. 6

in honour, my gratitude shall afford you the information your threats could not extort: we are three hundred, the foremost youths of Rome, who have conspired to assail you in this fashion. I drew the first lot; the others, in whatever order it falls to them, will attack you, each at his own time, until Fortune shall have delivered you into our hands."

XIII. The release of Mucius, who was afterwards known as Scaevola,[1] from the loss of his right hand, was followed by the arrival in Rome of envoys from Porsinna. The king had been so disturbed, what with the hazard of the first attack upon his life, from which nothing but the blunder of his assailant had preserved him, and what with the anticipation of having to undergo the danger as many times more as there were conspirators remaining, that he voluntarily proposed terms of peace to the Romans. In these terms Porsinna suggested, but without effect, that the Tarquinii should be restored to power, more because he had been unable to refuse the princes this demand upon their behalf than that he was ignorant that the Romans would refuse it. In obtaining the return of their lands to the Veientes he was successful; and the Romans were compelled to give hostages if they wished the garrison to be withdrawn from Janiculum. On these terms peace was made, and Porsinna led his army down from Janiculum and evacuated the Roman territory. The Fathers bestowed on Gaius Mucius, for his bravery, a field across the Tiber, which was later known as the Mucian Meadows.

Now when courage had been thus distinguished, even the women were inspired to deeds of patriotism. Thus the maiden Cloelia, one of the hostages, eluded

LIVY

dibus, cum castra Etruscorum forte haud procul ripa Tiberis locata essent, frustrata custodes, dux agminis virginum inter tela hostium Tiberim tranavit sospitesque omnes Romam ad propinquos restituit. Quod ubi regi nuntiatum est, primo incensus ira oratores Romam misit ad Cloeliam obsidem deposcendam: alias haud magni facere; deinde in admirationem versus supra Coclites Muciosque dicere id facinus esse, et prae se ferre quemadmodum, si non dedatur obses, pro rupto foedus se habiturum, sic deditam intactam inviolatamque[1] ad suos remissurum. Utrimque constitit fides: et Romani pignus pacis ex foedere restituerunt, et apud regem Etruscum non tuta solum sed honorata etiam virtus fuit, laudataque virginem parte obsidum se donare dixit; ipsa quos vellet legeret. Productis omnibus elegisse impubes dicitur, quod et virginitati decorum et consensu obsidum ipsorum probabile erat eam aetatem potissimum liberari ab hoste quae maxime opportuna iniuriae esset. Pace redintegrata Romani novam in femina virtutem novo genere honoris, statua equestri, donavere: in summa Sacra via fuit posita[2] virgo insidens equo.

XIV. Huic tam pacatae profectioni ab urbe regis Etrusci abhorrens mos traditus ab antiquis usque ad

[1] intactam inviolatamque *Frobenius*: inuiolatamque Ω.
[2] fuit posita Ω : posita *Novák, Weissenborn-Müller*.

BOOK II. XIII. 6–XIV. 1

the sentinels, when it chanced that the Etruscans had B.C. 508
encamped not far from the bank of the Tiber, and
heading a band of girls swam the river and, under a
rain of hostile darts, brought them all back in safety
to their kinsmen in Rome. When this had been
reported to the king, he was at first enraged and sent
emissaries to Rome to demand that the hostage
Cloelia be given up, for he made no great account of
the others. Then, admiration getting the better of
anger, he asserted that her feat was a greater one
than those of Cocles and Mucius, and declared that
although in case the hostage was not returned he
should regard the treaty as broken, yet if she were
restored to him he would send her back safe and
inviolate to her friends. Both parties kept their
word. The Romans returned the pledge of peace, as
the treaty required; and the Etruscan king not only
protected the brave girl but even honoured her, for
after praising her heroism he said that he would
present her with half the hostages, and that she
herself should choose the ones she wished. When
they had all been brought out it is said that she
selected the young boys, because it was not only
more seemly in a maiden, but was unanimously approved by the hostages themselves, that in delivering
them from the enemy she should give the preference
to those who were of an age which particularly
exposed them to injury. When peace had been established the Romans rewarded this new valour in a
woman with a new kind of honour, an equestrian
statue, which was set up on the summit of the Sacred
Way, and represented the maiden seated on a horse.

XIV. This peaceful departure of the Etruscan
king from Rome is inconsistent with the custom
handed down from antiquity even to our own age,

LIVY

A.U.C. 246

nostram aetatem inter cetera sollemnia manet, bona
2 Porsinnae regis vendendi. Cuius originem moris
necesse est aut inter bellum natam esse neque omis-
sam in pace, aut a mitiore crevisse principio quam
hic prae se ferat titulus bona hostiliter vendendi.
3 Proximum vero est ex iis quae traduntur Porsinnam
discedentem ab Ianiculo castra opulenta convecto ex
propinquis ac fertilibus Etruriae arvis commeatu
Romanis dono dedisse, inopi tum urbe ab longinqua
4 obsidione; ea deinde, ne populo immisso diriperen-
tur hostiliter, venisse, bonaque Porsinnae appellata,
gratiam muneris magis significante titulo quam
auctionem fortunae regiae quae ne in potestate quidem populi Romani esset.

5 Omisso Romano bello Porsinna, ne frustra in ea
loca exercitus adductus videretur, cum parte copiarum filium Arruntem Ariciam oppugnatum mittit.
6 Primo Aricinos res necopinata perculerat; arcessita
deinde auxilia et a Latinis populis et a Cumis tantum
spei fecere ut acie decernere auderent. Proelio inito
adeo concitato impetu se intulerant Etrusci ut fun-
7 derent ipso incursu Aricinos; Cumanae cohortes arte
adversus vim usae declinavere paululum, effuseque
praelatos hostes conversis signis ab tergo adortae

among other formalities observed at sales of booty, of proclaiming "the goods of King Porsinna." Such a practice must either have arisen during the war and have been retained when peace was made, or else have had its origin in some kindlier circumstance than would be suggested by the notice that an enemy's goods were to be sold. The most credible of the traditional explanations is that when Porsinna retired from Janiculum he handed over his camp, well stocked with provisions brought in from the neighbouring fertile fields of Etruria, as a gift to the Romans, who were then in a destitute condition after the long siege. These supplies were then sold, lest, if people were given a free hand, they might plunder the camp like an enemy; and they were called the goods of Porsinna rather by way of implying thankfulness for the gift than an auction of the king's property, which was not even in the possession of the Roman People.

On relinquishing his campaign against the Romans, Porsinna was unwilling that he should appear to have led his army into that region to no purpose, and accordingly sent a part of his forces, under his son Arruns, to besiege Aricia. At first the Aricini were paralysed with surprise. Afterwards the auxiliaries whom they called in from the Latin peoples, and also from Cumae, so encouraged them that they ventured to measure their strength with the enemy in the open field. When the battle began, the attack of the Etruscans was so impetuous that they routed the Aricini at the first charge. The Cumaean levies, employing skill to meet force, swerved a little to one side, and when the enemy had swept by them, faced about and attacked them in the rear, with the

LIVY

A.U.C. 246

sunt. Ita in medio prope iam victores caesi Etrusci.
8 Pars perexigua duce amisso, quia nullum propius
perfugium erat, Romam inermes et fortuna et specie
supplicum delati sunt. Ibi benigne excepti divisique
9 in hospitia. Curatis volneribus alii profecti domos,
nuntii hospitalium beneficiorum; multos Romae hospitum urbisque caritas tenuit. His locus ad habitandum datus quem deinde Tuscum vicum appellarunt.

A.U.C. 247–248

XV. Sp. Larcius inde et T. Herminius, P. Lucretius
inde et[1] P. Valerius Publicola consules facti. Eo
anno postremum legati a Porsinna de reducendo in
regnum Tarquinio venerunt. Quibus cum responsum
esset missurum ad regem senatum legatos, missi con-
2 festim honoratissimus quisque e patribus: non quin
breviter reddi responsum potuerit non recipi reges,
ideo potius delectos patrum ad eum missos quam
legatis eius Romae daretur responsum, sed ut in perpetuum mentio eius rei finiretur, neu in tantis mutuis beneficiis in vicem animi sollicitarentur, cum ille peteret quod contra libertatem populi Romani esset,

---

[1] Sp. Larcius inde et T. Herminius, P. Lucretius inde et
Madvig: *the name* Larcius *is not in the MSS.; his praenomen
is added to that of* Lucretius *or put in its place;* T. Herminius
is missing in the best MSS.; Dion. Hal. v. 36, *and Cassiodorius
give only the names of* Sp. Larcius *and* T. Hermenius, *and
Mommsen* (C.I.L. i². p. 99) *therefore deletes the others. See
note in Conway and Walters.*

BOOK II. xiv. 7–xv. 2

result that the Etruscans, caught between two lines, almost in the moment of victory, were cut to pieces. A very small number of them, having lost their leader and finding no nearer refuge, drifted to Rome, unarmed and with all the helplessness and the dejected aspect of suppliants. There they were kindly received and were quartered about among the citizens. When their wounds had healed, some departed for their homes to report the hospitality and kindness they had met with, but many were persuaded to remain in Rome by the affection they felt for their hosts and for the City. To these a place of residence was allotted which was afterwards called the Vicus Tuscus.

XV. Spurius Larcius and Titus Herminius were the next consuls, and after them came Publius Lucretius and Publius Valerius Publicola. In the latter year an embassy was sent to Rome for the last time by Porsinna to negotiate for the restoration of Tarquinius to power. To these envoys the senate replied that they would send representatives to the king, and they forthwith dispatched those of the Fathers who were held in the highest esteem. It would not have been impossible, they said, to reply shortly that the royal family would not be received. It was not for that reason that they had preferred to send chosen members of the senate to him rather than to give their answer to his ambassadors in Rome. But they had desired that for all time discussion of that question might be ended, and that where there were so great obligations on both sides there might not be mutual irritation, from the king's seeking that which was incompatible with the liberty of the Roman people, while the Romans, unless they were willing

B.C. 508

B.C. 507-506

LIVY

Romani, nisi in perniciem suam faciles esse vellent, negarent, cui nihil negatum vellent. Non in regno populum Romanum sed in libertate esse. Ita induxisse in animum, hostibus potius quam regibus portas patefacere; ea esse vota[1] omnium ut qui libertati erit in illa urbe finis, idem urbi sit. Proinde si salvam esse vellet Romam, ut patiatur liberam esse orare. Rex verecundia victus "Quando id certum atque obstinatum est," inquit, "neque ego obtundam saepius eadem nequiquam agendo, nec Tarquinios spe auxilii, quod nullum in me est, frustrabor. Alium hinc, seu bello opus est seu quiete, exilio quaerant locum, ne quid meam vobiscum pacem distineat." Dictis facta amiciora adiecit: obsidum quod reliquum erat reddidit, agrum Veientem foedere ad Ianiculum icto ademptum restituit. Tarquinius spe omni reditus incisa exsulatum ad generum Mamilium Octavium Tusculum abiit. Romanis pax fida[2] cum Porsinna fuit.

XVI. Consules M. Valerius P. Postumius. Eo anno bene pugnatum cum Sabinis; consules triumpharunt. Maiore inde mole Sabini bellum parabant. Adversus eos et ne quid simul ab Tusculo, unde etsi non apertum, suspectum tamen bellum erat, repentini

[1] ea esse vota *Hertz*; eam ea esse vota esse voluntatem *P*: eam esse voluntatem Ω.
[2] fida *Madvig*: fida ita Ω.

BOOK II. xv. 2–XVI. 2

to sacrifice their existence to their good nature, denied the request of a man whom they would not willingly have denied anything. The Roman people were not living under a monarchy, but were free. They had resolved to throw open their gates to enemies sooner than to kings; in this prayer they were all united, that the day which saw the end of liberty in their City might also see the City's end. They therefore entreated him, if he desired the welfare of Rome, to permit her to be free. The king, yielding to his better feelings, made answer: "Since this is your fixed resolve, I will neither importune you with repeated insistence upon a hopeless plea, nor will I deceive the Tarquinii with the hope of aid which it is not in my power to grant. Let them seek elsewhere, whether war or peace be their object, for a place of exile, that nothing may hinder my being at peace with you." His words were followed by yet more friendly deeds. The hostages remaining in his hands he returned, and he gave back the Veientine land which he had taken from the Romans by the treaty made on Janiculum. Tarquinius, cut off from all hope of returning, departed for Tusculum, to spend his exile in the home of his son-in-law, Mamilius Octavius. The Romans enjoyed an unbroken peace with Porsinna.

B.C. 507–506

XVI. The consulship of Marcus Valerius and Publius Postumius. This year a successful war was waged against the Sabines, and the consuls triumphed. More elaborate preparations for war were then made by the Sabines. To confront them, and to prevent any sudden peril arising from Tusculum, in which quarter hostility, though not openly avowed, was none the

B.C. 505–503

LIVY

periculi oreretur, P. Valerius quartum T. Lucretius
3 iterum consules facti. Seditio inter belli pacisque
auctores orta in Sabinis aliquantum inde virium
4 transtulit ad Romanos. Namque Attius Clausus,
cui postea Appio Claudio fuit Romae nomen, cum
pacis ipse auctor a turbatoribus belli premeretur nec
par factioni esset, ab Inregillo,[1] magna clientium
5 comitatus manu, Romam transfugit. His civitas data
agerque trans Anienem; vetus Claudia tribus additis
postea novis tribulibus qui ex eo venirent agro appellati.[2] Appius inter patres lectus haud ita multo post
6 in principum dignationem pervenit. Consules infesto exercitu in agrum Sabinum profecti cum ita
vastatione, dein proelio adflixissent opes hostium ut
diu nihil inde rebellionis timeri posset,[3] triumphantes
7 Romam redierunt. P. Valerius, omnium consensu
princeps belli pacisque artibus, anno post Agrippa
Menenio P. Postumio consulibus moritur, gloria ingenti, copiis familiaribus adeo exiguis ut funeri
sumptus deesset; de publico est datus. Luxere
8 matronae ut Brutum. Eodem anno duae coloniae
Latinae, Pometia et Cora, ad Auruncos deficiunt.

[1] Inregillo *Weissenborn* (*cf. Mommsen, C.I.L.* i¹. 444): ciñ regillo *M*: cñ rigillo *M²PFUO*: nc̄ rigillo *B*: ō rigillo *DL*: g̅rigillo *H*: . . . . . . gillo *R*: Cn. Regillo ϛ.
[2] appellati *Madvig*: appellata Ω.
[3] timeri posset *Duker*: timere possent Ω.

[1] By 241 B.C. the number of tribes had grown to thirty-five. After this date no new tribes were added, but newly incorporated districts were assigned to one or another of the already existing tribes. Thus certain members of the

BOOK II. xvi. 2-8

less suspected, Publius Valerius was made consul for the fourth time and Titus Lucretius for the second. A schism which occurred between the advocates of war and those of peace amongst the Sabines resulted in the transfer of some part of their strength to the Romans. For Attius Clausus, afterwards known at Rome as Appius Claudius, himself a champion of peace, was hard beset by the turbulent war-party, and finding himself no match for them, left Inregillus, with a large band of clients, and fled to Rome. These people were made citizens and given land across the Anio. The "Old Claudian Tribe" was the name used later, when new tribesmen had been added, to designate those who came from this territory.[1] Appius, having been enrolled in the senate, came in a short time to be regarded as one of its leading members. The consuls led an army into the country of the Sabines, and by wasting their fields, and afterwards by a battle, so crushed the enemy's strength that there could be no fear for a long time of any outbreak of hostilities in that region. They then returned to Rome and triumphed. Publius Valerius, universally regarded as the foremost citizen, both in military and in civil qualities, died in the following year, when Agrippa Menenius and Publius Postumius were consuls. He was a man of extraordinary reputation, but so poor that money was wanting for his burial, and it was furnished from the treasury of the state. He was mourned by the matrons as Brutus had been. In the same year two Latin colonies, Pometia and Cora, revolted to the Aurunci. The

B.C. 505-503

Claudian Tribe lived elsewhere than in the district "across the Anio," and those who came to Rome for elections from the original seat of the tribe were called the "Old Claudian Tribe." See note in Conway's edition of this Book.

LIVY

A.U.C.
249-251

Cum Auruncis bellum initum, fusoque ingenti exercitu, qui se ingredientibus fines consulibus ferociter obtulerat, omne Auruncum bellum Pometiam compulsum est. Nec magis post proelium quam in proelio caedibus temperatum est; et caesi aliquanto plures erant quam capti, et captos passim trucidaverunt; ne ab obsidibus quidem, qui trecenti accepti numero erant, ira belli abstinuit. Et hoc anno Romae triumphatum.

A.U.C.
252

XVII. Secuti consules Opiter Verginius Sp. Cassius Pometiam primo vi, deinde vineis aliisque operibus oppugnarunt. In quos Aurunci, magis iam inexpiabili odio quam spe aliqua aut occasione coorti, cum plures igni quam ferro armati excucurrissent, caede incendioque cuncta complent. Vineis incensis, multis hostium volneratis et occisis, consulum quoque alterum—sed utrum[1] auctores non adiciunt—gravi volnere ex equo deiectum prope interfecerunt. Romam inde male gesta re reditum. Inter multos saucios consul spe incerta vitae relatus.[2] Interiecto deinde haud magno spatio quod volneribus curandis supplendoque exercitui satis esset, cum ira maiore[3] tum viribus etiam auctis Pometiae arma inlata. Et cum vineis refectis aliaque mole belli iam in eo esset ut

[1] sed utrum *Hertz*: sed verum nomen Ω: verum nomen *Alschefski*.   [2] relatus *Duker*: relictus Ω.
[3] ira maiore ϛ: ira maiore bellum Ω.

---

[1] Livy has nowhere told us about these hostages. In chap. xxii. 2 the same towns give the same number of hostages. Obviously he has made distinct episodes out of

BOOK II. xvi. 8–xvii. 5

Aurunci were the first to be attacked. Upon the defeat of the great army which had boldly issued forth to meet the invasion of their territory by the consuls, the whole weight of the Auruncan war fell upon Pometia. After the battle, as well as during its progress, no quarter was given. The slain had somewhat outnumbered the prisoners, and the prisoners were indiscriminately slaughtered. Even the hostages, of whom three hundred had been received, were not spared in the rage of war.[1] This year also a triumph was celebrated at Rome.

XVII. The consuls of the next year, Opiter Verginius and Spurius Cassius, attempted to capture Pometia, first by assault and then by the use of mantlets and other engines. Against their besiegers the Aurunci, rather of an implacable hatred than for any hope or opportunity offered, rushed out, armed with firebrands for the most part, instead of swords, and carried death and flames in all directions. The mantlets were burned, many of their enemies were wounded or slain, and one of the consuls—which one the historians do not add—was seriously wounded, thrown from his horse, and almost killed. The Romans then marched home, defeated. Amongst the many wounded they brought the consul, hovering betwixt life and death. When a short time had elapsed, long enough for healing wounds and recruiting the army, they returned, with heightened resentment and also with augmented forces, to the attack of Pometia. They had repaired their mantlets and the rest of their equipment, and they were already upon the

different versions of the same story, misled no doubt by the different dates assigned by different annalists to the affair of Pometia.

LIVY

A.U.C. 252

6 in muros evaderet miles, deditio est facta. Ceterum nihilo minus foeda dedita urbe quam si capta foret Aurunci passi:[1] principes securi percussi, sub corona venierunt coloni alii; oppidum dirutum, ager veniit.
7 Consules magis ob iras graviter ultas quam ob magnitudinem perfecti belli triumpharunt.

A.U.C. 253

XVIII. Insequens annus Postumum Cominium et
2 T. Largium[2] consules habuit. Eo anno Romae, cum per ludos ab Sabinorum iuventute per lasciviam scorta raperentur, concursu hominum rixa ac prope proelium fuit, parvaque ex re[3] ad rebellionem spec-
3 tare videbatur. Super[4] belli Sabini[5] metum id quoque accesserat, quod triginta iam coniurasse populos
4 concitante Octavio Mamilio satis constabat. In hac tantarum exspectatione rerum sollicita civitate dictatoris primum creandi mentio orta. Sed nec quo anno, nec quibus consulibus, quia ex factione Tarquiniana essent — id quoque enim traditur — parum creditum sit, nec quis primum dictator creatus sit,
5 satis constat. Apud veterrimos tamen auctores T. Largium[6] dictatorem primum, Sp. Cassium magis-

---

[1] foeda ... passi *Madvig*: foede ... passim Ω.
[2] Largium Ω: Larcium *Madvig (with Dion. Hal.* v. l. 1) *from chap.* xxi. 1. *But Cassiodorius gives* Largus, *and it is safer (with Conway and Walters) to follow the MSS. where, as here, they agree.*
[3] ex re *Gronov.*: ex re res (*or* ex re ... spectare res) Ω.
[4] super *Duker*: supra Ω.
[5] Sabini *R²ς*: Latini Ω: *Conway and Walters bracket* supra ... metum *as a marginal summary.*
[6] Largium Ω: Larcium *Uς* (*so in* § 6, *below*).

BOOK II. xvii. 5–xviii. 5

point of sending their men against the walls when the town capitulated. But the fate of the Aurunci was no less awful from their having surrendered their city than if it had been stormed. Their chief men were beheaded, and the rest of the colonists were sold as slaves.[1] The town was razed; its land was sold. The consuls obtained a triumph, more because they had heavily avenged Rome's wrongs than because of the magnitude of the war which they had successfully concluded.

XVIII. The year after had as its consuls Postumius Cominius and Titus Largius. In this year, during the celebration of the games at Rome, the Sabine youths, in a spirit of wantonness, forcibly abducted certain harlots. Men gathered hastily and there was a brawl which was almost a battle, and, trifling as its origin was, it seemed to threaten a fresh outbreak of the war.[2] Besides the Sabine peril, it was generally known that the thirty Latin cities had already conspired, at the instigation of Octavius Mamilius. These grave apprehensions having occasioned a general anxiety, the appointment of a dictator was suggested, for the first time. But there is no general agreement as to the year, or which consuls were distrusted as being of the Tarquinian faction—for this is included in the tradition—or who it was that was first named dictator. In the oldest writers, however, I find it said that Titus Largius was the first to be made dictator, and that Spurius Cassius was

B.C. 502

B.C. 501

---

[1] Literally "under the crown," meaning a chaplet placed on the head of a captive as an indication that he was a part of the spoils.
[2] Despite the apparently conclusive victory recorded in chap. xvi. 6.

LIVY

trum equitum creatos invenio. Consulares legere;
6 ita lex iubebat de dictatore creando lata. Eo magis
adducor ut credam Largium, qui consularis erat,
potius quam M'. Valerium[1] Marci filium[2] Volesi nepotem, qui nondum consul fuerat, moderatorem et
7 magistrum consulibus appositum; quin,[3] si maxime
ex ea familia legi dictatorem vellent, patrem multo
potius M. Valerium spectatae virtutis et consularem
virum legissent.

8 Creato dictatore primum Romae, postquam praeferri secures viderunt, magnus plebem metus incessit, ut intentiores essent ad dicto parendum.
Neque enim, ut in consulibus qui pari potestate
essent, alterius auxilium, neque provocatio erat neque
9 ullum usquam nisi in cura parendi auxilium. Sabinis
etiam creatus Romae dictator, eo magis quod propter
10 se creatum crediderant, metum incussit. Itaque
legatos de pace mittunt. Quibus orantibus dictatorem senatumque ut veniam erroris hominibus
adulescentibus darent, responsum, ignosci adulescentibus posse, senibus non posse, qui bella ex bellis
11 sererent. Actum tamen est de pace, impetrataque
foret, si, quod impensae factum in bellum erat, praestare Sabini—id enim postulatum erat—in animum
induxissent. Bellum indictum: tacitae indutiae
quietum annum tenuere.

[1] M'. Valerium *Gruter*: M. Valerium Ω.
[2] Marci filium *Rhenanus*: marci fufium (*or the like*) Ω.
[3] quin *Lehnert*: qui (quis *P*) Ω.

---

[1] But in 300 B.C. a *lex Valeria de provocatione* gave the people the right to appeal from the dictator.

BOOK II. XVIII. 5-11

master of the horse. They chose men of consular B.C. 501
rank, for so the law prescribed which had been passed
to regulate the selection of a dictator. I am therefore the more disposed to believe that Largius, a
consular, rather than Manius Valerius, the son of
Marcus and grandson of Volesus, a man who had
not yet held the consulship, was assigned to be the
director and superior of consuls; and indeed if men
had been specially desirous of choosing the dictator
from that family, they would much sooner have
selected Marcus Valerius the father, a man of proven
worth and an ex-consul.

When they had named a dictator for the first time
at Rome, and men saw the axes borne before him, a
great fear came over the plebs and caused them to
be more zealous in obeying orders. For there was
no recourse in this case, as with the consuls, who
shared the powers of their office equally, to the assistance of the man's colleague, nor was there any
appeal nor any help anywhere but in scrupulous
obedience.[1] The Sabines, too, were inspired with
fear by the appointment of the dictator, especially
since they believed that it was on their account that
he had been created. Accordingly they sent legates
to treat for peace. When they requested the dictator and the senate to pardon an error committed
by young men, the answer was given that to pardon
young men was possible, but not old men who contrived one war after another. Nevertheless negotiations for peace were begun, and it would have been
granted to the Sabines, could they have made up
their minds to guarantee, as the Romans demanded,
the sum which had been expended for the war.
Hostilities were declared, but a tacit truce preserved
a state of peace through the year.

LIVY

XIX. Consules Ser.[1] Sulpicius M'. Tullius;[2] nihil dignum memoria actum. T. Aebutius deinde et 2 C. Vetusius. His consulibus Fidenae obsessae, Crustumeria capta, Praeneste ab Latinis ad Romanos descivit. Nec ultra bellum Latinum gliscens iam 3 per aliquot annos dilatum. A. Postumius[3] dictator T. Aebutius magister equitum magnis copiis peditum equitumque profecti ad lacum Regillum in agro Tus- 4 culano agmini hostium occurrerunt, et, quia Tarquinios esse in exercitu Latinorum auditum est, sustineri ira non potuit quin extemplo confligerent. 5 Ergo etiam proelium aliquanto quam cetera gravius atque atrocius fuit. Non enim duces ad regendam modo consilio rem adfuere, sed suismet ipsi[4] corporibus dimicantes miscuere certamina, nec quisquam procerum ferme hac aut illa ex acie sine 6 volnere praeter dictatorem Romanum excessit. In Postumium prima in acie suos adhortantem instruentemque Tarquinius Superbus, quamquam iam aetate et viribus erat gravior, equum infestus admisit, ictusque ab latere concursu suorum receptus in tutum 7 est. Et ad alterum cornu Aebutius magister equitum in Octavium Mamilium impetum dederat, nec

[1] Ser. *Sigonius (from Cic. Brut. 62, cf. Cassiod. C.I.L.* i². *p.* 99): Servilius Ω (*Dion. Hal.* v. lii. 1).
[2] M'. Tullius *Sigonius* (*Dion. Hal. l.c.*): m̄ manlius tullus (*or the like*) Ω.
[3] A. Postumius *Sabellicus* (*Dion. Hal.* VI. ii. 1): aurelius postumius Ω.   [4] ipsi *Gronov.*: ipsis Ω.

BOOK II. xix. 1-7

XIX. In the consulship of Servius Sulpicius and Manius Tullius nothing worthy of note occurred. They were succeeded by Titus Aebutius and Gaius Vetusius. During their year of office Fidenae was besieged, Crustumeria taken; Praeneste went over from the Latins to the Romans, and it was no longer possible to postpone the Latin war, which had now been smouldering for several years. Aulus Postumius as dictator,[1] and Titus Aebutius as master of the horse, set out with large forces of infantry and cavalry, and at Lake Regillus, in the territory of Tusculum, met the enemy's advancing column. The Romans had learned that the Tarquinii were with the Latin army, and were so enraged that they could not be withheld from instantly attacking, and the battle itself, in consequence of this report, was fought with a good deal more determination and bitterness than any other had been. For the leaders were not only in the field to direct the engagement with their strategy, but joined battle and fought in their own persons. Almost none of the nobles on either side came off unscathed, except the Roman dictator. Postumius was in the front rank encouraging his men and forming them, when Tarquinius Superbus, though now burdened with years and broken in strength, rode full-tilt against him. But the old man received a thrust in the side, and his followers rushed in and rescued him. Similarly on the other wing, Aebutius, the master of the horse, charged Octavius Mamilius. But the Tusculan commander

B.C. 500-499

---

[1] Postumius had not held the consulship, which in chap. xviii. 5 Livy stated to have been a necessary qualification for the dictatorship.

LIVY

A.U.C.
254-255

fefellit veniens Tusculanum ducem, contra quem[1] et
8 ille concitat equum. Tantaque vis infestis venientium hastis fuit, ut bracchium Aebutio traiectum sit,
9 Mamilio pectus percussum. Hunc quidem in secundam aciem Latini recepere: Aebutius cum saucio
bracchio tenere telum non posset, pugna excessit.
10 Latinus dux nihil deterritus volnere proelium ciet
et, quia suos perculsos videbat, arcessit cohortem
exsulum Romanorum, cui L. Tarquini filius praeerat. Ea, quo[2] maiore pugnabat ira ob erepta bona
patriamque ademptam, pugnam parumper restituit.

XX. Referentibus iam pedem ab ea parte Romanis
M. Valerius Publicolae frater conspicatus ferocem
iuvenem Tarquinium ostentantem se in prima exsulum acie, domestica etiam gloria accensus, ut cuius
2 familiae decus eiecti reges erant, eiusdem interfecti
forent, subdit calcaria equo et Tarquinium infesto
3 spiculo petit. Tarquinius retro in agmen suorum
infenso cessit hosti. Valerium temere invectum in
exsulum aciem ex transverso quidam adortus transfigit, nec quicquam equitis volnere equo retardato
moribundus Romanus labentibus super corpus armis
4 ad terram defluxit. Dictator Postumius postquam
cecidisse talem virum, exsules ferociter citato agmine
5 invehi, suos perculsos cedere animadvertit, cohorti

[1] contra quem Ω: contraque *Madvig.*
[2] Ea, quo *MPRD*: ea q̄uo *HL*: ea quoniam *O*: eo quo
P²FUB: eoque *M³*.

---

[1] Of the sons of Tarquinius, Sextus's death is mentioned
in I. lx. 2 and that of Arruns in II. vi. 9. This must therefore have been Titus (I. lvi. 6).

BOOK II. xix. 7–xx. 5

saw him coming, and he too spurred his horse to the encounter; and so great was the force in their levelled lances as they met, that the arm of Aebutius was transfixed, while Mamilius was struck in the breast. Mamilius was received by the Latins within their second line: Aebutius, being unable to manage a weapon with his wounded arm, retired from the battle. The Latin leader, not a jot discouraged by his wound, urged on the fighting, and, because he saw that his men were in retreat, called up a cohort of Roman exiles, commanded by a son of Lucius Tarquinius,[1] and these, fighting with greater fury on account of the loss of their property and native land, restored the battle for a while.

XX. When the Romans were now beginning to give way in that part of the field, Marcus Valerius, Publicola's brother, espied the young Tarquinius, who was boldly inviting attack in the front rank of the exiles. Valerius found in his brother's glory an additional incentive, and resolving that the family which had the honour of expelling the tyrants should also gain the credit for their death, he dug his spurs into his charger and rode at Tarquinius with levelled spear. Tarquinius drew back within the company of his followers to avoid his desperate antagonist. Valerius was plunging blindly into the exiles' line when one of them attacked him in the flank and ran him through the body. But the rider's wound did not check the career of his horse, and the dying Roman came down in a heap upon the ground with his arms upon him. When the dictator Postumius perceived that so brave a soldier had fallen, that the exiles were advancing boldly at the double, and that his troops were checked and were giving

suae, quam delectam manum praesidii causa circa se habebat, dat signum ut quem suorum fugientem viderint pro hoste habeant. Ita metu ancipiti versi 6 a fuga Romani in hostem et restituta acies. Cohors dictatoris tum primum proelium iniit; integris corporibus 7 animisque fessos adorti exsules caedunt. Ibi alia inter proceres coorta pugna. Imperator Latinus ubi cohortem exsulum a dictatore Romano prope circumventam vidit, ex subsidiariis manipulos aliquot in 8 primam aciem secum rapit. Hos agmine venientes T. Herminius legatus conspicatus interque eos insignem veste armisque Mamilium noscitans tanto vi maiore quam paulo ante magister equitum cum hostium 9 duce proelium iniit, ut et uno ictu transfixum per latus occiderit Mamilium et ipse inter spoliandum corpus hostis veruto percussus, cum victor in castra esset relatus, inter primam curationem exspi-10 raverit. Tum ad equites dictator advolat obtestans ut fesso iam pedite descendant ex equis et pugnam capessant. Dicto paruere: desiliunt ex equis, provolant in primum et pro antesignanis parmas obi-11 ciunt. Recipit extemplo animum pedestris acies, postquam iuventutis proceres aequato genere pugnae secum partem periculi sustinentes vidit. Tum de-

BOOK II. xx. 5-11

ground, he issued orders to his own cohort, a picked body of men which he kept about his person as a guard, that if they saw any Roman running away they should treat him as an enemy. Being thus between two dangers, the Romans faced about to meet the foe, and the battle-line was formed again. The cohort of the dictator then entered the engagement for the first time. With fresh strength and spirit they attacked the weary exiles and cut them to pieces. Then began another combat between leaders. The Latin general, perceiving that the cohort of the exiles was nearly cut off by the Roman dictator, took a few companies of his reserves and hurried them to the front. As they came marching up, Titus Herminius, the lieutenant, caught sight of them, and in their midst, conspicuous in dress and accoutrements, he saw and recognized Mamilius. Whereupon he hurled himself upon the enemy's commander with so much more violence than the master of the horse had done a little before, that not only did he pierce Mamilius through the side and slay him with a single lunge, but in the act of stripping the body of his antagonist he was himself struck by a hostile javelin, and after being borne off in the moment of victory to the Roman camp, expired just as they began to dress his wound. The dictator then dashed up to the knights and besought them, since the foot-soldiers were exhausted, to dismount and enter the fight. They obeyed: they leaped down from their horses, hastened to the front, and covered the front-rankers with their shields. It restored at once the courage of the foot to see the young nobles on even terms with themselves and sharing in the danger. Then at last the

LIVY

mum impulsi Latini, perculsaque inclinavit acies.
12 Equiti admoti equi ut persequi hostem posset;
secuta et pedestris acies. Ibi nihil nec divinae nec
humanae opis dictator praetermittens aedem Castori
vovisse fertur ac pronuntiasse militi praemia qui
13 primus, qui secundus castra hostium intrasset; tantusque ardor fuit ut eodem impetu quo fuderant
hostem Romani castra caperent. Hoc modo ad
lacum Regillum pugnatum est. Dictator et magister equitum triumphantes in urbem rediere.

XXI. Triennio deinde nec certa pax nec bellum
fuit. Consules Q. Cloelius et T. Larcius,[1] inde
2 A. Sempronius et M. Minucius. His consulibus aedis
Saturno dedicata, Saturnalia institutus festus dies.
3 A. deinde Postumius et T. Verginius consules facti.
Hoc demum anno ad Regillum lacum pugnatum
apud quosdam invenio; A. Postumium, quia collega
dubiae fidei fuerit, se consulatu abdicasse; dictato-
4 rem inde factum. Tanti errores implicant temporum
aliter apud alios ordinatis magistratibus ut nec qui
consules secundum quos,[2] nec quid quoque anno
actum sit in tanta vetustate non rerum modo sed
etiam auctorum digerere possis.

[1] Larcius Ω : Lartius *UO* : Largius ς : Largus *Cassiod.*,
Mommsen, C.I.L. i.[2] p. 99 (*but Dion. Hal.* v. lix. 1, *has*
Λάρκιος).
[2] quos *Crevier*: quosdam Ω.

---

[1] The Saturnalia proper fell on December 17, though as
many as seven days came to be devoted to the popular cele-

BOOK II. xx. 11–xxi. 4

Latins received a check, and their battle-line was forced to yield. The knights had their horses brought up that they might be able to pursue the enemy, and they were followed by the infantry. Then the dictator, neglecting no help, divine or human, is said to have vowed a temple to Castor, and to have promised rewards to the soldiers who should be first and second to enter the camp of the enemy; and so great was the ardour of the Romans, that with a single rush they routed their opponents and took their camp. Such was the battle at Lake Regillus. The dictator and his master of the horse returned to the City and triumphed.

XXI. For the next three years there was neither a stable peace nor war. The consuls Quintus Cloelius and Titus Larcius were followed by Aulus Sempronius and Marcus Minucius. In the latter year a temple to Saturn was dedicated and the Saturnalia was established as a festal day.[1] Next Aulus Postumius and Titus Verginius were made consuls. It was not until this year, according to some authorities I have consulted, that the battle of Lake Regillus was fought. They say that Aulus Postumius, because his colleague was of doubtful loyalty, resigned the consulship, and was then made dictator. One is involved in so many uncertainties regarding dates by the varying order of the magistrates in different lists that it is impossible to make out which consuls followed which, or what was done in each particular year, when not only events but even authorities are so shrouded in antiquity.

bration of the festival (Macrobius, I. x. 24), which was a sort of carnival. As an old Italic feast it probably originated earlier than Livy thought. See Macrobius I. viii. 1.

LIVY

A.U.C. 259

5 Ap. Claudius deinde et P. Servilius consules facti. Insignis hic annus est nuntio Tarquini mortis. Mortuus Cumis, quo se post fractas opes Latinorum ad 6 Aristodemum tyrannum contulerat. Eo nuntio erecti patres, erecta plebes. Sed patribus nimis luxuriosa ea fuit laetitia: plebi, cui ad eam diem summa ope inservitum erat, iniuriae a primoribus fieri coepere. 7 Eodem anno Signia colonia, quam rex Tarquinius deduxerat, suppleto numero colonorum iterum deducta est. Romae tribus una et viginti factae. Aedes Mercuri dedicata est idibus Maiis.

XXII. Cum Volscorum gente Latino bello neque pax neque bellum fuerat; nam et Volsci comparaverant auxilia quae mitterent Latinis, ni maturatum ab dictatore Romano esset, et maturavit Romanus, ne proelio uno cum Latino Volscoque contenderet. 2 Hac ira consules in Volscum agrum legiones duxere. Volscos consilii poenam non metuentes necopinata res perculit; armorum immemores obsides dant trecentos principum a Cora atque Pometia liberos. Ita 3 sine certamine inde abductae legiones. Nec ita multo post Volscis levatis metu suum rediit ingenium; rursus occultum parant bellum Hernicis in 4 societatem armorum adsumptis. Legatos quoque ad

BOOK II. xxi. 5–xxii. 4

At the next election Appius Claudius and Publius Servilius were chosen consuls. This year was marked by the announcement of Tarquinius's death. He died at Cumae, whither he had gone to the court of Aristodemus after the downfall of the Latin cause. These tidings cheered the Fathers and encouraged the plebs. But the Fathers were too inconsiderate, in consequence of their rejoicing at this event; and the plebs, who up to this time had been most studiously deferred to, began to feel the oppression of the nobles. The same year the colony of Signia, which King Tarquinius had planted, was recruited with new colonists and established for the second time. At Rome twenty-one tribes were formed. The temple of Mercury was consecrated on the fifteenth of May.

XXII. With the Volscian race there had been during the Latin war neither peace nor open hostilities; for while the Volsci had raised levies to send to the aid of the Latins, had the Roman dictator not moved quickly, yet the Romans did move quickly, that they might not have to fight both nations in the same battle Upon this quarrel the consuls led their legions into the country of the Volsci, who, not expecting to be held to account for their design, were surprised and overwhelmed. They had no thought of resisting, and surrendered as hostages three hundred children of the nobility of Cora and Pometia, and so the legions were withdrawn without a conflict. Yet it was not long before the Volsci, being relieved of their alarm, resumed their native duplicity; again they made secret preparations for war, and formed a military alliance with the Hernici, while they also sent out envoys, this

LIVY

sollicitandum Latium passim dimittunt; sed recens ad Regillum lacum accepta cladis Latinos ira odioque eius, quicumque arma suaderet, ne ab legatis quidem violandis abstinuit; comprehensos Volscos Romam duxere. Ibi traditi consulibus, indicatumque est 5 Volscos Hernicosque parare bellum Romanis. Relata re ad senatum adeo fuit gratum patribus ut et captivorum sex milia Latinis remitterent et de foedere, quod prope in perpetuum negatum fuerat, rem ad 6 novos magistratus traicerent. Enimvero tum Latini gaudere facto; pacis auctores in ingenti gloria esse. Coronam auream Iovi donum in Capitolium mittunt. Cum legatis donoque qui captivorum remissi ad suos 7 fuerant, magna circumfusa multitudo, venit. Pergunt domos eorum apud quem quisque servierant; gratias agunt liberaliter habiti cultique in calamitate sua; inde hospitia iungunt. Nunquam alias ante publice privatimque Latinum nomen Romano imperio coniunctius fuit.

XXIII. Sed et bellum Volscum imminebat, et civitas secum ipsa discors intestino inter patres plebemque flagrabat odio, maxime propter nexos ob aes 2 alienum. Fremebant se foris pro libertate et im-

---

[1] Neither captives nor treaty were mentioned in chap. xx., and Livy seems here to be following a different authority, possibly Valerius of Antium, whom at XXXIII. x. 8 he accuses of exaggerating numbers.

[2] The word *nexus* was used (1) of one who had borrowed money by "binding" himself to work out the debt as a virtual slave of his creditor, if unable to repay the money; (2) of one so "bound" and actually serving.

BOOK II. XXII. 4–XXIII. 2

way and that, to instigate the Latins to rebellion. B.C. 495
But the disaster which had recently befallen the
Latins at Lake Regillus so filled them with rage and
hate against anyone who advised them to go to war,
that they did not even abstain from violating an
embassy, but seized the Volsci and brought them
to Rome. There they delivered them up to the
consuls with the information that the Volsci and
the Hernici were preparing to attack the Romans.
When this service had been reported to the senate
the Fathers were so grateful that they released to
the Latins six thousand captives, and referred the
question of a treaty, which they had all but refused
in perpetuity, to the incoming magistrates.[1] Then,
indeed, the Latins rejoiced at the action they had
taken, and the advocates of peace were in great
repute. They sent a golden crown as a gift to the
Capitoline Jupiter. With the envoys who brought
the gift came the captives who had been restored to
their friends, a vast attendant multitude. Proceeding
to the homes of those whom they had severally
served, they thanked them for the liberality and
consideration which had been shown them in their
adversity, and entered into covenants of hospitality
with them. Never before had there been so close a
union, both official and personal, between the Latin
name and the Roman state.

XXIII. But not only was war with the Volsci imminent; the citizens were at loggerheads among
themselves, and internal dissensions between the
Fathers and the plebs had burst into a blaze of
hatred, chiefly on account of those who had been
bound over to service for their debts.[2] These men
complained loudly that while they were abroad fight-

289

LIVY

perio dimicantes domi a civibus captos et oppressos
esse, tutioremque in bello quam in pace et inter
hostis quam inter civis libertatem plebis esse; invi-
diamque eam sua sponte gliscentem insignis unius
3 calamitas accendit. Magno natu quidam cum omnium malorum[1] suorum insignibus se in forum proie-
cit. Obsita erat squalore vestis, foedior corporis
4 habitus pallore ac macie perempti; ad hoc promissa
barba et capilli efferaverant speciem oris. Noscita-
batur tamen in tanta deformitate, et ordines duxisse
aiebant aliaque militiae decora volgo miserantes eum
iactabant; ipse testes honestarum aliquot locis pug-
5 narum cicatrices adverso pectore ostentabat. Sciscitantibus unde ille habitus, unde deformitas, cum
circumfusa turba esset prope in contionis modum
Sabino bello ait se militantem, quia propter populationes agri non fructu modo caruerit, sed villa incensa
fuerit, direpta omnia, pecora abacta, tributum inique
6 suo tempore imperatum, aes alienum fecisse. Id
cumulatum usuris primo se agro paterno avitoque
exuisse, deinde fortunis aliis, postremo velut tabem
pervenisse ad corpus; ductum se ab creditore non
in servitium, sed in ergastulum et carnificinam esse

[1] malorum *Lipsius*: maiorum Ω.

ing for liberty and dominion they had been enslaved B.C. 495
and oppressed at home by fellow-citizens, and that
the freedom of the plebeians was more secure in
war than in peace, amongst enemies than amongst
citizens. This bitter feeling, which was growing
spontaneously, the notable calamity of one man
fanned into a flame. Old, and bearing the marks of
all his misfortunes, the man rushed into the Forum.
His dress was covered with filth, and the condition
of his body was even worse, for he was pale and half
dead with emaciation. Besides this, his straggling
beard and hair had given a savage look to his countenance. He was recognized nevertheless, despite
the hideousness of his appearance, and the word
went round that he had commanded companies; yet
other military honours were openly ascribed to him
by the compassionate bystanders, and the man himself displayed the scars on his breast which bore
testimony to his honourable service in various battles.
When they asked the reason of his condition and
his squalor, he replied, while the crowd gathered
about him much as though it were an assembly,
that during his service in the Sabine war not only
had the enemy's depredations deprived him of his
crops, but his cottage had been burnt, all his belongings plundered, and his flocks driven off. Then
the taxes had been levied, in an untoward moment
for him, and he had contracted debts. When these
had been swelled by usury, they had first stripped
him of the farm which had been his father's and his
grandfather's, then of the remnants of his property,
and finally like an infection they had attacked his
person, and he had been carried off by his creditor,
not to slavery, but to the prison and the torture-

LIVY

7 Inde ostentare tergum foedum recentibus vestigiis verberum. Ad haec visa auditaque clamor ingens oritur. Non iam foro se tumultus continet[1] sed
8 passim totam urbem pervadit. Nexi[2] vincti solutique se undique in publicum proripiunt, implorant Quiritium fidem. Nullo loco deest seditionis voluntarius comes; multis passim agminibus per omnes
9 vias cum clamore in forum curritur. Magno cum periculo suo qui forte patrum in foro erant in eam
10 turbam inciderunt; nec temperatum manibus foret, ni propere consules, P. Servilius et Ap. Claudius, ad comprimendam seditionem intervenissent. At in eos multitudo versa ostentare vincula sua deformitatem-
11 que aliam. Haec se meritos dicere exprobrantes suam quisque alius alibi militiam; postulare multo minaciter magis quam suppliciter ut senatum vocarent; curiamque ipsi futuri arbitri moderatoresque
12 publici consilii circumsistunt. Pauci admodum patrum, quos casus obtulerat, contracti ab consulibus: ceteros metus non curia modo sed etiam foro arcebat, nec agi quicquam per infrequentiam poterat
13 senatus. Tum vero eludi atque extrahi se multitudo putare,[3] et patrum qui abessent non casu, non metu, sed impediendae rei causa abesse, et consules ipsos

---

[1] continet ς : sustinet Ω.
[2] nexi $R^2\varsigma$: inexsui M : nexu Ω.
[3] putare $HD^2\varsigma$: putaret Ω.

chamber. He then showed them his back, disfigured
with the wales of recent scourging. The sight of
these things and the man's recital produced a mighty
uproar. The disturbance was no longer confined to
the Forum, but spread in all directions through the
entire City. Those who had been bound over, whether
in chains or not, broke out into the streets from every
side, and implored the Quirites to protect them. At
no point was there any lack of volunteers to join the
rising; everywhere crowds were streaming through
the different streets and shouting as they hurried to
the Forum. Great was the peril of those senators
who happened to be in the Forum and fell in with
the mob, which would not indeed have stopped
short of violence had not the consuls, Publius Servilius and Appius Claudius, hurriedly intervened to
put down the insurrection. But the crowd turned
on them and displayed their chains and other hideous
tokens. These, they cried, were the rewards they
had earned, and they bitterly rehearsed the campaigns they had each served in various places. They
demanded, in a manner much more threatening than
suppliant, that the consuls should convene the senate;
and they surrounded the Curia, that they might themselves witness and control the deliberations of the
state. The consuls succeeded in collecting only a
few of the senators whom chance had thrown in their
way. The rest were afraid to enter not only the
Curia but even the Forum, and nothing could be done
because those present were too few. Whereat the
people concluded they were being flouted and put off,
and that the missing senators were absent not from
accident, nor fear, but with the intent to hinder action,
and that the consuls themselves were paltering;

tergiversari, nec dubie ludibrio esse miserias suas.
14 Iam prope erat ut ne consulum quidem maiestas coerceret iras hominum, cum, incerti morando an veniendo plus periculi contraherent, tandem in senatum veniunt; frequentique tandem curia non modo inter patres sed ne inter consules quidem ipsos satis
15 conveniebat. Appius, vehementis ingenii vir, imperio consulari rem agendam censebat: uno aut altero arrepto quieturos alios; Servilius, lenibus remediis aptior, concitatos animos flecti quam frangi putabat cum tutius tum facilius esse.

XXIV. Inter haec maior alius terror: Latini equites cum tumultuoso advolant nuntio Volscos infesto exercitu ad urbem oppugnandam venire. Quae audita—adeo duas ex una civitate discordia fecerat—
2 longe aliter patres ac plebem adfecere. Exsultare gaudio plebes, ultores superbiae patrum adesse dicere deos; alius alium confirmare, ne nomina darent: cum omnibus potius quam solos perituros; patres militarent, patres arma caperent, ut penes eosdem peri-
3 cula belli, penes quos praemia essent. At vero curia maesta ac trepida ancipiti metu et ab cive et ab hoste Servilium consulem, cui ingenium magis populare erat, orare ut tantis circumventam terroribus

BOOK II. XXIII. 13–XXIV. 3

nor did they doubt that their misery was made a jest. A little more and not even the majesty of the consuls could have held in check the angry crowd, when the absent Fathers, uncertain whether they should incur more danger by holding back or by coming forward, finally came into the senate, and the required number being at length assembled, not only the senators, but even the consuls themselves were unable to agree. Appius, a headstrong man, was for settling the matter by the exercise of consular authority; when one or two men had been arrested, the others, he said, would calm down. Servilius, more inclined to gentle measures, believed that it was safer, as well as easier, to assuage their fury than to quell it.

XXIV. In the midst of the debate a greater alarm arose from a new quarter, for some Latin horsemen galloped up with the disquieting news that a Volscian army was advancing to attack the City. This report awoke very different feelings—so completely had their dissensions divided the state into two—in the Fathers and the plebs. The commons were jubilant; they said that the gods were taking a hand in punishing the arrogance of the senators. They encouraged one another not to give in their names; it would be better to perish all together than alone. Let the Fathers serve, let the Fathers take up arms, that those might incur the hazards of war who received its rewards. The Curia, on the other hand, was downcast and dismayed. In their twofold fear —of their fellow-citizens and of the enemy—they begged Servilius the consul, whose character appealed more to the people than did that of his colleague, that he would extricate the state from

B.C. 495

LIVY

4 expediret rem publicam. Tum consul misso senatu in contionem prodit. Ibi curae esse patribus ostendit ut consulatur plebi; ceterum deliberationi de maxima quidem illa sed tamen parte civitatis metum 5 pro universa re publica intervenisse. Nec posse, cum hostes prope ad portas essent, bello praeverti se[1] quicquam, nec, si sit laxamenti aliquid, aut plebi honestum esse, nisi mercede prius accepta arma pro patria non cepisse, neque patribus satis decorum per metum potius quam postmodo voluntate adflictis 6 civium suorum fortunis consuluisse. Contioni deinde edicto addidit fidem, quo edixit ne quis civem Romanum vinctum aut clausum teneret, quo minus ei nominis edendi apud consules potestas fieret, neu quis militis, donec in castris esset, bona possideret 7 aut venderet, liberos nepotesve eius moraretur. Hoc proposito edicto et qui aderant nexi profiteri extemplo nomina, et undique ex tota urbe proripientium se ex privato, cum retinendi ius creditori non esset, concursus in forum, ut sacramento dicerent, fieri. 8 Magna ea manus fuit, neque aliorum magis in Volsco bello virtus atque opera enituit. Consul copias contra hostem educit; parvo dirimente intervallo castra ponit.

[1] praeverti se *Weissenborn* : praeuertisse Ω : peruetisse *M* : praeuerti *Hertz*.

BOOK II. XXIV. 3-8

the fearful perils with which it was beset. Thereupon the consul adjourned the senate and went before the people. There he declared that the Fathers were anxious to consult the interests of the plebs, but that their deliberations concerning that very important part—but only a part after all—of the state had been broken off by their fears for the entire nation. It was impossible, when the enemy was almost at the city gates, to consider anything before the war; and even if there should be some slight respite in that regard, it was neither to the credit of the plebs to refuse to arm for their country, unless they should first receive a recompense, nor honourable to the Fathers to be driven by fear into passing measures for the relief of their fellow-citizens which they would have passed later of their own free will. He then confirmed his speech by a proclamation in which he commanded that no one should hold a Roman citizen in chains or durance so that he should not be able to give in his name to the consuls, and that none should seize or sell a soldier's property so long as he was in camp, or interfere with his children or his grandchildren. When this edict had been published, the debtors who were present at once enlisted, and from every quarter, all over the City, they hastened from the houses where their creditors no longer had the right to detain them, and rushed into the Forum to take the military oath. It was a great throng, nor were there any soldiers whose courage and usefulness in the Volscian war were more conspicuous. The consul led his troops against the enemy, and pitched his camp at a short distance from theirs.

LIVY

XXV. Proxima inde nocte Volsci, discordia Romana freti, si qua nocturna transitio proditiove fieri posset,[1] temptant castra. Sensere vigiles, excitatus exercitus, signo dato concursum est ad arma; ita frustra id inceptum Volscis fuit; reliquum noctis utrimque quieti datum. Postero die prima luce Volsci fossis repletis vallum invadunt. Iamque ab omni parte munimenta vellebantur, cum consul, quamquam cuncti undique, et nexi ante omnes, ut signum daret clamabant, experiendi animos militum causa parumper moratus, postquam satis apparebat ingens ardor, dato tandem ad erumpendum signo militem avidum certaminis emittit. Primo statim incursu pulsi hostes; fugientibus, quoad insequi pedes potuit, terga caesa; eques usque ad castra pavidos egit. Mox ipsa castra legionibus circumdatis, cum Volscos inde etiam pavor expulisset, capta direptaque. Postero die ad Suessam Pometiam, quo confugerant hostes, legionibus ductis, intra paucos dies oppidum capitur, captum praedae datum. Inde paulum recreatus egens miles. Consul cum maxima gloria sua victorem exercitum Romam reducit. Decedentem Romam Ecetranorum[2] Volscorum legati,

---

[1] posset *MPFUBO* : possit *HRDL Ald.*

[2] Romam Ecetranorum *F*?*L* (*written* ec etr-) *ς* : roma mecetranorum *MPR* : roma matranorum (ce *written over* -at-) *B* : romam cetranorum *D* : romam mecetranorum *OH* : romam macetranorum *D*²ς⁻ : Ecetranorum *Crevier.*

XXV. The next night the Volsci, relying on the B.C. 495
lack of harmony among the Romans, attacked their
camp on the chance that the darkness might encourage desertions or treachery. But the sentries
perceived them, the army was roused, and, the signal
being given, rushed to arms. Thus the design of the
Volsci came to naught, and the remainder of the
night was devoted by both armies to sleeping. On
the following day at dawn the Volsci filled up the
trenches and assaulted the rampart, and soon they
were everywhere pulling down the palisades. On
every side the consul's men were clamouring for the
signal—none more loudly than the debtors. He
waited a moment, to test the temper of the soldiers.
When there could no longer be any doubt of their
great ardour, he finally gave the command for a
sortie and released them, eager for the fray. At the
very first onset the enemy were routed. While they
ran, the foot-soldiers struck at them from behind as
long as they could keep up the pursuit; then the
horsemen drove them panic-stricken clear to their
camp. Soon the camp itself had been surrounded
by the legions, and when the Volsci had fled from it
in terror, it was taken and plundered. Next day
Servilius led his forces to Suessa Pometia, where the
enemy had taken refuge, and within a few days took
the town and gave it up to be sacked.[1] This yielded
some slight relief to the soldiers, who needed it
badly. The consul led his army back to Rome, with
great honour to himself. As he was setting out on
his return thither ambassadors approached him from

[1] But it had already been razed, as we read in chap. xvii. 6—
another indication that Livy is reproducing different versions
of the same story (see chap. xvi. 9 and note).

LIVY

rebus suis timentes post Pometiam captam, adeunt. His ex senatus consulto data pax, ager ademptus.

XXVI. Confestim et Sabini Romanos territavere; tumultus enim fuit verius quam bellum. Nocte in urbem nuntiatum est exercitum Sabinum praedabundum ad Anienem amnem pervenisse; ibi passim 2 diripi atque incendi villas. Missus extemplo eo cum omnibus copiis equitum A. Postumius, qui dictator bello Latino fuerat; secutus consul Servilius cum 3 delecta peditum manu. Plerosque palantes eques circumvenit, nec advenienti peditum agmini restitit Sabina legio; fessi cum itinere tum populatione nocturna, magna pars in villis repleti cibo vinoque, vix fugae quod satis esset virium habuere.

4 Nocte una audito perfectoque bello Sabino postero die in magna iam spe undique partae pacis legati Aurunci senatum adeunt, ni decedatur Volsco agro 5 bellum indicentes. Cum legatis simul exercitus Auruncorum domo profectus erat; cuius fama haud procul iam ab Aricia visi tanto tumultu concivit Romanos ut nec consuli ordine patres nec pacatum responsum arma inferentibus arma ipsi capientes 6 dare possent. Ariciam infesto agmine itur, nec

BOOK II. xxv. 6–xxvi. 6

the Volsci of Ecetra, who were alarmed at their own prospects, in view of the capture of Pometia. A decree of the senate granted them peace, but took away their land.

XXVI. Directly after this the Sabines also caused an alarm at Rome—for it was indeed a turmoil rather than war. One night the City got word that a Sabine army bent on pillage had come as near as the river Anio, and was there plundering and burning farmhouses right and left. The Romans at once dispatched in that direction all their cavalry, under Aulus Postumius, who had been dictator in the Latin war. He was followed by the consul Servilius with a picked body of foot-soldiers. Many stragglers were cut off by the cavalry and, when the column of infantry drew near, no resistance was offered by the Sabine troops. Exhausted not only by their march but by their night of pillage as well, a great part of them had gorged themselves in the farmhouses with food and wine, and had scarcely vigour enough to run away.

A single night having sufficed for hearing of the Sabine war and ending it, men's hopes next day ran high that peace was now assured in every quarter, when legates from the Aurunci appeared before the senate to say that unless the territory of the Volsci were evacuated they should declare war. The Auruncan army had set out from home at the same time with the legates, and the report that it had already been seen not far from Aricia threw Rome into such a state of confusion that it was impossible to bring the matter regularly before the senate, or to return a peaceful answer to a people who had already drawn the sword, while they themselves were also arming. They marched on Aricia in fighting order, joined

B.C. 495

LIVY

procul inde cum Auruncis signa conlata proelioque uno debellatum est.

XXVII. Fusis Auruncis victor tot intra paucos dies bellis Romanus promissa consulis fidemque senatus exspectabat, cum Appius et insita superbia animo et ut collegae vanam faceret fidem, quam asperrime poterat, ius de creditis pecuniis dicere. Deinceps et qui ante nexi fuerant creditoribus tradebantur et 2 nectebantur alii. Quod ubi cui militi inciderat, collegam appellabat. Concursus ad Servilium fiebat; illius promissa iactabant; illi exprobrabant sua quisque belli merita cicatricesque acceptas. Postulabant ut aut referret ad senatum, aut[1] auxilio esset consul 3 civibus suis, imperator militibus. Movebant consulem haec, sed tergiversari res cogebat; adeo in alteram causam non collega solum praeceps erat[2] sed omnis factio nobilium. Ita medium se gerendo nec plebis vitavit odium nec apud patres gratiam iniit. 4 Patres mollem consulem et ambitiosum rati, plebes fallacem; brevique apparuit adaequasse eum Appi 5 odium. Certamen consulibus inciderat uter dedicaret Mercuri aedem. Senatus a se rem ad populum reiecit: utri eorum dedicatio iussu populi data esset,

---

[1] aut *Madvig*: aut ut Ω.   [2] praeceps erat ⲋ: praeceperat Ω.

BOOK II. xxvi. 6–xxvii. 5

battle with the Aurunci not far from the town, and B.C. 495
in a single engagement finished the war.

XXVII. Having routed the Aurunci, and having been, within a few days, victorious in so many wars, the Romans were looking for the help which the consul had promised and the senate guaranteed, when Appius, partly out of native arrogance, partly to discredit his colleague, began to pronounce judgment with the utmost rigour in suits to recover debts. In consequence, not only were those who had been bound over before delivered up to their creditors, but others were bound over. Whenever this happened to a soldier he would appeal to the other consul. The people flocked to the house of Servilius: it was he who had made them promises; it was he whom they reproached, as each rehearsed his services in the wars and displayed the scars he had received. They demanded that he should either lay the matter before the senate or lend his aid as consul to his fellow-citizens, as general to his soldiers. They moved the consul by this plea, but the situation forced him to temporize, so vehemently was the other side supported, not only by his colleague, but by the entire party of the nobles. And so he steered a middle course, and neither avoided the dislike of the plebs nor gained the goodwill of the Fathers. These considered him a pusillanimous consul and an agitator, while the commons held him to be dishonest; and it was soon apparent that he was as cordially hated as Appius. The consuls had got into a dispute as to which should dedicate the temple to Mercury. The senate referred the case to the people for decision. Whichever consul should, by command of the people, be entrusted with the dedication was to have charge

LIVY

eum praeesse annonae, mercatorum collegium instituere, sollemnia pro pontifice iussit suscipere. Populus dedicationem aedis dat M. Laetorio, primi pili centurioni, quod facile appareret non tam ad honorem eius, cui curatio altior fastigio suo data esset, factum quam ad consulum ignominiam. Saevire inde utique consulum alter patresque; sed plebi creverant animi, et longe alia quam primo instituerant via grassabantur. Desperato enim consulum senatusque auxilio, cum in ius duci debitorem vidissent, undique convolabant. Neque decretum exaudiri consulis prae strepitu et clamore poterat, neque cum decresset quisquam obtemperabat. Vi agebatur, metusque omnis et periculum,[1] cum in conspectu consulis singuli a pluribus violarentur, in creditores a debitoribus verterant. Super haec timor incessit Sabini belli; dilectuque decreto nemo nomen dedit, furente Appio et insectante ambitionem collegae, qui populari silentio rem publicam proderet, et ad id quod de credita pecunia ius non dixisset, adiceret ut ne dilectum quidem ex senatus consulto haberet: non esse tamen desertam omnino rem publicam neque proiectum consulare imperium, se unum et suae et patrum maiestatis vindicem fore. Cum circumstaret cotidiana multitudo licentia accensa, arripi unum insig-

[1] periculum *M*: periculum libertatis Ω.

---

[1] Mercury was the patron of trade.

BOOK II. XXVII. 5–12

of the corn-supply, to establish a guild of merchants,[1] B.C. 495
and perform the solemn rites in the presence of
the pontifex. The people assigned the dedication to
Marcus Laetorius, a centurion of the first rank—a
choice which would readily be understood as intended
not so much to honour Laetorius, to whom a com-
mission had been given which was too exalted for
his station in life, as to humiliate the consuls. Appius
and the Fathers were furious then, if they had not
been before; but the plebeians had plucked up heart
and threw themselves into the struggle with far more
spirit than they had shown at first. For, despairing
of help from consuls and senate, they no sooner beheld a debtor being haled away than they flew to
his assistance from every side. It was impossible
for the consul's decree to be heard above the din
and shouting, and when it had been pronounced
nobody obeyed it. Violence was the order of the
day, and fear and danger had quite shifted from the
debtors to the creditors, who were singled out and
maltreated by large numbers in full sight of the
consul. To crown these troubles came the fear of
a Sabine invasion. A levy was decreed, but no one
enlisted. Appius stormed and railed at the insidious
arts of his colleague, who, he said, to make himself
popular, was betraying the state by his inactivity;
and to his refusal to give judgment for debt was
adding a fresh offence in refusing to hold the levy
as the senate had directed. Nevertheless the welfare
of the state was not wholly forgotten, nor the authority of the consulate abandoned; he would himself, single-handed, assert both his own and the
senate's majesty. When the usual daily throng of
lawless men was standing about him, he gave orders

LIVY

nem ducem seditionum iussit. Ille cum a lictoribus iam traheretur, provocavit; nec cessisset provocationi consul, quia non dubium erat populi iudicium, nisi aegre victa pertinacia foret consilio magis et auctoritate principum quam populi clamore; adeo 13 supererant animi ad sustinendam invidiam. Crescere inde malum in dies non clamoribus modo apertis sed, quod multo perniciosius erat, secessione occultisque conloquiis. Tandem invisi plebi consules magistratu abeunt, Servilius neutris, Appius patribus mire gratus.

XXVIII. A. Verginius inde et T. Vetusius consulatum ineunt. Tum vero plebs, incerta quales habitura consules esset, coetus nocturnos, pars Esquiliis, pars in Aventino facere, ne in foro subitis trepidaret 2 consiliis et omnia temere ac fortuito ageret. Eam rem consules rati, ut erat, perniciosam ad patres deferunt, sed delatam consulere ordine non licuit; adeo tumultuose excepta est clamoribus undique et indignatione patrum, si, quod imperio consulari exsequendum esset, invidiam eius consules ad senatum 3 reicerent. Profecto, si essent in re publica magistratus, nullum futurum fuisse Romae nisi publicum concilium; nunc in mille curias contionesque [1] dis-

---

[1] *After* contionesque *the MSS.* give cum alia Esquiliis alia in Aventino fiant concilia, *which Wecklein ejects as a gloss derived from* xxviii. 1.

BOOK II. XXVII. 12–XXVIII. 3

to seize one who was a conspicuous leader in their disturbances. The lictors were already dragging the man away, when he appealed; nor would the consul have granted the appeal, for there was no question what the decision of the people would be, had not his obstinacy been with difficulty overcome, more by the advice and influence of the nobles than by the popular outcry, so steeled was he to endure men's hate. From that moment the trouble grew worse each day, and not only were there open disturbances, but what was far more pernicious, secret gatherings and conferences. At last the consuls whom the plebeians so hated went out of office. Servilius had the goodwill of neither party, but Appius was in high esteem with the senators.

XXVIII. Aulus Verginius and Titus Vetusius then entered upon the consulship. Whereat the plebs, uncertain what sort of consuls they would prove to be, held nightly gatherings, some on the Esquiline and others on the Aventine, lest if they met in the Forum they might be frightened into adopting ill-considered measures, and manage all their business rashly and at haphazard. This seemed to the consuls, as indeed it was, a mischievous practice. They laid the matter before the Fathers, but their report could not be discussed in an orderly fashion, so tumultuously was it received, with shouts from every part of the house and expressions of indignation from the senators, that a thing which ought to have been settled by an exercise of consular authority should be invidiously referred by the consuls to the senate. It was evident that if only there were magistrates in the nation there would have been no assembly in Rome but the assembly of the people; as it was, the

LIVY

4 persam et dissipatam esse rem publicam. Unum hercule virum—id enim plus esse quam consulem—qualis Ap. Claudius fuerit, momento temporis discus-
5 surum illos coetus fuisse. Correpti consules cum, quid ergo se facere vellent, nihil enim segnius molliusve quam patribus placeat acturos, percunctarentur, decernunt ut dilectum quam acerrimum
6 habeant: otio lascivire plebem. Dimisso senatu consules in tribunal escendunt; citant nominatim iuniores. Cum ad nomen nemo responderet, circumfusa multitudo in contionis modum negare[1] ultra
7 decipi plebem posse; nunquam unum militem habituros ni praestaretur fides publica; libertatem unicuique prius reddendam esse quam arma danda, ut pro patria civibusque, non pro dominis pugnent.
8 Consules quid mandatum esset a senatu videbant, sed eorum qui intra parietes curiae ferociter loquerentur neminem adesse invidiae suae participem;
9 et apparebat atrox cum plebe certamen. Prius itaque quam ultima experirentur, senatum iterum consulere placuit. Tum vero ad sellas consulum propere[2] convolavere[3] minimus quisque natu patrum, abdicare consulatum iubentes et deponere imperium ad quod tuendum animus deesset.

XXIX. Utraque re satis experta tum demum consules: "Ne praedictum negetis, patres con-

[1] negare M_5: negaret Ω.   [2] propere ς: prope Ω.
[3] convolavere Ω: conuolare VM.

---

[1] (1) to persuade the senate to content the people; (2) to coerce the people.

government was broken up into a thousand separate curias and meetings. One single *man*—a more significant word than *consul*—of the type of Appius Claudius, would have dispersed those assemblages in a moment. When the consuls, thus upbraided, asked the Fathers what then they desired them to do, and promised that their conduct of the matter should be no whit less strenuous and stern than the senate wished, it was resolved that they should hold a levy with the utmost severity: it was idleness that made the plebeians lawless. Having adjourned the senate, the consuls mounted the tribunal and cited the young men by name. When no one answered to his name, the crowd, which surrounded the speaker as in a public meeting, declared that it was impossible to deceive the commons any longer; the consuls would never have a single soldier unless a public guarantee were given: liberty must first be restored to every man before arms were given him, that he might fight for his country and his fellow-citizens, not for a master. It was clear to the consuls what the senate had bidden them do; but of all those who had uttered truculent speeches within the walls of the curia they found not one at their side to share their odium, and they saw before them a terrible struggle with the people. Accordingly they thought it best, before proceeding to extremities, to consult the senate a second time. When it met, the youngest senators all rushed up in hot haste to the seats of the consuls, bidding them to abdicate their office and to lay down an authority which they lacked the spirit to support.

XXIX. Having sufficiently weighed both the courses open to them,[1] the consuls finally said: "Lest you should say that you had not been warned, Con-

scripti, adest ingens seditio. Postulamus ut ii, qui maxime ignaviam increpant, adsint nobis habentibus dilectum. Acerrimi cuiusque arbitrio, quando 2 ita placet, rem agemus." Redeunt in tribunal; citari nominatim unum ex iis qui in conspectu erant dedita opera iubent. Cum staret tacitus et circa eum aliquot hominum, ne forte violaretur, constitisset globus, lictorem ad eum consules 3 mittunt. Quo repulso tum vero indignum facinus esse clamitantes qui patrum consulibus aderant, de- 4 volant de tribunali ut lictori auxilio essent. Sed ab lictore, nihil aliud quam prendere prohibito, cum conversus in patres impetus esset, consulum intercursu rixa sedata est, in qua tamen sine lapide, sine telo plus clamoris atque irarum quam iniuriae fuerat. 5 Senatus tumultuose vocatus tumultuosius consulitur, quaestionem postulantibus iis qui pulsati fuerant, decernente ferocissimo quoque non sententiis magis 6 quam clamore et strepitu. Tandem cum irae resedissent, exprobrantibus consulibus nihilo plus sanitatis in curia quam in foro esse, ordine consuli 7 coepit. Tres fuere sententiae. P. Verginius rem non volgabat; de iis tantum qui fidem secuti P. Servili consulis Volsco, Aurunco, Sabinoque militassent 8 bello, agendum censebat. T. Largius non id tempus esse ut merita tantummodo exsolverentur; totam

BOOK II. xxix. 1-8

script Fathers, we are on the verge of a great mutiny. We demand that those who are loudest in accusing us of cowardice stand by us while we hold the levy. The most severe amongst you, since such is your pleasure, shall guide our procedure." They returned to the tribunal, and purposely commanded to cite by name one of those who were present. When he stood still without answering, in the midst of a little knot of men who, fearing the possibility of violence, had gathered round him, the consuls sent a lictor to him. The lictor was driven back. Whereupon, with a cry of "Shame!" the senators who were attending the consul rushed down from the tribunal to assist the lictor. But when the mob turned from the officer, whom they had merely prevented from arresting the man, and assailed the senators, the consuls intervened and checked the brawl, in which no stones had been thrown nor any weapons used, and there were more shouts and expressions of rage than hurts. The senate was convened in confusion, and they deliberated in still greater confusion. Those who had been roughly handled demanded an investigation, and all the more violent members urged the resolution, not only with speeches but with shouts and uproar. When at length their passions had subsided, and the consuls berated them for showing as little sanity in the Curia as the people had shown in the Forum, they began to deliberate in an orderly manner. Three proposals were made. Publius Verginius advised against a general relief: only those who, relying on the promise of Publius Servilius the consul, had fought in the Volscian, Auruncan, and Sabine wars should, he thought, be considered. Titus Largius held that this was no time for merely requiting services;

B.C. 494

LIVY

plebem aere alieno demersam esse, nec sisti posse ni omnibus consulatur; quin, si alia aliorum sit condicio, accendi magis discordiam quam sedari. Ap. Claudius, et natura immitis et efferatus, hinc plebis odio illinc patrum laudibus, non miseriis ait sed licentia tantum concitum turbarum, et lascivire magis plebem quam saevire. Id adeo malum ex provocatione natum; quippe minas esse consulum, non imperium, ubi ad eos qui una peccaverint provocare liceat. "Agedum," inquit, "dictatorem, a quo provocatio non est, creemus; iam hic quo nunc omnia ardent conticescet furor. Pulset tum mihi lictorem qui sciet ius de tergo vitaque sua penes unum illum esse cuius maiestatem violarit."[1]

XXX. Multis, ut erat, horrida et atrox videbatur Appi sententia; rursus Vergini Largique exemplo haud salubres, utique Largi,[2] quae totam fidem tolleret. Medium maxime et moderatum utroque consilium Vergini habebatur; sed factione respectuque rerum privatarum, quae semper offecere officientque publicis consiliis, Appius vicit, ac prope fuit ut dictator ille idem crearetur; quae res utique alienasset plebem periculosissimo tempore, cum Volsci Aequi-

---

[1] violarit $R^2\varsigma$: uiolauit Ω.
[2] *After* Largi Ω *have* putabant sententiam, *which Gebhard deletes.*

BOOK II. xxix. 8–xxx. 3

the whole commons was submerged in debt, and B.C. 494
the situation could not be remedied unless provision
were made for all; indeed, if some were treated in
one way and some in another, it would heighten the
discontent instead of allaying it. Appius Claudius,
naturally harsh, and rendered savage by the hatred
of the plebs on the one hand and the praises of the
Fathers on the other, said that it was not misery but
licence that had stirred up so great a hubbub, and
that wantonness was what ailed the plebs rather than
anger. That was precisely the mischief which the
appeal occasioned; for the consuls might threaten
but could not command, when those who had shared
in the guilt might be constituted the court of appeal.
"Come," said he, "let us appoint a dictator, from
whom there is no appeal. At once this frenzy which
has now set everything ablaze will be stilled. Let
anybody strike a lictor then, knowing that the right
to scourge and behead him rests with that one man
whose majesty he has violated!"

XXX. Many felt, and with reason, that the proposal of Appius was stern and cruel; on the other hand those of Verginius and Largius were inexpedient because of the precedent; particularly that of Largius, since it destroyed all credit. The most reasonable and moderate plan, in its regard for both sides, was held to be that of Verginius. But owing to party spirit and consideration for private interests, things which have always been hurtful to public deliberations and always will be, Appius prevailed, and came very near to being himself appointed dictator, a step which would infallibly have estranged the commons, and that at a most dangerous moment, since the Volsci, the Aequi, and the Sabines were all, as it

313

LIVY

4 que et Sabini forte una omnes in armis essent. Sed curae fuit consulibus et senioribus patrum, ut magistratus[1] imperio suo vehemens mansueto permitte-
5 retur ingenio. M'. Valerium dictatorem Volesi filium creant. Plebes etsi adversus se creatum dictatorem videbat, tamen cum provocationem fratris lege haberet, nihil ex ea familia triste nec superbum timebat.
6 Edictum deinde a dictatore propositum confirmavit animos Servili fere consulis edicto conveniens; sed et homini et potestati melius rati credi omisso certa-
7 mine nomina dedere. Quantus nunquam ante exercitus, legiones decem effectae; ternae inde datae consulibus, quattuor dictator usus.

8 Nec iam poterat bellum differri. Aequi Latinum agrum invaserant. Oratores Latinorum ab senatu petebant ut aut mitterent subsidium aut se ipsos
9 tuendorum finium causa capere arma sinerent. Tutius visum est defendi inermes Latinos quam pati retractare arma. Vetusius consul missus est; is finis populationibus fuit. Cessere Aequi campis locoque magis quam armis freti summis se iugis montium
10 tutabantur. Alter consul in Volscos profectus, ne et ipse tereret tempus, vastandis maxime agris hostem

---

[1] magistratus *was inserted by Heerwagen.*

---

[1] That is to say, in general; from a dictator, however, there was no appeal until a later period.

BOOK II. xxx. 3-10

chanced, up in arms at once. But the consuls and B.C. 494
the older senators saw to it that a magistracy rendered formidable by its paramount authority should be committed to a man of gentle disposition, and chose for dictator Manius Valerius, son of Volesus. The plebs, though they perceived that it was against themselves that the creation of a dictator was aimed, still, since it was through a law proposed by a brother of Valerius that they possessed the right of appeal,[1] they had no fear of any harsh or oppressive act on the part of one of that family. An edict which the dictator soon promulgated strengthened their confidence. It conformed essentially to the edict of Servilius; but Valerius and the office he held commanded greater confidence, and, ceasing to struggle, men gave in their names. So large an army had never been enrolled before. Ten legions were embodied; each consul was given three of these, and the dictator had four.

Nor could war be deferred any longer, for the Aequi had invaded Latin territory. Emissaries from the Latins begged the senate either to send them help or permit them to take up arms themselves in defence of their country.[2] It seemed safer that the Latins should be defended without arming them, than that they should be suffered to resume their weapons. Vetusius the consul was dispatched to them, and this ended the pillaging. The Aequi left the fields, and trusting more to situation than to arms, secured themselves on the summits of the ridges. The other consul marched against the Volsci. Lest he too might waste his time, he provoked the

[2] Apparently the Latins, perhaps after the battle of Lake Regillus (chap. xix. f.), had been denied the right to make war, save at the pleasure of the Romans.

315

LIVY

ad conferenda propius castra dimicandumque acie excivit. Medio inter castra campo ante suum quisque vallum infestis signis constitere. Multitudine aliquantum Volsci superabant; itaque effusi et contemptim pugnam iniere. Consul Romanus nec promovit aciem nec clamorem reddi passus defixis pilis stare suos iussit: ubi ad manum venisset hostis, tum coortos[1] tota vi gladiis rem gerere. Volsci cursu et clamore fessi cum se velut stupentibus metu intulissent Romanis, postquam impressionem sensere ex adverso factam et ante oculos micare gladios, haud secus quam si in[2] insidias incidissent, turbati vertunt terga; et ne ad fugam quidem satis virium fuit, quia cursu in proelium ierant. Romani contra, quia principio pugnae quieti steterant, vigentes corporibus, facile adepti fessos et castra impetu ceperunt et castris exutum hostem Velitras persecuti uno agmine victores cum victis in urbem inrupere; plusque ibi sanguinis promiscua omnium generum caede quam in ipsa dimicatione factum. Paucis data venia, qui inermes in deditionem venerunt.

XXXI. Dum haec in Volscis geruntur, dictator Sabinos, ubi longe plurimum belli fuerat, fundit exuitque[3] castris. Equitatu immisso mediam turba-

---

[1] coortos *V*?: cohortos (*or* -es) Ω.
[2] quam si in ϛ: quam *M*: quam si Ω.
[3] exuitque *Walters*: fugatque exuit Ω: fugaque exuitque *M*.

BOOK II. xxx. 10–xxxi. 2

enemy, chiefly by ravaging their lands, to bring their camp nearer and do battle with him. In the plain between the camps the two armies formed their lines, each in front of its own stockade. In numbers the Volsci were somewhat superior, and accordingly they came on in a loose and careless order. The Roman consul did not advance, nor did he allow a response to the enemy's shout. He commanded his men to plant their spears in the ground and stand still until the enemy had come to close quarters; then they were to assail them with all their might, and settle the question with the sword. The Volsci, weary with running and shouting, hurled themselves upon the Romans, who seemed to be numb with fear. But when the attackers found that their charge was firmly met and saw the swords flash in their faces, they were no whit less confounded than if they had fallen into an ambush, and turned and fled; and even flight was beyond their strength, since they had been running as they entered the battle. The Romans on the contrary, having stood at ease at the beginning of the fight, were fresh and strong; they readily caught up with the exhausted Volsci, and having taken their camp with a rush, pursued their enemies beyond it to Velitrae, where vanquished and victors burst into the city in one body. More blood was shed there, in the promiscuous slaughter of all sorts of people, than had been in the battle itself. A very few were granted quarter, having come without arms and given themselves up.

XXXI. While these things were going on in the Volscian country, the dictator put to rout the Sabines —by far Rome's most important enemy—and captured their camp. Attacking with his cavalry, he

LIVY

A.U.C. 60

verat hostium aciem, quam,[1] dum se cornua latius pandunt, parum apte introrsum ordinibus[2] firmaverant; turbatos pedes invasit. Eodem impetu castra 3 capta debellatumque est. Post pugnam ad Regillum lacum non alia illis annis pugna clarior fuit. Dictator triumphans urbem invehitur. Super solitos honores locus in circo ipsi posterisque ad spectaculum datus, 4 sella in eo loco curulis posita. Volscis devictis Veliternus ager ademptus; Velitras coloni ab urbe missi et colonia deducta. Cum Aequis post aliquanto pugnatum est invito quidem consule, quia loco iniquo 5 subeundum erat ad hostes; sed milites extrahi rem criminantes ut dictator, priusquam ipsi redirent in urbem magistratu abiret, inritaque, sicut ante consulis, promissa eius caderent, perpulere ut forte 6 temere in adversos montes agmen erigeret. Id male commissum ignavia hostium in bonum vertit qui, priusquam ad coniectum teli veniretur, obstupefacti audacia Romanorum relictis castris, quae munitissimis tenuerant locis, in aversas[3] valles desiluere. Ibi[4] satis praedae et victoria incruenta fuit.

7 Ita trifariam re bello bene gesta, de domesticarum rerum eventu nec patribus nec plebi cura deces-

---

[1] quam *D*?: quia *OH*: qua Ω.
[2] ordinibus *Gronov.*: ordinibus aciem Ω.
[3] aversas *Tan. Faber*: aduersas Ω.   [4] Ibi ϛ: ubi Ω.

---

[1] That this apparently unique distinction was actually conferred on the Valerii is confirmed by an honorary inscription (*C.I.L.* i. 284).

BOOK II. XXXI. 2-7

made havoc of their centre, which, in extending B.C. 494
their wings too widely, they had unduly weakened;
and in the midst of the disorder the infantry assailed
them. By a single rush the camp was captured and
the war ended. From the time of the fight at Lake
Regillus no other battle of those days was more
famous. The dictator entered the City in triumph.
In addition to the customary honours a place was
assigned him in the circus, for himself and his descendants, to witness the games, and a curule chair
was put there for him.[1] The Volsci, having been
conquered, were deprived of the Veliternian land;
colonists were sent from the City to Velitrae and a
colony was planted. Soon after this there was a
battle with the Aequi, though the consul was against
it, for it was necessary to approach the enemy from
unfavourable ground; but his men accused him of
dragging out the campaign in order that the dictator
might relinquish his office before their return to the
City, and his promises thus come to naught, as
the consul's promises had done before. Vetusius was
thus driven to order an advance at random, up the
mountains which confronted him. This ill-advised
measure the enemy's cowardice turned into success,
for before the Romans had come within a spear's
throw, the Aequi, appalled at their audacity, abandoned the camp which they had maintained in a
highly defensible position, and threw themselves
down into the valleys on the other side. There the
Romans gained considerable booty and a bloodless
victory.

Though a threefold success had thus been gained
in the war, neither senators nor plebeians had been
relieved of their anxiety respecting the outcome of

LIVY

serat; tanta cum gratia tum arte praeparaverant faeneratores quae non modo plebem sed ipsum etiam 8 dictatorem frustrarentur. Namque Valerius post Vetusi consulis reditum omnium actionum in senatu[1] primam habuit pro victore populo, rettulitque quid 9 de nexis fieri placeret. Quae cum reiecta relatio esset, "Non placeo," inquit, "concordiae auctor; optabitis, mediusfidius, propediem ut mei similes Romana plebes patronos habeat. Quod ad me attinet, neque frustrabor ultra cives meos neque ipse 10 frustra dictator ero. Discordiae intestinae, bellum externum fecere ut hoc magistratu egeret res publica: pax foris parta est, domi impeditur; privatus potius quam dictator seditioni intererо." Ita curia 11 egressus dictatura se abdicavit. Apparuit causa plebi, suam vicem indignantem magistratu abisse. Itaque velut persoluta fide, quoniam per eum non stetisset quin praestaretur, decedentem domum cum favore ac laudibus prosecuti sunt.

XXXII. Timor inde patres incessit ne, si dimissus exercitus foret, rursus coetus occulti coniurationesque fierent. Itaque, quamquam per dictatorem dilectus habitus esset, tamen, quoniam in consulum verba iurassent, sacramento teneri militem rati, per causam

---

[1] in senatu F^3U_ς: in senatum Ω.

BOOK II XXXI. 7–XXXII. 1

affairs at home, so great was the artfulness, as well B.C. 494
as influence, with which the money-lenders had laid
their plans to baffle not only the commons but even
the dictator himself. For after the return of the
consul Vetusius, the first business which Valerius
brought before the senate was in behalf of the victorious people, that the senate might declare its
policy regarding the treatment of those bound over
for debt. This resolution having failed to pass, the
dictator said: "I do not please you in urging
harmony. You will soon wish, I warrant you, that
the Roman plebs had men like me for their spokesmen. For my own part I will not be the means of
further disappointing my fellow citizens, nor will
I be dictator to no purpose. Internal strife and
foreign war made this office necessary to the nation;
peace has been secured abroad, but at home it is
being thwarted; I will play my part as a private
citizen rather than as a dictator, when the mutiny
breaks out." So saying he left the Curia and
laid down his office. It was evident to the people
that resentment of their wrongs had caused him to
resign the magistracy. And so, as though he had
kept his pledge (for it had not been his fault that it
was not being carried out), they attended him as he
retired to his house with manifestations of favour and
approval.

XXXII. Thereupon the senators became alarmed,
fearing that if the army should be disbanded there
would again be secret gatherings and conspiracies.
And so, although the levy had been held by order of
the dictator, yet because the men had been sworn in
by the consuls they regarded the troops as bound by
their oath, and, under the pretext that the Aequi

LIVY

A.U.C. 260

renovati ab Aequis belli educi ex urbe legiones
2 iussere. Quo facto maturata est seditio. Et primo
agitatum dicitur de consulum caede, ut solverentur
sacramento; doctos deinde nullam scelere religionem
exsolvi, Sicinio quodam auctore iniussu consulum in
Sacrum montem secessisse—trans Anienem amnem
3 est, tria ab urbe milia passuum; ea frequentior fama
est quam, cuius Piso auctor est, in Aventinum seces-
4 sionem factam esse;—ibi sine ullo duce vallo fos-
saque communitis castris quieti, rem nullam nisi
necessariam ad victum sumendo, per aliquot dies
5 neque lacessiti neque lacessentes sese tenuere. Pavor
ingens in urbe, metuque mutuo suspensa erant omnia. Timere relicta ab suis plebes violentiam patrum; timere patres residem in urbe plebem, incerti
6 manere eam an abire mallent. Quamdiu autem tranquillam quae secesserit multitudinem fore? Quid
futurum deinde, si quod externum interim bellum
7 exsistat? Nullam profecto nisi in concordia civium
spem reliquam ducere; eam per aequa per iniqua
8 reconciliandam civitati esse. Placuit igitur oratorem
ad plebem mitti Menenium Agrippam, facundum
virum, et quod inde oriundus erat, plebi carum. Is
intromissus in castra prisco illo dicendi et horrido
9 modo nihil aliud quam hoc narrasse fertur: tempore

---

[1] Livy appears to have had the other tradition in mind when he wrote III. liv. 9.

[2] If Menenius was a plebeian, it is improbable that he was also, as Livy rather implies, a senator. *cf.* i. 11 and note.

322

BOOK II. xxxii. 1-9

had recommenced hostilities, gave orders to lead the legions out of the City. This brought the revolt to a head. At first, it is said, there was talk of killing the consuls, that men might thus be freed from their oath; but when it was explained to them that no sacred obligation could be dissolved by a crime, they took the advice of one Sicinius, and without orders from the consuls withdrew to the Sacred Mount, which is situated across the river Anio, three miles from the City.—This version of the story is more general than that given by Piso, namely that the Aventine was the place of their secession.[1]—There, without any leader, they fortified their camp with stockade and trench, and continued quietly, taking nothing but what they required for their subsistance, for several days, neither receiving provocation nor giving any. There was a great panic in the City, and mutual apprehension caused the suspension of all activities. The plebeians, having been abandoned by their friends, feared violence at the hands of the senators; the senators feared the plebeians who were left behind in Rome, being uncertain whether they had rather they stayed or went. Besides, how long would the seceding multitude continue peaceable? What would happen next if some foreign war should break out in the interim? Assuredly no hope was left save in harmony amongst the citizens, and this they concluded they must restore to the state by fair means or foul. They therefore decided to send as an ambassador to the commons Agrippa Menenius, an eloquent man and dear to the plebeians as being one of themselves by birth.[2] On being admitted to the camp he is said merely to have related the following apologue, in the quaint and uncouth

B.C. 494

LIVY

A.U.C. 260

quo in homine non, ut nunc, omnia in unum consentiant, sed singulis membris suum cuique consilium suus sermo fuerit, indignatas reliquas partes sua cura suo labore ac ministerio ventri omnia quaeri, ventrem in medio quietum nihil aliud quam datis voluptatibus frui; conspirasse inde ne manus ad os cibum ferrent, nec os acciperet datum, nec dentes quae acciperent conficerent.[1] Hac ira dum ventrem fame domare vellent, ipsa una membra totumque corpus ad extremam tabem venisse. Inde apparuisse ventris quoque haud segne ministerium esse, nec magis ali quam alere eum, reddentem in omnis corporis partes hunc quo vivimus vigemusque, divisum pariter in venas, maturum confecto cibo sanguinem. Comparando hinc quam intestina corporis seditio similis esset irae plebis in patres, flexisse mentes hominum.

A.U.C. 261

XXXIII. Agi deinde de concordia coeptum concessumque in condiciones ut plebi sui magistratus essent sacrosancti, quibus auxilii latio adversus consules esset, neve cui patrum capere eum magistratum liceret. Ita tribuni plebei creati duo, C. Licinius et L. Albinus. Ii[2] tres collegas sibi creaverunt. In his

---

[1] quae acciperent conficerent *Walters*: acciperent. que conficerent *O*: acciperentque conficerent Ω: conficerent *PFBD*⁵*U* (*which last has* ne *for* nec).
[2] Ii *Conway and Walters*: hii Ω: hi *UOH*.

---

[1] The same apologue is found in Xenophon, *Mem.* II. iii. 18; Cicero, *Off.* III. v. 22; and St. Paul, *Cor.* I. xii. 12.

324

style of that age: In the days when man's members did not all agree amongst themselves, as is now the case, but had each its own ideas and a voice of its own, the other parts thought it unfair that they should have the worry and the trouble and the labour of providing everything for the belly, while the belly remained quietly in their midst with nothing to do but to enjoy the good things which they bestowed upon it; they therefore conspired together that the hands should carry no food to the mouth, nor the mouth accept anything that was given it, nor the teeth grind up what they received. While they sought in this angry spirit to starve the belly into submission, the members themselves and the whole body were reduced to the utmost weakness. Hence it had become clear that even the belly had no idle task to perform, and was no more nourished than it nourished the rest, by giving out to all parts of the body that by which we live and thrive, when it has been divided equally amongst the veins and is enriched with digested food—that is, the blood. Drawing a parallel from this to show how like was the internal dissension of the bodily members to the anger of the plebs against the Fathers, he prevailed upon the minds of his hearers.[1] XXXIII. Steps were then taken towards harmony, and a compromise was effected on these terms: the plebeians were to have magistrates of their own, who should be inviolable, and in them should lie the right to aid the people against the consuls, nor should any senator be permitted to take this magistracy. And so they chose two "tribunes of the people," Gaius Licinius and Lucius Albinus. These appointed three others to be their colleagues. Amongst the latter,

LIVY

Sicinium fuisse, seditionis auctorem: de duobus, qui fuerint, minus convenit. Sunt qui duos tantum in Sacro monte creatos tribunos esse dicant ibique sacratam legem latam.

Per secessionem plebis Sp. Cassius et Postumus[1] Cominius consulatum inierunt. Iis[2] consulibus cum Latinis populis ictum foedus. Ad id feriendum consul alter Romae mansit: alter ad Volscum bellum missus Antiates Volscos fundit fugatque, compulsos in oppidum Longulam persecutus moenibus potitur. Inde protinus Poluscam, item[3] Volscorum, cepit; tum magna vi adortus est Coriolos. Erat tum in castris inter primores iuvenum Cn. Marcius,[4] adulescens et consilio et manu promptus, cui cognomen postea Coriolano fuit. Cum subito exercitum Romanum Coriolos obsidentem atque in oppidanos, quos intus clausos habebat, intentum sine ullo metu extrinsecus imminentis belli Volscae legiones profectae ab Antio invasissent, eodemque tempore ex oppido erupissent hostes, forte in statione Marcius fuit. Is cum delecta militum manu non modo impetum erumpentium rettudit,[5] sed per patentem portam ferox inrupit, caedeque in proxima parte[6] urbis facta ignem temere arreptum[7] imminentibus muro aedificiis

---

[1] Postumus ς Sigonius: Postumius Ω.
[2] iis MPFBO: his RDL: hiis UHς.
[3] protinus Poluscam, item Cluverius (cf. II. xxxix. 3): protinus (-mus M) mus camitem (P) or mucamitem Ω.
[4] Cn. Marcius ς: lē martius M: c (or c̄) marcius Ω.
[5] rettudit D: retrudit (or retudit or retulit) Ω.
[6] parte supplied by H. J. Müller.
[7] arreptum ed. Ald.: abreptum Ω.

BOOK II. xxxiii. 2-8

Sicinius, the promoter of the revolt, was one, as all agree; the identity of the other two is less certain. Some hold that there were only two tribunes elected on the Sacred Mount, and that the law of inviolability was enacted there.[1]

During the secession of the plebs Spurius Cassius and Postumus Cominius entered upon their consulship. In this year a treaty was made with the Latin peoples. In order to make this treaty one of the consuls remained in Rome, while the other was dispatched to the Volscian war, and defeated and put to flight the Volsci of Antium. Forcing them to take refuge in the town of Longula, he followed them up and captured the place. Thence he proceeded to take Polusca, another Volscian town, after which he directed a strong attack upon Corioli. There was in camp at that time amongst the young nobles Gnaeus Marcius, a youth of active mind and ready hand, who afterwards gained the surname of Coriolanus. The Romans were laying siege to Corioli and were intent upon the townspeople shut up within the walls, with no thought of danger from any attack which might be impending from without, when they found themselves suddenly assailed by a Volscian army from Antium, and simultaneously by the besieged, who made a sortie from the town. It happened that Marcius was on guard. Taking a picked body of men he not only repelled the sally, but boldly forced his way through the open gate, and having spread carnage through the adjacent part of the town, caught up a firebrand on the spur of the moment, and threw it upon the buildings which

[1] In either case the number was five from the year 471 on (lviii. 1), till it was raised to ten in the year 457.

LIVY

iniecit. Clamor inde oppidanorum mixtus muliebri puerilique ploratu ad terrorem, ut solet, primum orto[1] et Romanis auxit animum et turbavit Volscos, utpote capta urbe cui[2] ad ferendam opem venerant.
9 Ita fusi Volsci Antiates, Corioli oppidum captum; tantumque sua laude obstitit famae consulis Marcius ut, nisi foedus cum Latinis in[3] columna aenea insculptum monumento esset, ab Sp. Cassio uno, quia collega afuerat, ictum, Postumum[4] Cominium bellum gessisse cum Volscis memoria cessisset.

10 Eodem anno Agrippa Menenius moritur, vir omni in vita[5] pariter patribus ac plebi carus, post secessio-
11 nem carior plebi factus. Huic interpreti arbitroque concordiae civium, legato patrum ad plebem, reductori plebis Romanae in urbem, sumptus funeri defuit; extulit eum plebs sextantibus[6] conlatis in capita.

XXXIV. Consules deinde T. Geganius P. Minucius facti. Eo anno, cum et foris quieta omnia a bello essent et domi sanata discordia, aliud multo
2 gravius malum civitatem invasit, caritas primum annonae ex incultis per secessionem plebis agris,
3 fames deinde, qualis clausis solet. Ventumque ad interitum servitiorum utique et plebis esset, ni consules providissent dimissis passim ad frumentum co-

---

[1] primum orto *Madvig*: primo ortu Ω.
[2] cui ς: qui Ω.
[3] in *supplied by H. J. Müller.*
[4] Postumum ς: Postumium Ω.
[5] omni in vita ς: omnium uita Ω.
[6] sextantibus ς: extantibus Ω.

BOOK II. xxxiii. 8–xxxiv. 3

overhung the wall. Thereupon the townspeople raised a shout, mingled with such a wailing of women and children as is generally heard at the first alarm. This brought new courage to the Romans and covered the Volsci with confusion—as was natural when the city which they had come to relieve was taken. Thus the men of Antium were routed, and Corioli was won. So completely did the glory of Marcius overshadow the consul's fame, that, were it not for the record on a bronze column of the treaty with the Latins which was struck by Spurius Cassius alone, in the absence of his colleague, men would have forgotten that Postumus Cominius had waged war on the Volsci.

That same year saw the death of Agrippa Menenius, a man who throughout his life had been equally beloved by patricians and plebeians, and who after the secession was even dearer to the commons. This mediator and umpire of civil harmony, this ambassador of the senators to the people, this restorer of the plebs to Rome, did not leave sufficient wealth to pay for a funeral. He was buried by the commons, who contributed a *sextans*[1] each to the cost.

XXXIV. The consuls next chosen were Titus Geganius and Publius Minucius. This year, though there was no war to occasion trouble from without and the breach at home had been healed, another and a much more serious misfortune befell the nation; for first the price of corn went up, from men's failure to cultivate the fields during the withdrawal of the plebs; and this was followed by a famine, such as comes to a beleaguered city. It would have meant starvation for the slaves, at least, and the plebeians, had not the consuls met the situation by sending

---

[1] A *sextans* was the sixth part of an *as*, or pound of copper.

LIVY

emendum non in Etruriam modo dextris ab Ostia litoribus laevoque per Volscos mari usque ad Cumas, sed quaesitum in Sicilia[1] quoque; adeo finitimorum odia longinquis coegerant indigere auxiliis. Frumentum Cumis cum coemptum esset, naves pro bonis Tarquiniorum ab Aristodemo tyranno, qui heres erat, retentae sunt; in Volscis Pomptinoque ne emi quidem potuit; periculum quoque ab impetu hominum ipsis frumentatoribus fuit; ex Tuscis frumentum Tiberi venit; eo sustentata est plebs. Incommodo bello in tam artis commeatibus vexati forent, ni Volscos iam moventes arma pestilentia ingens invasisset. Ea clade conterritis hostium animis, ut etiam ubi ea remisisset terrore aliquo tenerentur, et Velitris auxere numerum colonorum Romani, et Norbam[2] in montis novam coloniam quae arx in Pomptino esset miserunt.

M. Minucio deinde et A. Sempronio consulibus magna vis frumenti ex Sicilia advecta, agitatumque in senatu quanti plebi daretur. Multi venisse tempus premendae plebis putabant recuperandique iura quae extorta secessione ac vi patribus essent. In primis Marcius Coriolanus, hostis tribuniciae potestatis, "Si annonam," inquit, "veterem volunt, ius pristinum reddant patribus. Cur ego plebeios magistratus, cur Sicinium potentem video sub iugum mis-

---

[1] quaesitum in Sicilia *FBO*: quaesitum in siciliam Ω: in Siciliam *Crevier*.

[2] Norbam *Duker*: norbae (*or* -be) Ω.

BOOK II. xxxiv. 3-9

agents far and wide to buy up corn, not only to Etruria, northwards along the coast from Ostia, and south past the Volsci by sea, all the way to Cumae, but even to Sicily—so far afield had the enmity of Rome's neighbours driven her to seek for help. When grain had been purchased at Cumae the ships were held back by Aristodemus, the tyrant, in satisfaction for the property of the Tarquinii, whose heir he was. Among the Volsci and Pomptini the agents could not even make any purchases, and they were actually in danger from the violence of the people. From the Tuscans corn came in by way of the Tiber, and with this the plebs were kept alive. A disastrous war would have been added to the distresses arising from the scarcity of provisions, had not a grievous pestilence descended upon the Volsci just as they were beginning hostilities. Its ravages so terrified the enemy that even after the worst of it was over they did not fully recover from their fear, and the Romans increased the number of colonists at Velitrae and sent out a new colony to Norba, in the mountains, as a stronghold for the Pomptine country.

Next year, in the consulship of Marcus Minucius and Aulus Sempronius, a large quantity of grain was imported from Sicily, and the senate debated at what price it should be sold to the plebeians. Many thought the time had come for repressing the commons, and resuming the rights which they had violently extorted from the Fathers by secession. Conspicuous among these was Marcius Coriolanus, an enemy to the tribunician power, who said: "If they want corn at the old price let them restore to the senate its ancient rights. Why do I see plebeian magistrates, why do I, after being sent beneath

LIVY

10 sus, et[1] tamquam ab latronibus redemptus? Egone has indignitates diutius patiar quam necesse est? Tarquinium regem qui non tulerim Sicinium feram? Secedat nunc, avocet plebem; patet via in Sacrum montem aliosque colles. Rapiant frumenta ex agris nostris, quem ad modum tertio anno rapuere; fruan-
11 tur[2] annona quam furore suo fecere. Audeo dicere hoc malo domitos ipsos potius cultores agrorum fore quam ut armati per secessionem coli prohibeant."
12 Haud tam facile dictu est faciendumne fuerit quam potuisse arbitror fieri ut condicionibus laxandi annonam et tribuniciam potestatem et omnia invitis iura imposita patres demerent sibi.

XXXV. Et senatui nimis atrox visa sententia est, et plebem ira prope armavit: fame se iam sicut hostes peti, cibo victuque fraudari; peregrinum frumentum, quae sola alimenta ex insperato fortuna dederit, ab ore rapi, nisi Cn. Marcio vincti dedantur tribuni, nisi de tergo plebis Romanae satisfiat. Eum sibi carnificem novum exor-
2 tum, qui aut mori aut servire iubeat. In exeuntem e curia impetus factus esset, ni peropportune tribuni diem dixissent. Ibi ira est suppressa; se iudicem

[1] et *inserted by Postgate.*
[2] fruantur ς: fruantur utantur *VM*: utantur Ω.

the yoke and ransomed, as it were, from brigands, behold Sicinius in power? Shall I endure these humiliations any longer than I must? When I would not brook Tarquinius as king, must I brook Sicinius? Let him secede now and call out the plebs; the way lies open to the Sacred Mount and the other hills. Let them seize grain from our fields as they did two years ago. Let them enjoy the corn-prices they have brought about by their own madness. I make bold to say that this evil plight will so tame them that they will sooner till the land themselves than withdraw under arms and prevent its cultivation by others." It is not so easy to say whether it would have been right to do this, as it is clear, I think, that it lay within the Fathers' power to have made such conditions for reducing the price of corn as to have freed themselves from the tribunician authority and all the terms which they had unwillingly agreed to.

XXXV. Even the senate deemed the proposal too harsh, and the plebs were so angry that they almost resorted to arms. Starvation, they said, was now being employed against them, as though they were public enemies, and they were being defrauded of their food and sustenance; the imported corn, their only supply, unexpectedly bestowed on them by Fortune, was to be snatched from their mouths unless the tribunes should be delivered up in chains to Gnaeus Marcius, unless he should work his will on the persons of the Roman plebeians; in him a new executioner had risen up against them, who bade them choose between death and slavery. When he came out from the Curia they would have set upon him, had not the tribunes, in the nick of time, appointed a day to try him; whereupon their anger subsided,

333

LIVY

quisque, se dominum vitae necisque inimici factum
videbat. Contemptim primo Marcius audiebat minas
tribunicias: auxilii, non poenae ius datum illi potestati, plebisque non patrum tribunos esse. Sed adeo
infensa erat coorta plebs, ut unius poena defungendum esset patribus. Restiterunt tamen adversae
invidiae[1] usique sunt qua suis quisque, qua totius
ordinis viribus. Ac primo temptata res est si dispositis clientibus absterrendo singulos a coitionibus
conciliisque disicere rem possent. Universi deinde
processere—quidquid erat patrum, reos diceres—
precibus plebem exposcentes unum sibi civem, unum
senatorem, si innocentem absolvere nollent, pro nocente donarent. Ipse cum die dicta non adesset,
perseveratum in ira est. Damnatus absens in Volscos
exsulatum abiit minitans patriae hostilesque iam tum
spiritus gerens. Venientem Volsci benigne excepere
benigniusque in dies colebant, quo maior ira in suos
eminebat crebraeque nunc querellae, nunc minae
percipiebantur.[2] Hospitio utebatur Atti Tulli. Longe
is tum princeps Volsci nominis erat Romanisque semper infestus. Ita cum alterum vetus odium, alterum

---

[1] adversae invidiae *H. J. Müller*: aduersa inuidia Ω.
[2] percipiebantur *ed. Ald.* (*in Errata*): praecipiebantur Ω.

---

[1] The clients were a class distinct both from the plebs and the patricians. To the latter they stood in the feudal relation of vassal to lord. They were perhaps originally citizens of conquered towns, and were recruited by manumissions and immigration.

BOOK II. xxxv. 2-7

for every man saw that he was himself made his enemy's judge, and held over him the power of life and death. With contempt at first Marcius heard the threats of the tribunes, alleging that the right to help, not to punish, had been granted to that office, and that they were tribunes not of the Fathers, but of the plebs. But the commons had risen in such a storm of anger that the Fathers had to sacrifice one man to appease them. For all that, they resisted the hatred of their adversaries and called upon the private resources of the several senators, as well as the strength of the entire order. At first they tried, by posting their clients[1] here and there, to frighten persons from coming together for deliberation, in the hope that they might thereby break up their plans. Then they came out in a body—you would have said all the members of the senate were on their trial— and entreated the plebs to release to them one citizen, one senator; if they were unwilling to acquit him as innocent let them give him up, though guilty, as a favour. But when Marcius himself, on the day appointed for the hearing, failed to appear, men's hearts were hardened against him. Condemned in his absence, he went into exile with the Volsci, uttering threats against his country, and even then breathing hostility. When he came among the Volsci they received him with a kindness which increased from one day to the next, in proportion as he allowed a greater hatred of his own people to appear, and was more and more frequently heard to utter both complaints and threats. His host was Attius Tullius, at that time by far the foremost of the Volscian name and ever unfriendly to the Romans. And so, spurred on, the one by his inveterate hatred and

B.C. 491

LIVY

ira recens stimularet, consilia conferunt de Romano
8 bello. Haud facile credebant plebem suam impelli
posse ut totiens infeliciter temptata arma caperent:
multis saepe bellis, pestilentia postremo amissa iuventute fractos spiritus esse; arte agendum in exoleto iam vetustate odio, ut recenti aliqua ira exacerbarentur animi.

XXXVI. Ludi forte ex instauratione magni Romae
parabantur. Instaurandi haec causa fuerat. Ludis
mane servum quidam pater familiae nondum commisso spectaculo sub furca caesum medio egerat
circo; coepti inde ludi, velut ea res nihil ad religio-
2 nem pertinuisset. Haud ita multo post T. Latinio,
de plebe homini, somnium fuit; visus Iuppiter dicere
sibi ludis praesultatorem displicuisse; nisi magnifice
instaurarentur ei ludi, periculum urbi fore; iret, ea
3 consulibus nuntiaret. Quamquam haud sane liber
erat religione animus, verecundia tamen maiestatis
magistratuum timorque[1] vicit, ne in ora hominum
4 pro ludibrio abiret. Magno illi ea cunctatio stetit;
filium namque intra paucos dies amisit. Cuius repentinae cladis ne causa dubia esset, aegro animi
eadem illa in somnis obversata species visa est rogi-

---

[1] timorque *H. J. Müller*: timorem Ω

---

[1] *i.e.* the Roman Games (cf. I. xxxv. 9).

BOOK II. xxxv. 7–xxxvi. 4

the other by fresh resentment, they took counsel together how they might make war on Rome. They believed that it would be no easy matter to induce the Volscian commons to take up the arms which they had so often unluckily essayed; the destruction of their young men in oft-repeated wars, and finally by the plague, had, they supposed, broken their spirit; artifice must be invoked, where hate had grown dull with lapse of time, that they might find some new cause of anger to exasperate men's hearts.

XXXVI. It so happened that at Rome preparations were making to repeat the Great Games.[1] The reason of the repetition was as follows: at an early hour of the day appointed for the games, before the show had begun, a certain householder had driven his slave, bearing a yoke, through the midst of the circus, scourging the culprit as he went. The games had then been begun, as though this circumstance had in no way affected their sanctity. Not long after, Titus Latinius, a plebeian, had a dream. He dreamt that Jupiter said that the leading dancer at the games[2] had not been to his liking; that unless there were a sumptuous repetition of the festival the City would be in danger; that Latinius was to go and announce this to the consuls. Though the man's conscience was by no means at ease, nevertheless the awe he felt at the majesty of the magistrates was too great; he was afraid of becoming a laughing-stock. Heavy was the price he paid for his hesitation, for a few days later he lost his son. Lest this sudden calamity should leave any uncertainty as to its cause in the mind of the wretched man, the same phantom appeared again before him in his dreams, and asked

B.C. 491

[2] *i.e.* the slave who had been scourged through the circus.

LIVY

tare, satin magnam spreti numinis haberet mercedem; maiorem instare, ni eat propere ac nuntiet consulibus. Iam praesentior res erat. Cunctantem tamen ac prolatantem ingens vis morbi adorta est debilitate subita. Tunc enimvero deorum ira admonuit. Fessus igitur malis praeteritis instantibusque consilio propinquorum adhibito cum visa atque audita et obversatum totiens somno Iovem, minas irasque caelestes repraesentatas casibus suis exposuisset, consensu inde haud dubio[1] omnium qui aderant in forum ad consules lectica defertur. Inde in curiam iussu consulum delatus eadem illa cum patribus ingenti omnium admiratione enarrasset, ecce aliud miraculum. Qui captus omnibus membris delatus in curiam esset, eum functum officio pedibus suis domum rediisse traditum memoriae est.

XXXVII. Ludi quam amplissimi ut fierent senatus decrevit. Ad eos ludos auctore Attio Tullio vis magna Volscorum venit. Priusquam committerentur ludi, Tullius, ut domi compositum cum Marcio fuerat, ad consules venit; dicit esse quae secreto agere de re publica velit. Arbitris remotis "Invitus," inquit, "quod sequius sit de meis civibus loquor. Non tamen admissum quicquam ab iis criminatum venio,

---

[1] dubio *ed. Ald.*: dubie (*or* -ae) Ω.

him, as he thought, whether he had been sufficiently B.C. 491
repaid for spurning the gods; for a greater recompense was at hand unless he went quickly and informed the consuls. This brought the matter nearer home. Yet he still delayed and put off going, till a violent attack of illness suddenly laid him low. Then at last the anger of the gods taught him wisdom. And so, worn out with his sufferings, past and present, he called a council of his kinsmen and explained to them what he had seen and heard, how Jupiter had so often confronted him in his sleep, and how the threats and anger of the god had been instantly fulfilled in his own misfortunes. Then, with the unhesitating approval of all who were present, he was carried on a litter to the consuls in the Forum; and thence, by their command, to the Curia, where he had no sooner told the same story to the Fathers, greatly to the wonder of them all, when— lo, another miracle! For it is related that he who had been carried into the senate-house afflicted in all his members, returned home, after discharging his duty, on his own feet.

XXXVII. Games of the greatest possible splendour were decreed by the senate, and to see them came, at the suggestion of Attius Tullius, a host of Volsci. Before the beginning of the spectacle Tullius, in pursuance of the plan he and Marcius had formed at home, went to the consuls and told them that he had something of public importance which he wished to discuss with them in private. When the bystanders had been removed, "I am loath," he said, "to tell concerning my countrymen what may discredit them. Still I do not come to charge them with having committed any crime, but to put you on your

339

LIVY

4 sed cautum ne admittant. Nimio plus quam velim
5 nostrorum ingenia sunt mobilia. Multis id cladibus
sensimus, quippe qui non nostro merito sed vestra
patientia incolumes simus. Magna hic nunc Volscorum multitudo est; ludi sunt; spectaculo intenta
6 civitas erit. Memini quid per eandem occasionem
ab Sabinorum iuventute in hac urbe commissum sit;
horret animus ne quid inconsulte ac temere fiat.
Haec nostra vestraque causa prius dicenda vobis,
7 consules, ratus sum. Quod ad me attinet, extemplo
hinc domum abire in animo est, ne cuius facti dictive contagione praesens violer." Haec locutus abiit.
8 Consules cum ad patres rem dubiam sub auctore certo
detulissent, auctor magis, ut fit, quam res ad praecavendum vel ex supervacuo movit; factoque senatus consulto ut urbe[1] excederent Volsci, praecones
dimittuntur qui omnes eos proficisci ante noctem
9 iuberent. Ingens pavor primo discurrentis ad suas
res tollendas in hospitia perculit; proficiscentibus
deinde indignatio oborta se ut consceleratos contaminatosque ab ludis, festis diebus, coetu quodam
modo hominum deorumque abactos esse. XXXVIII.
Cum prope continuato agmine irent, praegressus
Tullius ad caput Ferentinum, ut quisque veniret,[2]
primores eorum excipiens querendo indignandoque,

[1] urbe $H\varsigma$: urbem Ω.   [2] veniret ς : eueniret Ω.

BOOK II. XXXVII. 3–XXXVIII. 1

guard lest they should commit one. The disposition B.C. 491
of our people is far more fickle than I could wish.
Many disasters have taught us the truth of this,
since it is not to our own merit, but to your patience,
that we owe our preservation. A great crowd of
Volsci is now in Rome; there are games; the citizens
will be intent upon the spectacle. I remember what
the Sabine youths did in this City on the same opportunity arising; I tremble lest something ill-advised
and rash may happen. It has seemed to me that
both on our account and on yours I ought to tell you
this beforehand, consuls. For my own part I intend
to go home at once, lest being on the spot I might
be implicated in some act or word and be compro-
mised." With this he departed. The consuls laid
before the senate this vague warning which came
from so reliable a source. It was the source, as
often happens, rather than the story, which induced
them to take precautions, even though they might
prove superfluous. The senate decreed that the
Volsci should leave the City, and heralds were sent
about to command them all to depart before night-
fall. At first they were stricken with a great alarm,
as they hurried this way and that to the houses of
their hosts to get their things. But when they had
started, their hearts swelled with indignation, that
like malefactors and polluted persons, they should
have been driven off from the games at a time of
festival, and excluded, in a way, from intercourse
with men and gods. XXXVIII. As they journeyed
on in an almost unbroken line, Tullius, who had
gone ahead, arrived before them at the source of
the Ferentina. There, when any of their chief men
arrived, he met them with words of complaint and

LIVY

et eos ipsos sedulo audientes secunda irae verba et per eos multitudinem aliam in subiectum viae cam-2 pum deduxit. Ibi in contionis modum orationem exorsus, "Ut omnia," inquit, "obliviscamini alia, veteres populi Romani iniurias cladesque gentis Volscorum,[1] hodiernam hanc contumeliam quo tandem animo fertis, qua per nostram ignominiam ludos 3 commisere? An non sensistis triumphatum hodie de vobis esse? Vos omnibus, civibus, peregrinis, tot finitimis populis, spectaculo abeuntes fuisse, vestras coniuges, vestros liberos traductos per ora hominum? 4 Quid eos qui audivere vocem praeconis, quid qui nos videre abeuntes, quid eos qui huic ignominioso agmini fuere obvii existimasse putatis, nisi aliquod profecto nefas esse, quod, si intersimus spectaculo, violaturi simus ludos piaculumque merituri, ideo nos 5 ab sede piorum, coetu concilioque abigi? Quid deinde? Illud non succurrit, vivere nos quod maturarimus proficisci? Si hoc profectio et non fuga est. Et hanc urbem vos non hostium ducitis, ubi si unum diem morati essetis, moriendum omnibus fuit? Bellum vobis indictum est, magno eorum malo qui 6 indixere, si viri estis." Ita et sua sponte irarum

[1] *The words* veteres ... Volscorum, *placed here by Walters, are given in the MSS. after* exorsus.

indignation. These leaders, eagerly drinking in the words with which he ministered to their anger, he conducted and, thanks to their influence, the rest of the throng also, to a field which lay below the road. There he launched out upon a speech like a general's harangue. "Though you should forget all else," he cried, "the ancient wrongs done by the Roman People and the disasters that have overtaken the Volscian race, with what feelings, pray, can you bear the insult which this day has brought to us, making our humiliation serve as the opening of their festival? Or did you not feel that they were triumphing over you to-day? That you furnished a spectacle to everybody when you departed—to the citizens, to the strangers, to all the neighbouring nations? That your wives and children were made a mock in the eyes of the world? What of those who heard the words of the herald? What of those who saw us going away? What of those who have met this ignominious procession? What think you they all supposed, but that we were certainly attainted of some sin; that because, were we to be present at the spectacle, we should pollute the games and incur the god's displeasure—for that reason we were being expelled from the seat of the righteous and from their gathering and their council? Moreover, does it not occur to you that we are alive because we hastened to depart?—if, indeed, this is a departure and not rather a flight. And this City—do you not regard it as a city of enemies, when if you had delayed there a single day, you would all have had to die? War has been declared upon you, and greatly shall they rue it who have been responsible, if you are men." So, their spontaneous anger fanned to a

LIVY

<small>A.U.C. 263</small> pleni et incitati domos inde digressi sunt instigandoque suos quisque populos effecere ut omne Volscum nomen deficeret.

<small>A.U.C. 266</small> XXXIX. Imperatores ad id bellum de omnium populorum sententia lecti Attius Tullius et Cn. Marcius, exsul Romanus, in quo aliquanto plus spei re-
2 positum. Quam spem nequaquam fefellit, ut facile appareret ducibus validiorem quam exercitu rem Romanam esse. Circeios profectus primum colonos inde Romanos expulit liberamque eam urbem Volscis
3 tradidit; Satricum, Longulam, Poluscam, Coriolos,
4 novella haec Romanis oppida ademit; inde Lavinium recepit; inde in Latinam viam transversis tramitibus transgressus,[1] tunc deinceps Corbionem, Veteliam,
5 Trebium, Labicos, Pedum cepit. Postremum ad urbem a Pedo ducit et ad fossas Cluilias[2] quinque ab urbe milia passuum castris positis populatur inde
6 agrum Romanum custodibus inter populatores missis, qui patriciorum agros intactos servarent, sive infensus plebi magis, sive ut discordia inde inter patres
7 plebemque oreretur. Quae profecto orta esset— adeo tribuni iam ferocem per se plebem criminando in primores civitatis instigabant,—sed externus timor, maximum concordiae vinculum, quamvis suspectos
8 infensosque inter se iungebat animos. Id modo non conveniebat, quod senatus consulesque nusquam alibi spem quam in armis ponebant, plebes omnia quam
9 bellum malebat. Sp. Nautius iam et Sex. Furius

---

[1] *The words* inde in Latinam ... transgressus, *placed here by Conway and Walters, are found in the MSS. between* tradidit *and* Satricum.

[2] Cluilias *Glareanus* (*cf.* I. xxii. 4): cluuilias (*or* cluuillas *or* cliuillas *or* cluullas *or* duuillias) Ω.

flame, they dispersed to their several homes, and, B.C. 491
every man arousing his own people, they brought
about a revolt of the entire Volscian name.

XXXIX. As generals for this war the nations all B.C. 488
agreed in choosing Attius Tullius and Gnaeus Marcius, the Roman exile, who inspired rather more hope
than did his colleague. This hope he by no means
disappointed, so that it was easy to see that Rome's
commanders were a greater source of strength to
her than her armies were. Marching first to Circei,
he drove out the Roman colonists from that city
and turned it over, thus liberated, to the Volsci.
He took Satricum, Longula, Polusca, and Corioli,
places which the Romans had recently acquired.
He then recovered Lavinium, and then, passing over
by cross-roads into the Latin Way, captured in succession Corbio, Vetelia, Trebium, Labici, and Pedum.
From Pedum he finally led his army against Rome
and, pitching his camp at the Cluilian Trenches, five
miles from the City, laid waste the Roman territory
from that base, sending out guards with the pillagers
to preserve intact the farms of the patricians, whether
from anger at the plebs, or to sow dissension between
them and the Fathers. And no doubt it would have
sprung up, so vehemently did the tribunes seek by
their accusations to rouse the already headstrong
commons against the nation's leaders, but dread of
invasion, the strongest bond of harmony, tended to
unite their feelings, however they might suspect and
dislike one another. In this one point they were
unable to agree, that the senate and the consuls saw
no hope anywhere but in arms, while the plebs preferred anything to war. Spurius Nautius and Sextus

LIVY

A.U.C. 266

consules erant. Eos recensentes legiones, praesidia per muros aliaque in quibus stationes vigiliasque esse placuerat loca distribuentis multitudo ingens pacem poscentium primum seditioso clamore conterruit, deinde vocare senatum, referre de legatis ad Cn.
10 Marcium mittendis coegit. Acceperunt relationem patres, postquam apparuit labare plebis animos, mis-
11 sique de pace ad Marcium oratores. Atrox responsum rettulerunt: si Volscis ager redderetur, posse agi de pace; si praeda belli per otium frui velint, memorem se et civium iniuriae et hospitum beneficii adnisurum ut appareat exsilio sibi inritatos non
12 fractos animos esse. Iterum deinde iidem missi non recipiuntur in castra. Sacerdotes quoque suis insignibus velatos isse supplices ad castra hostium traditum est; nihilo magis quam legatos flexisse animum.

A.U.C. 266-267

XL. Tum matronae ad Veturiam, matrem Coriolani, Volumniamque uxorem frequentes coeunt. Id publicum consilium an muliebris timor fuerit parum
2 invenio; pervicere certe ut et Veturia, magno natu mulier, et Volumnia duos parvos ex Marcio ferens filios secum in castra hostium irent et, quoniam armis viri defendere urbem non possent, mulieres precibus
3 lacrimisque defenderent. Ubi ad castra ventum est

---

[1] Livy implies that they were not the immediate successors of the consuls for 491, and in fact he seems to have omitted two sets, Q. Sulpicius Camerinus and Serg. Larcius Flavus (490), and C. Julius Iulus and P. Pinarius Rufus (489), though at III. xxxiii. 1 and v. liv. 5 he reckons in these two years. The missing names are supplied by Dion. Hal. vii. 68 and viii. 1.

BOOK II. xxxix. 9–xl. 3

Furius were now consuls.[1] While they were reviewing their levies and distributing garrisons about the walls and the other places where they had seen fit to place pickets and sentries, a great multitude of people demanding peace first terrified them with their rebellious clamour, and then forced them to call the senate together and propose the sending of envoys to Gnaeus Marcius. The Fathers consented to propose it when they saw that the plebeians were growing discouraged, and ambassadors were sent to Marcius to treat for peace. Stern was the answer they brought back. If the land of the Volsci were restored to them the question of peace could be taken up; if the Romans wished to enjoy the spoils of war without doing anything, he would forget neither the wrong his fellow-citizens had done him nor the kindness of his hosts, but would strive to show that exile had quickened his courage, not broken it. When the same envoys were sent back a second time, they were denied admittance to the camp. Even priests, wearing the appropriate fillets, are said to have gone as suppliants to the enemy's camp, where they were no more able than the envoys had been to alter the determination of Marcius.

XL. Then the married women gathered in large numbers at the house of Veturia, the mother of Coriolanus, and Volumnia, his wife. Whether this was public policy or woman's fear I cannot find out; in any case they prevailed with them that both Veturia, an aged woman, and Volumnia should take the two little sons of Marcius and go with them to the camp of the enemy; and that, since the swords of the men could not defend the City, the women should defend it with their prayers and tears. When they reached

B.C. 488

B.C. 488–487

347

LIVY

nuntiatumque Coriolano est adesse ingens mulierum agmen, ut[1] qui nec publica maiestate in legatis nec in sacerdotibus tanta offusa oculis animoque religione motus esset, multo obstinatior adversus lacrimas muliebres erat. Dein familiarium quidam qui insignem maestitia inter ceteras cognoverat Veturiam inter nurum nepotesque stantem, "Nisi me frustrantur," inquit, "oculi, mater tibi coniunxque et liberi adsunt." Coriolanus prope ut amens consternatus ab sede sua cum ferret matri obviae complexum, mulier in iram ex precibus versa "Sine, priusquam complexum accipio, sciam," inquit, "ad hostem an ad filium venerim, captiva materne in castris tuis sim. In hoc me longa vita et infelix senecta traxit, ut exsulem te, deinde hostem viderem? Potuisti populari hanc terram, quae te genuit atque aluit? Non tibi quamvis infesto animo et minaci perveneras ingredienti fines ira cecidit? Non, cum in conspectu Roma fuit, succurrit 'Intra illa moenia domus ac penates mei sunt, mater coniunx liberique'? Ergo ego nisi peperissem, Roma non oppugnaretur; nisi filium haberem, libera in libera patria mortua essem. Sed ego nihil iam pati nec tibi turpius nec[2] mihi miserius possum nec, ut sum miserrima, diu futura sum: de his videris, quos, si pergis, aut immatura

---

[1] agmen ut O_5: agmen in (ut B) primo ut Ω.
[2] nec *Bekker*: quam Ω: *Conway and Walters read* <us>quam *with M. Müller, and order the words thus*, ego mihi miserius nihil iam pati nec tibi turpius usquam possum.

348

BOOK II. XL. 3–9

the camp, and the word came to Coriolanus that a great company of women was at hand, at first, as might have been expected of one whom neither the nation's majesty could move, as represented in its envoys, nor the awfulness of religion, as conveyed to heart and eye by the persons of her priests, he showed even greater obduracy in resisting women's tears. Then one of his friends, led by Veturia's conspicuous sadness to single her out from amongst the other women, as she stood between her son's wife and his babies, said: "Unless my eyes deceive me, your mother is here and your wife and children." Coriolanus started up like a madman from his seat, and running to meet his mother would have embraced her, but her entreaties turned to anger, and she said: "Suffer me to learn, before I accept your embrace, whether I have come to an enemy or a son; whether I am a captive or a mother in your camp. Is it this to which long life and an unhappy old age have brought me, that I should behold in you an exile and then an enemy? Could you bring yourself to ravage this country, which gave you birth and reared you? Did not your anger fall from you, no matter how hostile and threatening your spirit when you came, as you passed the boundary? Did it not come over you, when Rome lay before your eyes: 'Within those walls are my home and my gods, my mother, my wife, and my children?' So then, had I not been a mother Rome would not now be besieged! Had I no son I should have died a free woman, in a free land! But I can have nothing now to suffer which could be more disgraceful to you or more miserable for myself; nor, wretched though I am, shall I be so for long: it is these you must consider, for whom, if you keep on, untimely death or

LIVY

A.U.C. 266-267

mors aut longa servitus manet." Uxor deinde ac liberi amplexi, fletusque ab omni turba mulierum ortus et comploratio sui patriaeque fregere tandem 10 virum. Complexus inde suos dimittit: ipse retro ab urbe castra movit. Abductis deinde legionibus ex agro Romano invidia rei oppressum perisse tradunt alii alio leto. Apud Fabium, longe antiquissimum auctorem, usque ad senectutem vixisse eundem in- 11 venio; refert certe hanc saepe eum exacta aetate usurpasse vocem, multo miserius seni exsilium esse. Non inviderunt laude sua mulieribus viri Romani— 12 adeo sine obtrectatione gloriae alienae vivebatur,— monumentoque[1] quod esset, templum Fortunae muliebri aedificatum dedicatumque est.

Rediere deinde Volsci adiunctis Aequis in agrum Romanum, sed Aequi Attium Tullium haud ultra 13 tulere ducem. Hinc ex certamine, Volsci Aequine imperatorem coniuncto exercitui darent, seditio, deinde atrox proelium ortum. Ibi fortuna populi Romani duos hostium exercitus haud minus perniciOso quam pertinaci certamine confecit.

14 Consules T. Sicinius et C. Aquilius. Sicinio Volsci, Aquilio Hernici—nam ii quoque in armis erant—provincia evenit. Eo anno Hernici devicti: cum Volscis aequo Marte discessum est.

[1] monumentoque *Gronov.*: monumento quoque Ω.

---

[1] For another account of Coriolanus, see Dion. Hal. viii. 12 and viii. 17–56.

long enslavement is in store." The embraces of his wife and children, following this speech, and the tears of the entire company of women, and their lamentations for themselves and their country, at last broke through his resolution. He embraced his family and sent them back, and withdrew his forces from before the City. Having then led his army out of Rome's dominions he is said to have perished beneath the weight of resentment which this act caused, by a death which is variously described. I find in Fabius, by far the oldest authority, that Coriolanus lived on to old age. At least he reports that this saying was often on his lips, that exile was a far more wretched thing when one was old. There was no envy of the fame the women had earned, on the part of the men of Rome—so free was life in those days from disparagement of another's glory—and to preserve its memory the temple of Fortuna Muliebris was built and dedicated.[1]

B.C. 488-487

Afterwards the Volsci again invaded Roman soil, in conjunction with the Aequi, but these would no longer put up with Attius Tullius for their general. Whereupon the dispute as to whether the Volsci or the Aequi should furnish a commander for the allied army, led to a quarrel, and this to a bloody battle. There the good fortune of the Roman People destroyed two hostile armies in one struggle, which was no less ruinous than it was obstinately fought.

The consulship of Titus Sicinius and Gaius Aquilius. Sicinius got the Volscian war for his command, and Aquilius that with the Hernici—for they too were up in arms. This year the Hernici were conquered, while the campaign against the Volsci was indecisive.

LIVY

XLI. Sp. Cassius deinde et Proculus Verginius consules facti. Cum Hernicis foedus ictum; agri partes duae ademptae. Inde dimidium Latinis, dimidium plebi divisurus consul Cassius erat. Adiciebat huic muneri agri aliquantum, quem publicum possideri a privatis criminabatur. Id multos quidem patrum, ipsos possessores, periculo rerum suarum terrebat; sed et publica patribus sollicitudo inerat, largitione consulem periculosas libertati opes struere. Tum primum lex agraria promulgata est, numquam deinde usque ad hanc memoriam sine maximis motibus rerum agitata. Consul alter largitioni resistebat auctoribus patribus nec omni plebe adversante, quae primo coeperat fastidire munus volgatum a civibus esse in socios; saepe deinde et Verginium consulem in contionibus velut vaticinantem audiebat, pestilens collegae munus esse, agros illos servitutem iis qui acceperint[1] laturos, regno viam fieri. Quid ita enim adsumi socios et nomen Latinum? Quid attinuisse[2] Hernicis, paulo ante hostibus, capti agri partem tertiam reddi, nisi ut hae gentes pro Coriolano duce Cassium habeant? Popularis iam esse dissuasor et

---

[1] acceperint *Grynaeus*: acceperant Ω.
[2] attinuisse $R^2 D^2{-}$: attinuisset Ω.

BOOK II. XLI. 1-7

XLI. Spurius Cassius and Proculus Verginius were then made consuls. A treaty was struck with the Hernici, and two-thirds of their land was taken from them. Of this the consul Cassius proposed to divide one half amongst the Latins and the other half amongst the plebeians. To this gift he wished to add some part of that land which, he charged, was held by individuals, although it belonged to the state. Whereupon many of the Fathers, being themselves in possession of the land, took fright at the danger which threatened their interests. But the senators were also concerned on public grounds, namely, that the consul by his largesses should be building up an influence perilous to liberty. This was the first proposal for agrarian legislation, and from that day to within living memory it has never been brought up without occasioning the most serious disturbances. The other consul resisted the largess, and the Fathers supported him; nor were the commons solidly against him, for to begin with, they had taken offence that the bounty had been made general, being extended to include allies as well as citizens; and again, they often heard the consul Verginius declare in his speeches, as though he read the future, that destruction lurked in the gift proposed by his colleague; that those lands would bring servitude to the men who should receive them, and were being made a road to monarchy. For what reason had there been, he asked, in including the allies and the Latin name, and in restoring to the Hernici, who had been enemies a short time before, a third of the land which had been taken from them, if it were not that these tribes might have Cassius in the room of Coriolanus for their captain? Popular

B.C. 86-485

353

LIVY

intercessor legis agrariae coeperat. Uterque deinde consul, ut certatim, plebi indulgere. Verginius dicere passurum se adsignari agros, dum ne cui nisi civ 8 Romano adsignentur: Cassius, quia in agraria largi tione ambitiosus in socios eoque civibus vilior erat ut alio munere sibi reconciliaret civium animos, iu bere pro Siculo frumento pecuniam acceptam retribu 9 populo. Id vero haud secus quam praesentem mer cedem regni aspernata plebes; adeo propter suspi cionem insitam regni, velut abundarent omnia 10 munera eius[1] respuebantur. Quem, ubi primum magistratu abiit, damnatum necatumque constat Sunt qui patrem auctorem eius supplicii ferant: eum cognita domi causa verberasse ac necasse peculium que filii Cereri consecravisse; signum inde factum 11 esse et inscriptum, "ex Cassia familia datum." In venio apud quosdam, idque propius fidem est, a quaestoribus Caesone Fabio et L. Valerio diem dic tam perduellionis, damnatumque populi iudicio, diru tas publice aedes. Ea est area ante Telluris aedem 12 Ceterum, sive illud domesticum sive publicum fui iudicium, damnatur Servio Cornelio Q. Fabio consu libus.

[1] *After* eius *the MSS. give* in animis hominum, *which i bracketed by Conway (after Vielhaber, who also ejects* insitam)

BOOK II. XLI. 7-12

favour now began to go over to the opponent and vetoer of the land-legislation. Each consul then began, as if vying with the other, to pamper the plebs. Verginius said that he would permit lands to be assigned, provided they were assigned to none but Roman citizens. Cassius, having by his proposed agrarian grants made a bid for the support of the allies and thereby lowered himself in the eyes of the Romans, desired to regain the affection of his fellow-citizens by another donation, and proposed that the money received from the Sicilian corn should be paid back to the people. But this the people spurned, as a downright attempt to purchase regal power; to such an extent did their instinctive suspicion of monarchy render them scornful of his gifts, as if they had possessed a superfluity of everything; and Cassius had no sooner laid down his office than he was condemned and executed, as all authorities agree. There are those who say that his father was responsible for his punishment: that he tried the case in his house, and that, after causing his son to be scourged and put to death, he consecrated to Ceres his personal property, from the proceeds of which a statue was made and inscribed "the gift of the Cassian family." I find in certain authors, and this is the more credible account, that the quaestors Caeso Fabius and Lucius Valerius brought him to trial for treason, and that he was found guilty by judgment of the people and his house pulled down by popular decree. Its site is now the open space in front of the temple of Tellus. But whether it was a domestic or a state trial, he was condemned in the consulship of Servius Cornelius and Quintus Fabius.

LIVY

XLII. Haud diuturna ira populi in Cassium fuit. Dulcedo agrariae legis ipsa per se dempto auctore subibat animos, accensaque ea cupiditas est malignitate patrum, qui devictis eo anno Volscis Aequisque 2 militem praeda fraudavere. Quidquid captum ex hostibus est, vendidit Fabius consul ac redegit in publicum. Invisum erat Fabium nomen plebi propter novissimum consulem; tenuere tamen patres, ut 3 cum L. Aemilio Caeso Fabius consul crearetur. Eo infestior facta plebes seditione domestica bellum externum excivit. Bello deinde civiles discordiae intermissae. Uno animo patres ac plebs rebellantes Volscos et Aequos duce Aemilio prospera pugna 4 vicere. Plus tamen hostium fuga quam proelium absumpsit, adeo pertinaciter fusos insecuti sunt 5 equites. Castoris aedes eodem anno idibus Quintilibus dedicata est. Vota erat Latino bello a Postumio[1] dictatore: filius eius duumvir ad id ipsum creatus dedicavit.

6 Sollicitati et eo anno sunt dulcedine agrariae legis animi plebis. Tribuni plebi popularem potestatem lege populari celebrabant: patres satis superque gratuiti furoris in multitudine credentes esse, largi-

---

[1] a Postumio *du Rieu*: Postumio Ω.

---

[1] The temple was erected in honour of both Castor and Pollux, but was commonly referred to by the name of the former alone (*e.g.* Cicero, *Mil.* 91). The *duumviri* were a committee of two, appointed to oversee the construction and

BOOK II. XLII. 1-6

XLII. It was not long before the people forgot the anger they had felt against Cassius. The inherent attractiveness of the agrarian legislation appealed to them on its own account, when its author had been removed, and their desire for it was enhanced by the meanness of the Fathers, who after the defeat in that year of the Volsci and the Aequi defrauded the soldiers of their booty. Whatever was taken from the enemy Fabius sold and placed the proceeds in the public treasury. The Fabian name was hateful to the plebs, on the last consul's account; nevertheless the patricians succeeded in procuring the election of Caeso Fabius to that office, along with Lucius Aemilius. This increased the rancour of the plebeians, and by their seditions at home they brought about a foreign war. The war then caused domestic strife to be interrupted, while with one mind and purpose patricians and plebeians met the rebellious Volsci and Aequi and, led by Aemilius, defeated them in a successful action. Yet more of the enemy perished in flight than in the battle, so relentlessly did the cavalry pursue their routed forces. Castor's temple was dedicated the same year, on the fifteenth of July. It had been vowed during the Latin war by Postumius, the dictator. His son, being made duumvir for this special purpose, dedicated it.[1]

The desires of the plebs were this year again excited by the charms of the land-law. The tribunes of the plebs endeavoured to recommend their democratic office by a democratic law, while the senators, who thought there was frenzy enough and to spare in the populace, without rewarding it, shuddered at

---

dedication of a temple when the man who had vowed it died without accomplishing his task.

LIVY

7 tiones temeritatisque invitamenta horrebant. Acerrimi patribus duces ad resistendum consules fuere. Ea igitur pars rei publicae vicit nec in praesens modo sed in venientem etiam annum M. Fabium, Caesonis fratrem, et magis invisum alterum plebi accusatione 8 Sp. Cassi, L. Valerium, consules dedit. Certatum eo quoque anno cum tribunis est. Vana lex vanique legis auctores iactando inritum munus facti. Fabium inde nomen ingens post tres continuos consulatus unoque velut tenore omnes expertos tribuniciis certaminibus habitum; itaque, ut bene locatus, mansit in ea familia aliquamdiu honos. Bellum inde Veiens 9 initum, et Volsci rebellarunt. Sed ad bella externa prope supererant vires, abutebanturque iis inter 10 semet ipsos certando. Accessere ad aegras iam omnium mentes prodigia caelestia, prope cotidianas in urbe agrisque ostentantia minas; motique ita numinis causam nullam aliam vates canebant publice privatimque nunc extis nunc per aves consulti, quam haud 11 rite sacra fieri. Qui terrores tandem[1] eo evasere ut Oppia virgo Vestalis damnata incesti poenas dederit.

[1] tandem *Madvig*: tamen Ω: *omitted in O.*

---

[1] For the next four years, making seven successive years in all, the Fabii were represented in the consulate.

BOOK II. XLII. 6-11

the thought of land-grants and encouragements to rashness. The most strenuous of leaders were at hand for the senatorial opposition, in the persons of the consuls. Their party was therefore victorious and not only won an immediate success but, besides, elected as consuls for the approaching year Marcus Fabius, Caeso's brother, and one whom, on account of the prosecution of Spurius Cassius, the people hated even more, namely, Lucius Valerius. This year also there was a conflict with the tribunes. Nothing came of the legislation, and its supporters fell into contempt, from boasting of a measure which they could not carry through. The Fabii were thenceforward held in great repute, after their three successive consulships, which had all without interruption been subjected to the proof of struggles with the tribunes; accordingly the office, as if well invested, was permitted to remain some time in that family.[1] War then broke out with Veii, and the Volsci revolted. But for foreign wars there was almost a superabundance of resources, and men misused them in quarrelling amongst themselves. To increase the general anxiety which was now felt, portents implying the anger of the gods were of almost daily occurrence in the City and the country. For this expression of divine wrath no other reason was alleged by the soothsayers, when they had enquired into it both officially and privately, sometimes by inspecting entrails and sometimes by observing the flight of birds, than the failure duly to observe the rites of religion. These alarms at length resulted in the condemnation of Oppia, a Vestal virgin, for unchastity, and her punishment.

LIVY

XLIII. Q. Fabius inde et C. Iulius[1] consules facti. Eo anno non[2] segnior discordia domi et bellum foris atrocius fuit. Ab Aequis arma sumpta: Veientes agrum quoque Romanorum populantes inierunt. Quorum bellorum crescente cura Caeso Fabius et Sp. Furius consules fiunt. Ortonam, Latinam urbem, Aequi oppugnabant: Veientes pleni iam populationum Romam ipsam se oppugnaturos minabantur. Qui terrores cum compescere deberent, auxere insuper animos plebis; redibatque non sua sponte plebi mos detractandi militiam, sed Sp. Licinius tribunus plebis, venisse tempus ratus per ultimam necessitatem legis agrariae patribus iniungendae, susceperat rem militarem impediendam. Ceterum tota invidia tribuniciae potestatis versa in auctorem est, nec in eum consules acrius quam ipsius[3] collegae coorti sunt, auxilioque eorum dilectum consules habent. Ad duo simul bella exercitus scribitur; ducendus Fabio in Aequos, Furio datur in Veientes. In Veientes nihil dignum memoria gestum; et in Aequis quidem Fabio aliquanto plus negotii cum civibus quam cum hostibus fuit.[4] Unus ille vir, ipse consul, rem publicam sustinuit, quam exercitus odio consulis, quantum in se fuit, prodebat. Nam cum consul praeter ceteras imperatorias artes, quas parando gerendoque bello edidit plurimas, ita

---

[1] Iulius *Sigonius* (*from Dion. Hal.* viii. 90. 5 *and Cassiod. C.I.L.* i², *p.* 101) : tullius Ω.

[2] anno non Ω : anno *M* (*cf.* § 4).

[3] ipsius *M*ς : ipsius eius Ω.

[4] *The words* ducendus *to* fuit *give the text as restored by Conway and Walters* (*cf. Class. Quart.* 1910, *p.* 276) : *the good MSS. order the words thus*: ducendus Fabio in Veientes, in Aequos Furio datur, et in Aequis quidem nihil dignum memoria gestum est ; Fabio aliquanto plus negotii cum ciuibus quam cum hostibus fuit.

BOOK II. XLIII. 1–7

XLIII. Quintus Fabius and Gaius Julius were then made consuls. This year there was no less discord at home, and the menace of war was greater. The Aequi took up arms, and the Veientes even made a foray into Roman territory. During the increasing anxiety occasioned by these campaigns Caeso Fabius and Spurius Furius were elected to the consulship. Ortona, a Latin city, was being besieged by the Aequi; while the Veientes, who by this time had their fill of rapine, were threatening to attack Rome itself. These alarms, though they should have restrained the animosity of the plebeians, actually heightened it; and they resumed their custom of refusing service, though not of their own initiative; for it was Spurius Licinius, tribune of the plebs, who, deeming that the moment had come for forcing a land-law on the patricians by the direst necessity, had undertaken to obstruct the preparations for war. But he drew upon his own head all the odium attaching to the tribunician office, nor did the consuls inveigh against him more fiercely than did his own colleagues, and with their help the consuls held a levy. Armies were enlisted for two wars at the same time; the command of one, which was to invade the Aequi, was given to Fabius, while with the other Furius was to oppose the Veientes. Against the Veientes nothing worth recording was accomplished; and in the Aequian campaign Fabius had somewhat more trouble with his fellow-Romans than with the enemy. That one man, the consul himself, preserved the state, which the army in its hatred of the consul would, so far as it was able, have betrayed. For when the consul, besides the many other instances of good generalship which he displayed in

LIVY

instruxisset aciem, ut solo equitatu emisso exercitum
8 hostium funderet, insequi fusos pedes noluit; nec
illos, etsi non adhortatio invisi ducis, suum saltem
flagitium et publicum in praesentia dedecus, postmodo periculum, si animus hosti redisset, cogere
potuit gradum adcelerare aut, si aliud nihil, stare[1]
9 instructos. Iniussu signa referunt maestique—cre-
deres victos—exsecrantes nunc imperatorem nunc
10 navatam ab equite operam, redeunt in castra. Nec
huic tam pestilenti exemplo remedia ulla ab imperatore quaesita sunt; adeo excellentibus ingeniis citius
defuerit ars qua civem regant, quam qua hostem
11 superent. Consul Romam rediit non tam belli gloria
aucta quam inritato exacerbatoque in se militum
odio. Obtinuere tamen patres ut in Fabia gente
consulatus maneret; M. Fabium consulem creant,
Fabio collega Cn. Manlius[2] datur.

XLIV. Et hic annus tribunum auctorem legis
agrariae habuit. Tib. Pontificius fuit. Is eandem
viam velut processisset Sp. Licinio ingressus dilec-
2 tum paulisper impediit. Perturbatis iterum patribus
Ap. Claudius victam tribuniciam potestatem dicere
priore anno, in praesentia re, exemplo in perpetuum,

---

[1] stare *Muretus*: instare (instrare *O*) Ω.
[2] Manlius *ed. Ald.* (*from* II. xlvii. 1, *Dion. Hal.* ix. 5. 1, *and Diod.* xi. 50; *but Cassiod. C.I.L.* i², *p.* 101 *has* Cn. Mallius): Manilius (*or* Mam-) Ω.

BOOK II. XLIII. 7–XLIV. 2

preparing for the war and in his conduct of it, had so drawn up the battle-line that a charge of the cavalry alone sufficed to rout the enemy's army, the foot refused to pursue the flying foe; nor could even their own sense of guilt—to say nothing of the exhortation of their hated general,—nor even the thought of the immediate disgrace to all, and the danger they must presently incur if the enemy should recover his courage, compel them to quicken their pace, or, if nothing else, to stand in their ranks. Contrary to orders they retreated and returned to their camp, in such dejection that you would have supposed them beaten, now uttering execrations against their leader and now against the efficient services of the horse. Ruinous though their example was, the general found no remedy for it; so true is it that noble minds are oftener lacking in the qualities by which men govern their fellow-citizens than in those by which they conquer an enemy. The consul returned to Rome, having purchased more hatred of his irritated and embittered soldiers than won increase in military fame. Nevertheless the Fathers held out for the retention of the consulship in the Fabian family. Marcus Fabius was the man they elected, and they gave him Gnaeus Manlius as a colleague.

XLIV. This year also had a tribune who advocated a land-law, Tiberius Pontificius. He set out on the same path that Spurius Licinius had trodden, as though Licinius had been successful, and for a time obstructed the levy. The senators were again thrown into consternation, but Appius Claudius told them that the tribunician power had been overcome the year before, actually for the time being, and potentially

LIVY

quando inventum sit suis ipsam viribus dissolvi.
3 Neque enim umquam defuturum qui et ex collega victoriam sibi et gratiam melioris partis bono publico velit quaesitam; et plures, si pluribus opus sit, tribunos ad auxilium consulum paratos fore, et unum
4 vel adversus omnes satis esse. Darent modo et consules et primores patrum operam ut, si minus omnes, aliquos tamen ex tribunis rei publicae ac senatui
5 conciliarent. Praeceptis Appi moniti patres et universi comiter ac benigne tribunos appellare, et consulares, ut cuique eorum privatim aliquid iuris adversus singulos erat, partim gratia partim auctoritate obtinuere ut tribuniciae potestatis vires salubres
6 vellent rei publicae esse; quattuorque[1] tribunorum adversus unum moratorem publici commodi auxilio dilectum consules habent.

7 Inde ad Veiens bellum profecti, quo undique ex Etruria auxilia convenerant, non tam Veientium gratia concitata quam quod in spem ventum erat discordia intestina dissolvi rem Romanam posse.
8 Principesque in omnium Etruriae populorum conciliis fremebant aeternas opes esse Romanas, nisi inter semet ipsi seditionibus saeviant. Id unum venenum, eam labem civitatibus opulentis repertam,

---

[1] quattuorque ς (cf. II. xxxiii. 2; III. xxx. 7): nouemque (noque M) Ω (? ix for iv).

BOOK II. XLIV. 2-8

for ever, since a way had been discovered for employing its resources to its own undoing. For there would always be some tribune who would be willing to gain a personal victory over his colleague, and obtain the favour of the better element, while doing the nation a service. There would be a number of tribunes, if a number should be needed, who would be ready to help the consuls; and a single one was enough, though opposed to all the rest. Only let the consuls, and the leading senators as well, make a point of winning over, if not all, at any rate some of the tribunes to the state and the senate. Acting on the instructions of Appius, the Fathers began as a class to address the tribunes in a courteous and kindly manner; and those who were of consular rank, when it happened that any of them had any private claim upon an individual tribune, brought it about, in part by personal influence, in part by political, that those officials were disposed to use their powers for the good of the state; and four of them, as against one who would have hindered the general good, assisted the consuls to hold the muster.

B.C. 480

The army then set out for a war with the Veientes, to whose help forces had rallied from every quarter of Etruria, not so much roused by goodwill towards the men of Veii as by hopes that civil discord might effect the downfall of the Roman state. And indeed the leading men in the councils of all the Etrurian peoples were wrathfully complaining that there would be no end to the power of the Romans unless factional quarrels should set them to fighting amongst themselves. They asserted that this was the only poison, the only decay which had been found to work upon

LIVY

A.U.C. 274

9 ut magna imperia mortalia essent. Diu sustentatum id malum, partim patrum consiliis partim patientia plebis, iam ad extrema venisse. Duas civitates ex una factas, suos cuique parti magistratus, suas leges 10 esse. Primum in dilectibus saevire solitos, eosdem in bello tamen paruisse ducibus. Qualicumque urbis statu manente disciplina militari sisti potuisse ; iam non parendi magistratibus morem in castra quoque 11 Romanum militem sequi. Proximo bello in ipsa acie, in ipso certamine consensu exercitus traditam ultro victoriam victis Aequis, signa deserta, imperatorem 12 in acie relictum, iniussu in castra reditum. Profecto, si instetur, suo milite vinci Romam posse. Nihil aliud opus esse quam indici ostendique bellum; cetera sua sponte fata et deos gesturos. Hae spes Etruscos armaverant, multis in vicem casibus victos victoresque. XLV. Consules quoque Romani nihil praeterea aliud quam suas vires, sua arma horrebant. Memoria pessimi proximo bello exempli terrebat ne rem committerent eo ubi duae simul acies timendae 2 essent. Itaque castris se tenebant, tam ancipiti periculo aversi : diem tempusque forsitan ipsum leni-

opulent states, so as to make great empires transitory. B.C. 480
For a long time the Romans had withstood this evil,
thanks partly to the prudence of the senate, partly to
the patience of the plebs; but they had now come
to a crisis. Two states had been created out of one:
each faction had its own magistrates, its own laws.
At first, though they had a way of fiercely opposing
the levies, yet when war began they had obeyed
their generals. No matter what the condition of
things in the City, so long as military discipline held
it had been possible to make a stand; but now the
fashion of disobeying magistrates was following the
Roman soldier even to his camp. In their latest war,
when the army was already drawn up for battle, and
at the very instant of conflict, they had with one
accord actually handed over the victory to the conquered Aequi, had deserted their standards, had left
their general on the field, and had returned, against
his orders, to their camp. Assuredly if her enemies
pressed forward they could vanquish Rome by means
of her own soldiers. There needed nothing more
than to make a declaration and a show of war; Fate
and the gods would of their own will do the rest.
Such were the hopes which had led the Etruscans
to take up arms, after many a shifting hazard of defeat and victory. XLV. The Roman consuls also felt
that they had nothing else to dread but their own
forces and their own arms. The recollection of the
heinous example set in the last war deterred them
from offering battle in a situation where they would
be in danger from two armies at the same time. Accordingly they kept within their camp, restrained by
the thought of so grave a peril: time and circumstances would perhaps assuage the anger of the men

LIVY

3 turum iras sanitatemque animis allaturum. Veiens hostis Etruscique eo magis praepropere agere; lacessere ad pugnam primo obequitando castris provocandoque, postremo, ut nihil movebant, qua consules 4 ipsos qua exercitum increpando: simulationem intestinae discordiae remedium timoris inventum, et consules magis non confidere quam non credere suis militibus; novum seditionis genus, silentium otiumque inter armatos. Ad haec in novitatem generis 5 originisque qua falsa, qua vera iacere. Haec cum sub ipso vallo portisque streperent, haud aegre consules pati; at imperitae multitudini nunc indignatio, nunc pudor pectora versare et ab intestinis avertere malis; nolle inultos hostes, nolle successum non patribus, non consulibus; externa et domestica odia 6 certare in animis. Tandem superant externa, adeo superbe insolenterque hostis eludebat. Frequentes in praetorium conveniunt; poscunt pugnam, postu- 7 lant ut signum detur. Consules velut deliberabundi capita conferunt, diu conloquuntur. Pugnare cupiebant, sed retro revocanda et abdenda[1] cupiditas erat, ut adversando remorandoque incitato semel militi 8 adderent impetum. Redditur responsum immaturam

[1] abdenda ⛬ *Gebhard* : addenda Ω.

---

[1] The headquarters of the consul, who was originally called praetor.

BOOK II. xlv. 2-8

and bring them to their senses. Their enemies the B.C. 480
Veientes and the other Etruscans were for that reason
the more in haste to act; they attempted to provoke
the Romans to fight, at first by riding up to their
camp and challenging them to come out, and finally,
when they gained nothing by this, by shouting insults
both at the consuls themselves and at the army. They
said that their pretended want of harmony amongst
themselves had been resorted to in order to conceal
their fear, and that the consuls distrusted the courage
of their men even more than their loyalty; it was a
strange kind of mutiny where armed men were silent
and inactive. To these taunts they added others upon
the newness of their race and origin, partly false and
partly true. This abuse, noisily uttered beneath the
very rampart and the gates, was endured unconcern-
edly enough by the consuls. But the inexperienced
rank and file, stirred now by indignation and now
by shame, were diverted from the thought of their
domestic troubles; they were unwilling that their
enemies should go unpunished; they were unwilling
that the patricians, that the consuls should obtain a
success; hatred of the foe contended in their bosoms
with hatred of their fellow-citizens. At length the
former feeling got the upper hand, so proud and insolent was the jeering of the enemy. They gathered
in crowds at the praetorium,[1] demanded battle, requested that the signal should be given. The consuls, as though considering the matter, put their
heads together and conferred for a long time. They
desired to fight, but it was needful to keep back
their desire and conceal it, that by opposition and
delay they might stimulate to fury the already eager
soldiery. The men were therefore told that the

LIVY

rem agi, nondum tempus pugnae esse; castris se tenerent. Edicunt inde ut abstineant pugna : si quis 9 iniussu pugnaverit, ut in hostem animadversuros. Ita dimissis, quo minus consules velle credunt, crescit ardor pugnandi. Accendunt insuper hostes ferocius multo, ut statuisse non pugnare consules cognitum 10 est: quippe impune se insultaturos, non credi militi arma, rem ad ultimum seditionis erupturam, finemque venisse Romano imperio. His freti occursant portis, ingerunt probra, aegre abstinent quin castra oppug- 11 nent. Enimvero non ultra contumeliam pati Romanus posse; totis castris undique ad consules curritur; non iam[1] sensim, ut ante, per centurionum principes postulant, sed passim omnes clamoribus agunt. Ma- 12 tura res erat; tergiversantur tamen. Fabius deinde ad crescentem tumultum iam metu seditionis collega concedente, cum silentium classico fecisset: "Ego istos, Cn. Manli,[2] posse vincere scio; velle ne scirem 13 ipsi fecerunt. Itaque certum atque decretum est non dare signum, nisi victores se redituros ex hac pugna iurant. Consulem Romanum miles semel in acie fefellit, deos numquam fallet." Centurio erat

[1] iam R_5: tam Ω.   [2] Manli $_5$: Manili Ω.

370

BOOK II. XLV. 8-13

thing was premature, that the time for battle had not yet come; that they must keep within the camp. Then the consuls issued an order to abstain from fighting, declaring that if any man fought without orders they should treat him as an enemy. Dismissed with these words, the less inclination the soldiers discovered in the consuls the greater became their own eagerness for the fray. They were still further exasperated by the enemy, who were much bolder even than before, when the consuls' determination not to fight became known: it was clear that they could insult the Romans with impunity; their soldiers were not trusted with weapons, the affair would culminate in absolute mutiny, and the end of the Roman power had come. Relying on these convictions, they charged up to the gates, flung gibes at their defenders, and scarcely refrained from assaulting the camp. At this the Romans could no longer brook their insults; from all over the camp they came running to the consuls. There were no more cautious requests, preferred through the chief centurions, but on all sides arose a general clamour. The time was ripe; nevertheless the consuls hung back. Then Fabius, when his colleague, beginning to fear mutiny, was on the point of yielding to the growing tumult, commanded silence by a trumpet-blast and said: "I know, Gnaeus Manlius, that these men have the power to conquer, but their will to do so I know not; and for this they are themselves to blame. I am therefore resolved and determined not to give the signal unless they swear that they will return victorious from this engagement. Once, in a battle, the soldiers betrayed a Roman consul: they will never betray the gods." There was a centurion named

LIVY

M. Flavoleius, inter primores pugnae flagitator. "Victor," inquit, "M. Fabi, revertar ex acie." Si fallat, Iovem patrem Gradivumque Martem aliosque iratos invocat deos. Idem deinceps omnis exercitus in se quisque iurat. Iuratis datur signum; arma capiunt; eunt in pugnam irarum speique pleni. Nunc iubent Etruscos probra iacere, nunc armati sibi quisque lingua promptum hostem offerri. Omnium illo die, qua plebis qua patrum, eximia virtus fuit; Fabium nomen[1] maxime enituit. Multis civilibus certaminibus infensos plebis animos illa pugna sibi reconciliare statuunt.

XLVI. Instruitur acies, nec Veiens hostis Etruscaeque legiones detractant. Prope certa spes erat non magis secum pugnaturos quam pugnaverint cum Aequis; maius quoque aliquod in tam inritatis animis et occasione ancipiti haud desperandum esse facinus. Res aliter longe evenit; nam non alio ante bello infestior Romanus—adeo hinc contumeliis hostes, hinc consules mora exacerbaverant—proelium iniit. Vix explicandi ordinis spatium Etruscis fuit, cum pilis inter primam trepidationem abiectis temere magis quam emissis pugna iam in manus, iam ad gladios, ubi Mars est atrocissimus, venerat. Inter

---

[1] Fabium nomen *Madvig*: fabium nomen fabia gens Ω.

BOOK II. XLV. 13–XLVI. 4

Marcus Flavoleius, who had been among the foremost in demanding battle. "I will return victorious from the field, Marcus Fabius," he cried, and invoked the wrath of Father Jupiter, Mars Gradivus, and the other gods, if he failed to keep his vow. The same pledge was then taken in order by the entire army, each man invoking its penalties upon himself. When they had sworn, the signal sounded. They armed and entered the fight, angry and confident. Now let the Etruscans fling their taunts! Now —they all cried—now, when they were armed, let the lip-bold enemy face them! On that day they all showed splendid courage, both commoners and nobles, but the Fabian name was especially distinguished. In the course of many political struggles they had estranged the plebs, and they resolved to regain their goodwill in that battle.

XLVI. The line was drawn up, nor did the Veientes and the Etruscan levies shun the encounter. They felt almost certain that the Romans would no more fight with them than they had fought with the Aequi. That they might even be guilty of some greater enormity, exasperated as they were, and possessed of a critical opportunity, was not too much to hope. But it turned out quite otherwise. For there had never been a war when the Romans went into battle with a keener hostility—so embittered had they been, on the one hand by the enemy's insults, on the other by the procrastination of the consuls. The Etruscans had barely had time to deploy when their enemies, who in the first excitement had rather cast their javelins at random than fairly aimed them, were already come to sword-strokes at close quarters, where fighting is the fiercest. The Fabian clan was

LIVY

primores genus Fabium insigne spectaculo exemploque civibus erat. Ex his Q. Fabium—tertio hic anno ante consul fuerat—principem in confertos Veientes euntem ferox viribus et armorum arte Tuscus, incautum inter multas versantem[1] hostium manus, gladio per pectus transfigit; telo extracto 5 praeceps Fabius in volnus cadit.[2] Sensit utraque acies unius viri casum, cedebatque inde Romanus, cum M. Fabius consul transiluit iacentis corpus obiectaque parma, "Hoc iurastis," inquit, "milites, 6 fugientes vos in castra redituros? Adeo ignavissimos hostes magis timetis quam Iovem Martemque, per quos iurastis? At ego iniuratus aut victor revertar aut prope te hic, Q. Fabi, dimicans cadam." Consuli tum Caeso[3] Fabius, prioris anni consul: "Verbisne istis, frater, ut pugnent te impetraturum 7 credis? Di impetrabunt, per quos iuravere; et nos, ut decet proceres, ut Fabio nomine est dignum, pugnando potius quam adhortando accendamus militum animos!" Sic in primum infensis hastis provolant duo Fabii totamque moverunt secum aciem.

XLVII. Proelio ex parte una restituto nihilo segnius in cornu altero Cn. Manlius consul pugnam 2 ciebat, ubi prope similis fortuna est versata. Nam ut altero in cornu Q. Fabium, sic in hoc ipsum

---

[1] versantem D^2 (or D^1) ς: uersantes Ω.
[2] cadit *H. J. Müller*: abiit Ω.
[3] Caeso ς: gaius Ω: c̄ U: graus H.

374

conspicuous among the foremost, a spectacle and encouragement to their fellow-citizens. One of them, the Quintus Fabius who had been consul three years before, was leading the attack on the closely marshalled Veientes, when a Tuscan, exulting in his strength and skill at arms, caught him unawares in the midst of a crowd of his enemies and drove his sword through his breast. As the blade was withdrawn Fabius fell headlong upon his wound. It was but the fall of one man, but both armies felt it; and the Romans were giving way at that point, when Marcus Fabius the consul leaped over the prostrate corpse and, covering himself with his target, cried, "Was this your oath, men, that you would return to your camp in flight? Do you then fear the most dastardly of foes more than Jupiter and Mars, by whom you swore? But I, though I have sworn no oath, will either return victorious or fall fighting here by you, Quintus Fabius!" To this speech of the consul Caeso Fabius, consul of the year before, made answer, "Think you that your words will persuade them to fight, brother? The gods will persuade them, by whom they have sworn. And let us, as is meet for nobles, as is worthy of the name of Fabius, kindle by fighting rather than by exhortation the courage of our soldiers!" With that the two Fabii rushed into the press with levelled spears and carried the whole line forward with them.

XLVII. Thus the fortune of the day was retrieved in one part of the field. On the other wing Gnaeus Manlius the consul was urging on the fight with no less vigour, when almost the same thing happened. For as Quintus Fabius had done on the

LIVY

consulem Manlium iam velut fusos agentem hostes et inpigre milites secuti sunt et, ut ille gravi volnere ictus ex acie cessit, interfectum rati 3 gradum rettulere; cessissentque loco, ni consul alter cum aliquot turmis equitum in eam partem citato equo advectus, vivere clamitans collegam, se victorem fuso altero cornu adesse, rem inclinatam 4 sustinuisset. Manlius quoque ad restituendam aciem se ipse coram offert. Duorum consulum cognita ora accendunt militum animos. Simul et vanior iam erat hostium acies, dum abundante multitudine freti subtracta subsidia mittunt ad castra op- 5 pugnanda. In quae haud magno certamine impetu facto, dum[1] praedae magis quam pugnae memores tererent tempus, triarii Romani, qui primam inruptionem sustinere non potuerant, missis ad consules nuntiis quo loco res essent, conglobati ad praetorium 6 redeunt et sua sponte ipsi proelium renovant. Et Manlius consul revectus in castra ad omnes portas milite opposito hostibus viam clauserat. Ea desperatio Tuscis rabiem magis quam audaciam accendit. Nam cum incursantes, quacumque exitum ostenderet spes, vano aliquotiens impetu issent, globus iuvenum unus in ipsum consulem insignem armis invadit.

[1] dum Ω (*including* M[1] *or* M[2]) : cum *Gronov. M.*

BOOK II. XLVII. 2–6

other flank, so here the consul Manlius was personally leading the attack upon the enemy, whom he had almost routed, for his soldiers followed him valiantly, when he was severely wounded and retired from the fighting line. His men believed him to be dead, and faltered; and they would have yielded the position, had not the other consul ridden up at a gallop, with some few troops of horse, and calling out that his colleague was alive, and that he himself had defeated and routed the other wing and was come to help them, in that way put a stop to their wavering. Manlius also showed himself among them, helping to restore the line; and the soldiers, recognizing the features of their two consuls, plucked up courage. At the same time the battle-line of the enemy was now less strong, for, relying on their excess of numbers, they had withdrawn their reserves and dispatched them to storm the Roman camp. There, having forced an entrance without encountering much opposition, they were frittering away their time, their thoughts more taken up with the booty than with the battle, when the Roman reserves, which had been unable to withstand the first onset, sent word to the consuls how things stood, and then closed up their ranks, returned to the praetorium, and of themselves resumed the battle. Meanwhile Manlius the consul had ridden back to the camp, and by posting men at all the gates had cut off the enemy's egress. In desperation at this turn the Etruscans had been inflamed to the point rather of madness than of recklessness. For when, as they rushed in whatever direction there seemed a prospect of escape, they had made several charges to no purpose, one band of youths made a dash at the consul himself, whose arms made him con-

LIVY

7 Prima excepta a circumstantibus tela; sustineri deinde vis nequit. Consul mortifero volnere ictus
8 cadit, fusique circa omnes. Tuscis crescit audacia; Romanos terror per tota castra trepidos agit, et ad extrema ventum foret, ni legati rapto consulis cor-
9 pore patefecissent una porta hostibus viam. Ea erumpunt; consternatoque agmine abeuntes in victorem alterum incidunt consulem. Ibi iterum caesi fusique passim. Victoria egregia parta, tristis tamen
10 duobus tam claris funeribus. Itaque consul decernente senatu triumphum, si exercitus sine imperatore triumphare possit, pro eximia eo bello opera facile passurum respondit; se, familia funesta Q. Fabi fratris morte, re publica ex parte orba, consule altero amisso, publico privatoque deformem luctu lauream
11 non accepturum. Omni acto triumpho depositus triumphus clarior fuit; adeo spreta in tempore gloria interdum cumulatior rediit. Funera deinde duo deinceps collegae fratrisque ducit, idem in utroque laudator, cum concedendo illis suas laudes ipse maxi-
12 mam partem earum ferret. Neque immemor eius, quod initio consulatus imbiberat, reconciliandi ani-

spicuous. Their first discharge of javelins was parried by the soldiers who surrounded him, but after that there was no withstanding their violence. The consul fell, mortally wounded, and all about him fled. The Etruscans grew more reckless than before; the Romans were driven, quaking with terror, right across the camp, and their case would have been desperate, had not the lieutenants caught up the body of the consul and opened a way for the enemy by one of the gates. By that they burst forth, and escaping in a disordered column, fell in the way of the other, the victorious consul, where they were again cut to pieces, and dispersed in all directions. A victory of great importance had been won, but it was saddened by the death of two so famous men. The consul therefore made answer to the senate, when it would have voted him a triumph, that if the army could triumph without its general, its services in that war had been so remarkable that he would readily grant his consent; as for himself, when his family was in mourning for the death of Quintus Fabius his brother, and the state was half orphaned by the loss of the other consul, he would not accept a laurel which was blighted with national and private sorrow. No triumph ever celebrated was more famous than was his refusal to accept a triumph, so true is it that a seasonable rejection of glory sometimes but increases it. The consul then solemnized, one after the other, the funerals of his colleague and his brother, and pronounced the eulogy of each; but while yielding their meed of praise to them, he gained for himself the very highest praises. Nor was he unmindful of that policy which he had adopted in the beginning of his consulship, of winning the affections of the plebs, but billeted the

LIVY

A.U.C. 274

mos plebis, saucios milites curandos dividit patribus. Fabiis plurimi dati, nec alibi maiore cura habiti. Inde populares iam esse Fabii nec hoc ulla[1] nisi salubri rei publicae arte.[2]

A.U.C. 275

XLVIII. Igitur non patrum magis quam plebis studiis Caeso[3] Fabius cum T. Verginio consul factus neque belli[4] neque dilectus neque ullam aliam priorem curam agere quam ut iam aliqua ex parte incohata concordiae spe primo quoque tempore cum 2 patribus coalescerent animi plebis. Itaque principio anni censuit, priusquam quisquam agrariae legis auctor tribunus exsisteret, occuparent patres ipsi suum munus facere, captivum agrum plebi quam maxime aequaliter darent: verum esse habere eos quorum 3 sanguine ac sudore partus sit. Aspernati patres sunt; questi quoque quidam nimia gloria luxuriare et evanescere vividum quondam illud Caesonis ingenium. Nullae deinde urbanae factiones fuere. 4 Vexabantur incursionibus Aequorum Latini. Eo cum exercitu Caeso missus in ipsorum Aequorum agrum depopulandum transit. Aequi se in oppida receperunt murisque se tenebant. Eo nulla pugna memorabilis fuit.

5 At a Veiente hoste clades accepta temeritate alte-

[1] ulla *Gruter*: ulla re Ω: nulla re *PFB*: ualerem *DL*.
[2] rei publicae arte *Gruter* (*now confirmed by* reiparte *FB*): reip. parte Ω.
[3] Caeso (*i.e.* Ceso) $R^2\varsigma$- (*cf. C.I.L.* i², p. 101): c, *M* (*Conway and Walters think this may be a corruption of* ce = cae-): c. (*or* g. *or* q.) Ω.   [4] belli *Hearne D ?*: bella Ω.

380

BOOK II. XLVII. 12–XLVIII. 5

wounded soldiers on the patricians, to be cared for. To the Fabii he assigned the largest number, nor did they anywhere receive greater attention. For this the Fabii now began to enjoy the favour of the people, nor was this end achieved by aught but a demeanour wholesome for the state.

XLVIII. The senators were now therefore not more forward than the plebeians in choosing Caeso Fabius to be consul, along with Titus Verginius. On taking office his first concern was neither war nor the raising of troops nor anything else, save that the prospect of harmony which had been already partly realized should ripen at the earliest possible moment into a good understanding between the patricians and the plebs. He therefore proposed at the outset of his term that before one of the tribunes should rise up and advocate a land-law, the Fathers themselves should anticipate him by making it their own affair and bestowing the conquered territory upon the plebs with the utmost impartiality; for it was right that they should possess it by whose blood and toil it had been won. The senators scorned the proposal, and some even complained that too much glory was spoiling and dissipating that vigorous intellect which Caeso had once possessed. In the sequel there were no outbreaks of strife and faction in the City, but the Latins were plagued with incursions of the Aequi. Thither Caeso was dispatched with an army, and passed over into the Aequians' own country to lay it waste. The Aequi retired to their towns and kept within their walls. For this reason there was no memorable battle.

But the Veientes inflicted a defeat on the Romans owing to the rashness of the other consul; and the

LIVY

rius consulis, actumque de exercitu foret, ni K. Fabius in tempore subsidio venisset. Ex eo tempore neque pax neque bellum cum Veientibus fuit; res proxime formam[1] latrocinii venerat. Legionibus Romanis cedebant in urbem; ubi abductas senserant legiones, agros incursabant, bellum quiete quietem bello in vicem eludentes. Ita neque omitti tota res nec perfici poterat. Et alia bella aut praesentia instabant, ut ab Aequis Volscisque, non diutius quam recens dolor proximae cladis transiret quiescentibus, aut mox moturos[2] esse apparebat Sabinos semper infestos Etruriamque omnem. Sed Veiens hostis, adsiduus magis quam gravis, contumeliis saepius quam periculo animos agitabat, quod nullo tempore neglegi poterat aut averti alio sinebat. Tum Fabia gens senatum adiit. Consul pro gente loquitur: "Adsiduo magis quam magno praesidio, ut scitis, patres conscripti, bellum Veiens eget. Vos alia bella curate, Fabios hostes Veientibus date. Auctores sumus tutam ibi maiestatem Romani nominis fore. Nostrum id nobis velut familiare bellum privato sumptu gerere in animo est: res publica et milite illic et pecunia vacet." Gratiae ingentes actae. Consul e curia egressus comitante Fabiorum agmine, qui in vestibulo curiae senatus consultum exspectantes stet-

---

[1] formam ς: in formam Ω.
[2] moturos *Madvig*: moturos se Ω.

BOOK II. XLVIII. 5–10

army would have been destroyed if Caeso Fabius B.C. 479
had not come, in the nick of time, to its rescue.
Thenceforward there was neither peace nor war with
the Veientes, but something very like freebooting.
In the face of the Roman legions they would retreat
into their city; when they perceived the legions to
be withdrawn they would make raids upon the fields,
evading war by a semblance of peace, and peace in
turn by war. Hence it was impossible either to let
the whole matter go or to end it. Other wars, too,
were immediately threatening—like the one with
the Aequi and the Volsci, who would observe peace
only so long as the suffering involved in their latest
defeat was passing away,—or were soon to be begun,
by the always hostile Sabines and all Etruria. But
the enmity of the Veientes, persistent rather than
perilous, and issuing in insults oftener than in
danger, kept the Romans in suspense, for they were
never permitted to forget it or to turn their attention elsewhere. Then the Fabian clan went before
the senate, and the consul said, speaking for the
clan: "A standing body of defenders rather than a
large one is required, Conscript Fathers, as you know,
for the war with Veii. Do you attend to the other
wars, and assign to the Fabii the task of opposing
the Veientes. We undertake that the majesty of
the Roman name shall be safe in that quarter. It
is our purpose to wage this war as if it were our
own family feud, at our private costs: the state may
dispense with furnishing men and money for this
cause." The thanks of the Fathers were voted with
enthusiasm. The consul came out from the senatehouse, and escorted by a column of the Fabii, who
had halted in the vestibule of the curia while awaiting

LIVY

erant, domum redit. Iussi armati postero die ad limen consulis adesse; domos inde discedunt.

XLIX. Manat tota urbe rumor; Fabios ad caelum laudibus ferunt: familiam unam subisse civitatis onus, Veiens bellum in privatam curam, in privata 2 arma versum. Si sint duae roboris eiusdem in urbe gentes, deposcant haec Volscos sibi, illa Aequos, populo Romano tranquillam pacem agente omnes finitimos subigi populos posse. Fabii postera die 3 arma capiunt; quo iussi erant conveniunt. Consul paludatus egrediens in vestibulo gentem omnem suam instructo agmine videt; acceptus in medium signa ferri iubet. Numquam exercitus neque minor numero neque clarior fama et admiratione hominum 4 per urbem incessit. Sex et trecenti milites, omnes patricii, omnes unius gentis, quorum neminem ducem sperneres,[1] egregius quibuslibet temporibus senatus, ibant, unius familiae viribus Veienti populo pestem 5 minitantes. Sequebatur turba, propria alia cognatorum sodaliumque, nihil medium, nec spem nec curam, sed immensa omnia volventium animo, alia publica sollicitudine excitata, favore et admiratione 6 stupens. Ire fortes, ire felices iubent, inceptis even-

---

[1] sperneres *Madvig*: sperneret Ω.

---

[1] The crimson *paludamentum*.

BOOK II. XLVIII. 10–XLIX. 6

the senate's decision, returned to his house. After receiving the command to present themselves armed next day at the consul's threshold, they dispersed to their homes.

XLIX. The news spreads to every part of the City and the Fabii are lauded to the skies. Men tell how a single family has taken upon its shoulders the burden of a state, how the war with Veii has been turned over to private citizens and private arms. If there were two other clans of equal strength in the City, the one might undertake the Volsci, the other the Aequi, and the Roman People might enjoy the tranquillity of peace, while all the neighbouring nations were being subdued. On the following day the Fabii arm and assemble at the designated place. The consul, coming forth in the cloak of a general,[1] sees his entire clan drawn up in his vestibule, and being received into their midst gives the order to march. Never did an army march through the City less in number or more distinguished by the applause and the wonder of men: three hundred and six soldiers, all patricians, all of one blood, no one of whom you would have rejected as a leader, and who would have made an admirable senate in any period, were going out to threaten the existence of the Veientine nation with the resources of a single house. They were followed by a throng partly made up of people belonging to them, their kinsmen and close friends, whose thoughts were busy with no mean matters, whether of hope or of fear, but with boundless possibilities; partly of those who were moved with concern for the commonwealth, and were beside themselves with enthusiasm and amazement. "Go," they cry, "in your valour, go with good

LIVY

tus pares reddere; consulatus inde ac triumphos,
7 omnia praemia ab se, omnes honores sperare. Praetereuntibus Capitolium arcemque et alia templa, quidquid deorum oculis, quidquid animo occurrit, precantur ut illud agmen faustum atque felix mittant, sospites brevi in patriam ad parentes restituant.
8 In cassum missae preces. Infelici via, dextro iano portae Carmentalis, profecti ad Cremeram flumen perveniunt. Is opportunus visus locus communiendo praesidio.

9 L. Aemilius inde et C. Servilius consules facti. Et donec nihil aliud quam in populationibus res fuit, non ad praesidium modo tutandum Fabii satis erant, sed tota regione qua Tuscus ager Romano adiacet, sua tuta omnia, infesta hostium vagantes per utrum-
10 que finem fecere. Intervallum deinde haud magnum populationibus fuit, dum et Veientes accito ex Etruria exercitu praesidium Cremerae oppugnant, et Romanae legiones ab L. Aemilio consule adductae cominus cum Etruscis dimicant acie. Quamquam
11 vix dirigendi aciem spatium Veientibus fuit; adeo inter primam trepidationem, dum post signa ordines introeunt subsidiaque locant, invecta subito ab latere Romana equitum ala non pugnae modo incipiendae
12 sed consistendi ademit locum. Ita fusi retro ad Saxa Rubra—ibi castra habebant—pacem supplices

---

[1] A name afterwards given to the arch from the result of this expedition.

fortune, and crown your undertaking with success as great!" They bid them look forward to receiving consulships at their hands for this work, and triumphs, and all rewards and all honours. As they pass by the Capitol and the citadel and the other temples, they beseech whatever gods present themselves to their eyes and their thoughts to attend that noble band with blessings and prosperity, and restore them soon in safety to their native land and their kindred. Their prayers were uttered in vain. Setting out by the Unlucky Way,[1] the right arch of the Porta Carmentalis, they came to the river Cremera, a position which seemed favourable for the erection of a fort.

B.C. 479-478

Lucius Aemilius and Gaius Servilius were then chosen consuls. And so long as nothing more than plundering was afoot the Fabii were not only an adequate garrison for the fort, but in all that region where the Tuscan territory marches with the Roman they afforded universal security to their own countrymen and annoyance to the enemy, by ranging along the border on both sides. Then came a brief interruption to these depredations, while the men of Veii, having called in an army from Etruria, attacked the post on the Cremera, and the Roman legions, led thither by Lucius Aemilius the consul, engaged them in a pitched battle; though in truth the Veientes had scarcely time to draw up a battle-line, for at the first alarm, while the ranks were falling in behind the standards and the reserves were being posted, a division of Roman cavalry made a sudden charge on their flank and deprived them of the power not only of attacking first, but even of standing their ground. And so they were driven back upon Saxa Rubra, where they had their camp, and sued for peace. It

387

LIVY

petunt; cuius impetratae ab insita animis levitate ante deductum Cremera Romanum praesidium paenituit.

L. Rursus cum Fabiis erat Veienti populo sine ullo maioris belli apparatu certamen, nec erant incursiones modo in agros aut subiti impetus in incursantes,[1] sed aliquotiens aequo campo conlatisque signis certatum, gensque una populi Romani saepe ex opulentissima, ut tum res erant, Etrusca civitate victoriam tulit. Id primo acerbum indignumque Veientibus est visum; inde consilium ex re natum insidiis ferocem hostem captandi; gaudere etiam multo successu Fabiis audaciam crescere. Itaque et pecora praedantibus aliquotiens, velut casu incidissent, obviam acta, et agrestium fuga vasti relicti agri, et subsidia armatorum ad arcendas populationes missa saepius simulato quam vero pavore refugerunt. Iamque Fabii adeo contempserant hostem ut sua invicta arma neque loco neque tempore ullo crederent sustineri posse. Haec spes provexit ut ad conspecta procul a Cremera magno campi intervallo pecora, quamquam rara hostium apparebant arma, decurrerent. Et cum improvidi effuso cursu insidias circa ipsum iter locatas superassent, palatique passim vaga, ut fit pavore iniecto, raperent pecora, subito ex

[1] in incursantes *Goebel*: incursantes ium *P*: incursantes lupi *M*: incursantium Ω.

was granted, but their instinctive fickleness caused them to weary of the pact before the Roman garrison was withdrawn from the Cremera.

B.C. 479-478

L. Again the Fabii were pitted against the people of Veii. No preparations had been made for a great war, yet not only were raids made upon farming lands, and surprise attacks upon raiding parties, but at times they fought in the open field and in serried ranks; and a single clan of the Roman People often carried off the victory from that most mighty state, for those days, in all Etruria. At first the Veientes bitterly resented this; but they presently adopted a plan, suggested by the situation, for trapping their bold enemy, and they even rejoiced as they saw that the frequent successes of the Fabii were causing them to grow more rash. And so they now and then drove flocks in the way of the invaders, as if they had come there by accident; and the country folk would flee from their farms and leave them deserted; and rescuing parties of armed men, sent to keep off pillagers, would flee before them in a panic more often feigned than real. By this time the Fabii had conceived such scorn for the enemy that they believed themselves invincible and not to be withstood, no matter what the place or time. This confidence so won upon them that on catching sight of some flocks at a distance from the Cremera, across a wide interval of plain, they disregarded the appearance here and there of hostile arms, and ran down to capture them. Their rashness carried them on at a swift pace past an ambuscade which had been laid on both sides of their very road. They had scattered this way and that and were seizing the flocks, which had dispersed in all directions, as they do if terrified,

B.C. 477

LIVY

A.U.C. 277

insidiis consurgitur, et adversi et undique hostes 7 erant. Primo clamor circumlatus exterruit, dein tela ab omni parte accidebant;[1] coeuntibusque Etruscis iam continenti agmine armatorum saepti, quo magis se hostis inferebat, cogebantur breviore spatio et 8 ipsi orbem colligere, quae res et paucitatem[2] eorum insignem et multitudinem Etruscorum multiplicatis 9 in arto ordinibus faciebat. Tum omissa pugna quam in omnes partes parem intenderant, in unum locum se omnes inclinant. Eo nisi corporibus armisque 10 rupere cuneo viam. Duxit via in editum leniter[3] collem. Inde primo restitere; mox, ut respirandi superior locus spatium dedit recipiendique a pavore tanto animum, pepulere etiam subeuntes; vincebatque auxilio loci paucitas, ni iugo circummissus Veiens in verticem collis evasisset. Ita superior rursus hostis 11 factus. Fabii caesi ad unum omnes praesidiumque expugnatum. Trecentos sex perisse satis convenit, unum prope puberem aetate relictum, stirpem genti Fabiae dubiisque rebus populi Romani saepe domi bellique vel maximum futurum auxilium.

A.U.C. 277-278

LI. Cum haec accepta clades est,[4] iam C. Horatius et T. Menenius consules erant. Menenius adversus

[1] accidebant *Gebhard* : accedebant Ω.
[2] et paucitatem *V? M*ς : paucitatem Ω.
[3] leniter ς : leuiter Ω.
[4] est *Crevier* : esset Ω (*but* clade se etiam *DV*).

---

[1] This was that Fabius, according to the legend, who was to become consul ten years later! See III. x.

390

when suddenly the ambush rose up, and enemies were in front and on every side of them. First the shout which echoed all along the Etruscan line filled them with consternation, and then the javelins began to fall upon them from every quarter; and as the Etruscans drew together and the Romans were now fenced in by a continuous line of armed men, the harder the enemy pressed them the smaller was the space within which they themselves were forced to contract their circle, a thing which clearly revealed both their own fewness and the vast numbers of the Etruscans, whose ranks were multiplied in the narrow space. The Romans then gave up the fight which they had been directing equally at every point, and all turned in one direction. Thither, by dint of main strength and arms, they forced their way with a wedge. Their road led up a gentle acclivity. There they at first made a stand; presently, when their superior position had afforded them time to breathe and to collect their spirits after so great a fright, they actually routed the troops which were advancing to dislodge them; and a handful of men, with the aid of a good position, were winning the victory, when the Veientes who had been sent round by the ridge emerged upon the crest of the hill, thus giving the enemy the advantage again. The Fabii were all slain to a man, and their fort was stormed. Three hundred and six men perished, as is generally agreed; one, who was little more than a boy in years,[1] survived to maintain the Fabian stock, and so to afford the very greatest help to the Roman People in its dark hours, on many occasions, at home and in the field.

LI. When this disaster befel, Gaius Horatius and Titus Menenius had begun their consulship.

LIVY

A.U.C. 277-278

2 Tuscos victoria elatos confestim missus. Tum quoque male pugnatum est, et Ianiculum hostes occupavere; obsessaque urbs foret super bellum annona premente—transierant enim Etrusci Tiberim,—ni Horatius consul ex Volscis esset revocatus. Adeoque id bellum ipsis institit moenibus ut primo pugnatum ad Spei sit aequo Marte, iterum ad portam
3 Collinam. Ibi quamquam parvo momento superior Romana res fuit, meliorem tamen militem recepto pristino animo in futura proelia id certamen fecit.

4 A. Verginius et Sp. Servilius consules fiunt. Post acceptam proxima pugna[1] cladem Veientes abstinuere acie; populationes erant, et velut ab arce Ianiculo[2] passim in Romanum agrum impetus dabant; non usquam pecora tuta, non agrestes erant.
5 Capti deinde eadem arte sunt qua ceperant Fabios. Secuti dedita opera passim ad inlecebras propulsa pecora praecipitavere in insidias. Quo plures erant,
6 maior caedes fuit. Ex hac clade atrox ira maioris cladis causa atque initium fuit. Traiecto enim nocte Tiberi castra Servili consulis adorti sunt oppugnare. Inde fusi magna caede in Ianiculum se aegre rece-
7 pere. Confestim consul et ipse transit Tiberim,

[1] proxima pugna *Gronov. D*?: proxime pugna *D or D*[1]: proxime pugnae *D*[2]: proximam pugnae Ω.
[2] Ianiculo *Madvig*: Ianiculi Ω.

BOOK II. LI. 1-7

Menenius was at once sent out to confront the Etruscans, elated by their victory. Again the Roman arms were unsuccessful, and Janiculum was taken by the enemy. They would also have laid siege to Rome, which was suffering not only from war but from a scarcity of corn—for the Etruscans had crossed the Tiber—had not the consul Horatius been recalled from the Volscian country; and so nearly did that invasion approach the very walls of the City that battles were fought first at the temple of Hope, where the result was indecisive, and again at the Colline Gate. There, although the advantage to the Roman side was but slight, still the engagement restored their old-time spirit to the troops and made them the better soldiers for the battles that were to come.

Aulus Verginius and Spurius Servilius were made consuls. After the defeat the Veientes had suffered in the last fight, they avoided a battle and took to pillaging. From Janiculum, as from a citadel, they sent out expeditions far and wide into the territory of the Romans; there was no security anywhere for flocks or country-folk. After a time they were caught by the same trick with which they had caught the Fabii. Having pursued the flocks which had been driven out here and there on purpose to lure them on, they plunged into an ambush, and as their numbers exceeded those of the Fabii so did their losses. This disaster threw them into a violent rage, which proved the cause and the beginning of a greater reverse. For they crossed the Tiber in the night and assaulted the camp of the consul Servilius. There they were routed with heavy losses and regained Janiculum with difficulty. Forthwith the

LIVY

castra sub Ianiculo communit. Postero die luce orta nonnihil et hesterna felicitate pugnae ferox, magis tamen quod inopia frumenti quamvis in praecipitia, dum celeriora essent, agebat[1] consilia, temere adverso 8 Ianiculo ad castra hostium aciem erexit, foediusque inde pulsus quam pridie pepulerat, interventu colle- 9 gae ipse exercitusque est servatus. Inter duas acies Etrusci, cum in vicem his atque illis terga darent, occidione occisi. Ita oppressum temeritate felici Veiens bellum.

LII. Urbi cum pace laxior etiam annona rediit, et advecto ex Campania frumento et, postquam timor sibi cuique futurae inopiae abiit, eo quod abditum 2 fuerat prolato. Ex copia deinde otioque lascivire rursus animi, et pristina mala, postquam foris de- 3 erant, domi quaerere. Tribuni plebem agitare suo veneno, agraria lege; in resistentes incitare patres nec in universos modo, sed in singulos. Q. Considius et T. Genucius, auctores agrariae legis, T. Menenio diem dicunt. Invidiae erat amissum Cremerae praesidium, cum haud procul inde stativa consul 4 habuisset; ea oppressit,[2] cum et patres haud minus

---

[1] agebat $R^2D^2U\varsigma$: agebant Ω.
[2] ea oppressit *Gronov. M*?: eam oppressit (*or* -erunt) Ω.

---

[1] What was the charge? Perhaps that he had failed to support the Fabii; perhaps that he had lost Janiculum by his incompetence.

BOOK II. LI. 7–LII. 4

consul himself crossed the Tiber and fortified a camp beneath the hill. Next day at dawn, partly because he was emboldened by the successful battle of the day before, but more because the want of corn drove him to the rashest kind of measures, provided only they were speedy, he was so reckless as to lead his army up Janiculum to the enemy's camp, and after suffering a more disgraceful repulse than he had administered the day before, owed his own rescue and that of his army to the arrival of his colleague. Caught between two lines, the Etruscans turned their backs first on one and then on the other, and were cut down with great slaughter. Thus the Veientine invasion was defeated by a lucky temerity.

B.C. 477-476

LII. There came to the City with the return of peace a relaxation in the corn-market; for not only was grain imported from Campania, but now that each had ceased to fear for his own future want, men brought out the stores which they had concealed. As a consequence of plenty and idleness a spirit of licence again began to affect men's minds, and they began to seek at home for the old troubles which were no longer to be met with abroad. The tribunes roused the plebs to madness with their usual poison, a land-law. The Fathers resisted, but the tribunes incited the people against them, not as a body merely, but as individuals. Quintus Considius and Titus Genucius, the proposers of the agrarian measure, cited Titus Menenius to appear for trial.[1] He had incurred the dislike of the plebs owing to the loss of the outpost on the Cremera, when he as consul had occupied a permanent camp not far away; and this unpopularity was his undoing, though the senators exerted themselves in his behalf no less

B.C. 476-475

LIVY

quam pro Coriolano adnisi essent, et patris Agrippae
5 favor hauddum exolevisset. In multa temperarunt
tribuni; cum capitis anquisissent, duorum milium[1]
aeris damnato multam dixerunt.[2] Ea in caput vertit.
Negant tulisse ignominiam aegritudinemque; inde
morbo absumptum esse.

6 Alius deinde reus Sp. Servilius, ut consulatu abiit,
C. Nautio et P. Valerio consulibus, initio statim anni
ab L. Caedicio et T. Statio tribunis die dicta non, ut
Menenius, precibus suis aut patrum, sed cum multa
fiducia innocentiae gratiaeque tribunicios impetus
7 tulit. Et huic proelium cum Tuscis ad Ianiculum
erat crimini. Sed fervidi animi vir, ut in publico
periculo ante, sic tum in suo, non tribunos modo sed
plebem oratione feroci refutando, exprobrandoque
T. Meneni damnationem mortemque, cuius patris
munere restituta quondam plebs eos ipsos quibus
tum saeviret magistratus, eas leges haberet, peri-
8 culum audacia discussit. Iuvit et Verginius collega
testis productus, participando laudes; magis tamen
Menenianum—adeo mutaverant animi—profuit iudicium.

LIII. Certamina domi finita: Veiens bellum exor-
tum, quibus Sabini arma coniunxerant. P. Valerius

---

[1] duorum milium *Reid*: duo milia Ω : duo *O*.
[2] multam dixerunt ς: multam (multa *R*) edixerunt (edux-
erunt *H*) Ω.

BOOK II. LII. 4–LIII. 1

than they had done for Coriolanus, and though the favour enjoyed by his father Agrippa had not yet passed away. In respect to the penalty the tribunes showed restraint; though they had charged him with a capital offence, they fixed the fine of the condemned at two thousand *asses*. But it cost him his life; they say that he could not endure the shame and grief, and from this cause fell ill and died.

Another man was then put upon his trial, namely Spurius Servilius. He had laid down the consulship and been succeeded by Gaius Nautius and Publius Valerius, when he was cited, in the very beginning of the year, by the tribunes Lucius Caedicius and Titus Statius. Unlike Menenius, he did not meet the attacks of the tribunes with entreaties, preferred by himself or the senators, but with high confidence in his innocence and popularity. He, too, was accused in connection with the battle against the Etruscans at Janiculum. But the fiery courage of the man had not been more in evidence in the nation's hour of peril than it was then in his own, and he confuted not only the tribunes but the plebs, upbraiding them, in a daring speech, with the condemnation and death of Menenius, to whose father, he declared, the plebs formerly owed their restoration and the possession of those very magistrates and laws which were the tools of their cruelty. This boldness swept away the danger. He was helped, too, by Verginius, his colleague, who, being called as a witness, shared his own credit with Servilius. But the trial of Menenius stood him in even better stead, so great a revulsion of feeling had set in.

LIII. Domestic strife was at an end; but war broke out with the Veientes, with whom the Sabines had united their arms. Publius Valerius the consul was

B.C. 476–475

LIVY

consul accitis Latinorum Hernicorumque auxiliis cum exercitu Veios missus castra Sabina, quae pro moenibus sociorum locata erant, confestim adgreditur tantamque trepidationem iniecit ut, dum dispersi alii alia manipulatim excurrunt ad arcendam hostium vim, ea porta cui signa primum intulerat caperetur.
2 Intra vallum deinde caedes magis quam proelium esse. Tumultus e castris et in urbem penetrat; tamquam Veiis captis, ita pavidi Veientes ad arma currunt. Pars Sabinis eunt subsidio, pars Romanos toto
3 impetu intentos in castra adoriuntur. Paulisper aversi turbatique sunt; deinde et ipsi utroque versis signis resistunt, et eques ab consule immissus Tuscos fundit fugatque; eademque hora duo exercitus, duae potentissimae et maximae finitimae gentes superatae sunt.

4 Dum haec ad Veios geruntur, Volsci Aequique in Latino agro posuerant castra populatique fines erant. Eos per se ipsi Latini adsumptis Hernicis sine Ro-
5 mano aut duce aut auxilio castris exuerunt; ingenti praeda praeter suas reciperatas res potiti sunt. Missus tamen ab Roma consul in Volscos C. Nautius; mos, credo, non placebat sine Romano duce exercituque socios propriis viribus consiliisque bella

BOOK II. LIII. 1-5

dispatched to Veii with an army to which had been added auxiliaries from the Latins and the Hernici. He at once advanced upon the Sabine camp, which had been established in front of the walls of their allies, and threw the enemy into such confusion that, while they were running out in small groups, some one way and some another, to repel the attack of the Romans, he captured the gate against which he had directed his first assault. What followed within the stockade was a massacre rather than a battle. The sounds of confusion in the camp penetrated even to the city, and the frightened inhabitants ran hastily to their weapons, as though Veii had been surprised. Some went to the rescue of the Sabines, others assailed the Romans, who were wholly preoccupied with the camp. For a moment the Romans were disconcerted and thrown into disorder; then they, too, faced both ways and made a stand, and the horse which the consul sent into the fight dispersed and routed the Etruscans. In one and the same hour two armies, two of the greatest and most powerful neighbouring nations, were defeated.

While these victories were being won at Veii, the Volsci and the Aequi had encamped on Latin soil, and had laid waste the country. These the Latins, acting independently, with the assistance of the Hernici, but without either general or aid from Rome, despoiled of their camp. Immense booty, in addition to property of their own which they recovered, fell into their hands. Nevertheless a consul, Gaius Nautius, was sent from Rome against the Volsci. The precedent, I suppose, of allies waging wars, without a Roman commander and army, by means of their own forces and their own strategy, was not welcome.

B.C.
476-475

LIVY

6 gerere. Nullum genus calamitatis contumeliaeque non editum in Volscos est, nec tamen perpelli[1] potuere ut acie dimicarent.

LIV. L. Furius inde et C. Manlius[2] consules. Manlio Veientes provincia evenit. Non tamen bellatum; indutiae in annos quadraginta petentibus datae 2 frumento stipendioque imperato. Paci[3] externae confestim continuatur discordia domi. Agrariae legis tribuniciis stimulis plebs furebat. Consules, nihil Meneni damnatione, nihil periculo deterriti Servili, summa vi resistunt. Abeuntes magistratu Cn. Genucius tribunus plebis arripuit.

3 L. Aemilius et Opiter Verginius consulatum ineunt; Vopiscum Iulium pro Verginio in quibusdam annalibus consulem invenio. Hoc anno—quoscumque consules habuit—rei ad populum Furius et Manlius[4] circumeunt sordidati non plebem magis quam 4 iuniores patrum. Suadent, monent, honoribus et administratione rei publicae abstineant; consulares vero fasces, praetextam curulemque sellam nihil aliud quam pompam funeris putent; claris insignibus velut 5 infulis velatos ad mortem destinari. Quod si consulatus tanta dulcedo sit, iam nunc ita in animum inducant consulatum captum et oppressum ab tribunicia potestate esse; consuli, velut apparitori tribunicio,

---

[1] perpelli $R^2 \varsigma$: perpeti Ω.
[2] Manlius O (*below* Manlio OM): Manilius (*below* Manilio) Ω, *and Cassiod. C.I.L.* i², *p.* 103. [3] paci ς: pacis Ω: facis M.
[4] Manlius $MOHRDL$: Manilius $PFUB$.

BOOK II. LIII. 5–LIV. 5

There was no species of disaster or indignity which was not visited upon the Volsci, yet they could not be forced into giving battle.

B.C. 476-475

LIV. Lucius Furius and Gaius Manlius were the next consuls. To Manlius fell the command against the Veientes. But there was no war; a truce for forty years was granted, at their solicitation, and corn and a money-indemnity were exacted of them. The foreign peace was immediately succeeded by quarrels at home. The land-law with which the tribunes goaded the plebs excited them to the pitch of madness. The consuls, not a jot intimidated by the condemnation of Menenius, not a jot by the danger of Servilius, resisted the measure with the utmost violence. As their term expired, Gnaeus Genucius, a plebeian tribune, haled them to trial.

B.C. 474-473

Lucius Aemilius and Opiter Verginius entered upon the consulship. Vopiscus Julius I find given as consul in certain annals, instead of Verginius. This year—whoever its consuls were—Furius and Manlius went about among the people as men accused, in garments of mourning, seeking out the younger patricians, as well as the plebeians. They advised them, they warned them to forbear from office-holding and the administration of the public business; as for the consular fasces, the purple-bordered toga, and the curule chair,—these they should regard in no other light than as the pageantry of burial; for splendid insignia, like the fillets placed on victims, doomed the wearer to death. But if the consulship was so alluring to them, let them recognize at once that it had been fettered and enslaved by the might of the tribunes; that the consul, as though an attendant upon those officials, must be subject in all

LIVY

omnia ad nutum imperiumque tribuni agenda esse; 6 si se commoverit, si respexerit patres, si aliud quam plebem esse in re publica crediderit, exsilium Cn. Marci, Meneni damnationem et mortem sibi propo- 7 nat[1] ante oculos. His accensi vocibus patres consilia[2] inde non publica, sed in privato seductaque a plurium conscientia habuere. Ubi cum id modo constaret, iure an iniuria eripiendos esse reos, atrocissima quaeque maxime placebat sententia, nec 8 auctor quamvis audaci facinori deerat. Igitur iudicii die, cum plebs in foro erecta exspectatione staret, mirari primo quod non descenderet tribunus; dein, cum iam mora suspectior fieret, deterritum a primoribus credere et desertam ac proditam causam publi- 9 cam queri; tandem qui obversati vestibulo tribuni fuerant nuntiant domi mortuum esse inventum. Quod ubi in totam contionem pertulit rumor, sicut acies funditur duce occiso, ita dilapsi passim alii alio. Praecipuus pavor tribunos invaserat, quam nihil auxilii sacratae leges haberent morte collegae moni- 10 tos. Nec patres satis moderate ferre laetitiam; adeoque neminem noxiae paenitebat ut etiam insontes fecisse videri vellent, palamque ferretur malo domandam tribuniciam potestatem.

[1] proponat U ?ς: proponant Ω.
[2] consilia Ω: concilia *Gronov*.

---

[1] *i.e.* from his home: the Forum was lower than the residential parts of Rome.

BOOK II. LIV. 5-10

he did to their beck and call; if he should bestir himself, if he should show consideration for the patricians, if he should believe that the state comprised any other element than the plebs—let him call to mind the exile of Gnaeus Marcius, the condemnation of Menenius and his death. Fired by these speeches, the senators began to hold councils, no longer publicly, but in private, where the people could not learn their plans. In these deliberations there was but one guiding principle, that by fair means or foul the defendants must be got off. The more truculent a suggestion was, the greater was the favour it evoked, and an agent was not wanting for the most daring crime. Well then, on the day of the trial the plebeians were in the Forum, on tiptoe with expectation. At first they were filled with amazement because the tribune did not come down;[1] then, when at length his delay began to look suspicious, they supposed he had been frightened away by the nobles, and fell to complaining of his desertion and betrayal of the people's cause; finally, those who had presented themselves at the tribune's vestibule brought back word that he had been found dead in his house. When this report had spread through all the gathering, the crowd, like an army which takes to flight at the fall of its general, melted away on every side. The tribunes were particularly dismayed, for the death of their colleague warned them how utterly ineffectual to protect them were the laws that proclaimed their sanctity. Nor did the senators place a proper restraint upon their satisfaction; so far, indeed, was anyone from repenting of the guilty deed that even the innocent desired to be thought its authors, and men openly asserted that chastisement must be employed to curb the power of the tribunes.

LIVY

LV. Sub hanc pessimi exempli victoriam[1] dilectus edicitur, paventibusque tribunis sine intercessione ulla consules rem peragunt. Tum vero irasci plebs tribunorum magis silentio quam consulum imperio, et dicere actum esse de libertate sua, rursus ad antiqua reditum; cum Genucio una mortuam ac sepultam tribuniciam potestatem. Aliud agendum ac cogitandum, quomodo resistatur patribus; id autem unum consilium esse ut se ipsa plebs, quando aliud nihil auxilii habeat, defendat. Quattuor et viginti lictores apparere consulibus et eos ipsos plebis homines; nihil contemptius neque infirmius, si sint qui contemnant; sibi quemque ea magna atque horrenda facere. His vocibus alii alios cum incitassent, ad Voleronem Publilium, de plebe hominem, quia, quod ordines duxisset, negaret se militem fieri debere, lictor missus est a consulibus. Volero appellat tribunos. Cum auxilio nemo esset, consules spoliari hominem et virgas expediri iubent. "Provoco," inquit "ad populum" Volero, "quoniam tribuni civem Romanum in conspectu suo virgis caedi malunt quam ipsi in lecto suo a vobis trucidari." Quo ferocius clamitabat, eo infestius circumscindere et spoliare lictor. Tum Volero et praevalens ipse et adiuvantibus advocatis repulso lictore, ubi indignantium pro

[1] hanc ... victoriam *Gronov.*: hac ... uictoria Ω.

---

[1] Livy mentions another instance of a conscript's objecting to serve in a rank lower than that he had previously held, in XLII. xxxiii. 3; but it does not appear that the men had any prescriptive right in the matter.

BOOK II. LV. 1-6

LV. Immediately following this pernicious victory a levy was proclaimed, which the timorousness of the tribunes allowed the consuls to push through without ever a veto. But this time the commons were fairly roused to anger, more by the silence of the tribunes than by the consuls' power. They declared that it was all up with their liberty; that men had gone back to their old ways; that with Genucius the tribunician power had suffered death and burial. They must adopt another course and other plans to resist the patricians; but the only way was this: that the plebs should undertake their own defence, since they had no one else to help them. Twenty-four lictors were all the retinue of the consuls, and even these were plebeians. Nothing was more contemptible or weaker, if there were any to contemn; it was every man's own imagination that made them great and awe-inspiring. They had incited one another with arguments of this sort when the consuls sent a lictor to arrest Volero Publilius, a plebeian, who, on the ground that he had been a centurion, denied their right to make him a common soldier.[1] Volero called upon the tribunes. When no one came to aid him, the consuls gave orders to strip the man and get out the rods. "I appeal," cried Volero, "to the people, since the tribunes would rather a Roman citizen should be scourged with rods before their eyes than themselves be murdered in their beds by you." But the more boldly he shouted the more roughly the lictor fell to tearing off his clothes and stripping him. Then Volero, who was himself a powerful man and was helped by those he had called to his assistance, beat off the lictor and, choosing the place where the uproar of his sympathisers

LIVY

se acerrimus erat clamor, eo se in turbam confertissimam recipit clamitans: " Provoco et fidem plebis
7 imploro. Adeste cives, adeste commilitones; nihil est quod exspectetis tribunos, quibus ipsis vestro
8 auxilio opus est." Concitati homines veluti ad proelium se expediunt; apparebatque omne discrimen adesse, nihil cuiquam sanctum non publici fore, non
9 privati iuris. Huic tantae tempestati cum se consules obtulissent, facile experti sunt parum tutam maiestatem sine viribus esse. Violatis lictoribus, fascibus fractis e foro in curiam compelluntur, incerti
10 quatenus Volero exerceret victoriam. Conticescente deinde tumultu cum in senatum vocari iussissent, queruntur iniurias suas, vim plebis, Voleronis auda-
11 ciam. Multis ferociter dictis sententiis vicere seniores, quibus ira patrum adversus temeritatem plebis certari non placuit.

LVI. Voleronem amplexa favore plebs proximis comitiis tribunum plebi creat in eum annum qui
2 L. Pinarium P. Furium consules habuit. Contraque omnium opinionem, qui eum vexandis prioris anni consulibus permissurum tribunatum credebant, post publicam causam privato dolore habito, ne verbo quidem violatis consulibus, rogationem tulit ad populum ut plebeii magistratus tributis comitiis fierent.
3 Haud parva res sub titulo prima specie minime

---

[1] It is not clear how Livy supposed that these officials had formerly been elected. Perhaps Volero merely aimed at securing by legal sanction what the state had always recognized in practice, viz. that plebeian magistrates should be chosen by none but plebeians. But this was not Livy's view, as is clear from lviii. 1.

BOOK II. LV. 6–LVI. 3

was the angriest, plunged into the thick of the crowd, calling out, "I appeal, and implore the protection of the plebs; help, citizens! help, fellow-soldiers! It is useless for you to wait for the tribunes, who themselves stand in need of aid from you." In their excitement men made ready as if to fight a battle, and it was evident that anything might happen, that nobody would respect any right, whether public or private. The consuls, exposed to this furious tempest, were quickly convinced of the insecurity of majesty when unaccompanied with force. The lictors were roughly handled and their rods were broken, while the consuls themselves were driven out of the Forum into the Curia, with no means of knowing how far Volero might use his victory. Afterwards, when the uproar began to die away, they summoned the Fathers into the senate-house and complained of the insults they had suffered, the violence of the plebs, and Volero's outrageous conduct. Though many daring opinions were expressed, the wishes of the older men prevailed, who had no mind to a conflict between an angry senate and a reckless plebs.

B.C. 473

LVI. Volero, having been taken into favour by the plebs, was at the next election made plebeian tribune for that year which had Lucius Pinarius and Publius Furius for consuls. And contrary to the expectation of all, who believed that he would employ his tribuneship in persecuting the consuls of the preceding year, he set the general welfare above his private grievance, and without attacking the consuls by so much as a word, brought a bill before the people providing that plebeian magistrates should be chosen in the tribal assembly.[1] It was no trivial matter which he proposed under this form, which at

B.C. 472-471

LIVY

atroci ferebatur, sed quae patriciis omnem potestatem per clientium suffragia creandi quos vellent tri-
4 bunos auferret. Huic actioni gratissimae plebi cum summa vi resisterent patres nec, quae una vis ad resistendum erat, ut intercederet aliquis ex collegio, auctoritate aut consulum aut principum adduci posset, res tamen suo ipsa molimine gravis certaminibus
5 in annum extrahitur. Plebs Voleronem tribunum reficit: patres, ad ultimum dimicationis rati rem venturam, Ap. Claudium Appi filium, iam inde a paternis certaminibus invisum infestumque plebi, consulem faciunt. Collega ei T. Quinctius datur.
6 Principio statim anni nihil prius quam de lege agebatur. Sed ut inventor legis Volero, sic Laetorius collega eius auctor cum recentior tum acrior
7 erat. Ferocem faciebat belli gloria ingens, quod aetatis eius haud quisquam manu promptior erat. Is, cum Volero nihil praeterquam de lege loqueretur, insectatione abstinens consulum, ipse accusationem[1] Appi familiaeque superbissimae ac crudelissimae in
8 plebem Romanam exorsus, cum a patribus non consulem, sed carnificem ad vexandam et lacerandam plebem creatum esse contenderet, rudis in militari homine lingua non suppetebat libertati animoque.
9 Itaque deficiente oratione, "Quando quidem non

[1] accusationem *Crevier*: in accusationem Ω.

first sight appeared so harmless, but one that completely deprived the patricians of the power of using their clients' votes to select what tribunes they liked. This measure was extremely welcome to the plebs; the Fathers opposed it with all their might, yet the only effectual resistance—to wit, a veto by some member of the tribunician college—neither consuls nor nobles were sufficiently influential to command. Nevertheless the legislation, which its very importance rendered difficult, was drawn out by party strife to the end of the year. The plebs re-elected Volero tribune: the senators, thinking the quarrel was sure to proceed to extremities, made Appius Claudius, son of Appius, consul, a man whose unpopularity with the plebs and hostility towards them went back to the struggles between their fathers. For colleague they gave him Titus Quinctius.

The new year was no sooner begun than discussion of the law took precedence of everything else, and it was urged not only by its author, Volero, but by his colleague Laetorius as well, whose advocacy of it was at once fresher and more acrimonious. He was emboldened by the great reputation he enjoyed as a soldier, since no one of that generation surpassed him in physical prowess. While Volero spoke of nothing but the law, and forbore to inveigh against the consuls' persons, Laetorius launched out into an arraignment of Appius and his family, as most cruel and arrogant towards the Roman plebs. But when he strove to show that the patricians had elected, not a consul, but an executioner, to harass and torture the plebeians, the inexperienced tongue of the soldier was inadequate to express his audacity and spirit. Accordingly when words began to fail him he cried,

LIVY

tam[1] facile loquor," inquit, "Quirites, quam quod locutus sum praesto, crastino die adeste. Ego hic aut in conspectu vestro moriar aut perferam legem." Occupant tribuni templum postero die; consules nobilitasque ad impediendam legem in contione consistunt. Summoveri Laetorius iubet, praeterquam qui suffragium ineant. Adulescentes nobiles stabant nihil cedentes viatori. Tum ex his prendi quosdam Laetorius iubet. Consul Appius negare ius esse tribuno in quemquam nisi in plebeium; non enim populi sed plebis eum magistratum esse; nec illum ipsum[2] summovere pro imperio posse more maiorum, quia ita dicatur: " Si vobis videtur, discedite, Quirites." Facile[3] contemptim de iure disserendo perturbare Laetorium poterat. Ardens igitur ira tribunus viatorem mittit ad consulem, consul lictorem ad tribunum, privatum esse clamitans, sine imperio, sine magistratu; violatusque esset tribunus, ni et contio omnis atrox coorta pro tribuno in consulem esset, et concursus hominum in forum ex tota urbe concitatae multitudinis fieret. Sustinebat tamen Appius pertinacia tantam tempestatem; certatumque haud incruento proelio foret, ni Quinctius, consul alter, consularibus negotio dato ut collegam vi, si aliter non

---

[1] tam *inserted by* ς *Madvig.*
[2] illum ipsum Ω: illam ipsam (*i.e.* plebem) *Conway.*
[3] facile *Drakenborch* ς: facile et Ω.

---

[1] The word *templum* might be applied to any space duly marked off by augural ceremonies. Here it means the speakers' platform in the *comitium*.

BOOK II. LVI. 9-15

"Since speech is not so easy for me, Quirites, as it is to make good what I have spoken, be at hand to-morrow. I will either die here in your sight or carry through the law." The tribunes were the first on the scene next day, and possessed themselves of the rostra;[1] the consuls and nobles took their stand in the assembly, with the purpose of obstructing the passage of the law. Laetorius ordered the removal of all but those who were voting. The youthful nobles stayed where they were and would not give way at the officer's behest. Then certain of them were ordered by Laetorius to be seized. The consul Appius declared that the tribune had no authority over anybody but a plebeian, seeing that he was not a magistrate of the people, but of the plebs; and even if he were, he could not, consistently with the custom of the Fathers, command the removal of anyone, by virtue of his authority, since the formula ran thus: "If it seems good to you, depart, Quirites." It was an easy matter to throw Laetorius into a passion by these contemptuous remarks about his rights. It was therefore in a blaze of anger that the tribune dispatched his attendant to the consul; while the consul sent his lictor to the tribune, crying out that Laetorius was a private citizen, without power, and no magistrate; and the tribune would have been mishandled, had not the whole assembly rallied fiercely to his support against the consul, while men rushed into the Forum from all over the City, in an excited throng. Still, Appius was obstinately holding out, despite the fury of the tempest, and a sanguinary battle would have ensued, if Quinctius, the other consul, had not entrusted the senators of consular rank with the task of getting his colleague out

LIVY

possent, de foro abducerent, ipse nunc plebem saevientem precibus lenisset, nunc orasset tribunos ut 16 concilium dimitterent: darent irae spatium; non vim suam illis tempus adempturum, sed consilium viribus additurum, et patres in populi et consulem in patrum fore potestate.

LVII. Aegre sedata ab Quinctio plebs, multo 2 aegrius consul alter a patribus. Dimisso tandem concilio plebis senatum consules habent. Ubi cum timor atque ira in vicem sententias variassent, quo magis spatio interposito ab impetu ad consultandum avocabantur,[1] eo plus abhorrebant a certatione animi, adeo ut Quinctio gratias agerent, quod 3 eius opera mitigata discordia esset. Ab Appio petitur ut tantam consularem maiestatem esse vellet quanta esse in concordi civitate posset: dum tribuni consulesque ad se quisque omnia trahant, nihil relictum esse virium in medio; distractam laceratamque rem publicam; magis quorum in manu sit quam ut 4 incolumis sit quaeri. Appius contra testari deos atque homines rem publicam prodi per metum ac deseri, non consulem senatui sed senatum consuli deesse; graviores accipi leges quam in Sacro monte acceptae sint. Victus tamen patrum consensu quie-

[1] avocabantur ⲋ: aduocabantur (-batur *M*) Ω.

BOOK II. LVI. 15–LVII. 4

of the Forum, by force, if they could not achieve it otherwise; while he himself now appealed to the raging populace with soothing entreaties, and now besought the tribunes to dismiss the council. Let them give their anger time: time would not rob them of their power, but would add wisdom to their strength; the Fathers would be subject to the people, and the consul to the Fathers.

LVII. It was hard for Quinctius to still the plebs; much harder for the senators to quiet the other consul. At length the council of the plebs was adjourned, and the consuls convened the senate. At this meeting alternating hope and fear gave rise to conflicting opinions. But in proportion as their passions cooled with the lapse of time and gave way to deliberation, their minds more and more revolted from the struggle; insomuch that they passed a vote of thanks to Quinctius, because it was due to him that the quarrel had been abated. They desired Appius to be content that the majesty of the consul should be no greater than was compatible with harmony in the state, pointing out that while tribunes and consuls were each striving to carry things his own way there was no strength left in the nation at large, and the commonwealth was torn and mangled, the question being rather in whose power it was than how it might be safe. Appius, on the other hand, called gods and men to witness that the state was being betrayed through cowardice, and abandoned; that it was not the consul who was failing the senate, but the senate the consul; that harder terms were being accepted than had been accepted on the Sacred Mount. Nevertheless he was borne down by the senate's unanimity and held his peace.

LIVY

A.U.C. 283

vit. Lex silentio perfertur. LVIII. Tum primum tributis comitiis creati tribuni sunt. Numero etiam additos[1] tres, perinde ac duo antea fuerint, Piso 2 auctor est. Nominat quoque tribunos, Cn. Siccium, L. Numitorium, M. Duillium,[2] Sp. Icilium,[3] L. Maecilium.[4]

3 Volscum Aequicumque[5] inter seditionem Romanam est[6] bellum coortum. Vastaverant agros ut, si qua secessio plebis fieret, ad se receptum haberet; 4 compositis deinde rebus castra retro movere. Ap. Claudius in Volscos missus, Quinctio Aequi provincia evenit. Eadem in militia saevitia Appi quae domi esse, liberior quod sine tribuniciis vinculis erat. 5 Odisse plebem plus quam paterno odio: quid? se[7] victum ab ea, se unico consule electo adversus tribuniciam potestatem perlatam legem esse, quam minore conatu, nequaquam tanta patrum spe, priores impe-6 dierint[8] consules? Haec ira indignatioque ferocem animum ad vexandum saevo imperio exercitum stimulabat. Nec ulla vi domari poterat, tantum certamen 7 animis imbiberant. Segniter, otiose, neglegenter, contumaciter omnia agere; nec pudor nec metus coercebat; si citius agi vellet agmen, tardius sedulo

---

[1] additos ⑤: addito Ω.   [2] Duillium ⑤: Duellium Ω.
[3] Icilium ⑤: ilicium (*or* illi-) Ω.
[4] Maecilium *Conway*: Mecilium (*or* melicium) Ω.
[5] Aequicumque ⑤: et quicumque Ω.
[6] est ⑤: et Ω.
[7] odio: quid? se *Weissenborn*: odio quod se (*or* odio se) Ω.
[8] impedierint *Rhenanus*: impedierunt (*or* -rant) Ω.

BOOK II. LVII. 4–LVIII. 7

The law was passed without opposition. LVIII. Then B.C. 471 for the first time tribunes were elected in the tribal assembly. That their number was also increased by three, as if there had been only two before, is stated by Piso. He also gives the names of the tribunes: Gnaeus Siccius, Lucius Numitorius, Marcus Duillius, Spurius Icilius, Lucius Maecilius.

While Rome was thus distracted, the Volsci and the Aequi began war. They had laid waste the fields in order that the plebeians, if they should secede, might find a refuge with them.[1] Then, when the matter was settled, they withdrew their camp. Appius Claudius was sent against the Volsci; to Quinctius fell the command against the Aequi. In his conduct in the field Appius displayed the same violence that he had shown in Rome, and it now had freer play because it was not hampered by the tribunes. He hated the plebs with a hatred that surpassed his father's: What? Had he been beaten by them? Was it in his consulship, who had been chosen as pre-eminently fitted to resist the tribunician power, that a law had been passed which former consuls had prevented, with less effort and by no means so much hope of success on the part of the patricians? His wrath and indignation at this thought drove his fierce spirit to torment the army with a savage exercise of authority. Yet he was unable by any violence to subdue them, so deeply had their spirits drunk ot opposition. Sloth, idleness, neglect, and obstinacy were in all they did. Neither shame nor fear restrained them. If he wished the column to advance more rapidly they deliberately retarded their pace;

[1] To *lay waste* Roman lands they must first *enter* them, and the purpose clause depends really upon this implied meaning of *vastaverant*.

LIVY

incedere; si adhortator operis adesset, omnes sua
8 sponte motam remittere industriam; praesenti voltus demittere,[1] tacite praetereuntem exsecrari, ut invictus ille odio plebeio animus interdum moveretur.
9 Omni nequiquam acerbitate prompta nihil iam cum militibus agere, a centurionibus corruptum exercitum dicere, tribunos plebei cavillans interdum et Volerones vocare.

LIX. Nihil eorum Volsci nesciebant, instabantque eo magis sperantes idem certamen animorum adversus Appium habiturum exercitum Romanum
2 quod adversus Fabium consulem habuisset. Ceterum multo Appio quam Fabio violentior fuit; non enim vincere tantum noluit, ut Fabianus exercitus, sed vinci voluit. Productus in aciem turpi fuga petit castra, nec ante restitit quam signa inferentem Volscum munimentis vidit foedamque ex-
3 tremi agminis caedem. Tum expressa vis ad pugnandum ut victor iam a vallo submoveretur hostis, satis tamen appareret capi tantum castra militem Romanum noluisse, alibi[2] gaudere sua clade atque
4 ignominia. Quibus nihil infractus ferox Appi animus cum insuper saevire vellet contionemque advocaret, concurrunt ad eum legati tribunique monentes

[1] demittere ϛ: dimittere Ω.
[2] alibi *Weissenborn*: alii Ω: alioqui *Walters*.

BOOK II. LVIII. 7–LIX. 4

if he stood by to encourage their work, they would B.C. 471 all relax the industry they had manifested of their own accord. In his presence they sunk their gaze; as he passed by they cursed him under their breath; till that proud spirit, which the hatred of the plebs had never broken, was at times disturbed. After exhausting every species of severity without effect, he would have no more to do with the men; the centurions, he said, had corrupted the army, and he sometimes sneeringly dubbed them "tribunes of the plebs" and "Voleros."

LIX. Every one of these circumstances was known to the Volsci, and they pressed their enemy the harder, hoping that the Roman army would exhibit the same spirited opposition to Appius which it had evinced towards the consul Fabius. But Appius found his men far more unruly than had Fabius; for not only were they unwilling to conquer, as the Fabian army had been, but they wished to be conquered. Being drawn out into battle-order, they basely fled and sought their camp; nor did they make a stand until they saw the Volsci advancing against their fortifications and inflicting a disgraceful slaughter upon their rearguard. This compelled them to exert themselves and fight, with the result that the enemy was dislodged from the stockade in the moment of victory. Yet it was evident enough that the capture of their camp was the only thing at which the Roman soldiers balked, and that elsewhere they rejoiced at their own defeat and ignominy. These things in no wise daunted the haughty spirit of Appius. But when he would have gone further and have vented his rage upon the army, and was issuing orders for an assembly, the lieutenants and tribunes gathered hurriedly about

LIVY

ne utique experiri vellet imperium cuius vis omnis in
5 consensu oboedientium esset. Negare volgo milites
se ad contionem ituros, passimque exaudiri voces
postulantium ut castra ex Volsco agro moveantur.
hostem victorem paulo ante prope in portis ac vallo
fuisse, ingentisque mali non suspicionem modo sed
6 apertam speciem obversari ante oculos. Victus tandem, quando quidem nihil praeter tempus noxae
lucrarentur, remissa contione iter in insequentem
diem pronuntiari cum iussisset, prima luce classico
7 signum profectionis dedit. Cum maxime agmen e
castris explicaretur, Volsci, ut eodem signo excitati,
novissimos adoriuntur. A quibus perlatus ad primos
tumultus eo pavore signaque et ordines turbavit ut
neque imperia exaudiri neque instrui acies posset.
8 Nemo ullius nisi fugae memor. Ita effuso agmine
per stragem corporum armorumque evasere ut prius
9 hostis desisteret sequi quam Romanus fugere. Tandem conlectis ex dissipato cursu militibus consul,
cum revocando nequiquam suos persecutus esset, in
pacato agro castra posuit; advocataque contione invectus haud falso in proditorem exercitum militaris
10 disciplinae, desertorem signorum, ubi signa, ubi
arma essent singulos rogitans, inermes milites, signo

him and warned him upon no account to seek a test of his authority, when its effectiveness all depended on the goodwill of those obeying it. The men, they reported, were saying that they would not go to be harangued, and everywhere voices were overheard demanding that the camp be removed from Volscian territory. The victorious enemy had a little while before been almost in their gates and on their wall, and a great disaster was not merely to be apprehended, but was openly hovering before their eyes. Giving way at last, since the soldiers were gaining nothing but a postponement of their punishment, he relinquished the idea of an assembly, and commanded a march for the following day. At daybreak he caused the signal for departure to be sounded on the trumpet. At the very instant when the column was getting clear of the camp, the Volsci, as though set in motion by the same signal, fell upon their rear. Thence the confusion spread to the van, and the panic so disordered the standards and the ranks that it was impossible either to hear commands or to form a line. Nobody thought of anything but flight, and so demoralised was the rout, as the men escaped over fallen bodies and discarded weapons, that the enemy sooner ceased to pursue than the Romans to flee. When at last the soldiers had been collected from their scattered flight, the consul, who had followed his men in a vain attempt to call them back, pitched his camp on friendly soil. Then he summoned an assembly and soundly rated them, not without reason, as an army which had been false to military discipline and had deserted its standards. Asking them all in turn where their arms and where their standards were, he caused the unarmed soldiers and

LIVY

A.U.C. 283

11 amisso signiferos, ad hoc centuriones duplicariosque qui reliquerant ordines virgis caesos securi percussit; cetera multitudo sorte decimus quisque ad supplicium lecti.

LX. Contra ea in Aequis inter consulem ac milites comitate ac beneficiis certatum est. Et natura Quinctius erat lenior, et saevitia infelix collegae quo
2 is magis gauderet ingenio suo effecerat. Huic tantae concordiae ducis exercitusque non ausi offerre se Aequi, vagari populabundum hostem per agros passi;
3 nec ullo ante bello latius inde acta est praeda. Ea omnis[1] militi data est. Addebantur et laudes, quibus haud minus quam praemio gaudent militum animi. Cum duci tum propter ducem patribus quoque placatior exercitus rediit, sibi parentem alteri exercitui dominum datum ab senatu memorans.
4 Varia fortuna belli, atroci discordia domi forisque annum exactum insignem maxime comitia tributa efficiunt, res maior victoria suscepti certaminis quam
5 usu; plus enim dignitatis comitus ipsis detractum est patres[2] ex concilio summovendo quam virium aut plebi additum est aut demptum patribus.

[1] acta est praeda. Ea omnis *Conway*: acte (*or* -ae) praede (*or* -ae) ea (*omitted by all but M*) omnis (domn *M*, omnes *H*) Ω.   [2] patres ⊊ *Alschefski*: patribus Ω.

---

[1] This was granted in recognition of unusual valour. So the Victoria Cross is accompanied by a small stipend.

BOOK II. LIX. 10–LX 5

the standard-bearers who had lost their standards, B.C. 471 and in addition to these the centurions and the recipients of a double ration[1] who had quitted their ranks, to be scourged with rods and beheaded; of the remaining number every tenth man was selected by lot for punishment.

LX. To contrast with all this, in the Aequian campaign there subsisted between consul and soldiers an emulation of goodwill and kindness. Not only was it natural to Quinctius to be more gentle, but the unfortunate harshness of his colleague had given him the more reason to be content with his own disposition. Against this complete harmony between commander and army the Aequi ventured no opposition, but suffered their enemies to devastate their fields at will; and in fact no previous war had ever yielded a larger booty from that country. This was all given to the troops, and to the spoils were added encomiums, which are no less efficacious than rewards in rejoicing a soldier's heart. Not only their leader, but for their leader's sake the Fathers, too, were looked upon with greater kindness by the army when they returned. They declared that to them the senate had given a parent, to the other army a tyrant.

Varying fortune in war, grievous discord at home and in the field, had characterized the year just ended; but it was chiefly distinguished by the tribal assembly, a matter more important because the men had won a victory in the struggle which they had undertaken than in its practical results; for the loss of dignity to the assembly itself, caused by the removal from it of the patricians, was greater than the gain in strength by the plebeians or the loss of it by the Fathers.

LIVY

LXI. Turbulentior inde annus excepit L. Valerio T. Aemilio consulibus, cum propter certamina ordinum de lege agraria tum propter iudicium Ap. Claudi, cui, acerrimo adversario legis causamque possessorum publici agri tamquam tertio consuli sustinenti, M. Duillius et Cn. Siccius diem dixere. Numquam ante tam invisus plebi reus ad iudicium vocatus populi est, plenus suarum, plenus paternarum irarum. Patres quoque non temere pro ullo aeque adnisi sunt: propugnatorem senatus maiestatisque vindicem suae, ad omnes tribunicios plebeiosque oppositum tumultus, modum dumtaxat in certamine egressum, iratae obici plebi. Unus e patribus, ipse Ap. Claudius, et tribunos et plebem et suum iudicium pro nihilo habebat. Illum non minae plebis, non senatus preces perpellere umquam potuere, non modo ut vestem mutaret aut supplex prensaret homines, sed ne ut ex consueta quidem asperitate orationis, cum ad populum agenda causa esset, aliquid leniret atque submitteret. Idem habitus oris, eadem contumacia in voltu, idem in oratione spiritus erat, adeo ut magna pars plebis Appium non minus reum timeret, quam consulem timuerat. Semel causam dixit, quo semper agere omnia solitus erat accusatorio spiritu;

BOOK II. LXI. 1-7

LXI. A stormier year succeeded, under the consuls Lucius Valerius and Titus Aemilius, partly owing to strife between the classes about the land-law, partly to the trial of Appius Claudius. He was the bitterest opponent of the law, and was upholding the claim of those who had possession of the public domain as if he had been a third consul, when Marcus Duillius and Gnaeus Siccius lodged an accusation against him. Never before had a defendant whom the plebs so detested been brought to trial before the people, burdened as he was with men's hatred, both of himself and of his father. The patricians, for their part, had not lightly put forth such exertions in behalf of any man. They felt that the champion of the senate and the guardian of their own dignity, who had stood firm against all sorts of tribunician and plebeian outbreaks, though he had possibly gone too far in the heat of the struggle, was being exposed to the angry commons. Alone amongst the Fathers, Appius Claudius himself regarded tribunes, plebs, and his own trial with perfect unconcern. He was not one whom the threats of the plebeians or the entreaties of the senate could ever prevail upon, I do not say to put on mourning, or to seek men out with appeals for mercy, but even to soften and subdue in a slight degree the accustomed sharpness of his tongue, though it was before the people he must plead. There was the same expression on his countenance, the same arrogance in his glance, the same fire in his speech; so markedly, in fact, that a great part of the plebs feared Appius no less when a defendant than they had feared him as consul. Once only did he plead his cause, in the tone he had been wont to use on all occasions, namely, that of a

B.C. 470

LIVY

adeoque constantia sua et tribunos obstupefecit et plebem ut diem ipsi sua voluntate prodicerent,[1] trahi deinde rem sinerent. Haud ita multum interim temporis fuit; ante tamen quam prodicta dies veniret morbo moritur. Cuius laudationem cum[2] tribuni plebis[3] impedire conarentur,[4] plebs fraudari sollemni honore supremum diem tanti viri noluit et laudationem tam aequis auribus mortui audivit quam vivi accusationem audierat, et exsequias frequens celebravit.

LXII. Eodem anno Valerius consul cum exercitu in Aequos profectus cum hostem ad proelium elicere non posset, castra oppugnare est adortus. Prohibuit foeda tempestas cum grandine ac tonitribus caelo deiecta. Admirationem deinde auxit signo receptui dato adeo tranquilla serenitas reddita ut velut[5] numine aliquo defensa castra oppugnare iterum religio fuerit. Omnis ira belli ad populationem agri vertit. Alter consul Aemilius in Sabinis bellum gessit. Et ibi, quia hostis moenibus se tenebat, vastati agri sunt. Incendiis deinde non villarum modo sed etiam vicorum, quibus frequenter habitabatur, Sabini exciti cum praedatoribus occurrissent, ancipiti proelio digressi postero die rettulere castra in tutiora loca. Id satis consuli visum cur pro victo relinqueret hostem, integro inde decedens bello.

---

[1] prodicerent *OH*: prodiicerent *M*: producerent (*om. L*) Ω.

[2] laudationem cum *V Conway and Walters*: cum laudationem Ω (*but RD have* conlaudationem cum, *and L* conlaudationem).

[3] tribuni plebis *V*?ς: tr. pl. Ω: tribunus plebis ς.

[4] conarentur *V*ς: conaretur Ω.   [5] velut *H*ς: uel Ω.

BOOK II. LXI. 7–LXII. 5

prosecutor; and so completely did his firmness overwhelm the tribunes and the commons that they themselves voluntarily adjourned the trial to a later day, and then allowed the affair to drag. The interval was not very long, but before the appointed day came round Appius fell sick and died. When his eulogy was being pronounced, the tribunes of the plebs attempted to interfere, but the plebs were not willing that the funeral-day of so great a man should be defrauded of the customary honours. They listened to his praises with as great goodwill, now he was dead, as they had heard the living man accused, and attended his burial in crowds.

LXII. The same year Valerius the consul, having marched with an army against the Aequi, was unable to entice the enemy into a battle, and directed an assault upon their camp. This was foiled by an awful storm that descended upon them with hail and claps of thunder. Their amazement was soon increased, on the signal for retreat being given, by the reappearance of so tranquil and cloudless a sky, that, as though some god had defended the camp, they scrupled to attack it a second time, and directed all their hostility towards devastating the fields. The other consul, Aemilius, conducted a campaign in the Sabine country. There, too, the enemy kept within his walls, and the Romans laid waste his fields. Afterwards, by setting fire not only to farmhouses but even to the villages, where the people lived close together, they aroused the Sabines, who, having met the pillagers and fought a drawn battle with them, next day withdrew their camp to a safer position. This seemed to the consul a sufficient pretext for leaving the enemy, as conquered, and he retired ere the campaign had fairly begun.

LIVY

LXIII. Inter haec bella manente discordia domi consules T. Numicius Priscus A. Verginius facti. 2 Non ultra videbatur latura plebes dilationem agrariae legis, ultimaque vis parabatur, cum Volscos adesse fumo ex incendiis villarum fugaque agrestium cognitum est. Ea res maturam iam seditionem ac 3 prope erumpentem repressit. Consules, coacti extemplo ab senatu, ad bellum educta ex urbe iuven- 4 tute tranquilliorem ceteram plebem fecerunt. Et hostes quidem, nihil aliud quam perfusis vano timore 5 Romanis, citato agmine abeunt: Numicius Antium adversus Volscos, Verginius contra Aequos profectus. Ibi ex insidiis prope magna accepta clade virtus militum rem prolapsam neglegentia consulis restituit. 6 Melius in Volscis imperatum est; fusi primo proelio hostes fugaque in urbem Antium, ut tum res erant, opulentissimam, acti. Quam consul oppugnare non ausus, Caenonem, aliud oppidum nequaquam tam 7 opulentum, ab Antiatibus cepit. Dum Aequi Volscique Romanos exercitus tenent, Sabini usque ad portas urbis populantes incessere. Deinde ipsi paucis post diebus ab duobus exercitibus, utroque per iram consule ingresso in finis, plus cladium quam intulerant acceperunt.

BOOK II. LXIII. 1-7

LXIII. While these wars were going on and there B.C. 469
was still discord at home, Titus Numicius Priscus and
Aulus Verginius were elected consuls. It was clear
that the plebs would endure no further postponement
of the land-law, and were preparing to use violent
measures, when the approach of a Volscian army was
announced by the smoke which rose from burning
farmhouses and by the flight of the country people.
By this circumstance the insurrection, which was
already matured and on the point of breaking out,
was repressed. The consuls, being at once commanded to do so by the senate, led the young men
out of the City to the war, a policy which diminished
the restlessness of the plebeians who were left behind.
As for the enemy, they did no more than cause the
Romans a needless panic, and hastily retreated.
Numicius marched to Antium against the Volsci,
Verginius against the Aequi. In the Aequian campaign an ambush nearly resulted in a severe defeat
for the Romans, but the courage of the soldiers
restored the day, which the carelessness of the
consul had almost lost. The Volscian expedition
was better directed: the enemy were routed in the
first engagement and driven in flight to Antium, a
very opulent city for those days. This place the
consul did not venture to assail, but he captured
from the Antiates another town, named Caeno, of
far less wealth. While the Aequi and Volsci kept
the Roman armies busy, the Sabines advanced clear
to the gates of the City on a plundering raid. A
few days after this they themselves had to confront
two armies, for both the consuls indignantly invaded
their borders, and they suffered greater losses than
they had themselves inflicted.

427

LIVY

LXIV. Extremo anno pacis aliquid fuit sed, ut semper alias, sollicitae[1] certamine patrum et plebis.
2 Irata plebs interesse consularibus comitiis noluit; per patres clientesque patrum consules creati T. Quinctius Q. Servilius. Similem annum priori habent,[2] seditiosa initia, bello deinde externo tran-
3 quilla. Sabini Crustuminos campos citato agmine transgressi cum caedes et incendia circum Anienem flumen fecissent, a porta prope Collina moenibusque pulsi ingentes tamen praedas hominum pecorumque
4 egere. Quos Servilius consul infesto exercitu insecutus ipsum quidem agmen adipisci aequis locis non potuit, populationem adeo effuse fecit ut nihil bello intactum relinqueret, multiplicique capta praeda re-
5 diret. Et in Volscis res publica egregie gesta cum ducis tum militum opera. Primum aequo campo signis conlatis pugnatum ingenti caede utrimque,
6 plurimo sanguine. Et Romani, quia paucitas damno sentiendo propior erat, gradum rettulissent, ni salubri mendacio consul fugere hostes ab cornu altero clamitans concitasset aciem. Impetu facto, dum se putant
7 vincere vicere. Consul metuens ne nimis instando
8 renovaret certamen, signum receptui dedit. Inter-

---

[1] sollicitae ϛ: sollicitae pacis Ω.
[2] habent *Gronov.*: consules habent Ω.

---

[1] Held in the centuriate comitia.

BOOK II. LXIV. 1-8

LXIV. Towards the close of the year there was a brief season of peace, but, as always on other occasions, a peace distracted by the strife of patricians and plebeians. The angry plebs refused to take part in the consular elections:[1] by the votes of the patricians and their clients Titus Quinctius and Quintus Servilius were chosen consuls. They experienced a year like the preceding one: dissensions, to begin with, then a foreign war and tranquillity. The Sabines executed a rapid march across the Crustuminian plains, bringing fire and sword to the country about the river Anio. When almost at the Colline Gate and the City walls they were beaten back, yet they carried off immense spoils of men and cattle. Servilius the consul pursued them with an army, and though he could not overtake the column itself on ground which was suitable for offering battle, he devastated the country so extensively as to leave nothing untouched by the ravages of war, and returned with many times the plunder which the Romans had lost. Operations in the Volscian country, too, were very successful, thanks both to the general and to his soldiers. First, there was a pitched battle in the open field, with enormous numbers killed and wounded on both sides. The Romans indeed, whose fewness made them feel their loss more sensibly, would have fallen back, had it not been for a salutary falsehood told by the consul, who shouted that the enemy were running away on the other wing, and so aroused the spirits of his troops. The Romans charged and, believing themselves to be conquering, they conquered. The consul feared lest by pressing the enemy too hard he might cause a renewal of the struggle. He therefore gave the signal for the recall. For a few

B.C. 469-468

LIVY

A.U.C. 285–286

cessere pauci dies, velut tacitis indutiis utrimque quiete sumpta, per quos ingens vis hominum ex omnibus Volscis Aequisque populis in castra venit, haud 9 dubitans si senserint Romanos nocte abituros. Itaque tertia fere vigilia ad castra oppugnanda veniunt. 10 Quinctius sedato tumultu quem terror subitus exciverat, cum manere in tentoriis quietum militem iussisset, Hernicorum cohortem in stationem educit, cornicines tubicinesque in equos impositos canere ante vallum iubet sollicitumque hostem ad lucem 11 tenere. Reliquum noctis adeo tranquilla omnia in castris fuere, ut somni quoque Romanis copia esset. Volscos species armatorum peditum, quos et plures esse et Romanos putabant, fremitus hinnitusque equorum, qui et insueto sedente equite et insuper aures agitante sonitu saeviebant, intentos velut ad impetum hostium tenuit.

A.U.C. 286

LXV. Ubi inluxit, Romanus integer satiatusque somno productus in aciem fessum stando et vigiliis 2 Volscum primo impetu perculit; quamquam cessere magis quam pulsi hostes sunt, quia ab tergo erant clivi, in quos post principia integris ordinibus tutus receptus fuit. Consul, ubi ad iniquum locum ventum est, sistit aciem. Miles aegre teneri, clamare, et 3 poscere ut perculsis instare liceat. Ferocius agunt equites; circumfusi duci vociferantur se ante signa

---

[1] The Romans divided the night into four equal watches, beginning at sunset.

430

BOOK II. LXIV. 8–LXV. 3

days both sides rested, as if they had tacitly agreed on a truce. Meanwhile a great force of men came in from all their tribes to the camp of the Volsci and Aequi. They made no question but that the Romans, if they had perceived them, would retreat in the night, and accordingly at about the third watch[1] they came to attack the camp. Quinctius stilled the tumult which the sudden alarm had raised, and bidding the soldiers remain quietly in their tents, led out a cohort of Hernici to an outpost, and mounting trumpeters and buglers upon horses, ordered them to blow their instruments in front of the rampart and keep the enemy in suspense till daybreak. For the remainder of the night all was so peaceful in camp that the Romans were even able to sleep. But the Volsci, beholding armed footsoldiers, whom they supposed to be more numerous than they were, and to be Romans; and hearing the stamping and neighing of the horses, which were infuriated not only at finding unaccustomed riders on their backs, but also by the blare of the trumpets, were kept on the alert in anticipation of an attack.

LXV. As soon as it was light, the Romans, who were fresh and had enjoyed a good sleep, were led out into line of battle. The Volsci, weary from standing and from loss of sleep, were driven back at the first assault; though it was rather a retreat than a rout, for behind them were hills, to which, under cover of the first line, they withdrew safely and in good order. The consul ordered a halt when his army reached rising ground. The infantry could hardly be restrained, noisily demanding permission to press on after the fleeing enemy. Still more ardent were the cavalry. They swarmed about the general, and shouted that

LIVY

ituros. Dum cunctatur consul virtute militum fretus, loco parum fidens, conclamant se ituros, clamoremque res est secuta. Fixis in terram pilis, quo leviores ardua evaderent, cursu subeunt. Volscus effusis ad primum impetum missilibus telis saxa obiacentia pedibus ingerit in subeuntes, turbatosque ictibus crebris urget ex superiore loco. Sic prope oneratum est sinistrum Romanis cornu, ni referentibus iam gradum consul increpando simul temeritatem simul ignaviam pudore metum excussisset. Restitere primo obstinatis animis; deinde, ut obtinentes locum vim pro vi referebant,[1] audent ultro gradum inferre et clamore renovato commovent aciem; tum rursus impetu capto enituntur atque exsuperant iniquitatem loci. Iam prope erat ut in summum clivi iugum evaderent, cum terga hostes dedere effusoque cursu paene agmine uno fugientes sequentesque castris incidere. In eo pavore castra capiuntur. Qui Volscorum effugere potuerunt Antium petunt. Antium et Romanus exercitus ductus. Paucos circumsessum dies deditur, nulla oppugnantium nova vi, sed quod iam inde ab infelici pugna castrisque amissis ceciderant animi.

[1] vim pro vi referebant *Conway and Walters*: uires ferebant Ω: vires refecerant *Weissenborn*: vires reficiebant *Madvig*.

BOOK II. LXV. 3–7

they were going on before the standards. While the consul was hesitating, feeling certain of the valour of his troops but doubtful of the ground, the men cried out that they were going, and instantly made good their word. Planting their spears in the ground, that they might be the lighter for the ascent, they went up at a run. The Volsci, having discharged their javelins at the first onset, picked up the stones which lay about under their feet, and flung them at their enemies as they mounted. Confused by this rain of missiles from above, the left wing of the Romans was nearly overwhelmed, and had already begun to retreat, when the consul, reproaching them at once with rashness and with cowardice, succeeded in shaming them out of their fear. First they made a resolute stand; then, after holding their ground and returning blow for blow, they even dared to press forward and, renewing their cheers, set their line in motion; then with another rush they struggled upward and scaled the height; and they were just emerging upon the summit of the ridge, when the enemy turned and fled. Running at full speed, and almost in one body, the pursued and the pursuers reached the Volscian camp, which was captured in the panic. Those of the Volsci who succeeded in escaping made for Antium, and to Antium marched the Roman army also. After a blockade of a few days the place surrendered; the besiegers had not delivered any new attack, but the Volsci had lost heart from the moment of their unsuccessful battle and the capture of their camp.

B.C. 468

LIBRI II PERIOCHA

Brutus iureiurando populum adstrinxit neminem Romae regnare passuros. Tarquinium Collatinum collegam suum propter adfinitatem Tarquiniorum suspectum coegit consulatu se abdicare et civitate cedere. Bona regum diripi iussit, agrum Marti consecravit, qui campus Martius nominatus est. Adulescentes nobiles, in quibus suos quoque et fratris filios, quia coniuraverant de recipiendis regibus, securi percussit. Servo indici, cui Vindicio nomen fuit, libertatem dedit; ex cuius nomine vindicta appellata. Cum adversus reges, qui contractis Veientum et Tarquiniensium copiis bellum intulerant, exercitum duxisset, in acie cum Arrunte filio Superbi commortuus est; eumque matronae anno luxerunt. P. Valerius[1] consul legem de provocatione ad populum tulit. Capitolium dedicatum est. Porsenna, Clusinorum rex, bello pro Tarquinis suscepto cum ad Ianiculum venisset, ne Tiberim transiret virtute Coclitis Horati prohibitus est, qui, dum alii pontem Sublicium rescindunt, solus Etruscos sustinuit et ponte rupto armatus in flumen se misit et ad suos transnavit. Accessit alterum virtutis exemplum in Mucio. Qui cum ad feriendum Porsennam castra hostium intrasset, occiso scriba, quem regem esse existimaverat, conprehensus inpositam manum altaribus, in quibus sacrificatum erat, exuri passus est dixitque tales ccc esse. Quorum admiratione coactus Porsenna pacis con-

---

[1] P. Valerius *Sigonius*: l. ualerius *MSS*.

SUMMARY OF BOOK II

BRUTUS bound the people with an oath to allow no one to reign in Rome. Tarquinius Collatinus, his colleague, who had incurred suspicion because of his relationship to the Tarquinii, he forced to abdicate the consulship and withdraw from the state. He ordered the king's goods to be plundered, and consecrated his land to Mars. It was named the Campus Martius. Certain noble youths—among them his own sons and his brother's—he beheaded, because they had conspired to bring back the kings. To the slave who gave the information, a man called Vindicius, he gave his freedom; from his name came the word *vindicta*. Having led an army against the princes, who had collected forces from Veii and Tarquinii and begun a war, he fell in the battle, together with Arruns, the son of Superbus, and the matrons mourned for him a year. Publius Valerius the consul proposed a law about appealing to the people. The Capitol was dedicated. Porsenna, king of Clusium, made war in behalf of the Tarquinii and came to Janiculum, but was prevented from crossing the Tiber by the bravery of Horatius Cocles, who, while the others were cutting down the Sublician Bridge, kept the Etruscans at bay, single-handed, and when the bridge had been destroyed, threw himself armed into the river and swam across to his fellows. Another example of courage was exhibited by Mucius. Having entered the camp of the enemy with the purpose of killing Porsenna, he slew a secretary, whom he had taken for the king. Being arrested, he placed his hand upon the altar, where sacrifice had been made, and suffering it to be burned off, declared that there were three hundred others as determined as himself. Overcome with astonishment at their daring, Porsenna proposed terms of peace and, having

LIVY

diciones ferre bellum omisit acceptis obsidibus. Ex quibus virgo una Cloelia deceptis custodibus per Tiberim ad suos transnavit et cum reddita esset, a[1] Porsenna honorifice remissa equestri statua donata est. Adversus Tarquinium Superbum cum Latinorum exercitu bellum inferentem Aulus Postumius[2] dictator prospere pugnavit. Appius Claudius ex Sabinis Romam transfugit. Ob hoc Claudia tribus adiecta est numerusque tribuum ampliatus est, ut essent XXI. Plebs cum propter nexos ob aes alienum in Sacrum montem secessisset, consilio Meneni Agrippae a seditione revocata est. Idem Agrippa cum decessisset, propter paupertatem publico inpendio elatus est. Tribuni plebis quinque creati sunt. Oppidum Vulscorum Corioli captum est virtute et opera Cn. Marci, qui ob hoc Coriolanus vocatus est. T. Latinius,[3] vir de plebe, cum in visu admonitus ut de quibusdam religionibus ad senatum perferret id[4] neglexisset, amisso filio pedibus debilis factus, postquam delatus ad senatum lectica eadem illa indicaverat, usu pedum recepto domum reversus est. Cum Cn. Marcius Coriolanus, qui in exilium erat pulsus, dux Vulscorum factus exercitum hostium urbi admovisset, et missi ad eum primum legati, postea sacerdotes frustra deprecati essent ne bellum patriae inferret, Veturia mater et Volumnia uxor impetraverunt ab eo, ut recederet. Lex agraria primum lata est. Spurius Cassius consularis regni crimine damnatus est necatusque. Opillia[5] virgo Vestalis ob incestum viva defossa est. Cum vicini Veientes incommodi magis quam graves essent, familia Fabiorum id bellum gerendum depoposcit misitque in id trecentos et sex armatos, qui ad Cremeram praeter unum

---

[1] a *supplied by edd.*
[2] Postumius *edd.*: postumus *MSS.*
[3] Latinius *Sigonius*: latinus *MSS.*
[4] id *Drakenborch*: et *MSS.*
[5] Opillia *Hertz*: illia (ilia) *MSS.*: *Livy*, II. xlii. 11, *has* Oppia: *Dion. Hal.* viii. 89, Ὀπιμία: *Oros.* II. viii. 13, Popilia.

SUMMARY OF BOOK II

taken hostages, relinquished the war. One of the hostages, the maiden Cloelia, evaded the sentinels and swam across the Tiber to her people. She was given up to Porsenna, but was restored by him with marks of honour, and was presented with an equestrian statue. Aulus Postumius the dictator fought a successful battle against Tarquinius Superbus, who was advancing with an army of Latins. Appius Claudius came over from the Sabines to the Romans. On this account the Claudian tribe was added and the number of tribes was increased to twenty-one. The plebs, after seceding to the Sacred Mount because of those who had been enslaved for debt, were induced by the advice of Menenius Agrippa to cease from their rebellion. The same Agrippa when he died was buried, owing to his poverty, at the state's expense. Five plebeian tribunes were elected. The Volscian town of Corioli was captured by the valiant efforts of Gnaeus Marcius, who acquired from this circumstance the name of Coriolanus. Titus Latinius, a man of the plebs, was warned in a dream to inform the senate regarding certain offences against religion. Having neglected to do it, he lost a son and was paralysed in his feet. When he had been carried to the senate in a litter and had revealed these same matters, he recovered the use of his feet and returned to his house. When Gnaeus Marcius Coriolanus, who had been driven into exile and had been made general of the Volsci, had led a hostile army nearly to Rome, and when the envoys who had been sent to him at first and afterwards the priests had vainly besought him not to make war upon his native land, his mother Veturia and his wife Volumnia persuaded him to withdraw. For the first time a land-law was proposed. Spurius Cassius, the ex-consul, charged with aspiring to be king, was condemned and put to death. Opilia, a Vestal Virgin, was buried alive for unchastity. The neighbouring Veientes being a troublesome rather than a dangerous enemy, the Fabian family asked to be allowed to carry on that war, and dispatched thither 306 armed men,

ab hostibus caesi sunt. Appius Claudius cos. cum adversus Vulscos contumacia exercitus male pugnatum esset, decimum quemque militum fuste percussit. Res praeterea adversus Vulscos et Hernicos et Veientes et seditiones inter patres plebemque continet.

SUMMARY OF BOOK II

who were all but one killed by the enemy at the Cremera. When Appius Claudius the consul had sustained a defeat at the hands of the Volsci, owing to the contumacy of his army, he caused every tenth soldier to be scourged to death. It contains besides campaigns against the Volsci, the Hernici, and the Veientes, and the quarrels between the patricians and the plebs.

INDEX OF NAMES

INDEX OF NAMES

(*The References are to Pages.*)

ABORIGINES, 8, 10, 12
Achivi, 8
Actiacum bellum, 66
Aebutius, T., 278, 280
Aemilius, L., 356, 386, 400; T., 422, 424
Aeneas, 8–14; Aeneas Silvius, 16
Aequi, 184, 312, 314, 318, 322, 350, 356, 360, 366, 380, 382, 384, 398, 410, 414, 424, 426, 430.
Aequicum bellum, 414
Agrippa (Alban king), 16; Menenius Agrippa, *see* Menenius
Alba Longa, 14, 16, 24, 70, 76, 78, 90, 96, 104, 106, 180
Albani, 24, 76, 78, 80, 82, 94–110; Albanus mons, 14, 110
Albinus, L., 324
Albula, 14, 16
Alpes, 8, 12
Ameriola, 136
Amulius, 16, 20
Anchises, 10
Ancus Marcius, 112–128, 140, 142, 146, 180
Anio, 96, 130, 132, 270, 300, 322, 428
Antemnates, 34, 38, 40
Antenor, 8
Antiates, 326
Antium, 326, 426, 432
Apiolae, 128
Apollo, 196
Appius Claudius, 270–312, 362, 364; Appius Claudius (son), 408–422
Aquilii, 228–240; Aquilius, C., 350
Arcades, 20
Arcadica urbs, 20
Ardea, 196, 200, 208
Argiletum, 66
Aricia, 264, 300
Aricini, 264
Aristodemus, 286, 330
Arruns (brother of L. Tarquinius Priscus), 122; (son of Priscus), 146, 160
Arsia silva, 238
Ascanius, 10, 14, 16
Asia, 156
Attius Clausus (= Appius Claudius) 270; Attius Tullius, 334, 338, 344, 350
Attus Navius, 130, 132
Atys, 16
Augustus, 66
Aurunci, 270, 274, 300, 302
Aventinus (Alban king), 16; mons, 16, 24, 70, 118, 120, 306, 322

BRUTUS, *see* Iunius

CACUS, 26, 28
Caedicius, L., 396
Caelius mons, 106, 118, 254
Caeninenses, 34, 38
Caeno, 426
Caere, 12, 208
Caesar Augustus, 66
Camenae, 74
Cameria, 136
Campania, 394
Campus Martius, 154, 230
Capena porta, 90
Capetus, 16
Capitolinus collis, 44
Capitolium, 40, 138, 242, 244, 248, 288, 386
Caprae palus, 56
Capys, 16
Carmenta, 28
Carmentalis porta, 386
Cassius, Sp., 272, 274, 326, 328, 352, 354, 356, 358

LIVY I. 443

INDEX OF NAMES

Castor, 284, 356
Celeres, 56
Ceres, 354
Circa (Circe), 172
Circeii, 194, 344
Claudia tribus (vetus), 270; Claudius, *see* Appius
Cloelia, 260; Cloelii, 106; Cloelius, Q., 284
Cluilia fossa, 78, 344
Cluilius, C., 76, 78, 80
Cocles, *see* Horatius
Collatia, 134, 198, 204, 206
Collatini, 136; Collatinus, L. Tarquinius, 198–224
Collina porta, 254, 392, 428
Cominius, Postumus, 274, 326, 328
Considius, Q., 394
Consualia, 34
Cora, 270, 286
Corbio, 344
Corinthus, 164
Coriolanus, *see* Marcius, Cn.
Corioli, 326, 328, 344
Cornelius, Servius, 354
Corniculum, 136, 140
Cremera, 386, 388, 394
Creusa, 14
Croton, 64
Crustumeria, 278; Crustumerium, 136
Crustumini, 34, 38, 42; Crustumini campi, 428
Cumae, 246, 264, 286, 330
Cures, 48, 62, 124
Curia Hostilia, 106
Curiatii fratres, 82–94; Curiatii (gens), 106
Curtius, Mettius, 44, 46; Curtius lacus, 48
Cyprius vicus, 168

DELPHI, 194
Demaratus, 122
Dialis flamen, 70
Diana Ephesia, 156, **158**
Dianium, 168
Diespiter, 84
Duillius, M., 414, 422

ECETRANI VOLSCI, 298
Egeria, 68, 74; Egerius (Tarquinius, son of Arruns), 122, 134, 198

Elicius, *see* Iuppiter
Eneti, 8
Esquiliae, 154, 306
Esquilina, porta, 254
Etruria, 12, 108, 130, 192, 264, 330, 364, 382
Etrusca res, 80; Etrusci, 12, *et passim*.
Euganei, 8
Evander, 20, 26, 28, 30

FABIA GENS, 382, 388, 390, 392; Fabius, Q., 354, 356, 360, 374, 378; Caeso (= K.), 354, 356, 360, 374, 380, 382; M., 358, 362, 370, 372, 374; Pictor, 154, 192, 350
Faustulus, 18, 20
Ferentina, aqua, 180, Ferentinum caput, 340; Ferentinae lucus, 174, 182
Feretrius, *see* Iuppiter
Feronia, 108
Ficana, 118
Ficulea vetus, 136
Fidenae, 52, 96, 278
Fidenates, 50, 52, 54, 96, 98
Fides, 74
Flavoleius, M., 372
Fortuna, 80; muliebris, 350
Fufetius, *see* Mettius
Furius, Sex., 344; Sp., 360; L., 400; P., 406
Fusius, Sp., 84

GABII, 182, 184, 188, 190, 208
Gabina via, 254; Gabini, 184, 186
Geganii, 106; Geganius, T., 328
Genucius, T., 394; Cn., 400, 404
Geryones, 26
Gradivus, *see* Mars
Graecia, 194

HADRIATICUS, 8
Helena, 8
Heraclea, 64
Hercules, 26, 28
Herminius, T., 250, 254, 266, 282
Hernici, 184, 286, 288, 350, 398, 430
Hersilia, 42
Horatia gens, 94; pila, 92; Horatii fratres, 82–92; Horatius, M., Pulvillus, 242, 244; Cocles, 248, 250, 262; C., 390, 392
Hostilia, curia, 106; Hostilius, Hostius, 44; Tullus, 74–114, 180

444

INDEX OF NAMES

IANICULUM, 120, 124, 248, 260, 264, 268, 392, 394, 396
Ianus, 66, 116
Icilius, Sp., 414
Ilium, 14
Inregillum, 270
Inuus, 20
Italia, 12, 62
Iulia gens, 14; Iulii, 106; Iulius Proculus, 58; Iulius, C., 360; Iulius Vopiscus, 400
Iulus, 14
Iunia domus, 232; Iunius, L., Brutus, 194-204, 208, 218, 220-228, 236, 240, 244, 270
Iuppiter, 28, 44, 46, 66, 70, 84, 114, 116, 138, 182, 190, 244, 336, 338, 374; Elicius, 72, 112; Feretrius, 40, 122; Indiges, 14; Stator, 44, 144

LABICI, 344
Laetorius, M., 304, 408, 410
Larcius, Sp., 250, 254, 266; T., 284
Larentia, 18
Largius, T., 274, 276, 310, 312
Lars Porsinna (Porsena), *see* Porsinna
Latina res, 14; Latini, 12, *et passim*; Prisci Latini, 16, 116, 118, 136; Latinus (king of the Laurentes), 8, 10, 12; Silvius, 16
Latinius, T., 336, 436
Laurens ager, 8; Laurentinus ager, 10
Laurentes, 50
Laurentium, 50
Lavinia, 10, 14; Lavinium, 10, 14, 24, 50, 78, 224, 344
Licinius, C., 324; Sp., 360
Longula, 326, 344
Luceres, 50, 130
Lucretia, 198, 202, 206; Lucretius, Sp., Tricipitinus, 202, 206, 208, 224, 242, 244; T., 244, 254, 270; P., 266
Lucumo (= L. Tarquinius Priscus), 122, 124
Lupercal, 20
Lycaeus Pan, 20

MACEDONIA, 8
Maecilius, L., 414
Maesia silva, 122

Malitiosa silva, 108
Manlius, T., 66; Cn., 362, 370, 374, 376; C., 400
Marcius, Cn., Coriolanus, 326-352, 396, 402; *see also* Numa and Ancus
Mars, 2, 16, 70, 88, 120, 238, 374; Gradivus, 70
Medullia, 120, 136
Menenius Agrippa, 270, 322, 338, 396; Menenius, T., 390, 394, 396, 400, 402
Mercuri, aedes, 286, 302
Metapontum, 64
Mettius Curtius, 44, 46, 48; Fufetius, 78, 90, 96, 100, 102
Mezentius, 12, 14
Minucius, M., 284, 330; P., 328
Mucia prata, 260; Mucius, C., Scaevola, 254-262
Murcia, 120

NAEVIA, PORTA, 254
Nautius, Sp., 344; C., 396, 398
Navius, Attus, 130
Neptunus, 34
Nomentum, 136
Norba, 330
Nova via, 144
Numa Pompilius, 62-74, 112, 114, 124, 126, 148; Numa Marcius, 70
Numicius, T., Priscus, 426
Numicus, 14
Numitor, 16-24
Numitorius, L., 414

OCTAVIUS MAMILIUS, 172, 268-282
Opillia, 436
Opiter, Verginius, *see* Verginius
Oppia (Vestalis), 358
Ortona, 360
Ostia, 122, 330

PALATINUS, 44
Palatium, 20, 24, 26, 44, 46, 118, 120, 248
Pallanteum, 20
Pallantium, 20
Pallor, 98
Pan (Lycaeus), 20
Pavor, 98
Pedum, 344

445

INDEX OF NAMES

Peloponnesus, 28
Pinarii, 28, 30; Pinarius, L., 406
Piso (L. Calpurnius, Frugi), 192, 322
Politorium, 118
Polusca, 326
Pometia, 270, 272, 286
Pompilius, see Numa
Pomptinus ager, 330
Pontificius, Tib., 362
Porsinna, Lars, 244–268; Arruns, 264
Postumius, P., 268, 270; A., 278, 280, 284, 300, 356
Potitii, 28, 30
Praeneste, 278
Proca, 16
Proculus, see Iulius
Publicola, see Valerius, P.
Publilius, Volero, 404–408, 416
Pylaemenes, 8
Punicum bellum, 66
Pythagoras, 62

QUINCTII, 106; Quinctius, T., 408, 410, 412, 414, 428, 430
Quirinalis, collis, 154
Quirinus, 70, 116
Quirites, 48, 58, 62, 82, 84, 94, 242, 292

RAMNENSES, 50
Ramnes, 130
Rea Silvia, 16
Regillus, lacus, 284, 288, 318
Remus, 20, 22, 24
Roma, 40, *et passim*
Romani, 40, *et passim*
Romularis, ficus, 18
Romulus, 20–74, 108, 114, 130, 140, 152, 170; Romulus Silvius, 16
Ruminalis, ficus, 18
Rutuli, 10, 12, 196

SABINAE, 46, 48; Sabini, 34–48, 60, 64, 74, 106, 108, 110, 118, 132, 134, 158, 268, 270, 274, 276, 300, 314, 316, 382, 396, 398, 424, 426
Sacer mons, 322, 332, 412
Salii, 70, 98
Satricum, 344
Saturnalia, 284
Saturnus, 284

Saxa Rubra, 386
Scaevola, see Mucius, C.
Sceleratus vicus, 170
Sempronius, A., 284, 330
Servilii, 106; Servilius, P., 286–314; C., 386; Sp., 392, 396, 400; Q., 428
Servius Tullius, 62, 138–170, 206, 208, 222
Siccius, Cn., 414, 422
Sicilia, 8, 330
Sicinius quidam, 322, 330; T., 350
Siculum, fretum, 12
Signia, 194, 286
Silvanus, 238
Silvia gens, 16; Silvius, 16
Spei (aedes), 392
Statius, T., 396
Stator, see Iuppiter
Suessa Pometia, 146, 182, 298
Sulpicius, Ser., 278

TANAQUIL, 122, 138, 144, 164
Tarpeius, Sp., 42; Tarpeius, mons, 190
Tarquinia, 194; Tarquinii (town), 122, 124, 164; (family), 330; Tarquinius, L., Priscus (= Lucumo), 122, 124, 126–146, 164, 222; Arruns (brother of Priscus), 122; Arruns (son of Priscus), 146, 160; Lucius, Superbus, 146, 160–238, 266, 268, 278, 286, 332; Sextus (son of Superbus), 184–188, 196–208; Arruns (son of Superbus), 194, 280; Titus (son of Superbus), 194, 280; Tarquinius Collatinus, see Collatinus
Tatius, Titus, 38, 42, 50, 60, 108, 124, 126, 190
Tellenae, 118
Tellus, 354
Terminus, 190
Termo, 210
Thalassius, 36
Tiberinus (Alban king), 16; Tiberinus pater (river god), 250
Tiberis, 16, 18, 26, 54, 96, 120, 122, 134, 136, 230, 248, 250, 256, 260, 330, 392
Titienses, 50, 130
Trebium, 344
Tricipitinus, see Lucretius, Sp.

446

INDEX OF NAMES

Troia, 8, 78; Troiana proles, 76; Troiani, 8, 10, 12; Troianus, 8
Tullia, 162, 170, 208; Tuliius, M'., 278; Servius Tullius, *see* Servius
Tullus, *see* Hostilius
Turnus (king of the Rutuli), 10, 12; Turnus Herdonius, 174, 176, 178
Tusci, 190, *et passim*; Tuscus ager, 386; vicus, 266

ULIXES, 172
Urbius, clivus, 170

VALERIUS, M. (fetial), 84; P., Publicola (son of Volesus), 202, 204, 224, 236, 238, 242, 244, 252, 254, 266, 270; M. (consul 505 B.C.), 268, 280; M'. (dictator, son of Volesus), 314, 320; M'. (grandson of Volesus), 276; L., 354, 358, 422, 424; P., (consul 476 B.C.), 396
Veiens, 98, 390; Veiens bellum, 358, 364, 395; Veientes, 54, 56, 90, 96, 108, 122, 148, 234, 236, 238, 244, 260, 360, 364, 368, 374, 380, 382, 386, 388, 392, 400

Veii, 54, 398
Velia, 240, 242
Veliternus ager, 318
Velitrae, 316, 318
Veneti, 8
Venus, 10
Verginius Opiter, 272, 400; T., 284, 380; A., 306, 392, 396, 426; P., 310, 312; Verginius Proculus, 352, 354
Vesta, 70
Vestalis (virgo), 16, 358
Vetelia, 344
Veturia, 346, 348
Vetusius, C., 278; T., 306, 314, 320
Vica Pota, 242
Viminalis, collis, 154
Vindicius, 234
Vitellii, 228, 240; Vitellius, **T.**, 228; Tib., 228
Volcanus, 134
Volero, *see* Publilius; Volerones, 416
Volesus, 202, 204
Volsci, 182, *et passim*; Volsci Antiates, 328; Volscum bellum, 414; Volscus ager, 418; Ecetrani Volsci, 298
Volumnia, 346

447

*Printed in Great Britain by
Richard Clay (The Chaucer Press), Ltd.,
Bungay, Suffolk*

THE LOEB CLASSICAL LIBRARY

VOLUMES ALREADY PUBLISHED

Latin Authors

AMMIANUS MARCELLINUS. Translated by J. C. Rolfe. 3 Vols.
APULEIUS: THE GOLDEN ASS (METAMORPHOSES). W. Adlington (1566). Revised by S. Gaselee.
ST. AUGUSTINE: CITY OF GOD. 7 Vols. Vol. I. G. E. McCracken. Vol. II. W. M. Green. Vol. IV. P. Levine. Vol. V. E. M. Sanford and W. M. Green. Vol. VI. W. C. Greene.
ST. AUGUSTINE, CONFESSIONS OF. W. Watts (1631). 2 Vols.
ST. AUGUSTINE, SELECT LETTERS. J. H. Baxter.
AUSONIUS. H. G. Evelyn White. 2 Vols.
BEDE. J. E. King. 2 Vols.
BOETHIUS: TRACTS and DE CONSOLATIONE PHILOSOPHIAE. Rev. H. F. Stewart and E. K. Rand.
CAESAR: ALEXANDRIAN, AFRICAN and SPANISH WARS. A. G. Way.
CAESAR: CIVIL WARS. A. G. Peskett.
CAESAR: GALLIC WAR. H. J. Edwards.
CATO: DE RE RUSTICA; VARRO: DE RE RUSTICA. H. B. Ash and W. D. Hooper.
CATULLUS. F. W. Cornish; TIBULLUS. J. B. Postgate; PERVIGILIUM VENERIS. J. W. Mackail.
CELSUS: DE MEDICINA. W. G. Spencer. 3 Vols.
CICERO: BRUTUS, and ORATOR. G. L. Hendrickson and H. M. Hubbell.
[CICERO]: AD HERENNIUM. H. Caplan.
CICERO: DE ORATORE, etc. 2 Vols. Vol. I. DE ORATORE, Books I. and II. E. W. Sutton and H. Rackham. Vol. II. DE ORATORE, Book III. De Fato; Paradoxa Stoicorum; De Partitione Oratoria. H. Rackham.
CICERO: DE FINIBUS. H. Rackham.
CICERO: DE INVENTIONE, etc. H. M. Hubbell.
CICERO: DE NATURA DEORUM and ACADEMICA. H. Rackham.
CICERO: DE OFFICIIS. Walter Miller.
CICERO: DE REPUBLICA and DE LEGIBUS; SOMNIUM SCIPIONIS. Clinton W. Keyes.

CICERO: DE SENECTUTE, DE AMICITIA, DE DIVINATIONE. W. A. Falconer.
CICERO: IN CATILINAM, PRO FLACCO, PRO MURENA, PRO SULLA. Louis E. Lord.
CICERO: LETTERS to ATTICUS. E. O. Winstedt. 3 Vols.
CICERO: LETTERS TO HIS FRIENDS. W. Glynn Williams. 3 Vols.
CICERO: PHILIPPICS. W. C. A. Ker.
CICERO: PRO ARCHIA POST REDITUM, DE DOMO, DE HARUSPICUM RESPONSIS, PRO PLANCIO. N. H. Watts.
CICERO: PRO CAECINA, PRO LEGE MANILIA, PRO CLUENTIO, PRO RABIRIO. H. Grose Hodge.
CICERO: PRO CAELIO, DE PROVINCIIS CONSULARIBUS, PRO BALBO. R. Gardner.
CICERO: PRO MILONE, IN PISONEM, PRO SCAURO, PRO FONTEIO, PRO RABIRIO POSTUMO, PRO MARCELLO, PRO LIGARIO, PRO REGE DEIOTARO. N. H. Watts.
CICERO: PRO QUINCTIO, PRO ROSCIO AMERINO, PRO ROSCIO COMOEDO, CONTRA RULLUM. J. H. Freese.
CICERO: PRO SESTIO, IN VATINIUM. R. Gardner.
CICERO: TUSCULAN DISPUTATIONS. J. E. King.
CICERO: VERRINE ORATIONS. L. H. G. Greenwood. 2 Vols.
CLAUDIAN. M. Platnauer. 2 Vols.
COLUMELLA: DE RE RUSTICA. DE ARBORIBUS. H. B. Ash, E. S. Forster and E. Heffner. 3 Vols.
CURTIUS, Q.: HISTORY OF ALEXANDER. J. C. Rolfe. 2 Vols.
FLORUS. E. S. Forster; and CORNELIUS NEPOS. J. C. Rolfe.
FRONTINUS: STRATAGEMS and AQUEDUCTS. C. E. Bennett and M. B. McElwain.
FRONTO: CORRESPONDENCE. C. R. Haines. 2 Vols.
GELLIUS, J. C. Rolfe. 3 Vols.
HORACE: ODES AND EPODES. C. E. Bennett.
HORACE: SATIRES, EPISTLES, ARS POETICA. H. R. Fairclough.
JEROME: SELECTED LETTERS. F. A. Wright.
JUVENAL and PERSIUS. G. G. Ramsay.
LIVY. B. O. Foster, F. G. Moore, Evan T. Sage, and A. C. Schlesinger and R. M. Geer (General Index). 14 Vols.
LUCAN. J. D. Duff.
LUCRETIUS. W. H. D. Rouse.
MARTIAL. W. C. A. Ker. 2 Vols.
MINOR LATIN POETS: from PUBLILIUS SYRUS TO RUTILIUS NAMATIANUS, including GRATTIUS, CALPURNIUS SICULUS, NEMESIANUS, AVIANUS, and others with "Aetna" and the "Phoenix." J. Wight Duff and Arnold M. Duff.
OVID: THE ART OF LOVE and OTHER POEMS. J. H. Mozley.

OVID: FASTI. Sir James G. Frazer.
OVID: HEROIDES and AMORES. Grant Showerman.
OVID: METAMORPHOSES. F. J. Miller. 2 Vols.
OVID: TRISTIA and EX PONTO. A. L. Wheeler.
PERSIUS. Cf. JUVENAL.
PETRONIUS. M. Heseltine; SENECA; APOCOLOCYNTOSIS. W. H. D. Rouse.
PHAEDRUS AND BABRIUS (Greek). B. E. Perry.
PLAUTUS. Paul Nixon. 5 Vols.
PLINY: LETTERS. Melmoth's Translation revised by W. M. L. Hutchinson. 2 Vols.
PLINY: NATURAL HISTORY.
10 Vols. Vols. I.–V. and IX. H. Rackham. Vols. VI.–VIII. W. H. S. Jones. Vol. X. D. E. Eichholz.
PROPERTIUS. H. E. Butler.
PRUDENTIUS. H. J. Thomson. 2 Vols.
QUINTILIAN. H. E. Butler. 4 Vols.
REMAINS OF OLD LATIN. E. H. Warmington. 4 Vols. Vol. I. (ENNIUS AND CAECILIUS.) Vol. II. (LIVIUS, NAEVIUS, PACUVIUS, ACCIUS.) Vol. III. (LUCILIUS and LAWS OF XII TABLES.) Vol. IV. (ARCHAIC INSCRIPTIONS.)
SALLUST. J. C. Rolfe.
SCRIPTORES HISTORIAE AUGUSTAE. D. Magie. 3 Vols.
SENECA: APOCOLOCYNTOSIS. Cf. PETRONIUS.
SENECA: EPISTULAE MORALES. R. M. Gummere. 3 Vols.
SENECA: MORAL ESSAYS. J. W. Basore. 3 Vols.
SENECA: TRAGEDIES. F. J. Miller. 2 Vols.
SIDONIUS: POEMS and LETTERS. W. B. ANDERSON. 2 Vols.
SILIUS ITALICUS. J. D. Duff. 2 Vols.
STATIUS. J. H. Mozley. 2 Vols.
SUETONIUS. J. C. Rolfe. 2 Vols.
TACITUS: DIALOGUES. Sir Wm. Peterson. AGRICOLA and GERMANIA. Maurice Hutton.
TACITUS: HISTORIES AND ANNALS. C. H. Moore and J. Jackson. 4 Vols.
TERENCE. John Sargeaunt. 2 Vols.
TERTULLIAN: APOLOGIA and DE SPECTACULIS. T. R. Glover. MINUCIUS FELIX. G. H. Rendall.
VALERIUS FLACCUS. J. H. Mozley.
VARRO: DE LINGUA LATINA. R. G. Kent. 2 Vols.
VELLEIUS PATERCULUS and RES GESTAE DIVI AUGUSTI. F. W. Shipley.
VIRGIL. H. R. Fairclough. 2 Vols.
VITRUVIUS: DE ARCHITECTURA. F. Granger. 2 Vols.

Greek Authors

ACHILLES TATIUS. S. Gaselee.
AELIAN: ON THE NATURE OF ANIMALS. A. F. Scholfield. 3 Vols.
AENEAS TACTICUS, ASCLEPIODOTUS and ONASANDER. The Illinois Greek Club.
AESCHINES. C. D. Adams.
AESCHYLUS. H. Weir Smyth. 2 Vols.
ALCIPHRON, AELIAN, PHILOSTRATUS: LETTERS. A. R. Benner and F. H. Fobes.
ANDOCIDES, ANTIPHON, Cf. MINOR ATTIC ORATORS.
APOLLODORUS. Sir James G. Frazer. 2 Vols.
APOLLONIUS RHODIUS. R. C. Seaton.
THE APOSTOLIC FATHERS. Kirsopp Lake. 2 Vols.
APPIAN: ROMAN HISTORY. Horace White. 4 Vols.
ARATUS. Cf. CALLIMACHUS.
ARISTOPHANES. Benjamin Bickley Rogers. 3 Vols. Verse trans.
ARISTOTLE: ART OF RHETORIC. J. H. Freese.
ARISTOTLE: ATHENIAN CONSTITUTION, EUDEMIAN ETHICS, VICES AND VIRTUES. H. Rackham.
ARISTOTLE: GENERATION OF ANIMALS. A. L. Peck.
ARISTOTLE: HISTORIA ANIMALIUM. A. L. Peck. Vol. I.
ARISTOTLE: METAPHYSICS. H. Tredennick. 2 Vols.
ARISTOTLE: METEOROLOGICA. H. D. P. Lee.
ARISTOTLE: MINOR WORKS. W. S. Hett. On Colours, On Things Heard, On Physiognomies, On Plants, On Marvellous Things Heard, Mechanical Problems, On Indivisible Lines, On Situations and Names of Winds, On Melissus, Xenophanes, and Gorgias.
ARISTOTLE: NICOMACHEAN ETHICS. H. Rackham.
ARISTOTLE: OECONOMICA and MAGNA MORALIA. G. C. Armstrong; (with Metaphysics, Vol. II.).
ARISTOTLE: ON THE HEAVENS. W. K. C. Guthrie.
ARISTOTLE: ON THE SOUL. PARVA NATURALIA. ON BREATH. W. S. Hett.
ARISTOTLE: CATEGORIES, ON INTERPRETATION, PRIOR ANALYTICS. H. P. Cooke and H. Tredennick.
ARISTOTLE: POSTERIOR ANALYTICS, TOPICS. H. Tredennick and E. S. Forster.
ARISTOTLE: ON SOPHISTICAL REFUTATIONS.
On Coming to be and Passing Away, On the Cosmos. E. S. Forster and D. J. Furley.
ARISTOTLE: PARTS OF ANIMALS. A. L. Peck; MOTION AND PROGRESSION OF ANIMALS. E. S. Forster.

ARISTOTLE: PHYSICS. Rev. P. Wicksteed and F. M. Cornford. 2 Vols.
ARISTOTLE: POETICS and LONGINUS. W. Hamilton Fyfe; DEMETRIUS ON STYLE. W. Rhys Roberts.
ARISTOTLE: POLITICS. H. Rackham.
ARISTOTLE: PROBLEMS. W. S. Hett. 2 Vols.
ARISTOTLE: RHETORICA AD ALEXANDRUM (with PROBLEMS. Vol. II.) H. Rackham.
ARRIAN: HISTORY OF ALEXANDER and INDICA. Rev. E. Iliffe Robson. 2 Vols.
ATHENAEUS: DEIPNOSOPHISTAE. C. B. Gulick. 7 Vols.
BABRIUS AND PHAEDRUS (Latin). B. E. Perry.
ST. BASIL: LETTERS. R. J. Deferrari. 4 Vols.
CALLIMACHUS: FRAGMENTS. C. A. Trypanis.
CALLIMACHUS, Hymns and Epigrams, and LYCOPHRON. A. W. Mair; ARATUS. G. R. Mair.
CLEMENT of ALEXANDRIA. Rev. G. W. Butterworth.
COLLUTHUS. Cf. OPPIAN.
DAPHNIS AND CHLOE. Thornley's Translation revised by J. M. Edmonds; and PARTHENIUS. S. Gaselee.
DEMOSTHENES I.: OLYNTHIACS, PHILIPPICS and MINOR ORATIONS. I.–XVII. AND XX. J. H. Vince.
DEMOSTHENES II.: DE CORONA and DE FALSA LEGATIONE. C. A. Vince and J. H. Vince.
DEMOSTHENES III.: MEIDIAS, ANDROTION, ARISTOCRATES, TIMOCRATES and ARISTOGEITON, I. AND II. J. H. Vince.
DEMOSTHENES IV.–VI.: PRIVATE ORATIONS and IN NEAERAM. A. T. Murray.
DEMOSTHENES VII.: FUNERAL SPEECH, EROTIC ESSAY, EXORDIA and LETTERS. N. W. and N. J. DeWitt.
DIO CASSIUS: ROMAN HISTORY. E. Cary. 9 Vols.
DIO CHRYSOSTOM. J. W. Cohoon and H. Lamar Crosby. 5 Vols.
DIODORUS SICULUS. 12 Vols. Vols. I.–VI. C. H. Oldfather. Vol. VII. C. L. Sherman. Vol. VIII. C. B. Welles. Vols. IX. and X. R. M. Geer. Vols. XI.–XII. F. Walton, General Index, R. M. Geer.
DIOGENES LAERITIUS. R. D. Hicks. 2 Vols.
DIONYSIUS OF HALICARNASSUS: ROMAN ANTIQUITIES. Spelman's translation revised by E. Cary. 7 Vols.
EPICTETUS. W. A. Oldfather. 2 Vols.
EURIPIDES. A. S. Way. 4 Vols. Verse trans.
EUSEBIUS: ECCLESIASTICAL HISTORY. Kirsopp Lake and J. E. L. Oulton. 2 Vols.
GALEN: ON THE NATURAL FACULTIES. A. J. Brock.
THE GREEK ANTHOLOGY. W. R. Paton. 5 Vols.
GREEK ELEGY AND IAMBUS with the ANACREONTEA. J. M. Edmonds. 2 Vols.

THE GREEK BUCOLIC POETS (THEOCRITUS, BION, MOSCHUS). J. M. Edmonds.

GREEK MATHEMATICAL WORKS. Ivor Thomas. 2 Vols.

HERODES. Cf. THEOPHRASTUS: CHARACTERS.

HERODOTUS. A. D. Godley. 4 Vols.

HESIOD AND THE HOMERIC HYMNS. H. G. Evelyn White.

HIPPOCRATES and the FRAGMENTS OF HERACLEITUS. W. H. S. Jones and E. T. Withington. 4 Vols.

HOMER: ILIAD. A. T. Murray. 2 Vols.

HOMER: ODYSSEY. A. T. Murray. 2 Vols.

ISAEUS. E. W. Forster.

ISOCRATES. George Norlin and LaRue Van Hook. 3 Vols.

ST. JOHN DAMASCENE: BARLAAM AND IOASAPH. Rev. G. R. Woodward, Harold Mattingly and D. M. Lang.

JOSEPHUS. 9 Vols. Vols. I.–IV.; H. Thackeray. Vol. V.; H. Thackeray and R. Marcus. Vols. VI.–VII.; R. Marcus. Vol. VIII.; R. Marcus and Allen Wikgren. Vol. IX. L. H. Feldman.

JULIAN. Wilmer Cave Wright. 3 Vols.

LUCIAN. 8 Vols. Vols. I.–V. A. M. Harmon. Vol. VI. K. Kilburn. Vols. VII.–VIII. M. D. Macleod.

LYCOPHRON. Cf. CALLIMACHUS.

LYRA GRAECA. J. M. Edmonds. 3 Vols.

LYSIAS. W. R. M. Lamb.

MANETHO. W. G. Waddell: PTOLEMY: TETRABIBLOS. F. E. Robbins.

MARCUS AURELIUS. C. R. Haines.

MENANDER. F. G. Allinson.

MINOR ATTIC ORATORS (ANTIPHON, ANDOCIDES, LYCURGUS, DEMADES, DINARCHUS, HYPERIDES). K. J. Maidment and J. O. Burrt. 2 Vols.

NONNOS: DIONYSIACA. W. H. D. Rouse. 3 Vols.

OPPIAN, COLLUTHUS, TRYPHIODORUS. A. W. Mair.

PAPYRI. NON-LITERARY SELECTIONS. A. S. Hunt and C. C. Edgar. 2 Vols. LITERARY SELECTIONS (Poetry). D. L. Page.

PARTHENIUS. Cf. DAPHNIS and CHLOE.

PAUSANIAS: DESCRIPTION OF GREECE. W. H. S. Jones. 4 Vols. and Companion Vol. arranged by R. E. Wycherley.

PHILO. 10 Vols. Vols. I.–V.; F. H. Colson and Rev. G. H. Whitaker. Vols. VI.–IX.; F. H. Colson. Vol. X. F. H. Colson and the Rev. J. W. Earp.

PHILO: two supplementary Vols. (*Translation only.*) Ralph Marcus.

PHILOSTRATUS: THE LIFE OF APOLLONIUS OF TYANA. F. C. Conybeare. 2 Vols.

PHILOSTRATUS: IMAGINES; CALLISTRATUS: DESCRIPTIONS. A. Fairbanks.
PHILOSTRATUS and EUNAPIUS: LIVES OF THE SOPHISTS. Wilmer Cave Wright.
PINDAR. Sir J. E. Sandys.
PLATO: CHARMIDES, ALCIBIADES, HIPPARCHUS, THE LOVERS, THEAGES, MINOS and EPINOMIS. W. R. M. Lamb.
PLATO: CRATYLUS, PARMENIDES, GREATER HIPPIAS, LESSER HIPPIAS. H. N. Fowler.
PLATO: EUTHYPHRO, APOLOGY, CRITO, PHAEDO, PHAEDRUS. H. N. Fowler.
PLATO: LACHES, PROTAGORAS, MENO, EUTHYDEMUS. W. R. M. Lamb.
PLATO: LAWS. Rev. R. G. Bury. 2 Vols.
PLATO: LYSIS, SYMPOSIUM, GORGIAS. W. R. M. Lamb.
PLATO: REPUBLIC. Paul Shorey. 2 Vols.
PLATO: STATESMAN, PHILEBUS. H. N. Fowler; ION. W. R. M. Lamb.
PLATO: THEAETETUS and SOPHIST. H. N. Fowler.
PLATO: TIMAEUS, CRITIAS, CLITOPHO, MENEXENUS, EPISTULAE. Rev. R. G. Bury.
PLOTINUS: A. H. Armstrong. Vols. I.–III.
PLUTARCH: MORALIA. 15 Vols. Vols. I.–V. F. C. Babbitt. Vol. VI. W. C. Helmbold. Vols. VII. and XIV. P. H. De Lacy and B. Einarson. Vol. IX. E. L. Minar, Jr., F. H. Sandbach, W. C. Helmbold. Vol. X. H. N. Fowler. Vol. XI. L. Pearson and F. H. Sandbach. Vol. XII. H. Cherniss and W. C. Helmbold.
PLUTARCH: THE PARALLEL LIVES. B. Perrin. 11 Vols.
POLYBIUS. W. R. Paton. 6 Vols.
PROCOPIUS: HISTORY OF THE WARS. H. B. Dewing. 7 Vols.
PTOLEMY: TETRABIBLOS. Cf. MANETHO.
QUINTUS SMYRNAEUS. A. S. Way. Verse trans.
SEXTUS EMPIRICUS. Rev. R. G. Bury. 4 Vols.
SOPHOCLES. F. Storr. 2 Vols. Verse trans.
STRABO: GEOGRAPHY. Horace L. Jones. 8 Vols.
THEOPHRASTUS: CHARACTERS. J. M. Edmonds. HERODES, etc. A. D. Knox.
THEOPHRASTUS: ENQUIRY INTO PLANTS. Sir Arthur Hort, Bart. 2 Vols.
THUCYDIDES. C. F. Smith. 4 Vols.
TRYPHIODORUS. Cf. OPPIAN.
XENOPHON: CYROPAEDIA. Walter Miller. 2 Vols.
XENOPHON: HELLENICA, ANABASIS, APOLOGY, and SYMPOSIUM. C. L. Brownson and O. J. Todd. 3 Vols.
XENOPHON: MEMORABILIA and OECONOMICUS. E. C. Marchant.
XENOPHON: SCRIPTA MINORA. E. C. Marchant and G. W. Bowersock.

DESCRIPTIVE PROSPECTUS ON APPLICATION

London
Cambridge, Mass.

WILLIAM HEINEMANN LTD
HARVARD UNIVERSITY PRESS